pub: 12-18-68

FINLAND, GERMANY, AND THE

SOVIET UNION, 1940–1941

Finland, Germany, and the Soviet Union, 1940–1941

THE PETSAMO DISPUTE

by H. Peter Krosby

THE UNIVERSITY OF WISCONSIN PRESS

Madison, Milwaukee, and London: 1968

Published by
The University of Wisconsin Press
Box 1379, Madison, Wisconsin 53701

The University of Wisconsin Press, Ltd.
27–29 Whitfield Street, London, W.1

Printed in the United States of America by the
George Banta Company, Inc., Menasha, Wisconsin
Library of Congress Catalog Card Number 68–9833

FOR MAUREEN

Preface

ALTHOUGH much has already been written about Finland's tragic role in the dramatic events of World War II, a comprehensive and reasonably accurate history of that role is not likely to be written for some time yet. Even during the war itself fact and fiction began to mix, as conflicting versions of how and why Finland on three separate occasions became involved in the war were presented. In Finland, all three stages of the involvement were explained as three links in one brutal chain forged by Kremlin blacksmiths for the enslavement of the Finns: the first led inexorably to the second, which in turn led, equally inexorably, to the third.

Outside Finland, the three stages of the Finnish involvement were seen in a somewhat different light. The Russo-Finnish Winter War of 1939–40 was indeed acknowledged by all but the Russians themselves to have been a case of unprovoked aggression by the Soviet Union against a small if heroic neighbor. But the Russo-Finnish Continuation War of 1941–44 was generally regarded as an avoidable conflict which Finland had entered as an aggressor motivated by a desire for revenge and territorial aggrandizement in league with Hitler's Germany. The German-Finnish Lapland War of 1944–45, during which German forces destroyed most of northern Finland while retreating into Norway, went largely unnoticed by the outside world as attention was focused on the more spectacular destruction of the Third Reich by the victorious Allied armies.

Of the three wars fought by Finland between 1939 and 1945,

the Continuation War—so called by the Finns who saw it, and wanted others to see it, as an unavoidable resumption, or continuation, of the Winter War—was clearly the most significant, for it was that war which brought Finland into the larger world conflict on the "wrong" side and left it branded in the hour of reckoning as a German ally or satellite. Hence it became an impelling requirement for the Finns to persuade the world of the victors that their involvement had been inescapable, that they had been the victims and not the perpetrators of aggression. Immediately after the start of the Continuation War in the summer of 1941, the Finnish government published a collection of diplomatic documents which purported to demonstrate that the Soviet threat to Finland's independent existence had not ended with the conclusion of the Winter War fifteen months before. The peace treaty had merely terminated the shooting temporarily, while the Soviet Union sought to accomplish the destruction of independent Finland by constant diplomatic, economic, and psychological pressure.

The truth lies somewhere in between the extreme opposite versions of how the Continuation War originated. If it can be said that Finland took the road to cobelligerency with Germany against the Soviet Union because of compelling circumstances largely beyond its control, it must also be said that the Finns marched down that road without too much reluctance and without looking around overly energetically for an alternative road—if such were actually open to them. That, in fact, is one of the many questions which remain to be comprehensively investigated, and such an investigation cannot be completed until all the relevant official archives of all of the countries involved are made available to historians. Finland's own archives remain closed, and so do the archives of the Soviet Union. Neither the British nor the American archives have been thrown open to the historical profession, although a small number of chosen historians have been admitted for the purpose of producing "official" war histories. Less privileged historians must rely on these works, on the published volumes of selected declassified diplomatic documents, and on whatever other information may be available.

In these circumstances, an investigation of Finnish policy during the interval between the Winter War and the Continuation War must for the time being depend largely on the captured records of the Third Reich for its primary source materials. It goes without saying that these records are far more important than any other foreign records so long as we are dealing with a period during which German power was predominant in Europe and, specifically, with a subject of which the major theme is the development of Finland's relations with Germany toward a climax of military collaboration.

This book is actually an unintended by-product of a research project which started out as an investigation into the origins of Finland's participation at Germany's side in the war against the Soviet Union. There was scarcely a hint in the available published accounts of the period of the unique significance of the Petsamo question for the evolution of Finnish-German relations. Finnish and German memoir writers practically ignored it—with the single exception of the late President J. K. Paasikivi, who was Finland's envoy in Moscow in 1940–41. Historians tended to treat it as nothing more than a relatively minor irritant in Finnish-Soviet relations, and tight-lipped wartime Finnish diplomats, questioned by the author, concurred.

A survey of the published documentary materials, however, suggested another order of priorities. The official Finnish *Blue-White Book* of 1941 devoted more space to the Petsamo question than to any other issue, for example. A check of the U.S. State Department's publication of American diplomatic documents for the period reveals a similar emphasis. And more than one half of the German documents on relations with Finland published in the relevant volumes of *Documents on German Foreign Policy 1918–1945* (Series D) are exclusively or primarily concerned with the Petsamo question. If sheer bulk indicates anything, the tens of thousands of unpublished German diplomatic records involving relations with Finland in 1940–41 confirm, as do the German military records, that Petsamo loomed larger in those relations than any other problem.

The conclusion that the Petsamo question—combining, as it did, political, economic, and military factors of prime importance— occupied a central position among the many difficult and dangerous problems confronting the Finnish government in 1940–41 is unavoidable. Between the early summer of 1940 and the spring of 1941 it was constantly on the diplomatic agenda. Practically every

day, new memoranda, reports, and letters were added to the bulging
Petsamo files in the German Foreign Ministry, and all of them
testify to the nature and extent of the increasingly intimate working
relationship between Finns and Germans. In fact, it can easily be
demonstrated that the Petsamo question acted as a remarkably
accurate barometer of Finnish-German relations in general.

Thus there is no lack of justification for a separate study of the
Petsamo question. Such a study imposes itself on anyone who
delves into the primary sources.

It might be prudent to point out, lest misunderstandings arise,
what this book is *not* intended to be. First of all, it is not a study
in Soviet foreign policy or Finnish-Soviet relations. The author is
aware of the existence of fairly recent Soviet publications dealing
with Soviet policy during this period. The focus of this book, however, is on Finnish-German relations as seen through the prism—
or read on the barometer—of the Petsamo question. While the
shadow of the Soviet Union always loomed large over this relationship, what the Finns believed the intentions of the Soviet
Union to be was far more important than what those intentions in
reality were. In this book, therefore, Soviet policies are presented
as interpreted—or misinterpreted—by the Finns and the Germans.
There has been no serious attempt to place the Petsamo dispute
clearly in the larger context of European events. To do so would
have taken this study too far afield. Only the diplomacy of the
Petsamo question itself has been treated as comprehensively as
the underlying source materials would permit. Consequently, the
only claim that can be made for this book is that it is a contribution
to the knowledge of Finnish foreign policy, and perhaps German
foreign policy, during a crucial year of World War II. As such,
other historians concerned with larger issues may find it useful.

H. P. K.

Madison, Wisconsin
June 6, 1968

Acknowledgments

THE author gratefully acknowledges his indebtedness to many persons and institutions. Former Prime Minister Rainer von Fieandt, who served as Finland's chief negotiator in the Petsamo question in 1940–41 and from that vantage point acquired a unique knowledge of its scope and complexities, graciously agreed to read an earlier version of this study. The comments and new information which he subsequently provided were invaluable. His personal and unsolicited initiative in bringing the study to the attention of a Helsinki publishing house, which resulted in its publication in 1966 in Finnish translation, has placed the author lastingly in Minister von Fieandt's debt.

Former Finnish Justice Minister Dr. J. O. Söderhjelm, who guided the affairs of the Petsamo Nickel Company from cradle to grave, and who was in close touch with the Petsamo diplomacy in 1940–41, also willingly played the role of critic and informant, notably after the publication of the Finnish edition. The present version is better for Dr. Söderhjelm's contribution.

Much useful information and advice were provided by several past and present members of the staff of The International Nickel Company of Canada, Ltd., in New York City. Mr. Paul Queneau, assistant to the chairman and consulting engineer, went out of his way to find historical and technical literature about his company's Petsamo venture. He also arranged to have the author meet with Dr. John F. Thompson, the retired president and chairman of the board of directors of International Nickel; and Mr. Norman H. Kearns, the engineer in charge of constructing the mining facilities in Petsamo. Their reminiscences about their company's activities in Europe in general and in Finland in particular added life and flavor to events and personalities. And Mrs. Alice O. Riley, records coordinator, worked her way through company files in search of relevant records. The author is deeply grateful to all of them.

Bergdirektor Max Maczek, engineer, technical director, and member of the board of directors of Kupferbergbau Mitterberg Gesellschaft m.b.H. in Mühlbach am Hochkönig, Salzburg, Austria, was sent to Petsamo in late 1940 and again in the summer of 1941 by I. G. Farbenindustrie along with a team of mining engineers to evaluate the nickel ore body and prepare for production. The author is indebted to him for information and for an invaluable collection of photographs of the Petsamo Nickel Company's facilities.

General of the Infantry Erich Buschenhagen, chief of staff of the German Army in Norway (1940–42); and General of the Artillery Walter Warlimont, deputy chief of the Operations Staff in the High Command of the German Armed Forces (1938–44), both discussed the military aspects of the Petsamo question with the author, a task for which they possess unique qualifications. For similar assistance, the author is indebted to Colonel General Franz Halder, chief of staff of the German army (1939–42); the late General of the Infantry Erik Heinrichs, chief of staff of the Finnish Army (1940–41); General of the Infantry K. A. Tapola, chief of operations in the Finnish General Staff (1940–41); and General of the Infantry Paavo Talvela, who was in charge of all Petsamo traffic (1940–44).

The late Professor Arvi Korhonen, to whom a generation of Finnish history students is indebted, gave freely of his advice and encouragement for several years. The author is further indebted, for various reasons, to Mr. Matti Tuovinen, chief of the Press Bureau in the Finnish Ministry for Foreign Affairs; Mr. Aaro Pakaslahti, Finland's ambassador to Spain; Mr. Asko Ivalo, Finland's ambassador to India; Professor Erik Castrén of Helsinki University; Professor Earl F. Ziemke of the Department of History, University of Georgia; the staffs of the National Archives of Finland in Helsinki, the Foreign Office Library in London, the World War II Records Service of the National Archives and Records Service in Washington, and the Memorial Library of the University of Wisconsin in Madison. The Ford Foundation provided the initial and indispensable financial booster to get the project off the ground; the American-Scandinavian Foundation contributed toward a visit to Helsinki; and the Hattie M. Strong Foundation tided the venture over a rough spot.

Professor Emeritus John H. Wuorinen of Columbia University has earned much more than a former graduate student's perfunctory recognition for services rendered in the line of duty. His constant interest, support, and friendship were important factors in launching the investigation of which this book became a surprise by-product. But without the unwavering and indispensable support and understanding of the author's wife, that by-product, let alone the entire project, would never have been finished. To her this volume is dedicated.

Contents

Preface	vii
Acknowledgments	xi
Chapter I. A Problematical Property	3
Chapter II. In the Cross Fire of Great Power Interests	32
Chapter III. War Clouds	53
Chapter IV. Under Hitler's Umbrella	73
Chapter V. The Dilatory Negotiators	97
Chapter VI. In the Eye of the Hurricane	110
Chapter VII. No Supine Accommodation	126
Chapter VIII. The Coming of the Good Season	152
Chapter IX. "On Snow-Covered Tundras Under the Midnight Sun"	165
Chapter X. Epilogue: Mining the Precious Nickel, 1941–1944	186
Notes	205
Abbreviations	245
Bibliography	248
Index	265

Illustrations

following page 78

Pl. 1. German map of the Petsamo area, 1944
Pl. 2. Town of Kirkenes, Norway, 1941
Pl. 3. Jäniskoski power house, 1941
Pl. 4. J. O. Söderhjelm
Pl. 5. Wipert von Blücher
Pl. 6. Surface plant of the Kaula shaft, Kaulatunturi, 1941
Pl. 7. Rainer von Fieandt
Pl. 8. Henrik Ramsay
Pl. 9. Kolosjoki: entry to the adit, 1941

FINLAND, GERMANY, AND THE

SOVIET UNION, 1940–1941

CHAPTER I

A Problematical Property

For nearly a quarter of the twentieth century, Finland was in possession of the Petsamo area. This portion of the Northern Cap,* which the Russians call Pechenga, had historically been regarded as a condominium, populated only by a few fishermen and traders and by nomadic Lapps whose reindeer herds knew no country or international boundary. When the borderline was finally regulated in 1826 by Russia and Sweden-Norway, no account was taken of the need of Finland, a grand duchy under the Russian imperial throne, for an outlet to the Arctic Ocean. During the ensuing decades, the idea of giving Finland such an outlet in return for Russian territory on the Karelian Isthmus northwest of St. Petersburg was occasionally debated, but no action was ever taken.

On December 6, 1917, following the Bolshevik revolution in Russia, Finland proclaimed its independence. Nearly three years later, after a bloody civil war and sporadic fighting against the Russian Bolsheviks, Finland at last acquired the Petsamo area by the terms of the Russo-Finnish treaty of Tartu (Dorpat), signed on October 14, 1920.[1] In return, adjustments in favor of Russia were made in the disputed Karelian borderline, and Finland renounced its claims on the ethnically Finnish areas of Eastern Karelia north of Lake Ladoga. Finland also acquired the western littoral of the Rybachi Peninsula, which extends from the Petsamo area northward into the Artic Ocean. Thus Finland had gained a northern outlet

* This name is now commonly used to denote that portion of northern Europe which lies between the Atlantic Ocean and the White Sea north of the Arctic Circle.

3

to the world oceans through a narrow land corridor between Russia and Norway.

Beyond the potential economic significance of the permanently ice-free harbor of Liinahamari, a sleepy fishing village on the Petsamo Fiord, the area seemed to have little to recommend it. Its 4,041 square miles of tundra, lakes, and low rolling mountains were nearly devoid of population, had no rail or useful road communications, and could boast of no conspicuous exploitable natural resources other than their scenic beauty. But the Finns began to develop the area. New roads were built, including the crucial Arctic Ocean Highway running north from the railhead at Rovaniemi to the triple villages of Parkkina (often loosely referred to as Petsamo), Trifona, and Liinahamari. The latter soon became the center of a growing fishing industry based on the riches of the Barents Sea. Small passenger craft began to ply the fiords, rivers, and lakes of the area, and tourists anxious to see the midnight sun and willing to rough it began to flock into the new chalets and hotels of the barren hinterland. However, these improvements did not significantly alter the character of the Petsamo area as a remote, if quaint, outpost of civilization.

In 1924, surveys conducted by the Geological Commission of Finland revealed a nickel-copper ore deposit in the Kaulatunturi mountain range near the Norwegian border and close to the Arctic coast. The initial tests tended to indicate that the discovery was of major proportions, too large to be adequately exploited by Finland's limited capital resources. It was decided to approach The Mond Nickel Company of London,[2] a wholly owned subsidiary of The International Nickel Company of Canada, whose dominance in the field of nickel production amounted to a near world monopoly. It took both time and tempting inducements, however, to arouse the interest of the Anglo-Canadian trust in the newly discovered Finnish ore field. Not until the summer of 1933 was a representative of Mond Nickel sent to Finland in response to an offer by Professor J. Johannes Sederholm, the head of the Geological Commission of Finland, personally to assist the British company in the negotiation of a contract with the Finnish government for the right to explore and, if justified, exploit the Kaulatunturi property.[3] The contract was signed on June 22, 1934. It gave Mond Nickel exclusive rights to develop and exploit the ore field, described as twenty-eight miles long and two miles wide, for a period of forty years, and with an option to renew for another forty years. The contract also required Mond Nickel to form a Finnish subsidiary company to handle its operations in Finland, and the Petsamo Nickel Company was accordingly established with Edgar Pam of Mond Nickel as the chairman of the board of directors. The other two members of the board were Dr. Johan O. Söderhjelm, the Helsinki attorney and member of parliament who had been instrumental in negotiating the contract, and Dr. Henrik Ramsay, a prominent businessman and politician who would later serve as Finnish foreign minister. Dr. Söderhjelm also became the managing director of the new company.[4]

Test borings at Kaulatunturi quickly proved that the ore field was eminently exploitable, and in 1936 the construction of all necessary facilities at the site began. They included the town of Kolosjoki, a smelter plant adjoining it, an adit into the mountain, and a shaft down to the ore. In 1938, the construction of a dam and a major hydroelectric power station was begun at Jäniskoski some fifty miles to the southwest on the Pasvik River, just off the Arctic Ocean Highway. By November, 1939, these facilities were nearing their completion. International Nickel had by then invested $6,723,908 in the venture and expected to spend another $3,500,000 before production of nickel-copper matte could begin, probably "not later than 1941."[5] But the European war, and especially the Russo-Finnish Winter War and the German invasion of Norway, interrupted this schedule. Temporarily, at least, the risks involved were too great to justify further investments in Petsamo. As the president of International Nickel, Robert C. Stanley, told the company's stockholders in late April, 1940, the "future of this property in Finland is problematical."[6] It was indeed that. As things turned out, International Nickel would never extract a single ton of nickel at Kolosjoki.

In 1920, the agreement which gave the Petsamo area to Finland could hardly have seemed like much of a concession to Soviet leaders. The ensuing nineteen years produced no evidence of regrets on their part. When they did begin to do some renewed thinking about Finland in the 1930's, it was in the light of strategic rather than economic considerations. Nazi Germany was looming up on the western horizon as a major threat to the security of the

Soviet Union, and the more the Soviet leaders became obsessed with their fear of a German attack, the more they tended to look on their European neighbors as potential accomplices of Germany in such an attack. As this obsession grew, Finland came in for a vexing propaganda offensive by the Soviet press and radio, an offensive punctuated by occasional ominous pronouncements by Soviet leaders, notably from 1936 on.[7]

But the Petsamo area was never mentioned in these outbursts. Nor did it figure in the proposals for another territorial agreement, designed to improve the military defense position of Leningrad, which the Soviet government submitted to the Finnish government in 1938–39.[8] Not even the disastrous Finnish-Soviet negotiations in the fall of 1939, prior to the Winter War, yielded any indications of significant Soviet interest in the Petsamo area. The matter was raised, but apparently more for effect than for substantive reasons. Although it is difficult to determine exactly why the Russians brought Petsamo into the talks, the fact that they did so at all put the Finns on notice that their Soviet neighbors were paying some attention to it. Foreign Commissar Vyacheslav M. Molotov initiated a discussion about Petsamo during the very first meeting of the Finnish and Soviet negotiators in the Kremlin on October 12, but it seemed that his purpose was to suggest a legal basis for the desired acquisition of a Soviet military base in southwest Finland on the shores of the Gulf of Finland. As he put it: "Give us a concession in the western part of the Gulf of Finland similar to the one you have given England in Petsamo, but for military-political purposes." "Furthermore," he said, "the Petsamo border is a bad one." Evidently he was not referring to the Petsamo area itself, however, for he went on to propose that Finland give the Soviet Union its section of the Rybachi Peninsula in return for Soviet territory in Eastern Karelia.[9] Two days later, Molotov discussed Petsamo and the Anglo-Canadian mining concession again, but security was his primary concern. Both Germany and England threatened the Murman Coast, he asserted, but then he dropped the issue and returned to the problem of the border on the Karelian Isthmus and the demand for a base at Hanko in southwest Finland.[10]

Back in Helsinki for consultations with government and military leaders, the Finnish negotiators, headed by Dr. Juho Kusti Paasikivi, then the Finnish minister in Stockholm, found no under-

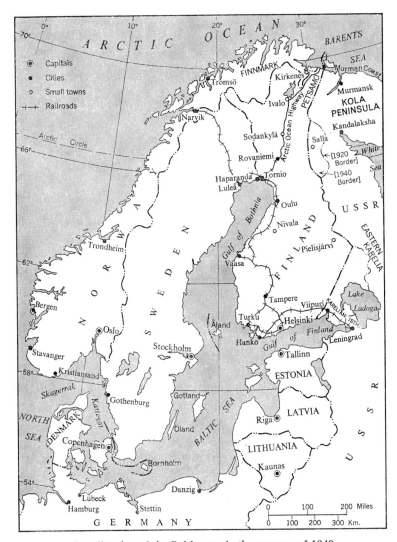

Scandinavia and the Baltic area in the summer of 1940

standing for either the Soviet demands or their own warnings. The
Finnish government regarded both the Petsamo area and the

Rybachi Peninsula as without either economic or military importance for the Soviet Union and refused to consider a cession of the western littoral of the peninsula that protected the entry to Liinahamari through Petsamo Bay.[11] When Paasikivi reported this as the negotiations resumed in Moscow on October 23, Joseph Stalin repeated that the Soviet Union required those areas on the Rybachi Peninsula from which a German or British naval expedition to Petsamo could be prevented.[12] Paasikivi was in no position to comply, but in his diary he noted that Finland ought to cede the northern tip of its territory on the peninsula,[13] and he suggested this to his government in Helsinki three days later.[14] The government agreed,[15] but when Paasikivi proposed it to Stalin on November 4, the only response he received was a curt "We will think about it."[16] The question was not discussed again before the negotiations were broken off on November 9.[17]

One may assume, then, that the Petsamo area held no great attraction for the Soviet Union between 1920 and 1939. The negotiations in Moscow had revealed a tentative Soviet military interest in the western littoral of the Rybachi Peninsula, but that was clearly the least of the concerns preoccupying Soviet leaders. The possibility of a German or British landing at Petsamo was not yet acute. For the Germans to have tried it before their occupation of Norway would have been sheer madness. For the British to have challenged the Soviet Union in Finland during the winter of 1939–40 would have been an extremely ill-conceived act. It is of course true that the French wanted to open up a second front in Scandinavia during the Winter War in the hope of easing the German pressure on France itself, but that scheme was firmly rejected by the British.[18] In other words, there was never sufficient cause for the Soviet leaders to be particularly concerned about the Petsamo area for any reason in late 1939.

The Winter War and its settlement underscored the Soviet Union's lack of immediate interest in the Petsamo area. During the war, the Finns concentrated their defensive efforts on meeting the major Soviet thrusts across the Karelian Isthmus and in the region just north of Lake Ladoga. Only two divisions were left to defend the remaining hundreds of miles of wild border running north to the Arctic Sea. The Petsamo area was practically undefended,[19] and it fell quickly to the attacking Soviet army corps.[20] Still, at the end of their victorious war, the Russians returned the Petsamo area to Finland and kept only the disputed western littoral of the Rybachi Peninsula. In view of the extensive territorial annexations made by the Soviet Union elsewhere in Finland, that was indeed remarkable, as Molotov with great emphasis pointed out to the Finnish peace negotiators in Moscow in the second week of March, 1940. No other great power would have condescended even to negotiate with "a country the size of Finland," he declared, but the Soviet Union appreciated Finland's needs and had no desire to cause undue hardships. "We have only one ice-free harbor," he said, "and you have another, Petsamo. We must see to it that the passage out to the world oceans is secured." Molotov seemed anxious to make his Finnish visitors understand the magnitude of this grand gesture. "No other great power would have agreed to withdraw its troops from an ice-free harbor," he said, and "significant, very significant, military circles" had insisted that Petsamo be retained by the Soviet Union. Although "we never go against popular opinion, the Soviet government is in this instance willing to give the Petsamo area back to Finland," Molotov concluded.[21]

And so the following provision was included in the Treaty of Moscow of March 12, 1940: "The USSR undertakes to withdraw its military forces from the Petsamo area which the USSR voluntarily ceded to Finland under the terms of the Peace Treaty of 1920." But the treaty prohibited Finland from maintaining warships on its northern coast, and the Soviet Union acquired the right of free passage through the Petsamo area for its goods and nationals and the right to establish a consulate in Petsamo.[22]

Why did the Soviet Union restore the Petsamo area to Finland? In his report to the Supreme Soviet on March 29, Molotov explained that the Soviet government had thought it "necessary to let Finland have an ice-free port," for Finland was "a northern and not merely a Baltic country."[23] In the peace talks with the Finns, on the other hand, Molotov had repeatedly emphasized that the Soviet demands, including the territorial demands, were based on the brutal fact that a war had been fought. War has its own logic, he had said, and the law of war ruled now.[24] If so, then the conqueror, by that same law and logic, should have kept what he had won, including the Petsamo area. But the conqueror relinquished a part of his spoils, a part which was not of negligible worth. One hesitates, therefore, to accept Molotov's explanation at face value.

Field Marshal Gustaf Mannerheim, the Finnish commander in chief, was of the opinion that Finland owed its retention of the Petsamo area to the foreign-owned nickel concession there.[25] Paasikivi, on the other hand, was convinced that this Anglo-Canadian interest "would not have prevented the Soviet Union from using its military power in Petsamo."[26] Paasikivi was probably wrong. Soviet leaders were apparently not prepared to test their military power against the English and French, and certainly not over a small piece of the Northern Cap which had not yet become vitally important to the Soviet Union. The military weakness of the Allied Powers had not yet been revealed in March, 1940, while startling shortcomings in the Soviet Union's ability to wage war effectively had been demonstrated in the Winter War. In fact, there is evidence to indicate that rumors of an imminent Anglo-French intervention on Finland's side caused the Soviet Union to break off the Winter War even as total victory was within its reach.[27]

This would also explain why the Finns, when they returned to Petsamo after the war, found the mining property at Kolosjoki under heavy guard and completely untouched by Soviet hands. There were not even tracks in the snow. Soviet officers explained that they had orders to return this "American property"* exactly as they had found it, and they made the Finns sign a protocol certifying that fact.[28]

Germany's interest in Finnish mineral resources dated back to the prewar period. According to the provisions of trade agreements signed in the fall of 1939 and valid through 1940, Germany was entitled to purchase the entire Finnish output of copper, estimated at 13,000 tons per year. The entire output of the Mätäsvaara molybdenum mine about to be opened up by the Vuoksenniska Company at Pielisjärvi in east Finland had also been promised to Germany. Furthermore, these agreements would give the Germans the output of a nickel mine soon to be opened at Nivala in Oulu

---

* American capital controlled The International Nickel Company, and its business headquarters was located on Wall Street in New York City.

province near the Gulf of Bothnia. But in return for the Nivala nickel ore, plus a Finnish promise to increase the deliveries of copper, Germany had committed itself to deliver to Finland 134 anti-aircraft guns, 50 of which were actually shipped to the Finns before the war began in late November. Finally, these prewar agreements provided for Finnish deliveries of cobalt.[29]

The Winter War led to a very serious deterioration of Finnish-German relations. Faithful to the Non-Aggression Pact of August 23, 1939, which had placed Finland within the Soviet sphere of interest, Germany did not raise a finger to aid the Finns. A circular telegram of December 2 from State Secretary Ernst von Weizsäcker in the German Foreign Ministry instructed all German diplomatic missions abroad to "avoid any anti-Russian note" in conversations regarding the Russo-Finnish conflict.[30] On December 7, Foreign Minister Joachim von Ribbentrop reinforced this with a second instruction ordering all diplomatic missions to express "sympathy with the Russian standpoint" and "refrain from any expression of sympathy for the Finnish position."[31] A plea by the pro-Finnish German minister in Helsinki, Wipert von Blücher, that Germany play the role of the "honest broker," went unanswered.[32]

Blücher then proceeded to bombard his colleagues in Berlin with suggestions that Germany ought to take an interest in Finland's welfare for economic reasons, if for no other. He also reported with brutal frankness the rapid deterioration of Germany's stature in the eyes of the Finnish people. Shortly after the war broke out, he reported that Finns "who have remained pro-German complain to me that Germany's policy is driving Finland into the arms of England."[33] In mid-January, he wrote to the head of the Scandinavian desk in the Foreign Ministry in Berlin that the Finnish attitude to Germany was "visibly deteriorating," and Finnish officers, traditionally friendly to Germany, were "taking off their Iron Crosses."[34]* He summed it all up in a telegram dispatched on the day the war ended: "Germany has caused deep disappointment in Finland and incurred hatred in many circles."[35]

In the latter telegram, Blücher also took note of another and

* A considerable number of Finns who had served in a Finnish volunteer battalion in the German army on the Russian front during World War I had been awarded this German military decoration for valor. Most of Finland's general officers in 1939–40 were veterans of that battalion.

more auspicious development. "Political realists," he reported, "are
becoming aware that actually only two great powers, Germany
and Russia, have any influence in the Baltic region and that a
correct orientation toward both is of vital importance to the Finnish
nation." He even anticipated, though he could hardly have realized
it fully at the time, the future course of Finland's foreign policy in
his concluding remark: "Since it is not to be expected that the Finns
will resign themselves definitely to the new boundary, and since it
is uncertain whether the Russians regard the peace as an interim
phase or temporary measure, further tension in the Baltic region
must be anticipated."[36] These were precisely the factors which
within a few months were to cause Finland's leaders to seek closer
ties with Germany.

Blücher was also the first within the German foreign service to
take up the problem of Petsamo. On the evening of March 2, he
had been privately informed by former Foreign Minister Antti
Hackzell about the Soviet peace terms as they were then known
in Helsinki, and he had noted that the Russians "put no value on
Petsamo."[37] The next morning, Blücher sent a telegram to Berlin
in which he stated that it was indeed in Germany's own interest
that the Finns retained an outlet on the Arctic Ocean, but it was
not in the interest of either Germany or Russia to permit the
British continued possession of the Petsamo nickel concession. He
proposed that the German Foreign Ministry ask the Soviet government to demand, in the course of the negotiations with the Finns,
that the British concession be annulled.[38]

No action was taken on his proposal, but Blücher's colleagues
in Berlin were not unaware of the problem of Petsamo. In fact,
the records of the German Foreign Ministry for this period reveal
not only a growing awareness of the vital importance of the Finnish
nickel, but also a fuller realization than could be discerned in
either Moscow or Helsinki of how potent Petsamo was politically.
The reason that Blücher's proposal of March 3 had not been acted
upon was obviously that it might backfire. If Germany were to
have any hope of eventually acquiring nickel from Kolosjoki, the
worst way to go about it would be to encourage the Soviet Union
to remove the Anglo-Canadian establishment at a time when
Germany had no plausible justification for filing a claim of its
own. And since a Soviet concession company was likely to replace

the Anglo-Canadian trust should the latter be forced to move out, the best policy for Germany was to let sleeping dogs lie while seeking to maneuver inconspicuously into a more advantageous position through quiet negotiations with the Finns.

That was in fact what the efforts of the German Foreign Ministry during the following three months were designed to accomplish. Germany and the Soviet Union had both scheduled trade talks with Finland for late spring or early summer. The German Foreign Ministry soon decided to give top priority to the acquisition of Petsamo nickel in its talks with the Finns, and the alarm was sounded when reports from Stockholm advised that the Soviet Union, according to news stories in the Swedish press, planned to eliminate England's influence in the Petsamo area in the course of the Finnish-Soviet trade talks. On March 22, Blücher received instructions from the Wilhelmstrasse to keep his ears open and his lips sealed: "Request telegraphic report if more is known there. Please do not mention in contacts with official authorities."[39]

The following Thursday, March 28, six officials of the Foreign Ministry and the Ministry of Economics met to draw up guidelines for the trade talks with Finland.[40] Among those present was Counselor Reiner Kreutzwald of the legation in Helsinki, who began the meeting with some disturbing remarks about the "outspokenly unfriendly" attitude to Germany then prevalent in Finland. The Finns though they had been "left in the lurch" and "sold out" by Germany, he reported. They were pinning their hopes on the western powers and expected that a German defeat would lead to the restoration of the old Finnish borders.

In view of this attitude, the six officials thought that the time was not yet ripe for a major expansion of Finnish-German trade, but it was necessary nevertheless to secure for Germany a number of "vital supplies" from Finland, notably certain raw materials. Because of the danger that the Finns might conclude agreements with the British, and possibly even with the Russians, Dr. Karl Schnurre, head of the Eastern European desk in the Economic Policy Department of the Foreign Ministry, suggested a crash program of limited negotiations with the Finns to obtain these, above all copper, molybdenum, nickel, and iron pyrites.

Getting the nickel posed the most difficult and delicate problem. The 1939 trade agreements entitled Germany to the output of the

Nivala mine, but this mine was not ready for production and could not be counted on for a while. Furthermore, in return for delivering Nivala nickel to Germany, Finland was entitled to receive the remaining 84 anti-aircraft guns which had not been shipped to the Finns by the time the Winter War broke out. To deliver arms to Finland now might be a very ticklish affair politically. But the promise of arms deliveries was tied up with Nivala nickel only, not with Petsamo nickel. Although no refined nickel or even nickel matte could be expected from the unfinished smelter plant at Kolosjoki for a considerable length of time, it might be possible to extract ore from the mine in the near future and transport it to Germany for processing. The Anglo-Canadian trust was not likely to resume work on the mining facilities for the duration of the war, but with some "political pressure from Germany" the Finns might be persuaded to start operations anyway. All of the officials attending the March 28 conference realized that "Russian support could hardly be expected" for such a venture, but it was worth an attempt nevertheless. They also expected that the German bid for the Petsamo nickel ore would be "the most difficult question" in the pending trade negotiations with Finland.

Although it was recorded in the minutes of this conference that arrangements had been made to send Minister Schnurre, accompanied by Counselor Waldemar Ludwig of the Ministry of Economics, to Helsinki on April 8 for preliminary talks with Prime Minister Risto Ryti,[41] the records of the German Foreign Ministry provide no evidence of it. Not until two weeks later, after further deliberations, was the German legation in Helsinki instructed to arrange for such a mission.

In the meantime, the problem was turned over to the expert staff of the Economic Policy Department in the Foreign Ministry, headed by Ministerialdirektor Emil Wiehl. Within this department, the two officials most closely involved were Counselor Hilger van Scherpenberg, head of the Northern European (Scandinavian) desk, and Minister Schnurre, head of the Eastern European desk, which included the Soviet Union, the three Baltic States, and Poland. It was up to Scherpenberg to translate the discussion of the conference on March 28 into practical proposals for an expedient course of action. By April 2 he had completed his assignment and submitted his findings and recommendations in the form of a six-page memorandum.[42] He considered the large deposit of nickel in the Petsamo area to be much more important to Germany than the Nivala nickel deposit, but because of the Anglo-Canadian interest it would be possible to "cause the Finnish government to make the nickel there available to us in some form or other" only by resorting to "the strongest political pressure or by the granting of considerable return favors." He was not certain what sort of pressure could be applied, since "our strongest means of pressure, the supply of coal, is of limited value as long as the coal can to a great extent be replaced by wood because of the Finnish riches of wood." Still, "in spite of the contrary commitments on the part of the Finnish government to the Canadian concessionaires, the attempt should be made to achieve the delivery of nickel ore from Petsamo."

Apparently Scherpenberg's superiors shared his view. A memorandum prepared in his department[43] was forwarded to the legation in Helsinki on April 11,[44] with instructions to Blücher to make the necessary arrangements for a visit by Schnurre and Ludwig. The telegram explained that the present state of affairs made it necessary to clarify a few things by direct conversations with Prime Minister Ryti before the Finnish-German trade talks began in Berlin. If Ryti agreed, the two German diplomats could come the following week. Speed was of the essence "in view of English and Russian endeavors in Finland." The question of delivery of Finnish metals, "especially nickel ore from Petsamo," was of "particular urgency for us in this connection," concluded the telegram. Strict secrecy was to be observed.

Although Ryti agreed at once to receive the two official delegates of the German government,[45] the high-level talks were not held until three weeks later. The records contain no explanation of the delay. Nor do they shed much light on what happened when the conversations finally took place at the turn of the month. In a brief cabled report to Dr. Karl Ritter, ambassador on special assignment in the Foreign Ministry, Schnurre merely said that his talks with "the Finnish government" had covered the "intensification of German-Finnish economic relations and Baltic questions."[46] The talks were concluded on May 6, and Schnurre promised to give an oral report on his return to Berlin after a side trip to Stockholm. He expected that formal negotiations with a Finnish trade delegation could begin in Berlin on May 23. No memorandum of Schnurre's oral report has been found. When he reported on his trip to Finland to a meeting of the Commercial Policy Committee on May 16,[47] the recording secretary merely noted in the minutes that the Finns were prepared to deliver 11,000 tons of copper annually and possibly 50 per cent more later, but in return they wanted Germany to deliver "a limited quantity of war material." The minutes noted further that this question would be investigated by the High Command of the Armed Forces (OKW) as soon as the Finns provided more details, while the Foreign Ministry would determine the political implications of the problem. It quickly developed, however, that Adolf Hitler was not ready to supply arms to the Finns "for the time being."[48]

If the German records provide no explicit information about the delay of the Schnurre mission to Helsinki and the Finnish response to the German requests for nickel and other vital goods, they do at least suggest what was going on in both of the foreign ministries involved. When Blücher on April 18 visited the new Finnish foreign minister, Professor Rolf Witting, to request that the conference between Ryti and Schnurre be scheduled for five days hence, Witting, while agreeing to try to arrange it, remarked that Finland could make deliveries to Germany only on a very limited scale. He included copper and iron pyrites in the list of items that could be delivered, but no mention was made of nickel from any source. Blücher would not discuss details, however, and he advised Witting that Schnurre's discussions "would be kept within a general framework."[49]

This interview took place nine days after the German invasion of Denmark and Norway. Denmark had surrendered at dawn on the day of the invasion, but Norway was fighting on.[50] On the outcome of this daring German military venture would depend whether Finland were to retain any freedom of action in its foreign trade or be at the mercy of Germany and its Soviet confederate. As Blücher put it in a telegram to Berlin on April 19: "Only if England occupies Narvik and an undamaged Narvik railroad can a part of Finnish transoceanic trade evade German control." In the opposite event, Finnish overseas trade would come "under complete German control."[51] As the German conquest of Norway progressed, the Finns began to realize what this meant for them.

During a conversation with Finnish Minister to Germany Aarne Wuorimaa on April 26, State Secretary Weizsäcker found "the conspicuous desire of the minister to restore the intimate relationship which he maintained with us previously" to be as noteworthy as the subject discussed.[52] And as Blücher reported from Helsinki a few days later, the latest news from Norway had "impressed Finnish public opinion deeply."[53]

Under the impact of these events, Witting, who had succeeded Väinö Tanner as foreign minister on March 27, proceeded to take certain steps designed to improve Finland's relations with Germany. At the time of his appointment, Blücher had described him as "friendly to Germany" and without significant contacts with the western powers.[54] Witting told the German minister that the new government under Ryti would pursue a foreign policy "like the Kivimäki cabinet,"[55] an illusion to the Scandinavian orientation of the government which Professor Toivo M. Kivimäki headed from December, 1932, to October, 1936. He also made a point of expressing himself "sharply" against Finland's failure to accept the German offer of a non-aggression pact in the spring of 1939.[56] On April 1, during a "strictly personal" conversation with Blücher, Witting committed the remarkable indiscretion of asking the German minister what he thought of Wuorimaa's effectiveness as Finland's minister in Berlin. Blücher said that he thought Wuorimaa had achieved an "excellent position and enjoyed confidence and favor" there, but Witting was not satisfied. He was of the opinion, he said, that "Wuorimaa was not sufficiently active," and perhaps a new man ought to be sent to Berlin in view of the "new attitude to Germany." He had in mind someone like Kivimäki.[57]

For the time being, Witting's obvious desire to improve Finland's relations with Germany was far ahead of Finnish public opinion,[58] but the German victories in Norway soon closed that gap considerably. On April 13, Blücher discussed Kivimäki's political views and his suitability as a diplomatic promoter of Finnish-German relations in a report to Berlin. It was a highly favorable assessment. Kivimäki was described as one of Finland's most capable and respected statesmen, an expert on German affairs, and "the Finnish politician best suited to represent Finland in Germany." With some exaggeration, Blücher wrote that Kivimäki, during his years as prime minister, had come under the influence of the highly conservative and pro-German President Per Evind Svinhufvud, as a result of which the Kivimäki cabinet had been "pronouncedly" right-wing.[59]

From that point on, things moved swiftly. On May 6, the Finnish government was informed that the German government would be pleased to have Kivimäki as Finland's new envoy in Berlin.[60] Henceforth, with Witting pursuing his foreign policy goals in Helsinki and Kivimäki backing him up in Berlin, Finland's political and economic reorientation toward Germany was to proceed smoothly under the growing impact of the violent European developments of the spring and summer of 1940.

The German camapign in Norway may also have had something to do with the postponement of the Schnurre mission to Helsinki. Once Germany were in full control of Norway, its bargaining position vis-à-vis Finland in the Petsamo nickel question would naturally be enhanced. This would also explain why Schnurre during his conversations in Helsinki apparently refrained from a detailed discussion of the sort of trade treaty Germany desired. The whole question of Germany's economic policy in northern Europe was under close and constant scrutiny in Berlin during the weeks following the invasion of Norway.[61] By the end of April, all of southern Norway, with the exception of one intrepid fort near Trondheim, was in German hands. With the German invasion of the Low Countries and the decisive assault on France in the second week of May, which soon caused the Anglo-French Expeditionary Corps in northern Norway to abandon its front in the Narvik area on the eve of victory, the fate of Blücher's "Narvik question" was settled. All of Norway would be occupied by Germany, and Finland's freedom of action would be circumscribed.

In the light of these developments, a lengthy statement of the new economic situation in Scandinavia and the Baltic was prepared in Scherpenberg's office and forwarded to all the German diplomatic missions within the precincts of Schnurre and Scherpenberg on May 11.[62] The report noted that the recent events in Denmark and Norway had altered the economic positions of all the Scandinavian states. Although it would be premature to predict the ultimate effects of those changes, it was already necessary to prepare for a new economic order, and the German diplomats in the capitals of northern Europe should keep that in mind. With Norway and Denmark in German hands and the Kattegat blocked by German mines, the "export, import, and transit routes of the northern states will almost all be controlled by Germany," the report noted. That such a favorable situation must be taken advantage of "as fully as possible for the aims of the economic warfare forced upon Germany" was obvious, and it was the intention of the German government to expand its trade relations with the Scandinavian states "as strongly as possible and bilaterally." The diplomatic missions were instructed to report to Berlin all developments which might serve to promote that purpose.

As far as Finland was concerned, said the report, the new situation meant that no exits to the outside world remained other than the route over Petsamo—"which cannot be of great significance in terms of volume"—and the transit route through the Soviet Union as well as trade with the Soviet Union itself. The latter possibility would have to be dealt with separately, suggested the report, "in view of the position of the Soviet Union and its special relations with Germany." In any event, Germany's aim in the impending negotiations with Finland would be to persuade the Finns to commit to Germany all those commodities which Germany required and which had not already been committed to the Soviet Union. Whether Finland and the other Scandinavian states were to be permitted to trade with other continental states at all would depend on their readiness to adjust their economic policies to the new situation created by German military successes. Germany would consider their import needs in terms of how they decided to "cooperate positively and constructively with Germany in the reorganization of economic relations in the northern region." The ultimate aim was to "turn the Baltic Sea into a free landlocked ocean [*freien Binnenmeer*] and a center of economic interchange" serving the purposes of Germany. The Soviet Union, incidentally, was not automatically to be regarded as a Baltic littoral state.

Given the nature of Germany's economic policy goals in northern Europe, goals reminiscent of the control exercised by the Hanseatic League in the late Middle Ages, and given the high stakes involved in the coming negotiations with Finland, Germany could not afford to move with carefree haste so long as the prey was not yet firmly in the trap. The Soviet interest in Finland must be examined, and the Soviet Union's reaction to an expansion of Finnish-German trade relations must be anticipated. Furthermore, Schnurre's visit to Helsinki in late April and early May revealed that the Finns were not willing to sell Petsamo nickel ore to Germany.[63] That fact alone would have been ample reason for Germany to postpone the trade negotiations with Finland from the date originally scheduled (May 23) to the second week of June. Presumably the imminent German victory in Norway and the expected victory in France would have a salutary effect on the Finns and cause them to reassess their negative attitude to Germany's desire for nickel.

Another possible reason for the postponement may have been the composition of the delegation which the Finnish government by the middle of May had named to represent it in the negotiations in Berlin. The German Foreign Ministry suspected that the chairman of the delegation would be very difficult to deal with. "Negotiations with him will probably lead very quickly to a negative result," complained Ambassador Ritter in a telegram to Blücher. The German government had therefore decided to "give the Finnish government an opportunity to alter its decision."[64] Blücher took the matter up with Foreign Minister Witting, and Witting was soon able to ascertain that the chairman of the delegation "would not be free for the new term set for the negotiations." His place was taken by Rainer von Fieandt, and other suitable personnel changes were also made before the delegation finally left for Berlin.[65]

For Fieandt, this was the beginning of what may well have been the most trying and nerve-racking year in his long public career. The Petsamo question was soon to develop into one of the most explosive of the many crises sprung upon the Finnish government during 1940–41, and Fieandt was destined to cope with it until it finally dissipated in the spring of 1941. A prominent financier, industrialist, businessman, and politician, who had served as minister of supply in 1939–40 and would eventually serve his country as prime minister, Fieandt was as distinguished a negotiator as the Germans could hope to face. His selection also seemed to meet with their pleasure. Blücher generously recommended him to the German Foreign Ministry as a man "regarded as friendly to Germany" and as one who "maintains intimate contacts with the legation."[66]

It is impossible to say what Fieandt's instructions might have been had he gone to Berlin in May, at the time of his appointment.

When he and his colleagues finally did leave Helsinki on June 8, much had happened to influence the Finnish attitude to Germany. The Norwegian situation was fully clarified, and spectacular German victories on the western front indicated that France would soon be out of the war and England out of the continent. Finland was rapidly being propelled by the force of events into an entirely new frame of mind. "The feats of German arms in the west have made the deepest impression everywhere in Finland," reported Blücher on May 22. They "pave the way for the realization that a new balance of power in Europe is in the making and are now silencing all criticism of the German march through Holland and Belgium."[67] Two weeks later he cabled: "Events in the western theater of war are forcing a rising awareness in many quarters of the errors of a British-oriented foreign policy and are giving the upper hand to social strata friendly to Germany."[68]

Thus it was perhaps not surprising that Fieandt should have given clear expression to a new Finnish foreign policy when he talked at length with Blücher prior to his departure for Berlin.[69] Acknowledging that the British-oriented trade policy had been a failure, the Finnish government was ready for "the most extensive adjustment of its economic policy to Germany," he announced. Even the Anglophile Prime Minister Ryti was now "ready for a change of mind."[70] If Germany would guarantee that the Finnish mines could be profitably operated, the Finns were prepared to deliver copper and molybdenum "to the limit of the technically possible." More than that, the previously submitted German request for Petsamo nickel was "not rejected any more." When Blücher suggested that International Nickel might give up its concession rights in Petsamo, Fieandt promised to discuss the prospect with Dr. Söderhjelm, the managing director of the Petsamo Nickel Company. His personal opinion, he said, was that "Germany could jump in" if the Anglo-Canadian trust were to pull out. In view of Fieandt's statements, it was not surprising that Blücher advised the Foreign Ministry in Berlin to instruct the German negotiators to deal with the chairman of the Finnish delegation in a friendly and open manner, for he was "animated by the very best intentions" and had thought for some time that Finland's geographical location dictated a German orientation of its economic policy.

In the course of the lengthy conversation, Fieandt also remarked that the Finns were worried about a possible British invasion of the Petsamo area. Blücher assured him that such a prospect was utterly impossible. He "evaded" Fieandt's question as to whether Germany considered Finland to belong to the Soviet sphere of interest. In fact, however, he was not at all confident on that score, and he was deeply concerned about a possible Soviet invasion of the Petsamo area. As Fieandt left for Berlin, Blücher informed the Foreign Ministry that the Russians appeared ready to set up a consulate in Petsamo, as was their privilege under the terms of the Treaty of Moscow. Blücher urged that a German consulate be established there also, and as quickly as possible. From such an observation post, Germany would be able to keep an eye on shipping through the port of Liinahamari as well as on the nickel operations at Kolosjoki.[71]

That proposal was the start of a persistent personal campaign by the German minister in Helsinki to arouse the interest of his government in the Petsamo area as a place which held a particularly great significance for Germany itself. Initially, Blücher's purpose seemed to be simply to bring home the point that the area was precariously located, and if Germany hoped to get the nickel ore from Kolosjoki it would be necessary to take certain concrete political and military steps. Eventually, however, as Blücher grew worried about a new Soviet threat to Finland's security, his campaign tended to overstate the importance of the Petsamo area and to tie its security in with the security of Finland as a whole. He seemed to be making the point that as Finland goes, so goes Petsamo; since Germany had a stake in Petsamo, it would therefore also have to take an interest in the security of Finland. As will be shown, he made his point regarding the significance of the Petsamo area for Germany, but failed in his larger purpose. While Hitler would soon decide that the Russians should never have the Petsamo area, his subsequent decision to keep them out of Finland altogether rested on entirely different premises.

On June 10, the day on which Norway's armed forces capitulated, Blücher advised the Foreign Ministry that the Anglo-French withdrawal from Narvik was of "great significance for our political and economic position in Finland." It would facilitate the establishment of German control of Petsamo shipping as well as "the achievement of our aims with respect to the nickel there."[72] It seemed necessary to act quickly, however, for even though the Norwegians had surrendered, the German forces in Norway had not yet advanced north of Narvik, leaving the large northernmost province of Finnmark—which in the east adjoined the Petsamo area—practically a military no-man's-land. Problems of logistics made an early occupation of Finnmark by German troops impossible. Because of that, paragraph 7 of the German-Norwegian armistice agreement, which stipulated that the Norwegian High Command in Tromsö would handle the demobilization of the Norwegian military units in Finnmark itself, called for two Norwegian infantry battalions and one artillery battery to remain under arms and guard the eastern border.[73]

But a few miles to the east, Russian troops stood poised on their border with Petsamo, and it was rumored that they planned to cross it and continue right into the military vacuum of Finnmark. Blücher brought this alarming prospect to the attention of the German Foreign Ministry on June 11. He reported that the Finnish General Staff feared that the Russians were about to acquire a foothold in Kirkenes, and Colonel Horst Rössing, the German military attaché, had been told by Finnish staff officers that they hoped the Germans themselves would quickly reach eastern Finnmark. Blücher also relayed the information that the Russians were hurriedly fortifying the western coast of the Rybachi Peninsula, "from where they command the entry to Petsamo harbor."[74]

The news was quickly relayed to the military authorities, and the rumor concerning the Russian intentions in North Norway stirred up a flurry of excitement in both the High Command of the Army (OKH) and the OKW. By evening, Blücher's telegram had been forwarded to the headquarters of the German Army in Norway,[75] whose chief of staff, Colonel Erich Buschenhagen, got off a radio message before midnight to his liaison officer with the Norwegian High Command in Tromsö: "Fuehrer has ordered that Norwegian border battalions in East Finnmark must be placed under German command. You will assume command until further notice."[76] By noon the next day, Buschenhagen was able to report to the OKW that the Finnish-Norwegian border was secured by two reinforced Norwegian battalions under the authority of the Norwegian governor of Finnmark province, who in turn took his orders directly from the German army. Buschenhagen also reported that the Norwegian High Command feared a Soviet occupation of Kirkenes and had asked that the Germans garrison the area themselves. He requested permission to send an available SS unit to the border at once.[77] Less than two hours later he cabled the OKW again, on the basis of information received from the Finnish General Staff through the Norwegian High Command, that the Russians were massing troops along the Murman Coast, ostensibly for the purpose of moving on Kirkenes.[78] The OKW, however, was inclined to doubt this information,[79] and it was decided that the Norwegian units could guard the border without SS reinforcements.[80]

But the excitement was not yet over. General Otto Ruge, the Norwegian commander in chief, told the German liaison officer attached to his staff that North Norway had been described on a Moscow radio broadcast as "presently ownerless, and a buffer state must be established."[81] It was Ruge's opinion that the Germans ought to carry out their occupation of Finnmark all the way to the Finnish border as speedily as possible. That this argument should have been made by Ruge, whose loyalty to the exiled Norwegian government was firmly established, is notable because it demonstrated that the Norwegians, like the Finns, chose Germany if the only alternative was the Soviet Union. To Ruge's military argument, Blücher added a political one: "If progress is not made in the German-Finnish negotiations over the Petsamo nickel question, it should be suggested that Kirkenes be occupied quickly. The German colors in Kirkenes would agreeably strengthen the accommodating tendencies of the Finnish government."[82]

Apparently the OKW was not persuaded by General Ruge's information, and the Foreign Ministry was unimpressed by Blücher's advice. Not until July 22 did an SS battalion take over the defense of the Norwegian-Finnish border in the Petsamo area,[83] and two days later the demobilization of the two Norwegian border guard battalions was finally completed.[84]

Blücher's suggestion to fly the German flag in Kirkenes was superfluous advice. The Finns no longer needed to be prodded into an agreement on the Petsamo nickel ore with Germany. The total collapse of France before the massive German onslaught came as a profound shock to most Finns and proved to be a sufficiently persuasive argument even in the nickel question. According to

Blücher, the Finnish reaction to the fall of France was as follows: "Recognition of the German leadership and of German soldiers finds spontaneous expression everywhere. Mixed in are voices which speak of a new and better Europe and perceive in a German hegemony a guarantee against the danger from the east."[85] The Finnish reaction was expressed more concretely by the government's decision to extend *de jure* recognition to the German puppet state of Slovakia, to withdraw its chargé d'affaires from the exiled Norwegian government in London, and to take up the question of Finland's membership in the League of Nations for renewed examination.[86]

In a political report written toward the end of June, Blücher gave further examples of the radical changes being wrought in Finnish attitudes. He noted that the conservative National Coalition Party was attempting to pressure the government into assuming its place in Hitler's New Order in Europe. And he reported that Foreign Minister Witting had become so favorably disposed toward him that they met almost daily and conferred with each other in complete confidence and candor. Not only did Witting keep him thoroughly informed about all important developments, but he even allowed Blücher to read for himself the actual "relevant telegrams" that passed across his desk.[87]

If the apparent victory of Hitler's New Order in Europe was one decisive propellant of the Finnish ship of state as its officers charted a new and, they hoped, safer foreign policy course, ingrained distrust and fear of the Soviet Union was the other. The Finns had long suspected that their country had been assigned to the Soviet sphere of interest. When the Russians in mid-June opened their drive to incorporate the Baltic states, Bessarabia, and Bukovina into the USSR, the Finns thought they knew what was in store for them. The Russian measures in the Baltic states "trigger nervousness in the Finnish people," reported Blücher on June 17.[88] Kivimäki, who on June 18 paid his first official visit as the new Finnish minister in Berlin to Minister Werner von Grundherr, head of the Scandinavian and Baltic States desk in the Political Department of the Foreign Ministry, claimed that the events in Estonia, Latvia, and Lithuania were viewed "with calmness" in Helsinki, but he added that "one can never be sure about the Russians."[89] The Helsinki correspondent of the German News Bureau (DNB) reported widespread fears in Finland,[90] and this was confirmed by Blücher.[91] The Swedish minister in Berlin, Arvid Richert, expressed the concern of his government to State Secretary Weizsäcker on June 19.[92] That same day, Minister Wilhelm Fabricius in Bucharest informed Berlin that "concrete information" received from the Rumanian General Staff indicated that "the Soviet Union has prepared strong forces against Finland and that Finland was in grave danger."[93] A spate of stories in the Soviet press, charging that the allegedly unpopular and incompetent regime in Finland was causing all sorts of distress for the suffering masses, further heightened Finnish apprehensions.[94]

But the signs of imminent danger to Finland abated temporarily while the Soviet Union went through the ritual procedure of annexing the three Baltic States, Bessarabia, and Bukovina. When the danger signals reappeared in late July, they were to trigger a swift and thorough German re-evaluation of Finland's role in the future German scheme of things.

The indications of sinister Soviet designs on Finland are recounted here because they served to pave the way for a growing Finnish conviction that only Germany could prevent the Soviet Union from completing the process, begun with the Winter War, of destroying independent Finland. If the Soviet Union had given concrete and credible evidence of a resolve to respect Finland's territorial integrity, the Finnish drift toward Germany might have been halted in time. Had the Soviet government made it possible for the Finns to satisfy their economic requirements by trading with their eastern neighbor and with the outside world through Soviet territory, Germany might not have been able to draw Finland into its economic web. But the Russians did none of these things. Instead they were constantly making new demands upon Finland, accusing the Finns of aggressive intentions, and interfering in domestic Finnish affairs.[95] They behaved in such a fashion that the Finns had to expect the worst. Even a vigorous critic of Finnish foreign policy during 1940–41, a critic whose purpose it was to investigate whether Finland had "maintained her virtue intact during the years of close association with the bully-boy of Europe, Nazi Germany," was moved to comment that "to a considerable degree the Soviet leaders were themselves responsible for this misfortune." By isolating Finland from the outside world, "they virtually forced it into close economic cooperation with Germany."[96]

Familiarity with this general background is important for an understanding of the very accommodating spirit of the Finnish trade negotiators in Berlin in June, 1940. While they could be tough enough on the business level, they seemed to be as anxious as their German colleagues to forge a stronger economic tie between the two countries than had been the case in the past. Unfortunately, the surviving records seem to contain very little information about the negotiations themselves, though the texts of the agreements concluded are available.[97] The records reveal nothing about the discussions of the Petsamo nickel question. We know that the negotiations lasted three weeks, and we also know that the representatives of the Finnish government readily agreed in principle to let Germany purchase the majority of the ore to be extracted in Kolosjoki, perhaps as much as 75 per cent of it. But the political agreement was to be implemented only after the business interests directly involved had worked out the practical details between themselves. In the nickel question, the firms involved were the Petsamo Nickel Company and the I.G. Farbenindustrie.

I.G. Farbenindustrie was a relative newcomer to the nickel industry. During the 1920's, experiments conducted by scientists of this firm in Oppau, near Ludwigshafen on the Rhine, led to the development of a process which, when applied to nickel ore, recovered the refined nickel in the form of a fine powder. The method, which was patented in 1932, proved to be particularly well suited for the refinement of nickel-copper ores and produced the metal in purer form than achieved by previously used methods. I.G. Farbenindustrie hoped that its newly patented process might enable it to challenge the position of International Nickel, which in 1932 controlled about 85 per cent of the world production, and which traditionally protected its near monopoly by refusing to sell either nickel ore or nickel matte, its unfinished concentrate. But efforts to obtain nickel ore from Finland, Norway, Greece, South Africa, Brazil, and Australia failed, and Germany's own ore fields were too small and too poor to be exploited economically. Eventually, in April, 1934, a deal was made with International Nickel. Interested in the new process patented by I.G. Farbenindustrie, International Nickel consented to deliver nickel-copper matte to the German firm for a period of ten years. With a guaranteed supply of raw material, I.G. Farbenindustrie expanded the capacity of its Oppau works, and in 1937 it began construction of a second plant at Frose near Nachterstedt in central Germany. Completed shortly before the outbreak of World War II, the Frose works remained idle when the hostilities cut off the Canadian source of matte. Nevertheless, I.G. Farbenindustrie had become an important producer of nickel. Of Germany's total consumption of about 9,000 metric tons of nickel in 1939, two-thirds were produced in Germany itself, and of this I.G. Farbenindustrie produced 4,168 tons (as compared with 110 tons in 1933), or more than twice the combined output of its three competitors—Friedrich Krupp, Norddeutsche Affinerie, and Blaufarbenwerke.[98]

Anticipating the martial conflict which began in September, 1939, I.G. Farbenindustrie had continued its search for a European source of nickel ore supplies. Early that year, it had reached an understanding with International Nickel and Mond Nickel whereby I.G. Farbenindustrie obtained the option to examine the newly discovered ore deposit at Nivala in Finland, and negotiations with the Finnish authorities were begun in June. Although no immediate results were achieved, the talks, coupled with the fact that the Finns became accustomed to think of I.G. Farbenindustrie as a business associate of the Anglo-Canadian trust, prepared the ground for the negotiations which were to follow a year later.[99]

The detailed diary notes of Eduard Weber-Andreae, director and member of the executive committee of I.G. Farbenindustrie, shed some light on this search for European nickel ore and on the close relationship between the firm and the Ministry of Economics. The man who was in charge of both of these activities was Paul Haefliger, also a director and member of I.G. Farbenindustrie's executive committee. On December 23, 1939, Weber-Andreae noted that Haefliger had briefed the Ministry of Economics on the firm's relations with International Nickel, and he had also drawn the Ministry's attention to the great significance of Petsamo as a source of nickel.[100] What Haefliger was obviously looking for was a plausible excuse for separating the Anglo-Canadian trust from its Petsamo mining concession. Within three months, he had found it. "Haefliger has determined," wrote Weber-Andreae in his diary, "that INCO has violated its agreement with us, and that we may therefore grab hold of the ore in Petsamo with the aid of the

Finnish government."[101] The nature of the alleged violation was not made clear, nor did the Finnish government seem anxious to cooperate. Weber-Andreae noted in late May that the question remained completely unsolved, and no deliveries from Petsamo could be expected for at least two years even in the best of circumstances.[102] For the time being, I.G. Farbenindustrie tried to work out an arrangement with Krupp for the day when the Petsamo ore should become available to Germany. Haefliger wanted a cooperative effort whereby I.G. Farbenindustrie would handle the production of nickel, Krupp would be the major consumer of it, and Metallgesellschaft in Frankfurt would handle the sale of the surplus to other consumers.[103]

In view of its predominant role in the German nickel industry, it was only logical that I.G. Farbenindustrie should be asked by the German government to participate in the negotiations with the Finns in June, 1940. On June 19, Haefliger was asked by the Foreign Ministry to join the negotiators the next day.[104] The implication of this would appear to be that delivery of Petsamo nickel ore to Germany had by then already been agreed upon in principle by the two government delegations, and that the time had come to turn the detailed negotiations of a commercial contract over to the firms concerned. As it turned out, these negotiations did not proceed as smoothly as the Germans had expected. One major problem was the fact that the Germans were reluctant to pay the price which the Petsamo Nickel Company regarded as a reasonable minimum, and it was to take a considerable time before all of the various contracts involved were signed. While the basic delivery contract was concluded on July 23, 1940, the last of the additional agreements went unsigned until February 19, 1941. I.G. Farbenindustrie also conducted negotiations with the Outokumpu Company, which on August 22, 1940, contracted to deliver the entire output of nickel and copper from its Nivala mine to the Germans until the end of 1947.[105]

The most important obstacle to a speedy conclusion of the Petsamo negotiations was political rather than economic, however. On June 23, at a moment when the Finns and the Germans were in sight of a final agreement, the Soviet government suddenly submitted a demand of its own to Finland, a demand which covered not only delivery of nickel from Petsamo, but also the transfer of the mining concession to the Soviet government in some suitable form. Finland found itself on the spot, and consternation reigned in Berlin.[106] As Weizsäcker told the German ambassador in Moscow, Count Friedrich W. von der Schulenburg, the "most important point in the German-Finnish trade negotiations was delivery of nickel from the Petsamo mines."[107] When the Russians began to use pressure on Finland to obtain the Petsamo concession, Blücher advised the German Foreign Ministry to hurry up and sign the trade treaty as it then stood and continue the Petsamo nickel negotiations separately. No risk was involved in such a procedure, said Blücher, for the Finns would not refuse to negotiate to a successful conclusion. "We need apply no pressure in this matter, since the Finnish government will give full consideration to our wishes and resistance exists only in Moscow," he cabled to Berlin.[108]

It was sound advice, as the Foreign Ministry instantly recognized. Within twenty-four hours, Blücher was notified that the Finnish-German trade treaty, incorporating a number of special agreements, had been signed in the afternoon of June 29 by Schnurre and Fieandt. In addition, an exchange of letters had been prepared and initialled by these two men, by which Finland committed itself to deliver nickel ore to Germany, even though blank spaces had to be left for dates and for the quantity of nickel involved. These spaces would be filled in and the actual exchange of the letters would take place whenever Petsamo Nickel and I.G. Farbenindustrie reached their agreement.[109]

That the general attitude of the Fieandt delegation had been a very accommodating one is clear. A final indication of it was given in a memorandum by Schnurre, signed on July 1.[110] Recapitulating the attitude of the Finnish delegation and summarizing the agreements arrived at, it referred to the nickel matter only in a brief sentence, noting that the "negotiations about delivery of nickel ore from the Petsamo area have not yet been brought to a conclusion and are being continued separately." It may be deduced from the unconcerned tone of the sentence that Schnurre shared Blücher's confidence regarding the eventual success of those negotiations. His memorandum also demonstrated the complete reorientation of Finland's economic policy which the treaty reflected. "There was full agreement," he wrote, "that Finnish foreign trade with our enemies either via Petsamo or via Russia is out of the question for the future." Fieandt had referred to this as "self-evident," even though Schnurre had not insisted that the Finns commit their benevolent attitude to paper.

The nickel negotiations were not yet completed, but the Finns and the Germans both knew that it was merely a matter of time before the commercial contracts would be signed. What the entry of the Soviet Union into the nickel picture might entail was a new and unknown factor, and it did worry the Germans as the Berlin negotiations ended, but the fact remained that the Finns had already committed themselves to Germany in the Petsamo question. Whether that move would pay political dividends was now the question uppermost in the minds of Finland's leaders.

CHAPTER II

In the Cross Fire of
Great Power Interests

W HEN Molotov summoned Paasikivi to the Kremlin on June 23, 1940, and asked that Finland "grant the nickel concession to the Soviet Union, or agree to the establishment of a Finnish-Russian company, or make some other arrangement,"[1] the Finnish minister was thoroughly taken aback.[2] After his painful negotiations in Moscow in October-November, 1939 and March, 1940, he had come to the conclusion that the Petsamo area was of no particular interest to the Russians. Their failure to bring it up at all during the three and a half months since the peace treaty had tended to confirm him in this belief. Only once during that period had Petsamo made news in the Soviet press. On May 1, the Reuter correspondent in Paris had circulated a report which claimed that the Soviet Union had offered to return to Finland the city of Viipuri and the naval lease area at Hanko if the Finns would surrender instead the Åland Islands and the Petsamo area to the Soviet Union. The story was emphatically denied three days later by the official Soviet news agency, Tass.[3]

That Paasikivi should have been so surprised by the Soviet démarche in the Petsamo question is puzzling. It would have been more surprising had it not occurred. In a series of talks and formal negotiations with the Finns since the spring of 1938, the Russians had consistently given expression to their fundamental fear of a future German aggression against the Soviet Union. That fear had been the basic cause of the Winter War, and it had been voiced again on various occasions since the Winter War by Soviet officials.[4] That the extension of German military power to the Arctic region of Norway, within easy striking distance of the Kola Peninsula, should have triggered a Soviet countermove was only logical. Paasikivi was not unaware of this logic. But somehow he was not fully persuaded that it was the real reason for the sudden Soviet demand. "All of this can get its full explanation only in the future," he wrote in his memoirs.[5]

Though a man of explosive temper, Paasikivi was not one to commit impulsive statements to paper. In this instance, however, he should have been capable of ending his speculation with a period rather than a question mark. The evidence fully reinforces Arvi Korhonen's conclusion: "Such as the situation was developing in the year 1940, the question of control over the [Petsamo] area should have appeared on the agenda even if there were nothing there but reindeer lichen."[6]

Paasikivi's immediate reaction to Molotov's disturbing request was to fall back on what he himself would probably have described as a typically Finnish argument: it was legally impossible. His memoirs are full of references to the frustrations of trying to establish a dialogue between Finns and Russians, basically because the Russians approached international relations from the point of view of power realities, while the Finns took their stand on the letter of the written law and the principles of justice. Paasikivi often chided his countrymen, including his colleagues in the foreign service, for failing to understand and adjust to the facts of life of power politics. He thought they lived in a world of illusions. Yet, when abruptly confronted with Molotov's demand, he took refuge instinctively in the same legalistic position. "I pointed out," he reported to Witting, "that the concession had been granted to an English corporation, and that we are probably legally bound in the matter, but that if we are free to act, we would be just as pleased to sell nickel to the Soviet Union as to others."[7] The main problem, he told Molotov, concerned the amount of nickel that Finland might be able to sell to the Russians, since he did not know how much of the Kolosjoki production had already been promised to Germany.[8] In his subsequent report to Helsinki, he recommended that the most favorable consideration be given to the wishes of the Soviet government.[9]

Paasikivi's instinctive reply to Molotov's demand had been the correct one, as the official Finnish response confirmed. Delivered to Molotov by the Finnish minister on June 27, it stressed the legal rights of the Anglo-Canadian trust, but it also declared that Finland was prepared to do everything possible to secure 50 per cent of the nickel production for the Soviet Union, provided that Germany would be willing to reduce its claim from 75 per cent to one-half. To Molotov, this was "not an answer." He had demanded the concession, not the nickel. The Russians were "not now interested in the ore, but in the area itself and the nickel in it, for all time," he said. The British "must be cleared out of the area." He was not impressed at all by the legal argument against that, for he was "convinced that if the Finnish government is desirous of annulling the concession given to the [British] corporation, the corporation will raise no obstacles." Nor would the Germans cause any difficulties, he asserted. He repeated his demand that the Anglo-Canadian concession be annulled in favor of the Soviet Union or a Finnish-Russian company.[10]

Two things emerged clearly from the Paasikivi-Molotov confrontation on June 27. First, the Soviet interest in the Petsamo area was political and not economic. Second, the Soviet Union expected to exercise exclusive influence in the area. Molotov's demand that the British be "cleared out of the area" was obviously directed against all other great powers also, including Germany. If this second conclusion was implicit in the demand for the removal of the British, it was explicit in the demand for the concession itself, because the elimination of the Petsamo Nickel Company entailed the annulment of the as yet unfinished contracts to be signed by that company and I.G. Farbenindustrie. Ultimately this meant that the political guarantee of these contracts, embodied in the still pending exchange of letters between the two governments, would not be worth the paper on which it was written. Finnish acceptance of the Soviet demand would force the Germans to deal with the Russians in the nickel matter.

One writer has suggested that the Soviet Union might have had an economic motive for stepping into the Petsamo question when it did: "She might have wanted to build up a semi-monopoly position in nickel production which would have been a valuable bargaining counter with Germany, who desperately needed this metal for her armaments industry, but there is little evidence to suggest that this was a primary motive."[11] There is in fact no evidence that this was any kind of a motive, although the suggestion does have the credible ring of intelligent speculation. However, as the same writer admits, the Soviet intervention in the Petsamo question "does not make much sense as a question of economics," and the reasons were therefore "probably political."[12]

Whether or not the Soviet motives were purely political and the German motives purely economic, Finland was caught squarely in the middle. Finland had already executed a complete reorientation of its economic policy to the German orbit without having obtained any assurances that Germany would, if necessary, restrain the Soviet Union from resorting to extreme measures against Finland. What Germany might do should the Soviet Union wave the big stick to get its way in Petsamo, as it was soon to do, was now the big question for Finland's leaders.

They also had to consider what England might do. It is too strong to say that Finland "could not afford to offend the British government by confiscating its [sic] concession" in Petsamo,[13] but it is true that England was capable of retaliating should the concession be menaced. The port of Liinahamari was Finland's only remaining outlet to overseas markets. Germany was in a position to plug it, but had not done so because Finland by this route obtained certain important goods from the United States and South America which Germany itself could not provide for Finland. England, of course, held the master key to the Petsamo traffic, as long as the British fleet dominated the Atlantic. And at the end of July, 1940, as a weapon in its economic war against Germany, the British government ordered the introduction of compulsory navicerts for neutral ships and cargoes. To obtain them, shipowners had to satisfy the British Ministry of Economic Warfare that their ships would not be used for the benefit of the enemy. Ships sailing without navicerts would be treated as blockade-runners by the Royal Navy.[14]

Finland's dilemma was, therefore, three-sided. It was caught, as Paasikivi expressed it, "in the cross fire of the interests of three great powers," Germany, the Soviet Union, and England. He seemed to think that this was the real tragedy of the situation. "From all three quarters demands were presented and pressure exerted on us," he lamented. "Without taking our predicament into account, each of the big three demanded that we solve the problem in complete accordance with its interests and stand firm against the others."[15] One must of course concede to Paasikivi that Finland's situation was not an enviable one, but there was also a brighter side to it, a side which Paasikivi's deeply pessimistic nature would perhaps not permit him to see. Had Finland faced the Soviet Union alone in the Petsamo question, the situation would have been hopeless, since everything would have depended on the intentions of the Soviet Union. As things stood, however, there might be room for the Finns to maneuver. Of the two alternatives, being caught in the cross fire was clearly the preferable one.

Witting, and his envoys, were fully aware of this from the outset. On June 29, Witting suggested to Blücher that the nickel problem ought to be worked out jointly by Finland, Germany, and the Soviet Union.[16] The same day, Kivimäki reported on the latest developments in the Petsamo question to Under State Secretary Ernst Woermann, director of the Political Department in the German Foreign Ministry, and he concluded his lengthy exposition by suggesting that a joint Finnish-German-Soviet concession company might solve the problem.[17] Two days later, Witting again suggested to Blücher that the conclusion of a three-way agreement was the most suitable solution.[18] And the Finnish minister in Stockholm, Professor Jarl Axel Wasastjerna, told Counselor Carl von Below of the German legation that "in the nickel question it was not for Finland to decide, but the decision must be made by Berlin and Moscow."[19]

None of these hints and suggestions succeeded in eliciting the German response that the Finns wanted. Blücher, Woermann, and Below listened attentively, perhaps even sympathetically, but they remained noncommittal. For obvious reasons, the Germans would not be pinned down to a commitment to Finland. The German policy vis-à-vis Finland had not yet been clarified. Soviet interests were involved, and the Germans feared that if they expressed any kind of support for the Finns, the Finns might embarrass and possibly compromise Germany in its relations with the Soviet Union.

But the Germans were far more interested than the Finns realized, and they kept in close touch with developments both in Helsinki and Moscow. It worried them that Molotov had brought up the Petsamo question before the Finnish-German agreements were completed, because it had provided him with a plausible excuse for rejecting the priority of the German claim. Since the Germans had signed Finland over to the Soviet Union less than one year before, it might be difficult for them to press an economic claim there in the face of a conflicting Soviet political claim. The fact that the German claim had not yet acquired the legal status of an international treaty at the time when the Soviet bid was put in did not make things any easier. As was to be expected, Molotov based his strategy squarely on this time element. It made no difference to him that the Finns and the Germans had actually reached an agreement in principle long before the signing of the trade treaty of June 29 and the delivery contract of July 23. Days before the actual signing of the treaty, German diplomatic correspondence referred to the agreement in the past tense.[20] By virtue of the Finnish promise to deliver "the major portion of the nickel ore production" to Germany, which supposedly justified the German priority claim, and with reference to "our needs, which the Russians surely appreciate," the Germans now appealed to Molotov to accept the Finnish-German agreement.[21]

Molotov's response bore out the worst forebodings of the German Foreign Ministry, and it set the stage for one of the most vexing German-Soviet controversies prior to the outbreak of war a year later. All the Soviet Union was trying to do in the Petsamo area, said Molotov to Schulenburg, was to get the British out. After the nickel concession had been taken over by a Soviet-Finnish company controlled by the Russians, the Germans could have their nickel. In fact, said Molotov, the Soviet government had "already decided to supply Germany with no less than one-half the Petsamo nickel ore output." If Germany wanted the full 75 per cent promised by the Finns, the Russians would give it "sympathetic" consideration.[22]

Although Molotov's position appeared to accommodate fully the German nickel interests, it did in fact endanger them alarmingly. It connoted a Soviet rejection of the Finnish-German nickel agreement by implicitly removing the Finnish government from the picture. The Soviet government now regarded itself as the rightful agent for all matters involving Petsamo. It had demanded that the nickel concession be turned over to a joint Soviet-Finnish company controlled by the Soviet Union, and it was so confident about the pending Finnish response that it was already making decisions about marketing the nickel output. In short, if the German government permitted Molotov's arrogant assumptions to go unchallenged, all of the arrangements already made with the Finns would automatically be cancelled, and the nickel negotiations would begin all over again—with the Russians. It was impossible to guess from Molotov's blandly benevolent words how such negotiations might turn out, for he had studiously avoided specifics, except for the promise to supply Germany with 50 per cent of the nickel ore produced. But even that promise was not adequately specific, since there was nothing in it to suggest for how long the Soviet Union might be willing to deliver the ore. As would later develop, his promise would have been worth no more than one or two months of deliveries.

There was also another alarming implication in Molotov's statements to Schulenburg. The reason why there was "no longer any room for the English in Petsamo" was, according to Molotov, that the Soviet Union had "secured special rights" there. He was to elaborate that point later,[23] unnecessarily, as it were, for the Germans understood him clearly enough the first time: no power other than the Soviet Union had any rights in the Petsamo area, and the door to Petsamo was Moscow.

In the light of the division of Europe into interest spheres, as agreed upon by the German and Soviet governments the previous August, it was not unreasonable of Molotov to expect that the Germans would bow out when the Soviet government decided to assert its rights in an area inside its own sphere. But Germany now had a vital interest at stake in the Petsamo area, and it was not about to renounce it without an argument. The problem was how to defend that interest without appearing to interfere unduly with the political rights previously conceded to the Soviet Union. The problem was turned over to van Scherpenberg as soon as Schulenburg's disturbing report came in from Moscow in the early morning of July 2. By the next day he had two documents ready for examination. The first was an informational telegram which was sent to Schulenburg over Ritter's signature right away to ensure that he avoid giving the Russians the impression that the Germans were satisfied with Molotov's attitude.[24] The other analyzed the nature of the German interest in Petsamo nickel and suggested possible ways of coping with the danger posed by the Soviet intervention. Over Weizsäcker's signature it was dispatched to Ribbentrop[25] along with a copy of Ritter's telegram, since the decision in this important matter would obviously have to be made by the foreign minister himself.

Both of these documents revealed the consternation prevailing in the German Foreign Ministry. "The Soviet government is now pretending," said the informational telegram to Schulenburg, "that it is complying with a German request. The fact, however, is that we have been in accord with the Finnish government for a long time, and that the Soviet government has now deprived us of our success through its intervention with Finland." To accept Molotov's proposal "would entail an unfavorable development in the future," since everything would become "wholly dependent on the good or bad will" of the Russians. This would be most unfortunate, for the Germans knew from experience that Soviet demands were "much harder to meet than Finnish demands." Weizsäcker's memorandum to Ribbentrop, like the Ritter telegram, characterized Molotov's reply as "unsatisfactory for us" and proposed a German response on these lines: Germany had a great interest in the nickel ore in Petsamo and therefore wished to get the production started as quickly as possible. This could be done regardless of how the concession problem was solved. If the Anglo-Canadian concession were annulled, Germany wished to participate in whatever new arrangements were made in view of its special interests. Either a German-Soviet or a German-Soviet-Finnish concession company would be acceptable and would underscore the friendly cooperation which Germany and the Soviet Union were both striving for. Since the German economic interest was greater than the Russian, Germany should be entrusted with the technical leadership of the mining operation.

This proposed response side-stepped Molotov's basic point regarding exclusive Soviet influence in the Petsamo area by announcing a German claim to participate in the concession. That could perhaps be justified on economic grounds, as Weizsäcker proposed to do, but the Germans could not resist the temptation to strengthen their claim by alleging that in the concession matter, too, they had practically reached agreement with the Finns during the Berlin negotiations.[26] In his telegram to Schulenburg, Ritter maintained that the Finns "had always been on notice" that Germany wanted to succeed the Anglo-Canadian concessionaires at the earliest possible opportunity, and that the demand for delivery was merely "a stopgap solution." The German demand for participation in the concession when the time came had been "recognized in principle" by the Finnish government, asserted Ritter.

The assertion was false, though it may have been made in good faith as a result of a misunderstanding. Fieandt had told Blücher in early June that Germany would be welcome to take over the concession should it ever be given up by the Anglo-Canadian trust.[27] Ritter himself, in a lengthy memorandum of June 1 in which he had discussed the economic reorganization of Europe, had suggested that Germany, in the peace treaties to be concluded at the end of the war, take possession of all enemy industrial establishments within the "Greater Economic Sphere," including the Anglo-Canadian nickel mines in Finland."[28] But these were plans for the future, and they had never been discussed with the Finnish government, as Witting emphatically pointed out on July 6 when Blücher reported to him the contents of Ritter's telegram to Schulenburg. During the Finnish-German negotiations in Berlin in June, the German demands had been "not for participation in the *concession,* but for a share of the *output,*" said Witting. He had been so informed by Fieandt and Dr. Ramsay, the leading members of the Finnish delegation.[29] Ritter's assertion, therefore, was not accurate.

A few days earlier, Witting had discussed the concession problem with Blücher. He had noted that the entire problem had been subjected to a thorough review by Finnish experts, and the conclusion they had arrived at was that the contract which the Finnish government had entered into with the Anglo-Canadian trust was without loopholes and could not be annulled "even by an act of God." Only if the present concessionaires were willing to sell their interest in the mine to the Finnish government could a three-way concession arrangement involving Finland, Germany, and the Soviet Union be achieved.[30] Blücher had also spoken with Dr. Ramsay about the matter and had noted the latter's thoughts as follows: "1) Finland to get the mine. 2) Canadians to keep the concession. 3) Output to be turned over to Germany or Russia. State must put itself in the picture and buy out English trust in order to pass it [i.e., concession] on to G[ermany] and R[ussia]."[31] These two conversations had been duly reported by Blücher to the German Foreign Ministry, where they had not been contradicted.[32] Hence it would appear that Ritter's misrepresentation was not accidental. This supposition is further reinforced by the fact that the Foreign Ministry continued to use Ritter's false claim in discussions with the Russians even after Witting had exposed it, a procedure which would soon cause Germany considerable embarrassment.[33]

On July 3, Paasikivi submitted the Finnish reply to Molotov's demands of June 27. The Finnish government was favorably inclined in the matter, he said, and negotiations would be started with the Anglo-Canadian trust with a view to buying it out. Molotov urged that these negotiations be expedited, but he foresaw no difficulties with the Canadians. The decision was up to the trust, said Paasikivi.[34]

If anything else was said during the interview, it has not been recorded. But almost at once it was rumored that a Finnish-Soviet agreement had been reached. Paasikivi's closest friend among the foreign diplomats in Moscow, the Swedish Minister Vilhelm Assarsson, told Ambassador Schulenburg that this agreement, about which he had been informed by Paasikivi, would transfer the nickel concession to the Soviet government "on a strictly commercial basis."[35] Alarmed by Schulenburg's report, the Foreign Ministry immediately requested Blücher to check the information with Witting.[36] Blücher, who could have ended the confusion at that point, compounded it by replying that the concession had "not yet" been given to the Russians.[37] Thus the rumor, which must have originated as a misunderstanding between Paasikivi and Assarsson, or between Assarsson and Schulenburg, remained alive. When viewed in the light of two recent telegrams from Blücher, it appeared to spell trouble. Blücher had reported on July 4 that the British and Canadians opposed any arrangement which might result in nickel deliveries to Germany. The Finns had been so informed by a Canadian spokesman and by Molotov. Even Witting had acted as if he no longer knew for sure whether deliveries to Germany could actually be made.[38] Two days later, Blücher reported that the British minister in Helsinki, Gordon Vereker, had notified the Finnish government that England would accept any reorganization of the nickel company "provided the entire output goes to Russia."[39]

As these communications were interpreted in the German Foreign Ministry, Germany's nickel interests in Petsamo were now seriously menaced. Haefliger of I.G. Farbenindustrie, who had come to Helsinki on July 5 to negotiate the delivery contract with the Petsamo Nickel Company,[40] was told by Blücher to do nothing which might create a "counterpoise to Russia." Specifically, he was instructed to do nothing about the concession matter and to leave open the volume of nickel ore to be delivered to Germany.[41] A cautious approach was necessary so long as the Foreign Ministry was still considering its next step in the Petsamo question. That study was proceeding rapidly.

On July 8, a memorandum[42] prepared in van Scherpenberg's division of the Economic Policy Department of the Foreign Ministry was forwarded to Ritter by Wiehl along with a brief typewritten comment by the latter.[43] This typewritten note, plus the handwritten comments made on it and on an additional appended page,[44] indicated the nature of the dilemma: how to encourage the Finns to resist the Soviet demands without implying German support for the Finnish position, lest the Finns play off the Germans against the Russians. One of Ritter's two comments on the note also revealed the urgency of the matter. If Ribbentrop found it impossible to reach an immediate decision on how the envoys in Helsinki and Moscow were to be instructed, then van Scherpenberg's memorandum, prepared as a draft telegram,[45] should be sent to Helsinki at once anyway "since there is danger in delay." Ritter regarded such a procedure as harmless, "since waiting for the foreign minister's instruction is necessary only with regard to Moscow, not with regard to Helsinki."

The telegram was forwarded to Helsinki the next day by Wiehl.[46] It reiterated the false assertion made by Ritter the week before and already denied by Witting, although this time it was phrased somewhat less categorically. "The course of the negotiations here could not have left the Finnish delegation in doubt that we are interested primarily in a concession," began the telegram. The Germans had "accepted the agreement about delivery of nickel ore only as an interim solution, since the Finnish government believed that there was no possibility at present of inducing the Canadians to give up the concession." However, the situation had changed since the Berlin negotiations, continued Wiehl. The English and Canadians had made an attempt to "play the concession into the hands of third parties to our disadvantage," and that could not go unchallenged. Hence the Finnish government should be warned against any "collaboration" in such an anti-German game. If it went along with the Anglo-Canadian schemes, Germany was bound to get the impression that the Finnish government, "contrary to assurances given us, is supporting English intrigues against us." Blücher was instructed to "warn the Finnish government urgently against taking any definitive steps without first having come to terms with us about them."

As an attempt to encourage Finnish resistance against Soviet demands in the Petsamo area without implying German support for Finland, this was a clumsy effort. The Finns understood the message too well, both the explicitly stated German interest in the concession and the implicit German support contained in the warning. Small countries do not normally react to a stern warning from the government of a great power with elation, but such was Witting's reaction in this case. It filled him with deep satisfaction, he told Blücher, that Germany was so interested in the Petsamo concession. Personally he could conceive of no better solution than to have Germany take over the concession. It had come to his attention, he said, that Germany planned to demand the concession in the peace negotiations with England, and he would welcome that, since it would establish an "incontestable legal basis" for the transfer.[47]

Witting was in an unusually good mood during this interview. He had just received a telegram from Paasikivi, according to which the Soviet government had declared itself willing to "limit its 1940 purchases of nickel ore from Finland to 40 per cent, on condition that the rest of the ore is sold to Germany."[48] Arkady A. Sobolev, the secretary general of the Commissariat for Foreign Affairs, had stated that his government was for the present interested in the nickel ore as well as the concession and the removal of the British from Petsamo. He had also said that Finland could purchase diesel oil in the Soviet Union, which Witting took as an indication of a more conciliatory Soviet attitude. On the basis of this information, he had already instructed Kivimäki, he told Blücher, to notify the

German government of Finland's intention to deliver 60 per cent of the Petsamo nickel ore production to Germany and to start operations at Kolosjoki at the earliest possible date. Other and more complex matters, "such as granting of the concession," could be settled in the course of the year. Blücher noted in his report to Berlin that Witting spoke of this new development "in a very gratified tone."[49]

Temporarily, Witting had a good reason to be satisfied. The Petsamo question seemed to have been taken partly out of his hands by the intervention of England and Germany. For the next seven or eight weeks the Russians were in fact to give him less trouble over this vexing problem than the British, as the diplomatic game over Petsamo shifted from Moscow-Helsinki to Moscow-Berlin, Berlin-Helsinki, and Helsinki-London.

On July 13, the German Foreign Ministry sent a copy of Blücher's report on the Sobolev proposal to the embassy in Moscow. Ambassador Schulenburg was instructed to inform Molotov that Germany was prepared to accept this proposal as an interim solution, even though it fell far short of what Germany stood to gain from its agreements with Finland. With the Sobolev proposal in mind, the German government would continue its talks with the Finnish government and proceed with the technical preparations for starting the production at Kolosjoki. As far as the concession went, the German government reserved the right "to make further proposals designed to safeguard German interests." In the meantime it was investigating the possibility of splitting the concession territorially into two parts, "since a joint German-Soviet concession could become a source of unpleasant difficulties."[50] This instruction was relayed to Blücher the same night, and he was told to have I.G. Farbenindustrie's negotiator in Helsinki, Haefliger, determine whether a division of the mining operation between German and Soviet concession companies could be effected.[51] After a trip to Kolosjoki, Haefliger reported this to be impossible, for the nickel deposit formed one continuous area.[52] The Finnish government, meanwhile, directed the Petsamo Nickel Company to put every effort into the job of getting the operation at Kolosjoki underway.[53]

That Haefligers' report on a divided concession was categorically negative was probably of very little consequence. The notion that such a solution should have met with greater favor in Moscow than any other, so long as Germany retained any influence at all in the Petsamo area, was an illusion. But if the report shattered this illusion, it also whetted Germany's appetite for the Petsamo area. Haefliger estimated the value of the nickel underground at one billion Reichsmarks, and he thought that it could be profitably exploited for at least twenty years. This meant, he said, that a share of 60 per cent of the output would cover the requirements of Greater Germany in full. If the necessary equipment could be installed promptly, he expected that up to 500 tons of nickel ore a day could be produced as of November, 1940. The ore could be shipped to Germany by way of Kirkenes, and the problems involved in facilitating the transport from the mine to the ore vessels could easily be worked out. Nickel matte and refined nickel could probably not be produced until the end of 1941. Haefliger did not yet have any reliable reports on the ore's nickel content, but he was optimistic. Cautiously, he speculated that the mine might yield some 10,000 tons of nickel matte and 5,000 tons of nickel a year.[54] Within four months, that estimate was revised upward fourfold.[55]

Ambassador Schulenburg saw Molotov on July 17 and presented the German position on the Petsamo question as explained to him in Ritter's telegram of July 3 and Weizsäcker's telegram of July 13. He had received no correction of the false allegation made in the former telegram. Consequently he told Molotov that the Finns had been notified during the Berlin negotiations in June that Germany was interested in the mining concession. Molotov was astonished and showed great displeasure. The Soviet government considered the Petsamo area "its exclusive domain, where it had stipulated new special privileges for itself in the peace treaty of 1940." No other power had any business there, "obviously not Germany either." The Soviet interest in the Petsamo area was primarily political and economic, and Germany's interest was "fully satisfied by the grant of the larger part of the nickel ore output there." That Germany should also wish to participate in the "readjustment of the conditions of the concession" was unwarranted and "something entirely new, of which thus far even Paasikivi had not informed him in any way," declared Molotov.[56]

Ritter's misrepresentation had come home to roost, and the German Foreign Ministry found itself in an embarrassing position. It could retreat gracefully and explain that there had been a misunderstanding, or it could stick to its guns and embarrass the Finns in their relations with the Soviet Union. Obviously a hasty retreat was the only possible course. Immediately after the arrival of Schulenburg's report, Schnurre drafted an instruction for the embassy in Moscow. It began with the categorical statement that "German-Finnish negotiations about a German concession in Petsamo have not taken place." The June negotiations had dealt only with the delivery of nickel ore to Germany. "There were no negotiations about the concession, since Finland would not touch the Canadian concession situation and we put off the matter until later peace negotiations with England." The Finns had merely been told that Germany would be interested in the concession whenever a change in the arrangements might occur. This explained why it had been impossible for Paasikivi to mention the matter to Molotov; there was nothing to tell. "In the interest of the Finnish position vis-à-vis the Soviet government it is important that this is made clear to the Soviet government," concluded Schnurre.[57]

He also drafted a four-part telegram for the legation in Helsinki, of which the first two parts merely repeated the telegram from Schulenburg and Schnurre's draft reply for Blücher's information. In the third part, Schnurre suggested a measure which had been made urgently necessary by the situation which had suddenly arisen: the commercial agreement between I.G. Farbenindustrie and Petsamo Nickel for delivery of 60 per cent of the nickel ore would have to be concluded "as fast as possible with legally binding effect," and I.G. Farbenindustrie's representatives in Finland should be told to get the technical apparatus at Kolosjoki in immediate shape for production. The question of whether Germany was to participate in the concession could remain open, suggested Schnurre in the last part of the telegram. Ribbentrop could make a decision on that later.[58]

Both of these draft telegrams were held back by the Foreign Ministry for several days. Only the last two parts of the telegram intended for Helsinki were dispatched at once, since there could be no doubt about the desirability of carrying out the suggested emergency measures designed to secure most of the nickel for Germany.[59] The instruction reached Blücher as he arrived in his office in the morning of July 20, and the final round of negotiations between the two sides got underway at once. On July 23, the delivery contract between I.G. Farbenindustrie and Petsamo Nickel was signed.[60] The next day Schnurre and Fieandt completed, signed, and exchanged the identical letters prepared in Berlin in late June.[61] Simultaneously, Fieandt addressed a strictly confidential letter to Blücher in which he pointed out that the removal of the original time limitation, which would have restricted deliveries to 1940 and 1941, signified that the two governments considered the agreement to constitute an "unlimited permanent arrangement." Even if one of the two firms involved in the private commercial contract should eventually wish to terminate it, the Finnish government would respect the wishes of the German government in any new arrangement.[62]

By this *fait accompli,* the German government had successfully established a plausible bargaining position versus the Soviet government in the Petsamo question. The Germans now had a valid legal contract, backed by a Finnish government guarantee, which stood in direct contradiction to the expressed wish of the Soviet government to limit deliveries of Petsamo nickel ore to Germany to the year 1940. The Finns had been fully aware of this Soviet wish. Whether they realized that they were now accomplices in a regular double cross perpetrated against the Soviet Union cannot be demonstrated, however. They knew that German-Soviet negotiations about the Petsamo question had been going on in Moscow, and they knew that these talks had been responsible for the Soviet agreement to let the Germans purchase 60 per cent of the nickel ore output. When I.G. Farbenindustrie suddenly announced its readiness to sign the long delayed delivery contract, the Finns may well have assumed that this, too, was a consequence of a German-Soviet understanding. At least this is how Witting explained the matter to Blücher on a later occasion, after it had become clear that the Soviet government was very upset about the contract having been signed behind its back, as it were.[63] At any rate, the Finns did not check on their assumption in Moscow at the time, and they could hardly have been expected to do so. For them, the greatest attainable measure of security seemed to be found in the cross fire of great power interests, and the nickel agreements with Germany promised to keep them in that position a while longer and more firmly than before. And if they really believed that the delivery contract had been made possible by advance Soviet consent, the failure of the Soviet government to protest against the contract confirmed such a belief.

Armed with their new trump card, the Germans were ready to take up Molotov's challenge of July 17. The pertinent points of the delivery contract were related to Schulenburg for his personal information on July 24,[64] but not until five days later did the Foreign Ministry instruct him what to tell Molotov. Apparently the emergency was over for the time being. The Germans had their legal contract, and they also had Witting's assurances that nobody could buy control of the Petsamo concession from International Nickel behind their backs, since shares in the Petsamo Nickel Company could not be traded without the explicit consent of the Finnish government.[65]

The draft of Schulenburg's instruction was completed on July 26. Incorporating Schnurre's draft telegram of eight days before, it also stated that the Germans would waive participation in the Petsamo concession and restrict themselves to the fulfillment of the Finnish-German delivery contract.[66] The telegram went out on July 30 over Weizsäcker's signature.[67] Whether Molotov would realize at once the full ramifications of the message he was about to receive remained to be seen. He would find out soon enough that a formidable roadblock had been placed in his path. The German Foreign Ministry awaited his reaction with interest and new-found confidence. However, for the time being there was no important reaction. Molotov seemed to have lost all interest in the Petsamo question.

England's interest, meanwhile, was just beginning to pick up. Witting told Blücher on July 19, without going into the details, that the English government was "suddenly causing trouble for Finnish shipping via Petsamo." He thought that this was England's answer to Finland's willingness to accommodate Germany in the nickel question.[68] Four days later, Witting noted that the British had illegally stopped a Finnish vessel en route from Petsamo to the United States and brought it into the Firth of Clyde. The Finnish minister in London, Georg A. Gripenberg, had reported that he expected the cargo of paper and cellulose to be confiscated. Also, only one of six Finnish vessels which for two weeks had been waiting for navicerts in American ports had received one. Previously, navicerts had always been granted without delay.[69] By the end of July, Witting was complaining to Blücher that the English were "causing new difficulties for Finland daily." They had denied navicerts to two Finnish vessels in the United States, vessels which were loaded with vitally important gasoline and aluminum. The Finns had been told that since they were selling their own products to the Soviet Union and Germany, they could buy their gasoline and aluminum in those countries also.[70]

That the stepped-up British interference with the Petsamo traffic was connected with the mounting evidence of an imminent Finnish-German agreement about nickel sales to Germany seems clear, and Minister Vereker filed a strong British protest with the Finnish government as soon as that agreement materialized.[71] Still, the British government was not without understanding or sympathy for Finland's difficult position. The formal protest against the nickel agreement was little more than a perfunctory diplomatic gesture. As Witting told the American minister, Arthur Schoenfeld, a few days later, the nickel agreement was of course "unpalatable" to the British, but they had acquiesced."[72]

However, Germany stood to gain considerable economic advantage from the availability of Finnish nickel ore, and England could not be unconcerned about that. Hence there was no good reason why Finland should be allowed to escape the consequences of its close economic relations with Engand's enemy by being exempted from the rules proclaimed by England for its conduct of the economic war. These rules, as they applied to trade between neutral European states and the Western Hemisphere, had been developed very cautiously since early in the war by the British, always mindful of avoiding anything which might offend the United States.[73] During the spring and early summer of 1940, the United States gradually came to accept the need for contraband control exercised by the British government, and a system was worked out whereby the U.S. State Department based its issuance of export licenses to foreign purchasing agents on the list of approved navicert applications provided by the British Ministry of Economic Warfare.[74] The upshot of this development was the British Reprisals Order of July 31, whereby a system of compulsory navicerts was extended to all shipping crossing the Atlantic and leaving or approaching the North Sea and the Mediterranean. Any ship not properly navicerted would be liable to seizure by British patrols.[75]

The new British blockade regulations were brought to the attention of the Finnish government by Minister Vereker on August 1.[76] At the same time he applied for permission to set up a British vice-consulate in Petsamo to facilitate the cargo inspection required for the issuance of navicerts to ships engaged in the Petsamo traffic. The request was granted as a matter of course. Blücher immediately advised the Foreign Ministry in Berlin that "the dispatch of a German consul should not be delayed" any longer.[77]

This extension of the British long-distance blockade posed a serious threat to the Finnish economy, even though it affected only the relatively limited Petsamo traffic. Germany's reaction to the British measure heightened its impact. The German Foreign Ministry warned that it would regard any compliance with the British blockage regulations as "active support of British measures in the economic warfare at sea." Germany's countermeasures would depend on what the Finnish government decided to do.[78]

As so often before, Blücher pleaded Finland's cause. He pointed out to his colleagues in Berlin that the Petsamo traffic was of vital importance to Finland, since only through that outlet could Finland acquire certain indispensable imports, such as fuel, from overseas. As long as England derived no advantages from this traffic, it would be in Germany's own interest to keep it alive, said Blücher. According to Witting, he reported, Finnish shipowners had already agreed not to trade with England if trade with the United States could be continued. In view of that, and on the basis of positive statements made by the Germans during the Berlin trade negotiations in June, Witting hoped that Germany would not obstruct the Petsamo traffic, even though it would henceforth depend on British navicerts.[79]

The German government did not immediately make up its mind about the Finnish appeal. Having no new instructions to go by since the circular telegram issued by the Foreign Ministry in Berlin on August 3, Blücher warned Witting that Finland, by accepting the British regulations, was embarking upon a dangerous course of supporting the enemy's economic blockade.[80] The Finnish government then sent Dr. Ramsay to Berlin for negotiations. Nothing is known about these talks other than that they were eventually successfully concluded, but there are at least a couple of reasons for assuming that they were difficult. One indication of this is the length of time it took to obtain Germany's consent. Another is the warning communicated by Ramsay to Helsinki toward the end of the month, that the Finnish government should completely terminate all further sailings from Petsamo until further notice from him.[81]

It must of course be recalled that the German government in August was concerned with much larger issues of policy, of which more will be said later. Involved in these larger issues was a fundamental reevaluation of Germany's policy vis-à-vis Finland in the light of Hitlers' recent decision to invade the Soviet Union in the spring of 1941. This led in turn, in view of the Soviet Union's annexation of the Baltic states and its concurrent pressure on Finland, to Hitler's decision to provide the Finns with arms and to a request for permission to use the Arctic Ocean Highway as part of a new transit route for German troops and equipment between Finnish Baltic ports and Kirkenes in North Norway. This request was linked by the Germans with the question of the Petsamo traffic.

On August 28, the same day that Witting informed Blücher that the Finnish government on Ramsay's suggestion had halted the Petsamo traffic, Field Marshal Mannerheim ordered Major General Paavo Talvela, who was in charge of the Petsamo traffic and all traffic on the Arctic Ocean Highway north of Rovaniemi, and Lieutenant Colonel M. K. Stewen, then chief of operations in the General Staff, to Berlin to negotiate the transit request.[82] Full agreement was quickly reached. The Finns consented to the German transit through north Finland, and the Germans agreed to let the Petsamo traffic continue on the condition that all details concerning arrivals, departures, and cargoes be submitted to the newly established German consulate in Petsamo. Swedish goods were not to be carried, and trade with North America would have to wait until satisfactory control procedures could be worked out, but trade with South America could proceed at once. Finally, according to the agreement concluded on September 7, a representative of the German Naval War Staff would be assigned to the consulate in Petsamo to assist with the implementation of the control provisions.[83]

The Germans were not again to cause difficulties for Finland's trade through Petsamo. Traffic between Petsamo and the United States was also quickly resumed. But as Finland continued to move closer to Germany during the ensuing months, England's harassment of the Petsamo traffic was to grow steadily more annoying.

It was due largely to the influence of the United States that the British government was persuaded not to plug the Petsamo leak in its blockade of continental Europe. According to what Witting told Blücher, the British government at first withheld navicerts from Finnish vessels after the new regulations went into effect, and they were granted only after an American protest had been made.[84] The details of the arrangement concerning the Petsamo traffic were then quickly worked out between the Finnish government and the British legation in Helsinki. The Finns agreed to let no ship leave Petsamo without a navicert, and the British agreed to issue navicerts after inspecting the cargoes.[85] Nevertheless, on several occasions during the fall of 1940, only direct American intervention with the British authorities enabled the Finns to obtain navicerts for important cargoes.[86]

CHAPTER III

War Clouds

T HE acute interest in the Petsamo question displayed by England and Germany during the month of August, 1940, found no echo in the Soviet Union. In fact, there had been no official Finnish-Soviet contact on the matter since Sobolev's conciliatory memorandum to Paasikivi on July 10 and no pressure at all since Molotov's last prompting on July 3. The puzzling Soviet silence continued unbroken until August 30, and the pressure was not really turned on again until September 13.

This Soviet non-activity in the Petsamo question extended to the Soviet-German diplomatic front as well. There had been no new Soviet moves since Molotov issued his deceptive challenge to Schulenburg on July 17. The German response to that challenge was apparently not submitted to the Soviet government, although Schulenburg received his instruction on July 30. A copy of this telegram was forwarded to Helsinki, where Foreign Minister Witting was quick to point out that the Russians, in their talks with the Finns, had limited their consent to Finnish nickel ore deliveries to Germany to the year 1940, while the new German position, as outlined in the telegram to Schulenburg, was based squarely on the contract between I.G. Farbenindustrie and Petsamo Nickel. That contract had no such time limit. Nor was any time limit given in the Finnish-German political agreement which covered the contract.[1]

The German Foreign Ministry immediately amended its instruction to Schulenburg. The new version, sent to him on August 7, instructed him to inform Molotov that the limitation of nickel ore deliveries to the year 1940 was totally unsatisfactory to Germany and injurious to German interests. Very little ore could be extracted in 1940, and substantial German investments were involved in getting the production in Petsamo started at all. The only reason that the Germans in their negotiations with the Finns had limited themselves to a discussion of 1940 and 1941 was that they expected to "obtain the concession itself by the end of 1941 at the latest." This should be made "entirely clear" to Molotov once again "in a suitable way."[2]

Schulenburg went to see Molotov at once. Molotov was unusually passive. He avoided a discussion of the matter and suggested merely that Anastas I. Mikoyan, people's commissar for foreign trade, was "the one competent for further conversations on this question." Schulenburg did not act on that suggestion, however,[3] and the Soviet and German governments did not take up the Petsamo question again until November 25.

On a different level, the Finns did make an effort during August to solve the difficult Petsamo question by direct negotiations with the Russians. On the strength of the Sobolev memorandum, in which the Soviet government had agreed to be content with 40 per cent of the nickel ore production in 1940, the Petsamo Nickel Company began discussions with the Soviet trade mission in Helsinki.[4] These commercial negotiations proceeded surprisingly smoothly. Not even when the representatives of the Petsamo Nickel Company gave the Soviet representatives a statement of the amounts of nickel ore to be delivered to Germany in 1941 under the contract of July 23 did the Russians show any signs of being perturbed, even though that statement was the first clear proof they had that the Finnish-German agreement was valid beyond the year 1940. By the second week of September, the Helsinki talks had reached a point where Dr. Söderhjelm was ready to go to Moscow for a final round of negotiations with the Soviet export organization Soyuzpromexport.[5] Fieandt had already been sent to Berlin in August to arrange the necessary financing of the construction that remained to be done at the Kolosjoki mine.[6]

It is impossible to say whether the Soviet government took the commercial negotiations between the Petsamo Nickel Company and Soyuzpromexport quite seriously. From mid-September to the end of November, these talks proceeded in Moscow as if in a vacuum, culminating in the signing of a commercial delivery contract on November 30,[7] while the Finnish-Soviet negotiations on the political level were deteriorating rapidly into a deepening crisis. The whole business, which required Dr. Söderhjelm's presence in Moscow for almost three months, seemed rather pointless. If the political negotiations were to result in the sort of arrangements which the Soviet government insisted on, then the commercial delivery contract would be completely superfluous. And if the Soviet government were unable to pressure Finland into the desired political settlement, then the commercial contract would only give the Soviet Union a few more tons of nickel, a metal available in abundance in the Soviet Union itself. Eventually, when the Russians were unable to get the political settlement they wanted, they ignored the commercial agreement completely.[8]

In order to try to explain the puzzling inactivity of the Soviet government in the Petsamo question during most of July and all of August, a period of over eight weeks, it is necessary to come to grips with the most controversial issue in Finnish-Soviet relations during the interwar period between March, 1940, and June, 1941, namely the question of whether the Soviet Union had intended to annex Finland in the late summer of 1940 through a military attack, possibly aided by subversive elements within Finland. Simple logic would seem to answer "yes" to this question. With the annexation of Estonia on August 6, the Soviet Union had incorporated into its territory all of the areas assigned to it in the Secret Protocol appended to the Nazi-Soviet Non-Aggression Pact of August 23, 1939, with the single exception of Finland. But simple logic is hardly a satisfactory or acceptable means of arriving at an answer to this problem. Nor is any documentary proof available as long as the records of the Soviet ministries of defense and foreign affairs remain inaccessible. In short, one is left with only circumstantial evidence, including diplomatic and intelligence reports, statements by Soviet leaders and diplomats, comments in the Soviet press, incomplete information about Soviet military movements, and other similar materials. Thus, the answer to the question depends on how this evidence is interpreted.

A possible clue may be discerned in the chronology of the events which led up to the Soviet annexation of the Baltic states. During the fall of 1939, the Soviet Union concentrated its efforts on the three Baltic states and did not make its demands on Finland until these states had already yielded to Soviet pressures. In mid-June, 1940, the Soviet government issued its ultimata to the three Baltic states, all of which submitted at once. An ultimatum to Rumania demanding the cession of Bessarabia and Bukovina followed immediately, and this was also accepted when Germany advised Rumania to yield. Only then did the Soviet Union turn its attention to Finland, starting with certain demands involving the Petsamo area and the Åland Islands. The Finns, as in October, 1939, did not yield, and suddenly the Soviet government ceased to press for a settlement. Instead it began to give conspicuous support to a Communist-inspired Finnish organization, called the Society for Peace and Friendship between Finland and the Soviet Union (*Suomen-Neuvostoliiton rauhan ja ystävyyden Seura,* or SNS), a group which celebrated the "liberation" of the Baltic states and called for a Soviet Finland. When the SNS stepped up its subversive activities and engaged in public rioting in several cities, the Finnish authorities arrested some of its more vigorous leaders and street brawlers, a step that Molotov officially protested and described as "persecution" of the only Finnish group which worked for good Finnish-Soviet relations.[9]

If the Soviet government had hoped to use the SNS as its instrument to achieve the subversion of Finland, these hopes were dashed by the resolute reaction of the Finnish government. The Finns believed that subversion was the Soviet purpose, since the recurring refrain of the SNS propaganda was that the road taken by the Baltic states was also the road for Finland. Even Paasikivi came to the conclusion that extremely sinister Soviet motives lay behind the activities of the SNS, and on August 9 he warned the Finnish government that the matter had become very serious: "If it continues like this, we must reckon with the danger of Soviet intervention."[10] Two weeks later he warned Witting "that Molotov and other Soviet leaders are hoping for a movement similar to that in the Baltic states and that Finland with its help can be united with the Soviet Union."[11] What Paasikivi saw and heard in Moscow gave him a feeling of hopelessness."[12]

Public statements made in the Soviet Union in connection with the annexation of the Baltic states could also be regarded as discouraging by the Finns. Reporting the Baltic developments, *Pravda,* the official mouthpiece of the Central Committee of the Communist Party, noted that the number of Soviet Socialist Republics had risen from twelve to sixteen within only a few days, and "history has not yet closed her account."[13] Molotov told the Supreme Soviet that even though considerable successes had been achieved already, "we do not intend to rest satisfied with what has been attained."[14] This was ominous enough, but the Finns would have been even more discouraged had they known what Molotov had said one month earlier to Professor Vincas Kreve-Mickevičius, deputy prime minister and foreign minister of Lithuania, in the course of a lengthy and brutally candid conversation: "You must take a good look at reality and understand that in the future small nations will have to disappear. Your Lithuania along with the other Baltic nations, including Finland, will have to join the glorious family of the Soviet Union."[15]

None of these events or statements proves anything about the alleged Soviet aggressive designs on Finland in August, 1940, but they may at least be viewed as indicative of such intentions. It has been argued that the case for such a theory is merely a "superficially attractive thesis" which is inconsistent with the other actions of the Soviet government—an argument based on the contention that there was an "apparent lack of any suitable military preparations during the critical period," the first ten days of August. "More solid objections," goes the second part of this contention, lie in the seriousness with which Molotov pursued his demands regarding the Åland islands, the Petsamo nickel concession, the Hanko transit agreement, and the resignation of Tanner. The argument is quite correctly summed up as follows: "These demands would have been superfluous if there had been any serious intention or expectation of taking Finland over within a few weeks of their being presented."[16]

The argument would indeed have been a convincing one if the contention on which it is based corresponded to the facts. However, each part of the contention is erroneous. As has already been shown, the Soviet government appeared to have lost all interest in the Petsamo question during most of July and all of August. The same can be said for the Åland question, which remained practically suspended from July 24 to September 4, except for one occasion when Paasikivi mentioned it to Molotov. In fact, there

was no serious Soviet pressure in the Åland question from June 27
to October 11, when the Finnish-Soviet agreement concerning this
question was signed.[17] The resignation of Tanner was asked for
by the Soviet government, indirectly, on the grounds that he
opposed the work of the SNS.[18] While this may be interpreted to
mean that the Soviet government hoped to take over Finland
through a revolt triggered by the SNS, or that the assignment of
the SNS was to create such chaotic conditions in Finland that the
Soviet Union could claim that its intervention was necessary in
order to restore peace and stability, it does in no way rule out the
hypothesis of a planned aggression.

Only with respect to the demand for a transit agreement
"whereby Soviet trains will be allowed to travel on Finnish railways
to and from Hanko"[19] was some Soviet pressure applied during
those weeks. The Russians were asking for the right of free and
unlimited transit on Finnish railroads between the border and
Hanko for thirty years. The only suggested restriction was that
the Finns would be notified five hours in advance of each border
crossing.[20] Later the Russians reduced their demand to two trains
in each direction per day and twenty-four hours' advance notice.[21]
From a military point of view, the initial proposal was disturbing,
since it conjured up visions of the Red Army pouring across the
border while Soviet trains blocked every important railroad junc-
tion in south Finland, upsetting the schedule of the Finnish mobilization. Mannerheim put it this way in his postwar memoirs: "This
traffic clear through all of south Finland could of course lead to
abuses, and we had to see to it that the most important junctions
and bridges were secured."[22] Paasikivi, who did not think that the
Russians had any sinister ulterior motives with their demand for
military transit to Hanko, also took note of the possible dangers
involved for Finnish security.[23] Whatever the Russians actually
had in mind, their insistence on sending trains through, loaded
with troops and military equipment and immune to Finnish inspection or control of any kind, inspired fear in Finland and
strengthened the suspicion that an attack was contemplated.

There remains to be investigated the contention that there was
an apparent lack of any suitable Soviet military preparations during
the critical period in early August, and that the rumors of an
imminent Soviet attack on Finland, current during the last week

of July and much of August, were without foundation, based on misreadings of Soviet military movements connected with the summer maneuvers of the Leningrad military district.[24] Again, in the absence of Soviet documentary evidence, this contention can be disproved no more than it can be proved, but it is worthwhile to take a closer look at the so-called rumors. They had begun to circulate immediately following the Soviet ultimata to the Baltic states, but the Finnish government did not share the fears which consequently spread throughout the nation.[25] Not until July 16 did Witting indicate to Blücher that these fears had begun to afflict members of the government. Blücher's reaction was to state that Finland should not count on any help from Germany.[26]

On July 24, a rumor to the effect that a Soviet ultimatum to Finland was imminent swept Europe and was given publicity by the United Press. The Soviet Union, it was said, would demand the full demobilization of the Finnish armed forces. The rumor was reported to the German Foreign Ministry as being without any apparent foundation,[27] but it was not entirely discounted. The German missions in the Soviet Union, Finland, Sweden, and the Baltic states were told to be alert for further developments.[28] Schulenburg, who took no stock in the rumor, described Soviet intentions toward Finland as "wholly obscure," but he noted that Finland was being kept under constant Soviet pressure "with ever new demands."[29] Blücher advised the Foreign Ministry in a similar vein.[30]

There were more ominous indications, however, of what the Soviet government might have in mind. A few hours after the German Foreign Ministry began to be flooded with reports of the alleged Soviet ultimatum, it received an alarming telegram from its mission in Lithuania. Minister Erich Wilhelm Zechlin reported from Kaunas that according to a "reliable military source" the Soviet Union was preparing for an attack on Finland in mid-August and was for that purpose withdrawing airplanes and motorized units from Lithuania and Latvia.[31] No further details were immediately available, but Ribbentrop asked to be kept informed about further developments.[32] Similar reports apparently reached many diplomatic missions in Berlin, for a number of foreign military attachés informed the Finnish legation that the Russians were concentrating forces in Estonia for a landing on the Finnish coast, and Kivimäki mentioned it to Under State Secretary Woermann on July 29.[33] Two days later, the German minister in Tallinn, Hans Frohwein, invited his Soviet colleague for breakfast and was treated to a violent tirade against Finland. There was a desire in the Finnish government for revenge against the Soviet Union, declared Botshkarev, and that desire tended to tempt the Finns to provoke the Soviet Union. Should they do so, the Soviet Union was thoroughly capable of "putting an end to Finland in from one to two weeks."[34]

By the beginning of August, Estonia was buzzing with rumors of an impending Soviet attack on Finland, possibly even a Soviet-German conflict. "Soviet naval circles are ostensibly in favor of immediate action," reported Frohwein.[35] Zechlin, whose brief telegram of July 24 had provided the first concrete indication of Soviet military movements, and whose diplomatic dispatches tended to separate facts from rumors, passed along a second item of apparent relevance on August 3: "Informant, a high ranking Lithuanian officer, reaffirms his report, which derives from General Staff circles, and asserts that Soviet troops are to be combat ready on the Finnish border by August 15." Zechlin commented that it was in any case a fact that the Russians had withdrawn about one-third of their planes and tanks and much extremely well-equipped cavalry.[36] Four days later he provided further details based on another source, whom he identified as someone "close to the Soviet legation here." Fifteen divisions, reinforced by "particularly good motorized tank units," would be on the Finnish border by mid-August, he said. By the second half of the month, Finland could expect a Soviet ultimatum which would presumably result in the "complete occupation of Finland."[37]

The information coming in to the German Foreign Ministry from the Baltic states was confirmed from Helsinki. The Finnish government had received information, reported Blücher on August 8, revealing that "Russian troops on the eastern border are being reinforced; heavy tanks and heavy artillery are arriving."[38] The next day he reported that there were fifteen Soviet divisions on the border. There would be no peaceful occupation, however, should the Russians present an ultimatum, since the Finns could be counted on to fight. This was the firm opinion of both Blücher and his military attaché.[39] By August 15, allegedly the deadline for the completion of the Soviet military preparations, Blücher suggested to Berlin that the number of Soviet divisions along the Finnish border might have increased to twenty-three.[40]

Foreign observers in the Soviet Union were also gathering information about the military developments along the Soviet-Finnish border, and the results they came up with tallied with German and Finnish conclusions. Walter Thurston, counselor in the American embassy in Moscow, reported to the State Department on August 8 that military observers in the Soviet Union had information about "new troop movements towards Finland during the last few days, and it is estimated that some 25 Soviet divisions are now adjacent to that country."[41] A few days later, the American military attaché in Moscow learned from "reliable sources" that the Russians were moving up thirty divisions against Finland, including twenty along the border and ten in Estonia facing the southern coast of Finland. By August 19, these movements were reported to have been completed.[42]

These reports do not necessarily prove that a Soviet attack against Finland was in fact contemplated, but they do indicate a remarkable consensus among non-Soviet observers about the existence of such a threat. And most observers believed that the threat would materialize, either as naked aggression or as a military intervention justified by the Soviet government on the grounds of alleged persecution in Finland of "democratic" elements, like the SNS, which looked to the Soviet Union for relief and liberation. The basis for such a crusade had already been prepared by a vicious Soviet press campaign and by the activities and statements of the SNS within Finland itself. To most observers, it seemed that only if one considered the puzzle as a preparation for Soviet intervention in Finland would all the pieces fall into place. A few, once the immediate danger appeared to be abating, had second thoughts about it and decided, like Paasikivi and his military attaché, that the whole affair had been merely a false alarm.[43] But by that time the damage was already done, if by damage one means the Finnish decision to seek security through commitment to Germany.

The Finns knew from experience, notably the Winter War, that "any pretext would serve the Soviet authorities if they were disposed to force an issue," as Witting reminded the American

minister on August 3.[44] Schoenfeld apparently agreed, for four
days later he had become so disturbed by the continuing Soviet
charges of Finnish persecution of the SNS, charges for which he
could find no justification whatever, that he consulted his colleague
in Moscow: "I should appreciate your telegraphing me on the
basis of your observation of developments leading up to the absorption of the Baltic states whether recent reports and comment in
Soviet newspapers regarding Finnish affairs may be considered
similar enough to those preceding annexation of those countries
to warrant the belief that they reflect similar intentions with regard
to Finland."[45] Counselor Thurston tended to think so: "In all
instances of Soviet aggression since my arrival here last year, the
ultimate decisive moves have been preceded by press campaigns
of varying degrees of intensity and duration. On the basis of this
observation alone, the present campaign against Finland should
be regarded as ominous." The military preparations which had
been observed strengthened his apprehensions, said Thurston, although it could "only be surmised" what form the expected Soviet
move against Finland would actually take. It might be "limited
demands for additional rights and facilities or political reorganization, or complete absorption."[46] On August 19, Thurston suggested
to the State Department that the military buildup was "designed to
reinforce the border troops in order to cover any operation which
the Soviet Government might undertake against Finland, the date
of which, it is believed will depend in the first instance on the
development of the German offensive against England."[47]

   The apprehensions expressed by these two American diplomats,
both as well informed as foreign diplomats could be during those
critical days in the rumor-ridden capitals of Finland and the Soviet
Union, were felt equally strongly in Stockholm. State Secretary
Erik Boheman in the Swedish Foreign Ministry told the German
minister, the Prince of Wied, on July 31 that he was "extra-
ordinarily concerned" about the recent developments in Finnish-
Soviet relations.[48] Two days later, the Swedish minister in Berlin,
Arvid Richert, who had just returned from a stay in Stockholm,
made similar statements to Weizsäcker and wanted to know what
Germany's attitude would be "in the event of a new Russo-Finnish
conflict." The state secretary disingenuously retorted that Molotov's
speech of the previous day demonstrated that all was well between

Finland and the Soviet Union.[49] On August 12, the Prince of Wied received an unannounced visit from the chief of the Intelligence Department of the Swedish General Staff, Colonel Carlos Adler-kreutz, who expressed his "most serious concern" about the "imminent Russian attack on Finland" and the occupation of the Åland Islands which would presumably accompany it. Like Richert ten days before, Adlerkreutz wanted to know what Germany intended to do. Like Weizsäcker, the Prince of Wied replied "according to instruction."[50] A few days later he reported that Foreign Minister Christian Günther had also brought up the subject with him and had spoken about his "serious concern about the Russian threat to Finland." Germany's attitude would be decisive for Sweden's reaction to a Soviet attack on Finland, he said.[51]

How the Finns interpreted the signs of the times is abundantly clear. Because of the censorship in effect since the Winter War, most Finns knew only what they read in the papers or heard by way of the grapevine, but they were generally inclined to see in the Soviet annexation of the Baltic states the handwriting on the wall for themselves. As early as July 4, Witting had remarked to Blücher that Finnish public opinion, recently markedly anti-German, was moving "like an avalanche" toward a pro-German attitude.[52] At the time, the remark probably reflected Witting's hope of getting German support for Finland more than it reflected the truth, but by the end of the month it had almost become true, under the double pressure of ever new Soviet demands and tension born of uncertainty about what might come next.

The Finnish government itself was developing an acute case of jitters. Unless the war could be brought to an end very soon, it might be too late for Finland, for "the appetite of the Russian bear grows and is assuming dangerous proportions." Those words reflected the sentiments of Finland's leaders at the end of July, according to Blücher.[53] By mid-August, Prime Minister Ryti himself, a known Anglophile, summoned Blücher for a long interview and stated that "it might sound strange, coming from his lips, but he hoped that England would be overpowered quickly. He did not doubt a German victory, but only if this victory came quickly could it free Europe from the terrible situation into which it was gradually sliding."[54] Blücher failed to rise to the bait, and two days later Ryti, obviously in an effort to calm the raw nerves of his people, described Finnish-Soviet relations in rosy terms on a national radio broadcast.[55]

Ryti's speech, which has been accurately characterized as "riddled with dishonesty,"[56] was probably intended to placate the Soviet government as much as it was designed to break the tension at home. It is hard to say how it was received in Moscow, but it fooled nobody in Finland. What Ryti said was the opposite of what he knew to be true, and his expressed optimism was contradicted by his real expectations. All the activities and energies of Finnish diplomacy were, during those days, aimed at securing support from Germany; without this, the situation could well become hopeless, as even Paasikivi noted on several occasions. He had himself on July 15 recommended to Witting that the Finnish government investigate "whether Germany is interested in our fate."[57] When he deduced from a speech by Hitler four days later that this was not the case, he decided that the only policy for Finland would be to reach an accommodation with the Soviet Union.[58]

But the Finnish government was not equally quick to draw a similar conclusion. Between July 29 and August 14, Kivimäki paid at least three visits to the German Foreign Ministry in an effort to elicit a more positive German response than that which had been implicit in Hitler's speech of July 19. He was not successful, however. He expressed his "grave concern for the future of his country" to Woermann, who remained noncommittal.[59] He tried to pump Weizsäcker about Germany's attitude in the event of a new Finnish-Soviet war, but Weizsäcker was evasive.[60] He called on Woermann a second time and "repeatedly brought up the question of whether we would not support Finland at least diplomatically in case of a renewed advance on the part of the Soviet Union," but again his questions were "evaded."[61] All that Kivimäki seemed to accomplish was to prove the accuracy of Blücher's observation that "the eyes of leading Finnish statesmen are turning to Berlin."[62] Kivimäki could not know that German support had already been decided upon by the time of his frustrating session with Woermann on August 14.

Most of the alarming telegrams about Soviet military movements which had reached the Foreign Ministry since July 24 had also been studied by the military authorities, who had taken them quite seriously. Hitler had started to consider operational plans for an eastern front as early as June, and on July 21 he had ordered the commander in chief of the army to turn his attention to this problem and prepare some plans. In these plans, Finland was to be included as one of the "gateways of attack."[63] Ten days later, Hitler made his decision to launch an attack against the Soviet Union in the spring of 1941. Finland again figured in the directives given to the military planners, although its rôle in the invasion "remains to be seen."[64] It may be assumed, however, that Germany would no longer stand passively aside should the Soviet Union attempt to gobble up Finland, now a potential staging area for the projected German invasion.

By the second week of August, Hitler had decided that the time had come to supply Finland with arms. It was to be done quietly and through commercial channels, notably by reactivating and expanding an arms transaction, conducted through a Danish intermediary, which had been interrupted by the Winter War. This news was broken to a small number of leading Finnish statesmen and military officers in Helsinki on August 18 by a special emissary of Marshal Hermann Göring. Among the early initiates were Field Marshal Mannerheim, Prime Minister Ryti, Foreign Minister Witting, and the defense minister, Major General Rudolf Waldén. Göring's emissary was an old friend and confidant of his since World War I, retired Air Force Lieutenant Colonel Joseph Veltjens, a prominent arms dealer who had also handled the arms deliveries to Finland prior to the Winter War. The reaction of the Finnish leaders to the news brought by Veltjens was summed up by General Waldén: "Now I am beginning to see a tiny ray of light in the intense darkness."[65]

Kivimäki, who had been informed by Veltjens in Berlin three days before,[66] received further confirmation of what was developing when he and Fieandt were told by Ribbentrop on August 19 that Germany was ready to release to Finland a cargo of arms which had been confiscated in Norway. The two Finns said nothing. They knew that the shipment in question consisted of old French artillery pieces, some of them reputedly of 1870 vintage. Finally Ribbentrop broke the awkward silence: "If you wish, Germany is ready to exchange these old cannons for modern ones." Now his Finnish guests were thoroughly impressed. Since Finland could have no conceivable other use for modern weapons than to defend itself against the Soviet Union, Ribbentrop's statement implied "a complete change in Germany's policy vis-à-vis Finland." "Now it was clear," remembers Fieandt, "that we had experienced a historic moment."[67]

Veltjens also brought up another matter during his stay in Helsinki. He wanted to know whether the Finns were willing to permit transit of German troops and equipment through Finland to the reinforced division in the Kirkenes area. The Finns were willing, the more so since Veltjens assured them that expenses incurred in connection with the German transit would be covered by Germany through arms deliveries. Indeed, both sides seemed very eager to conclude the double arrangement. The Finns had offered to put tonnage at Germany's disposal for the Baltic Sea leg of the transit route, and Göring, on Hitler's order, had instructed Veltjens to tell the Finns that they could obtain a large amount of land mines from Germany on credit. Veltjens also played on the Finnish fears of a Soviet attack by passing on Göring's "personal opinion" that Finland had better defend itself to the last man, for "Russia's goal in a new war could only be to annihilate Finland."[68]

By the end of August, Finnish-German talks were underway in Berlin about arms deliveries, German transit, and the conditions on which Germany would permit the Petsamo traffic to continue. All of these matters overlapped to a considerable extent, but no serious difficulties arose, in view of the mutual anxiety to come to a speedy settlement. The question of the Petsamo traffic was settled by an agreement signed on September 7.[69] Five days later the military agreement regarding German transit through Finland was signed,[70] and on September 22 it was provided with a political cover in the form of an exchange of letters between Weizsäcker and Kivimäki,[71] chiefly because the Finnish government wished to make the transit appear to be analogous to the transit permitted to the Soviet Union to and from Hanko on September 6.[72] The arms delivery agreement—commonly known as the Veltjens Agreement—was signed in Helsinki on October 1 by Veltjens and Waldén.[73] It is symptomatic of the spirit in which these negotiations were conducted that German arms and munitions began to flow into Finland long before the Veltjens Agreement was signed, and that the first German transports arrived in Finnish ports before the political transit agreement was concluded. The procedure was anything but normal.

This was not a normal situation, however. With Finland facing growing Soviet pressure and the prospect of sharing the fate of the Baltic states, its leaders were desperately seeking salvation where they could find it. They had no choice but to seek it in Germany, and every new indication of German interest in Finland encouraged them to walk another step down the road to Berlin. It seemed at the time to be the only realistic policy. After the Continuation War, when the Finns were compelled by the Soviet Union to prosecute and convict eight of their wartime leaders on charges of war guilt, the prosecution's case rested on the assertion that Finland's involvement with Germany began with the transit agreement. This corresponded with the Soviet version, which was also adopted by Finnish Communists and their allies. One such fellow-traveler, Carl Olof Frietsch, a member of parliament for the Swedish People's Party, rushed this version into print almost before the ink had dried on the Finnish-Soviet Armistice Agreement of 1944, and his sanctimonious memoirs would be read and accepted at face value by readers outside Finland. Frietsch conveniently summed up his views: "In this situation, Finland permitted itself, through the high-handedness of certain circles or persons, to drift *into Germany's arms*."[74]

Frietsch put the cart before the horse, for he neglected to mention that the transit agreement and all that followed in its train were direct consequences of Soviet policy in the summer of 1940. The Russians themselves, by their own actions, "turned Finland politically adrift in dangerous waters," and then they "blew up an economic storm which drove it straight to the nearest port offering succor—Germany."[75] To blame the pro-German turn of Finland's policy on "the spread of pro-Nazi views,"[76] as Frietsch and his disciples did, was to obscure the fundamental causes of that turn by exaggerating an insignificant phenomenon out of all sensible proportions.

In return for German support against the Soviet Union, Finland's leaders were prepared to pay almost any price. For them, the only alternatives open to Finland were probable destruction by the Soviet Union or a precarious independence under the wing of Nazi Germany. Put that way, the choice they had to make was obvious to most Finns. Frietsch, in his new-found postwar wisdom, branded that view as a "stupid simplification," though he noted that the view was shared even by "fairly intelligent people" who were not at all pro-German. Looking back upon the events of 1940–41, he recalled that he had been practically the only one around who had seen clearly a third alternative for which Finland could—and should—have opted.[77] His assertion must be taken with a large spoonful of salt, however, for Frietsch was not above misrepresenting his own past.[78]

One crucial question remains: if the Soviet Union made preparations for war with Finland in July and August, why did it not attack? A documented answer to that question is not available, but at least one reasonable hypothesis presents itself. On July 1, in an "extremely frank, realistic and outspoken" discussion with the newly arrived British ambassador in Moscow, Sir Stafford Cripps, Stalin had refused to be drawn into closer cooperation with England. Germany, he said, "constituted the only real threat to the Soviet Union," and the basic aim of his foreign policy was "to avoid the involvement of the Soviet Union in the war and, in particular to avoid a conflict with the German army."[79] Stalin's statement may well explain why the Soviet Union failed to complete the process of annexing the Baltic states during the so-called phony war on the western front in 1939–40. Although such a move seemed to be justified by the secret supplementary protocol of the German-Soviet Non-Aggression Pact, it was not made until Germany's armed forces were fully committed against the allied powers in France and the Low Countries in the early summer of 1940. After the military collapse of France, a German invasion of England itself was commonly expected, and the start in late July of the massive German air assault on England was seen as a prelude.[80] Simultaneously the reports of Soviet preparations for military action against Finland began to circulate. The conclusion suggests itself that the Russians intended to move against Finland as soon as the Germans began to cross the English Channel. When it became clear that there would be no German invasion of England after all in the early fall of 1940, the anticipated Soviet attack on Finland was presumably called off. Stalin could not afford—or so his statements to Cripps indicate—to risk incurring Hitler's possible displeasure at a moment when German arms were not committed to combat elsewhere, since they might be turned against the Soviet Union itself.

The Petsamo area figured prominently in the German military deliberations in August. The great significance of the Petsamo nickel ore for Germany's armaments industry was stressed in several diplomatic and military documents. Blücher wrote to Weizsäcker on August 2 that the Petsamo nickel could make Germany "completely independent of the world nickel market for at least 20 years." Coupled with other economic and strategic considerations, that ought to "justify Germany in taking a vital interest in future developments in Finland."[81] Weizsäcker conceded, in reply, that "the Finnish question is beginning to become somewhat more important than it seemed this summer."[82] It was in fact more important than Weizsäcker realized. On August 10, he was told by Captain Leopold Bürkner, head of the Foreign Intelligence Branch in the Office of Foreign Intelligence and Counterintelligence of the OKW, that Field Marshal Wilhelm Keitel saw a "danger of a new Russo-Finnish war" in the recent reports of Soviet troop movements. Such a war would disturb "the regular deliveries of raw materials from Finland to Germany," and Keitel therefore requested that "a word of restraint be spoken in Moscow, with stress laid on our economic interests in Finland."[83] Two days later, Keitel himself telephoned Weizsäcker to say that Hitler had authorized arms deliveries to Finland.[84]

Hitler's concern about developments in Finland was also noted that day, August 12, by Colonel General Franz Halder, chief of staff of the OKH, who wrote in his war diary that the Soviet readiness for operations against Finland was "said to be set for August 15," and Hitler had asked about Finland's military strength.[85] He "did not want to give the Finns over to the Russians," as General Georg Thomas, head of the War Economy and Armaments Office of the OKW, noted in a memorandum on August 14.[86] It was General Thomas and his staff who developed the economic case for securing the Petsamo area for Germany, as Blücher had already suggested, and they made a very strong case for doing so. They submitted it to Keitel on August 19 in the form of a two-page memorandum entitled "Finland's significance for the German war economy."[87] Six categories of commodities that Finland could provide Germany with were enumerated, and the first one dealt with the nickel available from Kolosjoki. The conclusion left no room for doubt: "As a source country for German supplies, Finland is *indispensable with regard to nickel*."

Hitler must have agreed, for on August 26 he told Field Marshal Walther von Brauchitsch, commander in chief of the German army, that if the Russians attacked Finland, "we will occupy Petsamo."[88] That did not necessarily mean that Hitler had decided to support Finland in the event of a Soviet invasion. Such a war would interfere with his plans. "We want no new theaters of war," wrote General Halder in his diary on August 20,[89] referring specifically to Yugoslavia and Greece, but obviously echoing Hitler's attitude concerning Europe in general. Still, Hitler must have been prepared to take on a quarrel with the Soviet Union over the Petsamo area, for he meant what he said about occupying it.

After an inspection trip to North Norway, the commander in chief of the German Army in Norway, Colonel General Nikolaus von Falkenhorst, saw Hitler in Berlin on August 13, and was ordered to take all necessary steps to build up his forces in North Norway at once—ostensibly to meet a possible English threat.[90] Three days later he was issued more detailed orders through the OKW. "For the protection of the German interests in the *entire* Scandinavian area" he was to move strong forces as quickly as possible to "North Norway from Narvik to Kirkenes" and make preparations to repel any attack by air or sea. Petsamo was not mentioned in this order, but Falkenhorst wrote a marginal note on it with reference to the need for anti-aircraft batteries in Kirkenes.[91] It seems clear that the anticipated enemy would be the Soviet Union rather than England, for the purpose of all of these measures was to create a sufficiently powerful force in North Norway to effect a successful occupation of Petsamo.

The memorandum of August 19 by the War Economy and Armaments Office of the OKW was forwarded the next day to the chief of staff of the German Army in Norway, Colonel Erich Buschenhagen, along with a letter from Major General Walter Warlimont, chief of the National Defense Branch of the OKW, explaining the real reason for the sudden military reinforcement ordered for North Norway. It was directly connected with the development in Finland, a development which might well make necessary "an attack by the forces under you." The enclosed

memorandum, wrote Warlimont, "confirms the decisive importance
of the Petsamo area and suggests the idea that all measures should
be taken in order to appear there first, if such a state of affairs
should come about, and to secure the deposits for Germany under
all circumstances."[92]

This communication, which was received and initialled by both
Buschenhagen and Falkenhorst on August 22, received prompt
attention. The following day, Buschenhagen had three studies
ready for consideration by Falkenhorst and the OKW. The first
was a geopolitical treatise entitled "How and where might Russia
cut off the northern part of Norway."[93] The second was a brief
draft of a plan for an operation which was given the code name
"Reindeer."[94] Its opening sentence explained the purpose of the
operation as follows: "The development of the situation can lead
to the requirement of seizing and securing Petsamo and the nickel
mines at Kolosjoki with a swift strike." The third document
enumerated a number of problems which were to be discussed
orally with General Eduard Dietl, commanding general of Mountain Corps Norway in North Norway.[95]

It follows from the preceding documentation that the motives
behind the initial planning for operation "Reindeer" were primarily,
perhaps even exclusively economic.[96] The indispensable Kolosjoki
nickel must be secured for Germany under all circumstances. "For
me," recalls Warlimont, "there has never been the slightest doubt
that the German decision to occupy Petsamo (Pechenga, Kolosjoki) before all else in Finland was—and remained even to the
end of 1944—based exclusively on the indispensability of the
nickel ore to the German warfare." All other considerations "could
only have been of secondary importance."[97] Buschenhagen, while
agreeing that the "great importance of the nickel supply (quite
indispensable to the submarine warfare, for instance) made the
timely occupation and securing of the Petsamo area by German
forces a compelling necessity," considers the military-political
motive behind "Reindeer" to have been coequal with the economic
motive.[98] This does not really mean that the two men disagree,
however. Both are probably right.

Buschenhagen was charged with the responsibility for planning
the occupation of the Petsamo area. He knew that a subsequent
operation to the east was contemplated, and he therefore had to

look at "Reindeer" in the light of that larger operation. For him the economic value of the Petsamo area was balanced by its military value, since "each step eastward along prepared roads and without enemy resistance meant a gain for the planned operation against Murmansk." Hence it was "of compelling military interest that the Petsamo area was seized in good time, namely at the time of the start of the main attack on the Soviet Union at the latest, as a starting point for 'Silver Fox'."[99] The planning for operation "Silver Fox" began in January, 1941, and "Reindeer" then became a component part of it, except that "Reindeer" was launched on June 22, 1941, the day of the main German attack on the Soviet Union, while "Silver Fox" got underway on June 29.

Warlimont, on the other hand, viewed "Reindeer" from the vantage point of Hitler's military headquarters, the OKW. Hence his opinion would more correctly reflect the motives behind the original decision to occupy the Petsamo area. And his opinion confirms the conclusion drawn here, namely that "Reindeer" was a direct consequence of the generally entertained expectation of a Soviet invasion of Finland in the late summer of 1940, and its purpose was the purely economic one of securing the Kolosjoki nickel ore for Germany. Hitler was not yet ready to take on the Soviet Union in a total conflict of arms, but he was willing to risk a quarrel over Petsamo if necessary. This new German position was to be reflected in the diplomatic game over Petsamo when it resumed, even though the German Foreign Office did not appear to be fully informed about Hitler's decision.

CHAPTER IV

Under Hitler's Umbrella

THE long Soviet silence in the Petsamo question was broken at last on August 30, when Molotov asked Paasikivi for an early reply to the demand last presented on July 3 for a transfer of the mining concession to a Soviet-controlled company. Paasikivi's retort, that his government had assumed that the Soviet Union was no longer interested in the concession, was dismissed by Molotov as totally unwarranted. In fact, said Molotov, all other interested parties would have to be excluded from the new concession company. Germany could have its 60 per cent of the nickel ore production until the end of 1940, but after that the Soviet government would no longer be satisfied with a mere 40 per cent share.[1] The Soviet minister in Helsinki, Ivan S. Zotov, reminded the Finnish government a week later that its reply was expected forthwith.[2]

Witting discussed the new situation with Blücher on September 3.[3] On the basis of Blücher's report, the German Foreign Ministry instructed Schulenburg to take the matter up with Molotov at once.[4] Schulenburg subsequently told Molotov that Germany's claim on at least 60 per cent of the Petsamo nickel ore output was without a time limit, and in view of the "very considerable material expenditures made by Germany in order to render the nickel mines productive," Germany expected the Soviet government to respect this claim. Molotov made no reply. He merely ended the conversation with the remark that Mikoyan was the expert on such matters, and Schulenburg ought to take the nickel question up with him.[5]

Minister Schnurre, temporarily in Moscow, thought that negotiations with Mikoyan would sidetrack the matter altogether. Germany would have to challenge Molotov's wishy-washy attitude directly, he suggested, and remind him that the German government was dealing with Finland, not the Soviet Union, in the nickel question. Germany wanted a clear Soviet declaration that a new concession company would honor the rights which Germany had already acquired, not new negotiations about those rights with the Soviet government.[6] The Foreign Ministry decided to recall Schnurre to Berlin for further discussions on how to proceed.[7]

The Finnish government, hoping that support might develop in Berlin, delayed its reply to Molotov. On September 9, Witting gave Blücher a memorandum in which the whole history of the Petsamo negotiations since June 23 was outlined, with particular emphasis on the involvement of German interests and on Finland's commitments to Germany.[8] He pointed out that Zotov was now pressing hard for Finland's reply to Molotov, and he suggested that the credit agreement covering the purchasing contract of July 23 between I.G. Farbenindustrie and Petsamo Nickel ought to be signed at once.[9] Since paragraph 10 of the credit agreement provided for indefinite nickel ore deliveries to Germany without any possibility of cancellation before December 1, 1947, Blücher surmised that Witting needed it to resist the Soviet pressure.[10] This implied plea for German support was made explicit by Kivimäki two days later when he conveyed to Weizsäcker his government's full endorsement of the as yet unsigned credit agreement and suggested that Germany might steer the Soviet Union away from the nickel concession by using its influence in Moscow.[11] At the same time he gave Weizsäcker a copy of the Finnish reply which Paasikivi was going to submit to Molotov,[12] a procedure amounting to clearing that reply with the German government.

This reply, given to Molotov on September 13, made two points. It reiterated that Finland had concluded a delivery agreement with Germany in the belief that a Soviet-German understanding existed regarding the division of the output, a belief which had led the Finns to assume that the concession was now a secondary issue. And it reported that Finland had acted on Molotov's suggestion that it negotiate directly with Mond Nickel about a recovery of the concession by the Finnish state, a proposition which the British company had rejected. Hence the Finnish government had no legal way of offering the concession to anyone else, including the Soviet government.

The argument did not impress Molotov, who asked whether the professed Finnish concern for the rights of the British company did not really mean that the matter could be arranged, "provided a proper legal formula is found." The question went straight to the heart of the matter. The Finns were indeed trying to use the rights of Mond Nickel as a legalistic shield against the Soviet Union in the concession question, while at the same time they were waiting for the Germans to come up with another legal formula for taking over the concession in the peace treaty with England.[13] Now Molotov's question raised the specter of destruction of the convenient existing legal formula by direct Russian negotiation with the British government. Paasikivi was quick to state that both Mond Nickel and International Nickel had refused categorically and definitively to give up their concession rights.

Molotov then resorted to a rather remarkable legalistic argument of his own, explaining to Paasikivi that the existing concession arrangement conflicted with the Finnish-Soviet peace treaties of 1920 and 1940. That highly dubious interpretation was promptly rejected by Paasikivi, who "brought forward all possible other arguments." Molotov stuck to his guns and insisted that no states other than Finland and the Soviet Union had any business in the Petsamo area. The fact that Finland had made agreements involving the area with Germany "revealed the unfriendly attitude of the Finnish government to the USSR," declared Molotov, and he suggested that it was impossible to negotiate with that government. "It appeared to me," reported Paasikivi on this point, in a masterful understatement, "that our conversations and agreements with Germany were not to his liking." Molotov finally terminated the "very disagreeable" confrontation by requesting that the Finnish government reconsider the whole matter in the light of the "great importance" attached to it by the Soviet government, and he urged that the concession be transferred to a joint Finnish-Soviet company.[14]

During the preceding couple of weeks, the Finns had begun to permit themselves a tentative optimism. Ryti's statements to the American minister on September 4 reflected this. Referring to the German-Soviet accord of August, 1939, and its assumed secret provisions, he expressed the opinion that the gains made by the Soviet Union in the Winter War "represented complete fulfillment of the German engagement" and had left Germany free to determine its future policy in the north "without this commitment to the Russians." He even considered a close alignment of Sweden, Finland, and Norway to be a distinct possibility. Schoenfeld got the impression that in the event of a new war with the Soviet Union, "both allies and hope" might be forthcoming for Finland,[15] an impression which was reinforced by Witting a few days later. There had been conspicuous indications of a new German interest in Finland, said Witting, an interest which might be taken to signify an "increasing disapproval in Germany of Russian policy." In his subsequent report to the State Department, Schoenfeld suggested that "there is increasing hope which may not be unfounded that Germany may find it expedient not again to sacrifice Finnish interests to the Russians."[16]

To be sure, all these signs of increasing German interest and sympathy were encouraging, but they had never been translated into an official promise of support against the Soviet Union. The Finns, therefore, did not know, when the Russians began to apply heavy pressure in the Petsamo question in mid-September, how long or how firmly they might be able to resist the Soviet demands. On September 17, Kivimäki called on Weizsäcker in an effort to find out. He had heard, he began, that Germany had renounced its claim on the Petsamo nickel concession, and he wanted to know precisely what this implied. Weizsäcker explained that the step had been based on the legal arguments against the revocation of the Anglo-Canadian concession advanced by the Finns during the Berlin negotiations in June, and the Russians had been so told. In other words, Germany had not renounced the concession "in favor of Russia." Kivimäki then asked Weizsäcker's advice on how the Finns, with German assistance, could evade the insistent Soviet demand for the concession, but the state secretary refused to give him any hope of German intervention in the matter "at this time." The Finnish minister then warned that without German support Finland was in no position to oppose the Soviet Union and might have to grant the concession to the Russians, even though this meant that the promise to Germany would be broken. A threat of conflict "lurked behind Molotov's words in this nickel question," and since Finland could not afford to get into one, its present policy was to stall for time, said Kivimäki.[17]

Although Weizsäcker's statements evaded the positive promise Kivimäki was after, they were not negative either. While German support seemed to be unobtainable for the present, there was a hint that this was a flexible policy which might change in the future. Furthermore, it was quite clear that the German interest in the concession had not been abandoned. Kivimäki's gloomy response appeared to be a tactical maneuver designed to bring the real German attitude to the surface. His report on the conversation did not reflect the pessimism he professed in the presence of Weizsäcker, it may be assumed, for it had a cheering effect on Witting. He said to Blücher that one might as well get the mining operations at Kolosjoki going and conclude a delivery contract with the Russians for 40 per cent of the output. Söderhjelm of Petsamo Nickel had just gone to Moscow for that purpose, said Witting, adding that he had been instructed to maintain contact with representatives of I.G. Farbenindustrie there, just as he had done during the negotiations with the Soviet trade mission in Helsinki.[18]

The Finnish-Soviet negotiations now continued on two levels. On the political level, the going was rough. Witting told Blücher on September 23 that Molotov was "pressing hard" and had "intimidated Paasikivi."[19] It was the first of many such remarks, made by both Finns and Germans in the course of the Petsamo negotiations, suggesting that Paasikivi had a tendency to push the panic button whenever he came under persistent and heavy Soviet pressure. It is true that Paasikivi, after his difficult confrontation with Molotov on September 13 and under the pressure subsequently exerted on him by Molotov, advised his government to adopt a much more conciliatory policy than Witting considered necessary,[20] and this may be what Witting had in mind when he made his rather disparaging remark to the German minister. It is also true that the picture of the Petsamo negotiations which emerges from Paasikivi's memoirs is considerably more gloomy than that which emerges from other sources. But to say that Paasikivi tended to panic under pressure is to do him an injustice.

Paasikivi's relatively compliant attitude to Soviet demands was based on a long-range estimate of the political and military situation which was not at that time shared by his colleagues in Helsinki or, for that matter, by anyone else. Paasikivi simply did not believe that Germany was capable of inflicting a decisive military defeat on the Soviet Union. For that reason alone it would be unrealistic, in his opinion, for Finland to base its security policy on German support against the Soviet Union. Moreover, in the course of his long life, he had developed a completely cynical philosophy of power politics. He was convinced that no great power, be it totalitarian or democratic, would stand up for the rights of small states if these conflicted with its own vital interests. He considered it entirely possible, indeed likely, that Germany and the Soviet Union would eventually iron out their various differences, and when that happened, Finland would be expendable as far as the Germans were concerned. The only realistic policy for Finland would therefore be to keep in mind the advice which Stalin had given during the Moscow negotiations before the Winter War, namely that nothing could be done about the realities of geography. Finland could never forget that it happened to be next door to the Soviet Union.

Paasikivi's compliant attitude greatly irritated Witting and quickly undermined his confidence in the minister in Moscow. In early October, Witting told Blücher that "because the impression here is that Paasikivi permits himself to be intimidated by Molotov," the Finnish minister in Tallinn, Paavo J. Hynninen, would be transferred to the legation in Moscow as Paasikivi's special assistant with the rank of minister-counselor. The official reason would be that the septuagenarian Paasikivi was carrying an oversized work load.[21] Hynninen arrived in Moscow in mid-October. "I was very pleased about that," wrote Paasikivi in his memoirs.[22] Quite possibly he never discovered the real reason that his burden was lightened. At any rate, he continued to carry most of the burden himself until his position, by February, 1941, became so untenable that he offered his resignation and was at once removed from the Moscow scene.

Meanwhile, on the commercial level of the Petsamo negotiations, Söderhjelm's reports to Helsinki provided some cause for optimism. On September 26, he was able to report that the two sides were moving close to an agreement on all points except the price.[23] Furthermore, even though the Russians seemed to want to pay less for the nickel ore than it would cost the Finns to produce it,

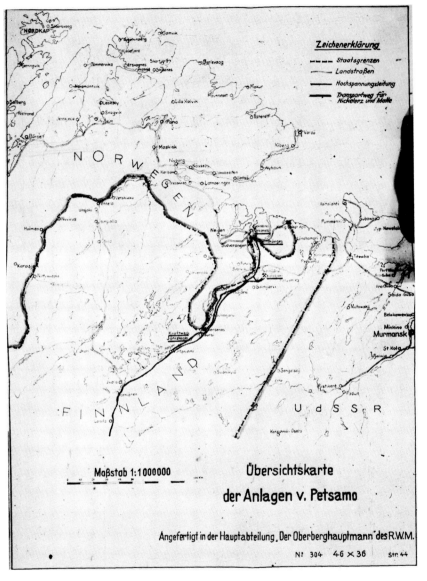

Pl. 1. German Ministry of Economics map of the Petsamo area, 1944 (Microfilm ref. T–84/99/1392504).

Pl. 2. Town of Kirkenes, Norway, May–June, 1941. Photo courtesy Max Maczek.

Pl. 3. Jäniskoski power house on the Pasvik River (under construction), May–June, 1941. Photo courtesy Max Maczek.

Pl. 4. J. O. Söderhjelm, managing director of Petsamo Nickel from its organization through 1940. Courtesy Pressfoto, Helsinki.

Pl. 5. Wipert von Blücher, minister of Germany to Finland. Courtesy Pressfoto, Helsinki.

Pl. 6. Surface plant of the Kaula shaft, May–June, 1941. Kaulatunturi mountains in background. Photo courtesy Max Maczek.

Pl. 7. Rainer von Fieandt, chief Finnish economic negotiator in the Petsamo question. Courtesy Pressfoto, Helsinki.

Pl. 8. Henrik Ramsay, Finnish negotiator with Germany and Great Britain. Courtesy Pressfoto, Helsinki.

Pl. 9. Kolosjoki: view toward the entry to the adit, May–June, 1941. Photo courtesy Max Maczek.

they were talking in terms of a contract extending beyond the year 1940, perhaps for as long as five or ten years. To the Finns, this was hopefully interpreted as an implicit recognition of the Finnish-German agreements, although Molotov seemed to be saying the opposite in his talks with Paasikivi. The divergence of the Soviet positions on the commercial and diplomatic levels confounded Witting.[24] But he rejected Paasikivi's plea for authorization to offer the Petsamo concession to the Soviet government on the condition that the Russians themselves first make the necessary arrangements with the Anglo-Canadian concession holders. Witting's argument was that Germany had been promised 60 per cent of the nickel ore output *"ad infinitum"* and planned to acquire the concession at the end of the war.[25]

The cooperative attitude displayed by the spokesmen of Soyuzpromexport in their negotiations with Söderhjelm did not survive the month of September. During the first week of October, the Russians avoided the representatives of the Petsamo Nickel Company altogether, and Paasikivi warned Witting of the likelihood of a "conflict of the first order" unless Finland gave in to the wishes of the Soviet government and shut out both Germany and England from the Petsamo area.[26] Then the Russians unceremoniously terminated the negotiations between Petsamo Nickel and Soyuzpromexport by rejecting Söderhjelm's application for an extension of his visa.[27]

Simultaneously, Molotov increased his pressure on Paasikivi. He had demanded an answer to his proposals on September 30,[28] and he inquired again with growing impatience on October 9. On the latter occasion he also came up with the surprising piece of information that the English government, through Ambassador Sir Stafford Cripps, had declared itself in favor of a Finnish-Soviet agreement concerning the nickel question. Cripps had said so in July, asserted Molotov.[29] This assertion, which was never substantiated but often repeated, contradicted information already available in the Finnish Foreign Ministry. At the time of the conversation between Cripps and Stalin in July, Minister Gripenberg was told in the British Foreign Office that English-Soviet trade had been discussed, "but nothing said about Finland."[30] Thus, the statement attributed to Cripps, if made at all, must have been an unauthorized one.

As the Soviet pressure in the Petsamo question mounted, the Finnish government grew increasingly concerned about the prolonged failure of the German government to make its position clear. Schnurre had not taken the matter up when he was in Moscow in mid-September, for instance, and he had suggested to Blücher that there was no particular hurry. "After all," he said, "this difference about the time limit is the only one we have with the Russians."[31] Still, rays of light continued to pierce the deepening shadow cast by the Soviet Union over Finland. The brightest of these was the Veltjens Agreement of October 1. Not only did it guarantee Finland an ample supply of German arms of all kinds, but it also had a direct bearing on the Petsamo question. During his visit to Helsinki in mid-August, Veltjens had extracted from Ryti the promise that Germany would get the privilege of first refusal on all concessions involving mineral deposits in Finland, including the Petsamo nickel concession. In paragraph 7 of the Veltjens Agreement, this promise was translated into a legal commitment:

The Finnish state pledges itself to grant to the Greater German Reich a right of pre-emption for the same consideration as might be asked of or offered by any other interested party, on any concessions in Finland of interest to the Greater German Reich, in so far as the Finnish state intends to offer these abroad at all and in so far as the Finnish state is subject to no previous commitment.[32]

By signing the Veltjens Agreement, Finland joined with Germany in erecting still another barrier to Soviet ambitions. Two Finnish legal commitments now blocked the Soviet Union's path to Petsamo: a contract with the Anglo-Canadian concession holders and a treaty with the German government. In order to acquire the Petsamo concession, the Russians would now have to go through Berlin.

Informed Finnish leaders realized that the Veltjens Agreement could turn out to be a boomerang. They had concluded it because it tied the interests of Germany more closely to Finland's own, so closely that Germany might be prepared to defend those interests against heavy Soviet pressure. Should that hope prove to be illusory, on the other hand, then the Finns would only have succeeded in provoking the Soviet Union still further and, in signing the treaty, might well have ventured beyond the point of no return.

They had, perhaps irrevocably, decided to gamble on the availability of German support, as implied by a German promise of
arms that could not conceivably be needed against anyone but the
Russians. The Finns hoped to turn this implication into a guarantee.
In a letter to Veltjens, Witting, referring to paragraph 7 of the
agreement, expressed the hope that Germany, "in case of possible
difficulties which might arise for the Finnish state from the Soviet
Union as a result of fulfilling the terms of the contract, would
lend its support in eliminating such difficulties."[33] But Veltjens
refused to make any promises.[34]

The absence of such a promise did not at all signify indifference
to Finland's plight on the part of the German Foreign Ministry.
The reports received from its missions in Helsinki and Moscow
were read with care and interpreted as indicative of a real Soviet
challenge to vital German interests. On October 8, Weizsäcker
wrote a memorandum to Ribbentrop in which he emphasized the
"daily-increasing pressure" exerted on Finland by the Soviet Union.
He feared that the Finns might be compelled to give in, which
would create "an unpleasant and unfavorable situation" for Germany, since the Soviet government "will not respect the German-
Finnish agreements." Weizsäcker pointed out that a Soviet acquisition of the nickel concession would have serious consequences for
Germany both economically and militarily. Germany's nickel
interests "would be completely wiped out," and the establishment
of exclusive territorial control in the Petsamo area would give the
Russians a military position detrimental to the German interests.
The German military, notably Göring, had expressed concern over
this, said Weizsäcker. They had "voiced the hope that we shall not
lose Petsamo." In that case the policy so far pursued by the Foreign
Ministry might prove inadequate: "It will now become necesary to
go beyond that and to strengthen the Finnish will to resist," Weizsäcker suggested. Although he did not think it was necessary to
support the Finns by intervening directly in Moscow, he did suggest
that Germany should tell the Finns to drag out their negotiations
with the Russians and not let them lead to an actual agreement
about a transfer of the concession. This much the Finns should be
told at once, since the matter was urgent, Weizsäcker concluded.[35]

Ribbentrop's reaction was not positive. He did not want the
Petsamo question "to become a controversial point with the Rus-

sians at the present moment," and therefore the Germans should not commit themselves to the Finns "any more than we have so far." Ribbentrop agreed that it was not ncessary to take the matter up with the Russians "for the present," but he would reexamine that problem in about ten days.[36]

Thus Schnurre was not in a position to give Finland any encouragement when he met with Fieandt in Berlin in late October for general economic talks. He did ask Fieandt how the Petsamo question was viewed in Helsinki, to which Fieandt replied that the Finnish government wanted to keep up its resistance against the Soviet pressure for a transfer of the concession "and to keep the matter in abeyance." The Finns intended to use the same three arguments they had employed so far, namely the legal commitment to the Anglo-Canadian concession holders, the agreements with Germany for nickel deliveries for an indefinite period of time, and the earlier rejection of a German request for the concession, a rejection based on the same legal grounds which prevented the Finns from granting the concession to the Soviet government. Although Schnurre refrained from discussing these arguments with Fieandt, he did say that he "considered it proper for the Finnish government to keep the question of the concession open as long as possible." And he advised the Foreign Ministry that, in view of "the great interest also at stake for us, it would be very desirable if we succeeded in keeping the Russians out of Petsamo."[37]

Kivimäki saw Weizsäcker on October 29 and repeated to him the statements which Fieandt had made to Schnurre. He was even less successful in eliciting a positive response. When he tried to draw out the state secretary by pointedly suggesting that the Veltjens Agreement seemed to him to indicate that Germany planned to take a hand in the game itself in Moscow should the Russians persist in their demands for the concession, Weizsäcker claimed to be uninformed about that agreement and said he would have to study it before discussing the matter further.[38]

Weizsäcker's excuse was less than candid. The Veltjens Agreement was already known in the Foreign Ministry. Even as Weizsäcker was talking with Kivimäki, van Scherpenberg was writing another memorandum on the Petsamo question. Recapitulating all the developments in the case since its origins, he concluded with the following statement: "In the V[eltjens] treaty the right of pre-emption on all concessions in Finland in favor of Germany was stipulated."³⁹ The following day, Wiehl discussed the Veltjens Agreement in general and its paragraph 7 in particular in a lengthy memorandum intended as a suitable answer to the many Finnish efforts to ascertain the position of the German Foreign Ministry on the Petsamo question. The Finns ought to continue to resist the Soviet demands, wrote Wiehl. How they preferred to do it was up to them, but the legal argument sounded all right. They should not drag Germany into it, however. As for German-Soviet talks on the subject, Wiehl would prefer to let the Russians take the initiative, and he considered it likely that they would do so in the near future.⁴⁰ Still, when Kivimäki called at the Foreign Ministry again on November 1, Wiehl claimed to be inadequately informed about the Veltjens Agreement, but he promised to take the matter up for consideration "with the utmost dispatch."⁴¹

Wiehl characterized Kivimäki's visit as "urgent," and well he might, for the Soviet government had just resumed the offensive in the Petsamo question with greater vigor than ever before. Andrei Y. Vyshinsky, first deputy commissar for foreign affairs, summoned Paasikivi on October 30 to discuss "a grave matter" with him. The Finnish government, he charged, had been delaying the Petsamo nickel question for months, and he was not aware of any justifiable reasons for such behavior. Paasikivi retorted that the present holders of the concession had refused to give up their rights, a position which the English government seemed to be in agreement with. There was unfortunately nothing that the Finnish government could do. Vyshinsky caustically asked whether Finland was a British colony or an independent state capable of making its own decisions. Assuming that the latter was the case, he expected to get an answer within two or three days. If no answer was received, the Soviet Union "would be compelled to take the measures which the situation demanded."⁴²

This attack was sufficiently alarming to cause Prime Minister Ryti to invite Minister Zotov to his office the next day and explain to him the Finnish position. Finland had not tried to evade a settlement with the Soviet Union in the Petsamo question, asserted Ryti. He explained that Finland was accustomed to honor its obligations, and, since it had already undertaken certain obligations involving the Petsamo nickel which would be compromised by the sort of agreement proposed by the Soviet government, Finland's integrity was at stake. If the Soviet government could obtain the German government's consent to such an agreement, as well as the consent of the British government and the Anglo-Canadian trust, the Finnish government would then be prepared to transfer the concession to a Finnish-Soviet company. Paasikivi was instructed to make a similar declaration to Vyshinsky.[43]

After another run-in with Molotov on November 1,[44] Paasikivi submitted the Finnish proposal to Vyshinsky on November 5. Vyshinsky declared that the matter was then as good as settled, for the consent of the other interested parties had already been obtained. Ambassador Cripps had recently reiterated his assertion of the previous July that the nickel concession could be transferred to the projected Finnish-Soviet company for the duration of the war, and the Germans had waived their claim, said Vyshinsky. All that the Finnish government had to do, therefore, was to annul the contract, take over the concession, and arrange the whole thing in accordance with the Soviet proposal. The statement was a glib falsification of the facts, but Paasikivi did not take issue with it. He merely noted that Finnish law required the formal consent of the present concession holders before an annulment could be effected, and such an annulment would have to be permanent.[45]

The Finns knew with certainty that Vyshinsky had misrepresented the German position on a transfer of the concession, for they had been told in Berlin that Germany had no intention of waiving its claims in favor of the Soviet Union. They knew also, from direct negotiations, that the Anglo-Canadian concession holders would not give up their rights. And they had been told in London that Cripps had never been authorized to make the sort of statement which the Russians claimed he had made in July. It was conceivable, however, that Cripps might have received new instructions since then, and Minister Gripenberg was ordered to check with the British Foreign Office. On November 7, he reported that Cripps "had never been sent any other directives than those reported by Minister Vereker" to the Finnish government. England would not accept any settlement of the nickel question "until the USSR undertakes not to export any nickel to Germany. This is a condition for any settlement which Great Britain would approve," reported Gripenberg.[46]

The hands of the Finnish government thus remained tied, and Paasikivi on November 12 so informed Vyshinsky. However, if the Soviet government would care to make the necessary arrangements with the various interested parties itself, the Finnish government would welcome it, he said. Vyshinsky would do no such thing. But he did not again resort to the glib assertions of the week before. He fell back on the argument that the Soviet Union was dealing with Finland in the Petsamo question, not with England or Germany, and if the Finnish government really wanted to do so, it could arrange the matter on its own authority. If existing Finnish laws stood in the way of unilateral Finnish action on the annulment proposal, then Finland should simply enact some suitable new law for the purpose. For that, only "good will" was needed, he maintained.[47]

Only three days later, Zotov used the discredited assertions again, however. Germany and England had already given their consent to a transfer of the concession to a Finnish-Soviet company, he said during a visit to the Finnish Foreign Ministry, and the Finnish government should therefore without delay put through the necessary legislation for the recovery of the concession.[48] That he should have linked his demand with these inaccurate assertions could be taken as a studied insult to the Finns—unless the Russians had got their signals crossed. But it could also mean that the English position had been misrepresented in Gripenberg's telegram of November 7, or that it had changed since then. As described by Witting to the American minister on November 14, the British position was not as reported by Gripenberg. The British, he asserted, were "prepared to give up their concession to the Finns for disposal in their discretion but in the hope that no nickel would go to Germany."[49] In short, non-delivery of nickel to Germany was only a hope, not a condition, as far as the British government was concerned. If so, the Russians were essentially right when they insisted that the matter could be arranged without English opposition. But only a few days later, Paasikivi told Molotov that "Great Britain had consented on condition Germany receives no nickel."[50]

That conversation took place on November 19, shortly after Molotov returned to Moscow from his talks with Hitler and Ribbentrop in Berlin. Molotov obviously tried to give Paasikivi the impression that the Petsamo question had practically been settled between Germany and the Soviet Union during those talks. "He told me," reported Paasikivi to Witting, "that Germany withdrew from the concession and had no objection to the transfer of the concession to the USSR." Furthermore, Molotov described England's alleged consent as "adequate," and he rejected the Finnish contention that the Anglo-Canadian companies also had to consent. England's reluctance to let Germany buy any nickel could be overcome simply by selling all of it to the Soviet Union, "which will take care of the matter." All of the Finnish objections had been removed, Molotov suggested, and he therefore "demanded in an insistent tone that the nickel affair be settled without delay." Paasikivi promised an early answer,[51] and he recommended to Witting that the Soviet demand be met.[52]

Finland was now in a very difficult position. The Finnish leaders knew that Molotov's assertions were false, but they did not know how to prove that to him without explicit German and English statements to back it up. Both England and Germany were playing their cards very close to the vest. They had made it plain to the Finns that they did not wish to see the Russians take over the concession, but they were not prepared to say so to the Russians. Both the Germans and the British left it up to the Finns to protect their interests against the Russians without providing them with the necessary diplomatic weapons to do it. England, powerless to influence the outcome of the concession dispute anyway, may well have been playing a double game, caught as it was between the fear of driving the Soviet Union closer to Germany by taking a stand in direct opposition to Soviet ambitions, on the one hand, and its sympathy for Finland, on the other. Besides, playing rough with Finland was likely to anger the United States, where Finland's cause was regularly supported.[53] The British were informed by the State Department that the United States "frankly did not see that the British Government had any sort of right to stop shipments of necessary foodstuffs to . . . Finland."[54] Germany refused to make its position clear in Moscow, but its continuous encouragement of Finnish resistance to Soviet demands hinted at its attitude. It is easy to understand Paasikivi's reasons for advising his government to yield, but Witting also had his reasons for being adamant. He had a strong hunch that Germany would keep the Soviet Union out of Petsamo.

Although Witting got no positive response to his request for German intervention in the face of the Soviet "ultimatum" of October 30,[55] the Germans were following the developments with the liveliest interest. They were also considering ways and means of strengthening Finland's bargaining position in Moscow. On October 30, Wiehl recommended, for instance, that it was "necessary in the future also to try to prevent the Finns, if possible, from transferring a concession to the Russians, without letting this become evident to the Russians."[56]

Blücher, who was in Berlin for consultations when the new Soviet diplomatic offensive against Finland opened, was doing all he could to influence his colleagues to give active support to the Finns. "Petsamo's significance for Germany can not be evaluated highly enough," he wrote in a memorandum on October 31, and he listed four different reasons why this was the case: (1) one of the richest nickel ore deposits in the world was located in the Petsamo area; (2) a fish flour plant in Petsamo was leased to German interests and was slated to become the center of German fisheries in the Barents Sea; (3) the Petsamo area offered Germany a short cut route to the rich mineral resources and fisheries of the Arctic region, an overland route connected with the Baltic Sea and safe from the British fleet; and (4) the Petsamo area constituted an essential part of the Northern Cap, which in turn formed a necessary economic, political, and military complement to *Mitteleuropa*.[57] In another memorandum prepared the following day, Blücher again emphasized the value of Finland to Germany, a value enhanced by the "creation of German interest in the immense Petsamo nickel deposits and by the centralization of the German Arctic Ocean fisheries in the port of Petsamo."[58] State Secretary Weizsäcker forwarded both of these memoranda to Ribbentrop.[59]

Minister Blücher was not alone in his efforts to prod the German Foreign Ministry to act in support of Finland. Words of warning about the possibly dire consequences of inaction also came from the embassy in Moscow, notably in a jointly authored telegram from Schnurre and Schulenburg. Although Schnurre said that Paasikivi appeared to view matters too pessimistically and tended to advise the Finnish government to observe exaggerated caution and tractability, he also declared that something had to be done by Germany as soon as possible to help the Finns withstand the Soviet pressure

in the Petsamo question. Unless Germany was prepared to let the
Finns off the hook by renouncing the Petsamo concession unconditionally, it must provide them with effective help to continue their
resistance. Schnurre recommended the second alternative. It would
be a serious mistake for Germany to abandon its claim, he suggested, and not only in an economic sense, for once the Russians
laid their hands on the concession, they would inevitably exclude
Germany from the Petsamo area altogether. Schulenburg expressed
greater optimism regarding the prospect of reaching an economic
agreement with the Soviet Union about the Petsamo nickel, but the
question went beyond that. *"In my view,"* said Schulenburg, *"the
Soviet interest in the Petsamo area is purely political, especially in
view of the proximity of the sole icefree port of Murmansk, which
gives the Soviet Union access to the oceans of the world."* Hence
the real motive behind the Soviet Union's demand on Finland was
to prevent any great power, including Germany, from getting a
foothold in the Petsamo area.[60] The German Foreign Ministry
reacted to this advice by instructing the embassy in Moscow to
"avoid repeating the renunciation previously expressed," pending
a decision by Ribbentrop.[61]

In order to aid Ribbentrop in reaching his decision, Wiehl wrote
to Göring, and asked whether Germany by the Veltjens Agreement
had "undertaken the obligation to give Finland some form of
support in the event that Russia maintains its claim on the nickel
concession, as it would appear from Mr. Kivimäki's statements."[62]
The reply, dated November 5 and prepared at Göring's request by
the Ministry of Economics, did not explicitly answer Wiehl's central
question, but it did spell out Göring's sentiments about the value of
the Kolosjoki nickel ore resources. Most of the letter consisted of
statistics supporting the contention that the Finnish nickel deliveries
would be of the most crucial importance for Germany. It was
pointed out that while Germany could expect only about 400 tons
of nickel in 1940, the year to which the Soviet government wished
to limit deliveries to Germany, ore containing some 3,500 tons of
nickel could be expected in 1941 and 5,000 tons in 1942. That
would cover 70 per cent of Germany's total wartime requirements,
a fact "of decisive importance." Admittedly the question of whether
the Soviet demand for the concession should be complied with was
"an exclusively political question," but if compliance was deemed

necessary, then Göring requested that "all means be employed to get the Soviet government to commit itself to deliver to Germany, under long-term contracts, the same amount of nickel which was to be expected under the German-Finnish contracts."[63]

Although the reply evaded Wiehls' main question, he already had his answer. Veltjens called on him on November 4 and related to him what had transpired during the Helsinki negotiations. No obligation to support Finland against the Soviet Union had been incurred, said Veltjens. The Finns had pressed strongly for such a commitment, and had repeatedly asked him what Germany intended to do if the Russians were to march against Finland as a consequence of Finland's fulfillment of the provisions contained in the agreement, but he had consistently stressed that nothing could be expected of Germany in such an event. He had also refused to confirm in any way the content of the letter given to him by Foreign Minister Witting in conjunction with the signing of the agreement.[64]

On the strength of this information, Wiehl proposed that the Foreign Ministry adopt a policy of simply awaiting further developments in the negotiations between Finland and the Soviet Union. If the Soviet government brought the concession matter up with the German government, it should be told that the German renunciation of the concession was based on the assumption that the German claims on nickel ore deliveries within the framework of existing Finnish-German agreements would be honored.[65] The German embassy in Moscow was instructed accordingly,[66] and Kivimäki and the German legation in Helsinki were also informed.[67]

But the Soviet government showed no inclination to negotiate with anyone but the Finns, and in those negotiations both Molotov and Vyshinsky were proceeding as if Germany and England had given their full consent to the sort of settlement demanded of the Finns by the Russians. Schulenburg reported this to Berlin on November 8 after a conversation with Paasikivi,[68] and the same information was given to the Foreign Ministry by the Finnish chargé d'affaires in Berlin.[69] The Finns suggested that Germany ought now to inform the Soviet government of its standpoint.

Wiehl promptly prepared another memorandum for Ribbentrop's attention. The Soviet government was obviously not going to raise the concession matter with Germany, he wrote, and it was therefore "urgently necessary on our part to approach Molotov regarding this matter." It should be impressed upon him that Germany could not "in any circumstances forego receiving 60 per cent of Petsamo's production, which will presumably amount to 6,000 to 12,000 tons yearly." Germany could not give up its claims and accept a Finnish-Soviet concession company unless such a company honored all the existing Finnish-German contracts for an unlimited period. If Molotov would agree to these German conditions, the German renunciation of the concession could be restated to him, suggested Wiehl.[70]

The anticipated volume of the nickel output quoted by Wiehl in this memorandum was corrected the same day in a letter from the Ministry of Economics, which had been informed by I.G. Farbenindustrie that the total production of refined nickel could within three years be increased to 20,000 tons annually. Germany's share of this would be enough to cover its total requirements both during and after the war.[71] Thus, on the eve of Molotov's visit to Berlin, the full scope of Germany's economic stake in the Petsamo area had become clarified.

A great deal was said about Finland in the course of Molotov's conversations with Hitler and Ribbentrop on November 12–13.[72] The emphasis was almost exclusively political, however, as Molotov sought to obtain Hitler's consent to a Soviet annexation of Finland. He reminded Hitler that the territorial revisions agreed upon in the Secret Protocol appended to the Non-Aggression Pact of the previous year had all been carried out "except for one point, namely Finland, and he wanted to know whether the agreement, "as far as it concerned Finland, was still in force." The Soviet government "considered it as its duty," said Molotov, "definitively to settle and clarify the Finnish question." He replied "somewhat evasively" when Hitler asked whether this meant another Soviet-Finnish war, but he thought that the settlement with Finland should be "on the same scale as in Bessarabia and in the adjacent countries." Hitler, while agreeing that Finland remained in the Soviet sphere of influence, insisted that Germany wanted peace in the Baltic area for the present, a statement he repeated often enough for Molotov to understand that it would be wise to postpone any military solution of the Finnish question.[73]

The conclusion that Molotov had hoped to obtain Hitler's consent to a Soviet annexation of Finland is confirmed by the first-hand account of the talks given to the American ambassador in Moscow, Laurence A. Steinhardt, shortly afterward. Steinhardt's informant was Counselor Gustav Hilger of the German embassy in Moscow, who had gone to Berlin with Molotov and had attended every talk which Molotov had there with German leaders.[74] Hilger told Steinhardt that Molotov's trip had probably been occasioned by "Soviet apprehensions and suspicions of Germany's future intentions which had resulted from the actions of Germany in regard to Rumania and Finland." In his statements in Berlin he had "made it quite clear" that the Soviet aims and aspirations "referred almost exclusively to territorial acquisitions and by implication had indicated that they related to Finland."[75]

There is no support in the records and accounts of the Berlin talks, however, for Molotov's statement to Paasikivi on November 19 that Germany had withdrawn its claim on the concession and was willing to see it transferred to the Soviet Union. Molotov apparently had not even brought the subject up in Berlin. Hitler had alluded to it briefly a couple of times, but only to emphasize the great German interest in nickel deliveries from Kolosjoki.[76] Schulenburg had also spoken with Molotov about the Petsamo question, but he had done so in accordance with Wiehl's memorandum of November 9. Thus Molotov knew that Germany would renounce its claim on the concession only if the Soviet government would guarantee to honor the Finnish-German delivery agreements indefinitely. Ribbentrop instructed Schnurre, who was in Moscow again, to pursue the matter with the Soviet government on that basis. Schnurre was also to insist that payments for the nickel ore be made through Finnish-German clearing in accordance with an agreement already concluded with Finland.[77]

Schnurre was inclined to think that stronger measures were called for. In reply to Ribbentrop's telegram he urged that no steps be taken to have the Petsamo nickel concession transferred to Soviet control unless and until the Soviet government had provided binding assurances of its willingness to honor all existing Finnish-German agreements without reservations. Should the concession be transferred before that was accomplished, he said, "then neither our negotiations in Moscow nor Finnish efforts in our behalf will secure our interests." He urged that the Finnish government also be asked to act in accordance with this procedure.[78]

His advice was accepted by the Foreign Ministry, and on November 19 instructions were cabled to the legation in Helsinki to inform the Finnish government that Germany would not object to the transfer of the concession to a mixed Finnish-Soviet company, provided that the Soviet government would commit itself in writing to the following four conditions:

(1) the German claim to 60 per cent of the yield for an unlimited period is upheld,

(2) the Soviet government recognizes the existing agreements between the German and Finnish governments with respect to these deliveries,

(3) the payments for these deliveries may continue to be made through the German-Finnish clearing,

(4) The Finnish-Russian concession company assumes the place of the Petsamo Nickel Company in the existing agreements between the latter company and the I.G. Farbenindustrie.

The Finnish government was further to be informed that the German government would itself bring these conditions to the attention of the Soviet government, and Minister Schnurre would be instructed to keep in close touch with Paasikivi about the continued handling of the question.[79]

This was encouraging news indeed. Blücher, who had just returned to his post in Helsinki after an extended visit to Berlin, informed Witting about the four German conditions on November 22. Although Witting would have preferred to see Germany as an active partner in a new concession company, he was obviously relieved by the new turn of events. He quickly expressed his acceptance of the German conditions and the proposed procedure to be followed in the talks with the Soviet government.[80]

Schnurre, with Schulenburg along for moral support, presented the German conditions to Molotov on November 25. Molotov's consternation was profound. Germany's position confused him, he complained. Twice he had been told that Germany renounced the concession, and he could not understand why conditions were now tagged on to that renunciation. He had said before that the Soviet government was prepared to let Germany have 60 per cent of the nickel output, and if the Germans wished it, the deliveries would continue "until the end of the war or for the year 1941 and 1942." But he "repeatedly rejected the taking on of obligations arising from the German-Finnish agreements," about which the Soviet government knew nothing. It was negotiating with the Finns about the concession, said Molotov, and it would negotiate with the Germans about deliveries to Germany. His statements were so categorical that Schnurre became convinced of the impossibility of changing his mind by further discussions. The only way to get Molotov to accept the German position would be to have the Finns refuse to transfer the concession until he did so, suggested Schnurre.[81]

The report on this conversation was relayed to Blücher by the Foreign Ministry with a request that he inform Witting.[82] Witting's reaction to the German démarche in Moscow was understandably enough the exact opposite of Molotov's. It seemed to reaffirm his faith in a policy of resistance to Soviet demands so much that he blurted out to Blücher, with greater candor than diplomatic prudence, that "the German interest in the nickel mines is now greater than the Finnish." And in the course of what Blücher described as a "comprehensive talk," Witting made statements which indicated that he had suddenly perceived that Finland now had a certain amount of freedom to bargain with the Germans, that Finland was no longer merely a beggar at Germany's door. He was quite willing to "go along with the German government in the anticipated fashion" in the Petsamo question, he declared, but Finland would "not let itself be pushed into the foreground." Hence the German government should not expect a "categorical behavior" on the part of Finland. The Finns were anxious to avoid conflicts with the Soviet Union, and they could not be expected to stick their necks out any farther than the Germans were willing to do, said Witting.[83] To make the Finns feel better about sticking their necks out, the Germans told them that "the Russian government was taking note of the fact that Germany did not wish any new disturbances in the north."[84]

Witting's unconcealed exultation about the news that Germany had at long last intervened directly in Moscow was understandable, for the Soviet pressure on Finland in the Petsamo question had become crushing by late November. The news gave the answer to a question which the Finns had put to the Germans insistently and with growing urgency for two weeks, starting with Molotov's arrival in Berlin. On the first day of Molotov's visit, Counselor Edvin Lundström of the Finnish legation went to the Foreign Ministry and called on both Under State Secretary Woermann and

Minister Grundherr of the Political Department.[85] With both of them he left a written statement, asking that it be regarded as a verbal note, in which Finnish apprehensions about what might come out of the Soviet-German discussions were implicit. The Finns assumed, said the note, that "political conversations regarding continental Europe" were in progress in Berlin. Should these talks also happen to affect Finland, it would be appreciated "if Germany in the course of them could strengthen Finland's position." Finland was "eager to strengthen and deepen the relations with Germany" and desired to live in peace with the Soviet Union on the basis of the new boundary of March, 1940.[86]

Four days later, Lundström was back again to report that Finland was now "under the strongest Russian pressure" to give the Petsamo concession to the Soviet Union at once. He said that the Finnish government would like to have a written confirmation from the German government of the existence of a Finnish commitment to give Germany the right of first refusal. He received no reply.[87]

On November 18, Weizsäcker recorded that Kivimäki had been in to see him and "wanted me to set his mind at ease" regarding rumors which were circulating in Berlin. The rumors had it that the Molotov visit would have serious consequences for Finland. Weizsäcker assured him that nothing had transpired during the visit, as far as he knew, which could justify these rumors. He also hinted that the Foreign Ministry might be able to tell Kivimäki something more definite about the Petsamo matter in a couple of days. For the time being he could only say that it looked as if Germany was not going to make any claims on the concession, but the "modalities" were yet to be worked out in detail.[88]

The same day, Field Marshal Mannerheim had a talk with the German military attaché in Helsinki, Colonel Rössing, to whom he pointed out that many dangers for Finland were "inherent in the transfer of the Petsamo concession to the Soviet government." For instance, said Mannerheim, the employment of Russian personnel in the mining operation at Kolosjoki was likely to constitute a veritable Communist propaganda center, which could have "far-reaching effects in the country."[89] This Trojan horse argument, obviously born of the recent experiences with the SNS, was probably used quite sincerely by Mannerheim, as it was to be used again and again with increasing emphasis during the ensuing months.

In view of the great fears which Molotov's Berlin visit stirred in Finland, the news that the German government had formulated its position on the Petsamo question and had subsequently revealed that position to the Soviet government was most welcome in Helsinki. Witting had good reason to allow himself the pleasure of feeling optimistic for a change, since indications were that the Molotov visit had at least not weakened Finland's situation. That it represented a major turning point in Germany's attitude toward Finland could not yet be clear to him, although Blücher was later to give that impression in his postwar memoirs. If one is to believe Blücher, Witting grasped at once the full significance of what the German minister told him upon his return from Berlin. Without a word being said beyond the cautious formula authorized by the German Foreign Ministry, Witting understood, according to Blücher, that "Hitler had blocked the Russian policy toward Finland and that as of this day a new political era was beginning."[90] That Witting was relieved is quite clear, but there is no indication in Blücher's contemporary reports from Helsinki that the Finnish foreign minister comprehended the full import of what Blücher said.

Before he left Berlin, Blücher had been told by Weizsäcker that Finland was safe, for Hitler had "held his umbrella firmly over Finland."[91] But such clear language was not yet to be used by German diplomats in conversations with Finns. The phrases which had been authorized were promising enough, of course, such as the formula suggested by Ribbentrop on November 22: "Finland should remain calm and firm in its negotiations and not become nervous, but also not provocative or insolent."[92] In a slightly altered form this formula was prescribed for both the German embassy in Moscow and the legation in Helsinki. The Finns were also told that "the Russians naturally realize that in the present situation we wish no new complications in the north," and they were to be encouraged to try to keep the Petsamo nickel concession for themselves if at all possible.[93]

What Weizsäcker had said to Blücher about Hitler's protection of Finland against the Soviet Union, he said in even more categorical terms to an officer of the General Staff of the army. As the statement was recorded in the war diary by Halder on November 16, any further Soviet move against Finland would constitute a "casus belli" for Germany.[94] Furthermore, by December 5, Hitler had decided to include Finland as a "participant" in the projected invasion of the Soviet Union,[95] and two weeks later Finland was referred to in Hitler's Directive No. 21 for Operation "Barbarossa" as one of Germany's "anticipated allies."[96]

The Finns knew nothing about these developments. And so long as they remained uninformed about the plans being made in Germany for an attack on the Soviet Union and the role assigned to Finland in those plans,[97] they could not know either that the German interest in the Petsamo nickel resources, which they knew to be great, had lost its top priority to a still more important German strategic interest in Finland as a whole. All that the best-informed Finns had to go on was a number of verbal assurances that Finland could remain "calm and firm" in its negotiations with the Soviet Union. They also noted with satisfaction certain concrete signs of an increasing German interest in Finland, such as the conclusion on November 22 of a new military agreement for continued German transit on an expanded scale.[98] And there was the remarkable fact that Finland had somehow been able to deny the Petsamo concession to the Soviet Union for five months, a feat which Finland could not realistically have been considered capable of accomplishing by itself. Germany had consistently refused to make any promises of support to Finland, but its actions were eloquent. The ray of light which had pierced the August darkness seemed brighter at the end of November.

CHAPTER V

The Dilatory Negotiators

M OLOTOV'S statement to Paasikivi on November 19 about the
German position on the concession matter had been a bluff, and
the Germans had been forced to call it. When they did so by intervening directly in Moscow at the end of the month, a temporary
impasse occurred in the Finnish-Soviet negotiations, though not the
complete peace and serenity suggested by the virtual absence of
comment in the official Finnish *Blue-White Book* for November,
1940, through January, 1941. And yet, during those eight weeks a
very significant Finnish-Soviet confrontation took place in Moscow.

It is inherent in the nature of official white books that they
present the policies and actions of the governments which issue
them in the most favorable light. As white books go, the Finnish
sample of 1941 was exceptionally truthful, though it did not reveal
the whole truth about everything. Aside from the obvious requirement of documenting the righteousness of Finland and the perfidy
and predaciousness of the Soviet Union, the editors of the *Blue-
White Book* had in addition to consider the interests of Germany,
which was Finland's cobelligerent after June 25, 1941. Presumably
for that reason, a number of the documents included in the publication were not reproduced in their entirety, as a comparison with
copies submitted to the Germans from time to time reveals. What
was eliminated concerned in most cases Finnish-German relations.
It would indeed have been difficult to include in this book a suitable
selection of diplomatic documents without revealing the fact that
Finland, in its Petsamo negotiations with the Soviet Union, was
dealing in bad faith with the Soviet side while constantly con-

ferring, surreptitiously, with the German Foreign Ministry about
the procedure to be followed. Given the situation Finland faced,
this was quite natural. Most of the action perforce took place in
the arena of Finnish-German consultations, as the Finns and
Germans together prepared Finland's defenses for the inevitable
resumption of the Soviet diplomatic offensive in the Petsamo
question.

As has already been shown, the Finns were informed in advance
about the four German conditions which Schnurre presented to
Molotov on November 25. Schnurre, who discussed the démarche
in advance with Paasikivi, discovered that the Finnish minister had
already been "accurately informed" from Helsinki. Paasikivi also
received a full report on Schnurre's conversation with Molotov
immediately after the German emissary returned from the Kremlin.[2]

The incident illustrates the sort of intimate contact between
German and Finnish diplomats which was already becoming a
routine practice in Moscow, Berlin, and Helsinki. Each side kept
the other informed at each new stage of the developing crisis, and
the accuracy of the information exchanged and dutifully recorded
at each corner of that geographical triangle was practically guaranteed by the procedure followed. For instance, the content of a conversation between Paasikivi and Schulenburg in Moscow would
be reported by both men to their respective foreign ministries. In
Berlin, Weizsäcker would forward Schulenburg's report to Blücher
in Helsinki, and he would also discuss it with Kivimäki who, in
turn, would send a report to Witting. Similarly, Witting would inform Kivimäki of Paasikivi's report and also discuss it with
Blücher, whose report would reach Weizsäcker in Berlin. Eventually, Paasikivi's account would reach Schulenburg by way of
Helsinki and Berlin, and Schulenburg's account would get to
Paasikivi by way of Berlin and Helsinki. Any discrepancy between
their two accounts of their conversation would be caught and
straightened out somewhere along the line. In other words, the
picture of the Finnish-Soviet negotiations which emerges from the
German diplomatic records would appear to be remarkably
accurate.

The day after the German démarche was made in Moscow, the
Finnish Foreign Ministry cabled instructions for Paasikivi to inform
the Soviet government that Finland proposed "that the two coun-

tries begin to work out the organization of a mixed Finnish-Russian
concession company." Two Finnish plenipotentiaries stood ready
to leave for Moscow whenever the Russians indicated their agreement. Paasikivi was to "take into account how Molotov reacts to
the German conditions," since that reaction would obviously have
an effect on how the Finnish government ought to proceed. He
should also tell Molotov that Finland agreed with the four German
conditions.[3] The instruction was a direct result of the hints of
German support which the Finns had been given after Molotov's
Berlin visit, notably the hints dropped by Veltjens during his brief
stay in Helsinki in late November.[4] What he told the Finnish
authorities had made them "grateful and extremely happy," he
reported upon his return to Berlin.[5] Apparently the German Foreign
Ministry felt that the Finns were taking undue advantage of the
new situation, however, and the Finnish Foreign Ministry was
asked to make a significant correction in its instruction to Paasikivi.
To have him tell Molotov that Finland passively agreed with the
four German conditions was not satisfactory, for those conditions
did after all reflect commitments which Finland had already made
to Germany. Paasikivi should be told instead to present those conditions to the Soviet government as Finnish conditions.[6] New instructions were promptly sent to Paasikivi in compliance with
the German request.[7]

Presumably the Russians had been pondering the unexpectedly
difficult problem of imposing their will on the Finns now that
Germany had made its objections to a military solution clear. The
problem had apparently not been solved by the time Paasikivi
called on Molotov on December 3. Molotov was in a bitter mood,
but he had no new ideas to air and no demands to make. He
recited a catalogue of insincerities of which the Finns were guilty
in their dealings with the Russians in the Petsamo question, but he
did not seem to know what to do about them. "With Germany you
have reached agreement readily enough," he complained, "but with
us you have dragged the matter out and hit upon all sorts of
prevarications; for five months you have put our patience to the
test." He wanted to know whether the new Finnish proposal for
the establishment of a mixed commission to work out the plans for
a joint company meant that Finland had at long last decided to
reach a definitive agreement with the Soviet Union in the nickel

matter. Paasikivi "had to answer evasively" and say that it depended on England's attitude. The Finnish government was waiting for the British to make up their minds on this question, and in view of the navicert situation this was an important consideration. Molotov disagreed. He asked whether the concession holders had lived up to their obligations under the contract. Paasikivi professed not to know anything about that. It was clear, then, said Molotov, that the Anglo-Canadian trust had not fulfilled its obligations, and the Finns could therefore annul the concession with a clear conscience if they really wanted to, but obviously they did not.

Once again Molotov went to the heart of the problem. He wanted to know how the Finns had managed to reach agreement with the Germans in spite of England's declared opposition to letting any nickel go to Germany, while they were resisting the Soviet Union on the grounds that England's position remained to be clarified. It was a question which Paasikivi had anticipated, and of which he had warned his government in advance. When his instructions reached him, he had immediately told Witting that it made no sense to propose negotiations for a joint company to the Russians without first deciding what to do about the British. Of the three great powers involved in the Petsamo question, England was farthest away. Finland could not afford to provoke the Soviet Union, and so long as Soviet and British interests were not reconcilable, England would simply have to be eliminated, at least for the duration of the war. If the Finnish government had not reached a firm decision on that question, it could not have reached a firm decision on the question of forming a mixed concession company with the Soviet Union either, Paasikivi reasoned. To propose negotiations for such a company to the Soviet government was therefore in itself an act of insincerity. Witting seemed to accept the logic of Paasikivi's argument, but he failed to make the decision which Paasikivi recommended.

Hence Molotov's question caused Paasikivi some embarrassment. As he recorded his reaction in his memoirs, he "tried to explain" that with the Germans it had been a matter of deliveries; with England it was a matter of the concession. "This did not appear to have any impact on Molotov, however," he noted dryly. Nor did any of his other explanations or arguments. As usual, Molotov also refused to accept any arguments based on the Finnish-German agreements. He knew nothing about those agreements, he insisted, and he asked to be shown the text of the delivery contract. Paasikivi evasively replied that the agreement had been made in Helsinki, but he had not seen it himself.

Finally, after raising various objections and warning that Finland's behavior "was not good for Russian-Finnish relations," Molotov agreed to the formation of a mixed commission to discuss the Finnish proposal, but he did so with obvious indifference.[8] He plainly realized, as did Paasikivi, that the Finnish proposal was merely another maneuver designed to "gain time."[9]

During the next two weeks, there were constant consultations between the Finnish and German Foreign Ministries as the strategy for the Finnish-Soviet negotiations in the mixed commission was worked out. The Germans even took a hand in selecting the two Finnish negotiators. Of the three candidates for the delegation— Fieandt and the industrial and business leaders, Berndt Grönblom and Åke Gartz,[10] the Finnish government chose Grönblom and Gartz.[11] The Germans regarded the choice as unfortunate. Schnurre, who learned the names of the three candidates from Paasikivi in Moscow before the final choice had been made, was opposed to the appointment of Grönblom, who "is known to us as difficult and unapproachable and opposed us vigorously during the first stage of the German-Finnish Petsamo negotiations;" he suggested that the Finnish government be urged to name Fieandt, "since he is more closely informed about the German-Finnish talks." Paasikivi agreed with the suggestion and would advise Helsinki accordingly, said Schnurre.[12] Blücher found Witting to be "open to my suggestion,"[13] and soon he was able to report to Berlin that Fieandt would be named in the place of Gartz. Grönblom was to remain on the delegation, but Fieandt would be the chairman. Minister Hynninen would be placed at the disposal of the delegation in Moscow.[14]

The Finnish-German consultations also covered Molotov's legitimate complaint that he could hardly be expected to accept responsibility for German rights under the Finnish-German agreements without having seen the agreements. The question of whether the texts of all or some of the agreements should be shown to him was discussed in Berlin by Wiehl and Kivimäki, who passed the delicate problem on to the representatives of I.G. Farbenindustrie and Petsamo Nickel, then engaged in talks in Berlin.[15] The two companies decided, by a formal agreement signed on December 11, that the Soviet government should be given the texts of five documents, namely the delivery agreement of July 23, the accompanying protocol of the same date, the exchange of letters of July 24, the credit agreement of September 16, and the draft of a still unsigned agreement whereby the Petsamo Nickel Company promised to deliver nickel matte to I.G. Farbenindustrie.[16]

The decision to let the Russians see the text of the draft nickel matte agreement was rescinded on the advice of Fieandt,[17] then reinstated at the suggestion of the Finnish government. Wiehl's reaction was to suspect that the Finnish government was trying to establish another *fait accompli,* so that Fieandt and Grönblom, once the mixed commission began its work in Moscow, could resist the Soviet demands from a position fortified by as many agreements involving German interests as possible. That would in effect force the Russians to work out a number of important matters with the Germans rather than the Finns, and that would take some of the pressure off Finland. Wiehl was probably right, but he thought that this Finnish tactic was quite harmless and instructed Schulenburg, provided he himself had no objections, to tell Fieandt that the Finns were welcome to go ahead and give the Russians the draft text of the nickel matte agreement.[18]

From Moscow, Schulenburg and Schnurre had already submitted a number of tactical proposals to Berlin regarding the imminent Finnish-Soviet negotiations. On December 14, they noted that it was indeed necessary to let the Soviet government have the texts of the various Finnish-German agreements, "but it should under all circumstances be done by the Finns." Germany ought not to take any new initiative in the Petsamo question if it could be avoided, since it might have a detrimental influence on the Soviet-German trade negotiations in which Schnurre was involved at the time. Schnurre also urged that the draft nickel matte agreement be signed before the Finnish-Soviet negotiations opened, and he suggested that a Finnish government guarantee, "which the credit agreement depends on," be formalized by that time as well. If it proved impossible to produce the government guarantee in time, then the Russians should be told that the credit agreement had already become operative by virtue of the interim guarantee provided by the Bank of Finland.[19]

The Foreign Ministry agreed with these tactical suggestions, since they appeared to offer plausible means of delaying the possible transfer of the Petsamo concession without necessitating overt German intervention in the matter in the near future. As Wiehl told Blücher, "the longer we can postpone our entry into the Moscow negotiations, the greater will be the possibilities of pursuing our stand in the Petsamo matter without having to worry about the parallel economic negotiations with Russia." It was also in Finland's interest to gain more time, he added. Finland could still use the argument that England had refused its consent to the transfer of the concession if any nickel was sold to Germany, and Germany had already tied its consent to a Soviet fulfillment of the familiar four conditions. The Russians had not accepted the English terms, and they had promised to deliver nickel ore to Germany. "Thereby a situation has been created which makes possible a dilatory treatment of all conditions," Wiehl pointed out, and he urged Blücher to have Witting instruct Fieandt to get in touch with Schnurre about this in Moscow at once.[20]

To negotiate dilatorily had been Finland's policy all along. Söderhjelm, upon his return to Helsinki following a final round of negotiations between the Petsamo Nickel Company and Soyuzpromexport,[21] made that quite clear in the course of a lengthy conversation with the American minister on December 8. The main reason why Ramsay had gone to Berlin, said Söderhjelm, was "to discuss with representatives of I.G. Farbenindustrie how present concession can be preserved." Schoenfeld informed the State Department that, according to Söderhjelm, "Ramsay still believes it may be possible to keep situation in suspense and to avoid an issue which is evidently the line of thought of Prime Minister Ryti."[22] Wiehl's advice was therefore most welcome. The Finnish government at once issued the requisite enabling act for the government guarantee of the credit agreement,[23] and the guarantee was granted upon application by the Petsamo Nickel Company.[24] On December 20, Fieandt was instructed to conduct his negotiations in the mixed commission "in dilatory fashion" and to establish immediate and close contact with Schnurre.[25]

As for revealing the draft text of the nickel matte agreement to the Russians, Fieandt's original counsel ultimately prevailed, and the Finnish government could not be moved to do it. Pressed by the Germans, a spokesman for the Finnish Foreign Ministry explained that Petsamo Nickel was not satisfied with the price offered for the nickel matte by I.G. Farbenindustrie and was therefore not prepared to do anything which implied that the document, which was in fact the latest proposal for an agreement submitted by I.G. Farbenindustrie, was a draft agreement between the two parties. Although the Germans argued that both the Finnish and the German positions would be weakened in their respective negotiations with the Russians unless the document in question was shown to the Soviet government,[26] the Finns stood their ground, and the agreement, in its conclusive form, was not submitted to the Russians until March 15, 1941.[27]

The Finnish government also made another attempt to ascertain the exact attitude of the British government before the mixed commission began its work. Several times during October and November, Minister Gripenberg had reported from London that the British Foreign Office, Admiralty, and Secret Service were receiving a steady stream of reports to the effect that pro-German sentiments were getting the upper hand in Finland while an anti-English mood was rising. The British understood, according to Gripenberg, why the Finns were buying arms in Germany, and they sympathized with Finland's hope of finding German support against the Soviet Union. But to let Germany develop a dominant position of influence in Finland was bound to have certain consequences for Finnish-English relations. Both in London and in Helsinki the British had hinted that the Finnish-German transit agreements, for instance, might result in British reprisals against Finland. So far there had been no action of that sort, but the Finns worried about what England might decide to do next.[28]

Gripenberg went to the British Foreign Office once more and had a long conversation with Under-Secretary of State Richard A. Butler about the Petsamo question. As in the past, he received no explicit answer to his questions, and at the end of the conversation he pointed out that he had now had a total of seven discussions about the nickel concession with responsible officials in the Foreign Office without getting any wiser. He would have to conclude, he told Butler, that the English government was not inclined to resist a transfer of the nickel concession "sufficiently energetically." If his assumption was correct, he would have to say that "nobody is entitled to criticize the Finnish government if the concession is taken away from the trust and if nickel is delivered to Germany." Butler admitted that, reported Gripenberg to Witting.[29]

Although Butler's admission did not constitute an official reply to the Finnish inquiry, Witting realized its great significance. It meant that England was for all practical purposes out of the Petsamo picture. Finland was henceforth dealing only with Germany and the Soviet Union.[30] However, as long as the British did not make their policy known in Moscow with the same candor with which Butler had revealed it to Gripenberg, the Finns could continue to tell the Russians that the British government was opposed to a transfer of the concession on the terms proposed to the Finns by the Russians.

This was the situation when the Finnish-Soviet mixed commission met in Moscow for the first time on December 19. The Soviet delegation which faced Fieandt and Grönblom consisted of Alexei D. Krutikov, deputy commissar for foreign trade and delegation chairman, and an official of the Commissariat for Foreign Affairs by the name of Kurotsev.[31] Although the negotiations were described as "formally agreeable," it quickly emerged that the two sides were as far apart as the proverbial east and west. The Finnish delegates had been instructed to keep in mind the four German conditions. They were to insist that Finland must have a clear majority of the stock in the projected Finnish-Soviet concession company. They were also to insist that this new company should handle only the marketing of the nickel and exercise certain limited powers of executive control, while the Petsamo Nickel company would continue to be responsible for the actual exploitation of the mine. Furthermore, before a transfer of the concession could take place, both Finland and the Soviet Union had to reach an agreement with the present concession holders about all matters connected with the transfer.[32] The Soviet delegation, on the other hand, made it clear that the Russians expected the new company to not only take over the concession, but also the entire mining operation with all executive powers. The Soviet government demanded 51 per cent of the capital stock, a controlling voice in the selection of the board of directors, and exclusive control of the business management.[33]

The gulf between the two positions seemed completely unbridgeable and full of dangers for Finland. Paasikivi was convinced that the dangers were very real. In his memoirs he described in almost contemptuous terms the rigid instructions given Fieandt. He thought they were more than simply naive. He also thought that Fieandt and Grönblom failed to understand what was at stake for Finland. He warned them of a possible Soviet occupation of the Petsamo area should Finland refuse to yield to Soviet demands. When Grönblom asked him "whether I was certain that the Russians would occupy Petsamo if we did not accomplish anything," Paasikivi, according to his diary, lectured Grönblom on "the problems of foreign policy." There was always an unknown factor in foreign affairs, he revealed, and he informed businessman Grönblom that "ordinary business affairs are quite simple in comparison with this." Because of the unknown factor always lurking in the shadows, Finland had to take into account the possibility of Soviet reprisals, and "we could not afford to let such a relatively small matter as the Petsamo nickel develop into conflict."[34]

If Paasikivi was worried about the possibly dire consequences of the rigid position taken by the Finnish government, Fieandt and Grönblom were skeptical about Paasikivi's pessimistic assessment of the situation too. On the same day that the minister lectured Grönblom on the problems of high diplomacy, Fieandt exchanged notes with Schnurre in a quiet Moscow side street, the sort of place they usually chose for their meetings in order to escape the long ears of the GPU, the Soviet secret police which made a habit of installing listening devices wherever foreign diplomats lived and worked. According to Schnurre, Fieandt told him that "Paasikivi has once again lost his nerve completely and is pressing for immediate capitulation in the Petsamo question."[35]

Whether Fieandt actually used the exact words reported by Schnurre is really a moot point. It was clear to Schnurre that the Soviet demands on Finland represented a serious threat to German interests both in the Petsamo area itself and in North Norway. It was therefore to be expected that he should have painted Paasikivi's attitude in the darkest possible colors in order to provoke the Foreign Ministry in Berlin to intervene in Moscow in Finland's behalf. It was equally clear that Fieandt, in spite of his close and respectful relationship with Paasikivi, represented a school of thought which was much less inclined to yield to Soviet pressures than Paasikivi was.[36] Ever since his interview with Ribbentrop on August 19, Fieandt had been rather confident that Germany could be relied upon to prevent a mortal Soviet blow against Finland, although he realized also that the danger was not over and Finland had to proceed with considerable caution. That Fieandt's attitude, which also reflected the view of Foreign Minister Witting, corresponded more closely to the interests of Germany is obvious, and Schnurre concluded his report on their conversation with a request to the German Foreign Ministry to have Witting order Paasikivi to support the position taken by Fieandt.

It is quite possible that Paasikivi was not kept as well informed by Witting about the tangled ramifications of the Petsamo question as his position in the Soviet capital would seem to entitle him to, and his memoirs indeed reveal that he was on occasion taken completely by surprise by Molotov's statements through lack of necessary information from Helsinki. Molotov was frequently able to embarrass Paasikivi by being better informed about affairs in Finland than Paasikivi was. On December 13, only a few days before the mixed commission began its work, Paasikivi had discussed in a letter to Witting the Finnish-Swedish union talks to which Molotov had put an abrupt end a week earlier. Paasikivi had referred to several factors involved in that problem, including "Germany's standpoint, which I do not know."[37] It is fairly clear that he did not know enough about Germany's standpoint on the Petsamo question either.

Fieandt, who was well acquainted with the whole picture, was able to remain calm in spite of the seemingly disastrous direction in which his negotiations were moving. The instructions he had been given left so little room for maneuver that he thought some changes would have to be made in them. As he told Schnurre on December 22, in the course of the conversation already referred to, "it seems more than doubtful that this Finnish standpoint can be maintained." However, the Soviet attitude was so intransigent that Krutikov would not even permit him to return to Helsinki for consultations and new instructions. Krutikov had made that clear "in unmistakable fashion," said Fieandt, and both he and Grönblom had found it impossible even to get travel permits to leave Moscow. The only advice that Schnurre was able to give him was that he would have to disentangle himself somehow without giving the Russians cause to break off the negotiations in the mixed commission.[38]

The chance to seek an amicable temporary adjournment of the talks came the very next day, when Krutikov for the first time revealed the full extent of the Soviet demands. Fieandt declared that the demands were unacceptable, and he would have to go to Helsinki and consult with his government before the talks could be continued. Krutikov agreed, and both Fieandt and Grönblom departed the following evening. Before they left, Schnurre told Fieandt to remain in Helsinki at least until Schnurre had completed his own negotiations for a German-Soviet trade treaty. In the meantime, the Finns should maintain contact with the Russians in the Petsamo question "in a cautious and dilatory manner."[39]

Upon his return to Helsinki, Fieandt gave a detailed description of the Moscow negotiations to Blücher. The Soviet negotiators, he related, had demanded that the board of directors of the projected mixed Finnish-Soviet concession company consist of three Russians and three Finns, with the chairmanship to rotate between the two sides. The managing director would always have to be a Russian, however. The Russians had refused to get involved in any negotiations with the British about the concession, but they were prepared to lend Finland the money to compensate the Anglo-Canadian trust for the loss of the concession. Not a single word had been uttered by the Russian negotiators about the four conditions presented earlier by the German government and repeated orally by Fieandt in the name of his government. It was his impression, said Fieandt to Blücher, that the Russians were primarily interested in gaining effective control of the mine itself and the operation of it. Once they had achieved that, he thought that they would probably expand the operation to its full capacity, which would enable them to hire as many Russian and Finnish Communist workers as possible. The end result would be a Communist reservation in the Petsamo area, a center of propaganda from which the work of promoting Finland's internal political disintegration could be carried on. In conclusion Fieandt said that he hoped to be able to find plausible excuses for postponing his return to Moscow for at least two weeks, which ought to be time enough for the German-Soviet trade negotiations to be completed. He would also like to know what Finnish concessions to the Russians might be tolerable to the German government.[40]

As it turned out, the Finnish government was able to come up with sufficient grounds for delaying the return of the delegates to Moscow for a full month. One of the arguments which Fieandt had used to obtain the adjournment of the talks in the mixed commission was that "certain data regarding relations with the English were available only in Helsinki, and that he could wind up the affairs with the English there only."[41] This argument was stretched nearly to the breaking point when the Finns decided that some of the data were not even available in Helsinki, but had to be sought in London. Soon Ramsay was on his way to England once again for talks with the British Foreign Office and officials of the Mond Nickel Company. Meanwhile a special committee was set up in Helsinki, consisting of Fieandt, Grönblom, and Dr. Erik Castrén, for the purpose of investigating the legal ramifications of the contract commitments to the Anglo-Canadian trust.[42] As long as one or both of those two fact-finding jobs could be continued without producing any facts, Finland could hope to keep stalling for more time.

A third excuse was also available. The reorganization of the Finnish government in the wake of Prime Minister Ryti's election to the presidency on December 19 proved to be a difficult and protracted affair. It was entirely reasonable to suggest to the Russians that a country without a government could hardly be expected to send delegates abroad for serious negotiations until the political situation at home had been returned to normal. Thus, when Minister Zotov reminded Witting—who had remained at his post as foreign minister in Acting Prime Minister Rudolf Waldén's interim cabinet—of the urgency of the Petsamo matter at the end of the year,[43] there was no positive Finnish response.

CHAPTER VI

In the Eye of the Hurricane

ALTHOUGH Minister Zotov's stern reminder of December 30 had evoked no particular sense of urgency or alarm in Helsinki—Zotov was perpetually stern and humorless—both the Finns and the Germans expected that the Petsamo question would continue to pose serious problems for them, perhaps also direct dangers to Finland. Schnurre, whose trade negotiations in Moscow were still in progress as 1941 opened, advised the German Foreign Ministry that the Finnish-Soviet Petsamo negotiations would, "provided Finland does not capitulate in the matter, move into another acute crisis." He expected the Soviet government to insist on the full acceptance of its demands, and it was quite likely that the Russians would refuse to assume responsibility for Finland's commitments to Germany by becoming a party to the existing Finnish-German agreements. Should it become necessary for Finland to make concessions to the Soviet side, then it would have to be concessions whereby the projected mixed company would take over the management of the mining operations. "In any case, Fieandt should not return to Moscow before my negotiations have been concluded," said Schnurre. He suggested that the Finns continue to blame the British for the delay.[1]

In relaying Schnurre's telegram to the legation in Helsinki, the Foreign Ministry requested Blücher not to mention anything to the Finns about possible Finnish concessions to the Soviet demands, "since this question is being weighed here." He should merely continue to work for the longest possible delay of the Finnish delegation's return to Moscow.[2] Blücher, who was already working for such a delay in his contacts with Foreign Minister Witting, asked what the German government was doing about strengthening the Finnish bargaining position.[3] There was no immediate response from Berlin, but Germany's ability to provide at least moral support was considerably improved by the conclusion on January 10 of the new German-Soviet trade agreement.[4] The Germans would not have to worry about that any more; the Finns had stalled for as long as Schnurre had asked them to do it.

The Russian pressure for the resumption of negotiations in the mixed commission had vanished, however. Nothing had been heard from the Soviet government in the Petsamo question since Zotov's reminder of late December. On January 8, Witting told the American minister that relations with the Soviet Union were "very quiet," though he feared that new difficulties might arise at any time.[5] The next day the Swedish envoy in Moscow gave his American colleague an accurate summary of the Soviet demands as presented to Finland earlier, but he described the current situation as "more or less quiescent."[6]

Witting's puzzlement, as expressed to Minister Schoenfeld, was understandable. For several months the Soviet Union had been whipping up a political hurricane over the Petsamo question, and then everything was suddenly deathly quiet. In fact, during the first ten days of January, 1941, Finland found itself in the eye of the hurricane. The other half of the storm was yet to come, and it was to be just as vicious as the first half, if somewhat briefer. By the time it had passed over and petered out, considerable damage had been done to Finnish nervous systems.

The first rumblings were soon heard as the Soviet press and radio resumed the temporarily interrupted anti-Finnish campaign. On January 11, the radio station in Petrozavodsk, capital of the Fenno-Karelian Soviet Socialist Republic, again beamed its powerful signal to Finland in a Finnish-language broadcast. In those times of press censorship, the Finnish public had learned to determine the current status of Finnish-Soviet relations by what was said about Finland in broadcasts from Petrozavodsk. Now they were informed that Finland was ogling the western powers while leaning tightly against "a certain imperialistic great power," whose protection it was seeking in return for adopting "certain ideologies." Because of the export of Finnish food to this great power, the masses of the Finnish people were in the grip of starvation, according to the broadcast.[7]

The Finns knew from past experiences that something unpleasant was afoot. In Moscow, Paasikivi automatically connected the resurgence of the anti-Finnish campaign with the protracted absence of the Finnish negotiators from Moscow, and he urged that they return at once.[8] Then, on January 18, Minister Zotov suddenly left Helsinki for the Soviet Union without giving official notification to the Finnish Foreign Ministry, and it was understood that "he might be absent for some time."[9] Simultaneously, the Finnish government began to receive reports from Finnish business people to the effect that they were not receiving scheduled Soviet shipments, and all transit of goods from or to Finland through the Soviet Union appeared to have been halted. There had been no statement from the Soviet government about any such embargo, and Witting speculated that it might be connected with Finland's procrastination in the Petsamo negotiations.[10] Schulenburg's opinion that the Soviet government was "no doubt exasperated by the Finnish government's protracted handling of the Petsamo question,"[11] seemed to confirm this. In Helsinki, Witting laconically told Schoenfeld on January 21 that "there had been considerable trouble with the Russians lately."[12] Watching the developments from Berlin, Wiehl considered that the Finnish-Soviet negotiations were "approaching their acute crisis."[13]

The last two weeks before the Finnish delegates to the mixed commission finally returned to Moscow were hectic ones for the Finnish and German officials concerned with the Petsamo question. By January 13, a sense of great urgency had filled most of them as a result of the familiar warning signals emitted by the Soviet propaganda machine. Paasikivi's appeal for the immediate return of the delegates and Blücher's inquiry to the German Foreign Ministry about whether he should "continue to try to retard the Finnish-Russian Petsamo talks"[14] were indications of this frame of mind. So was Kivimäki's visit to Wiehl on January 14, when he "emphasized that the opinion in Finland is that there is an inherent danger of an ultimative action by the Soviet Union in continued delaying tactics." He suggested that the Finnish and German governments synchronize their policies in the Petsamo question before the Finnish delegates returned to Moscow.[15]

Although Wiehl replied that such a decision ought not to be made until the imminent return of Schnurre to Berlin,[16] Kivimäki interpreted this as a positive answer, and he advised the Finnish Foreign Ministry to send Fieandt to Berlin for an exchange of views with Schnurre. Witting immediately sent Fieandt on his way by way of Stockholm.[17] When Wiehl found out about this, he hastened to inform Blücher that Fieandt's journey was "decidedly inopportune, since it might well give Moscow the impression that Fieandt received his instructions from Berlin."[18] Quick action by the Finnish Foreign Ministry succeeded in intercepting Fieandt in Stockholm, and he returned reluctantly to Helsinki. He still thought that an exchange of views with Schnurre in Berlin would have been desirable, according to what Blücher reported, and he suggested that his trip could plausibly have been explained as connected with the Finnish-German trade exchange. But Wiehl's view prevailed, and it was decided that an exchange of views could be undertaken more inconspicuously when Ramsay passed through Berlin on his way home from London.[19] If at all possible, Fieandt's return to Moscow should be delayed until then.

Meanwhile the tactical planning proceeded within and between the German and Finnish Foreign Ministries. The only key person who seemed to be inadequately informed about what was going on was Paasikivi, and this led to a brief tempest in a teapot. On January 16, Paasikivi told Minister Werner von Tippelskirch of the German embassy in Moscow that the Finnish delegates were due in Moscow that day. He also reported that the Russians were prepared to hold further talks in Helsinki.[20] Wiehl rushed off a telegram to Blücher demanding clarification of this "incomprehensible" news,[21] and he was promptly assured that the Fieandt delegation did not plan to leave Helsinki before Ramsay arrived there with the results of his discussions in Berlin.[22]

Wiehl then prepared a policy recommendation on the Petsamo question for Ribbentrop's consideration. He could see no benefits for Germany from a direct intervention in Moscow, he said. The Soviet government had twice been informed about Germany's wishes, and Molotov had interpreted them in his own peculiar fashion. He had not accepted the four German conditions, and yet he had considered the German representations to mean that Germany had no objections to the transfer of the concession. Even if Molotov were to accept the German conditions, Germany could not be sure that he would actually live up to his promise. The German government had all the while advised the Finns to remain uncompromising and not give the Russians the concession. Now, with the Finnish-Soviet negotiations approaching a stage of acute crisis, the time had come when the German government must make a choice, wrote Wiehl. Either the Finns must be encouraged to continue their resistance to the Soviet demands, or they must be advised to yield altogether. In Wiehl's opinion, Germany needed the Petsamo nickel so badly that the first alternative must be adopted. However, since this alternative might well result in Soviet military reprisals against Finland, he also urged that Germany be prepared to give the Finns "positive backing against the Russians."[23]

It was a radical recommendation, involving a policy change which affected German-Soviet relations in a fundamental way. The position which Wiehl now recommended could, if adopted, lead Germany into a situation where it would have to make an open stand against the Soviet Union in defense of Finland. For a diplomat of Wiehl's great caution to make such a bold proposal to Ribbentrop testified eloquently to the high value which Germany placed on the Petsamo nickel and the grave concern evoked in Berlin by the alarming indications of renewed Soviet pressure on Finland. That Schnurre, who had just returned to Berlin from Moscow, should make himself a spokesman for the hard line suggested by Wiehl was less surprising. He told Wiehl that he regarded the matter of offering concrete support to Finland in the Petsamo question to be essential, even though it might have detrimental repercussions for German-Soviet relations in all their aspects.[24]

The possibly enormous consequences of the recommended policy made Ribbentrop hesitate, and three days later a chance statement by Kivimäki that no immediate danger of a Soviet military move against Finland seemed to exist took him off the hook.[25] After discussing the matter with Schnurre, he chose to avoid a decisive stand for the time being. The Finnish government should merely be told that Germany remained interested in the retention of the nickel concession by Finland, and that the Germans shared the Finnish fear that a Soviet-dominated concession company would turn into a center for Communist agitation in Finland. "The Finnish government should accordingly be advised to continue to negotiate dilatorily and avoid an open rupture by granting minor concessions," Ribbentrop cabled Blücher. Should Ramsay fail to win the approval of the Anglo-Canadian trust for a transfer of the concession, the Finns should leave it to the Russians to seek such approval. The Finns should also request that the Soviet government clarify its position on the Finnish-German agreements.[26]

The time for putting off the decision was already past, however. Even as Ribbentrop's telegram was dispatched on January 24, events had rendered it obsolete. By the time Blücher received it the next day, it had become so obviously irrelevant that he saw no sense in passing on most of its contents to Witting. Ramsay's mission to England had failed, and the Soviet-generated hurricane was blowing with rapidly increasing force.

Ramsay's journey to London yielded no positive results whatever, except to the extent that his absence on such a mission served as an explanation for Finland's continuing procrastination. The British let Ramsay cool his heels in Lisbon for a considerable length of time before they allowed him to enter England, and he did not reach London until the middle of January.[27] After one week's labor he had nothing much to report to Helsinki. He had been received by some representatives of Mond Nickel for private and noncommittal talks. The representatives had politely assured him that they "believed him," and they would be happy to accept some changes which could ease Finland's difficult situation.[28] They would not sell their interest in Petsamo, but they might be willing to consider some temporary arrangement for the duration of the war.[29] Because the attitude of Mond Nickel did not go far enough to meet the categorical Soviet demand for a definitive transfer of the concession, it seemed like good news. It meant that Finland could continue to offer a compromise solution to the Soviet Union, a temporary solution which the Russians could be counted on to reject as inadequate. Thus Ramsay's report seemed to the Germans to confirm the wisdom of Ribbentrop's caution. But that illusion was short-lived.

Almost four weeks after he left Helsinki on his mission to England, Ramsay was finally able to discuss the Petsamo question with a representative of the English government.[30] He was told that the British would stand on the existing legal agreements concerning the concession and would reject any encroachments on the rights of British subjects. England would also oppose any solution which would give Petsamo nickel to Germany. However, the English government would not officially bring this standpoint to the attention of the Soviet government, although Ambassador Cripps would be informed and instructed to do whatever he pleased with the information unofficially. Ramsay drew the conclusion that England was not going to put up any kind of resistance to the Soviet designs on the Kolosjoki nickel ore resources. Witting agreed with that conclusion. As reported by Blücher to Berlin, the Finnish foreign minister thought that "the English card can no longer be played out against the Russians."[31]

This depressing news came as the Soviet demand for the resumption of the Moscow negotiations was becoming oppressively insistent. Vyshinsky told Paasikivi on January 14 that the patience of the Soviet government was exhausted, and the Finns had better submit their reply without further delay. Should they fail to accept an amicable settlement, the Soviet Union "would find ways to settle the matter." If necessary the Russians were prepared to negotiate in Helsinki.[32] The next day Zotov repeated this "in rather strong terms" and demanded that a date be fixed for the renewal of the talks.[33]

Simultaneously the Soviet trade embargo against Finland was quietly set in motion, to be followed by Zotov's disappearing act. As far as the embargo was concerned, Witting assured the Germans that he expected no serious economic consequences of it until the fall.[34] For good measure, the British government warned Gripenberg that there would be a further reduction in navicerts unless Finland cut down its export of molybdenum to Germany to about half the volume Finland was legally committed to export,[35] and Finnish intelligence reports revealed increased Soviet military activity along the border.[36] While Witting calmly assured Blücher that the British demand would not be complied with, Field Marshal Mannerheim reacted less calmly to the intelligence reports he received. He panicked and asked for President Ryti's authorization to order partial mobilization, a request supported by his chief of

staff and the minister of defense. But both Ryti and the new prime
minister, Johan (Jukka) Wilhelm Rangell, rejected Mannerheim's
advice, an act so unusual that he tried to resign.[37]

Although Mannerheim's fear of a Soviet invasion across the
Karelian Isthmus proved to be unwarranted, it was apparently
shared by a number of German political and military leaders.
Colonel General Halder noted in his war diary on January 18 that
there was currently some nervousness in the Foreign Ministry
based on the fear "that Russia will react to our entry into Bulgaria
with an attack on Finland."[38] Two days later, at the request of the
OKW, the Foreign Ministry asked Finland to take steps to protect
the mining facilities in the Petsamo area against possible sabotage
or "English disturbance measures."[39] Witting agreed,[40] and military
guards were quickly posted at the Kolosjoki mine, the Jäniskoski
power station, and the suspension bridge across the Pasvik River.[41]
It was a false alarm, however.

On January 21, Vyshinsky summoned Paasikivi again and insisted on an answer to the Soviet demands. He was not going to
listen to any more excuses, he said. When Paasikivi pointed out
that Ramsay was in England to try to clarify a matter which the
Russians themselves had refused to take up with the British,
Vyshinsky replied sarcastically that the Finns would probably send
Ramsay "right round the world, all the way to America." No
further delay would be tolerated, said Vyshinsky, and if the Finns
did not come up with a definitive answer within two days, the
Soviet government would regard that as a refusal to answer at all.

Paasikivi advised the Finnish government that this time it was
absolutely necessary for Finland to act, and the very least that
should be done was to tell the Russians, before the deadline set
by Vyshinsky, that the Finns stood ready to continue the negotiations in either Moscow or Helsinki. Witting agreed with the latter
point and sent Paasikivi the necessary instruction.[42] When Paasikivi
informed Vyshinsky about this on January 23, the first deputy
commissar appeared to be quite satisfied. He did repeat the old
suggestion that the Finnish government could, if it wanted to, find
some legal way of relieving Mond Nickel of the concession, but
he also listened patiently to Paasikivi's counter-arguments. He even
seemed to accept the idea that both sides would have to make

some concessions in order to reach a fair settlement of the Petsamo question.[43] This attitude, plus the fact that Finnish-Soviet trade relations were again showing signs of improvement, so encouraged Witting that he gave Blücher a rather optimistic account the next day of the most recent developments. He described the tension in Finnish-Soviet relations as "declining."[44]

It was at that juncture that Ribbentrop decided that no German intervention was required and dispatched his telegram to that effect to the legation in Helsinki, Blücher received the telegram just as Ramsay's bad news from London reached Witting. Blücher therefore made only limited use of Ribbentrop's telegram when he saw Witting on January 25. Witting pointed out that Ramsay's report altered the situation fundamentally, and the Finnish-Soviet negotiations, which he had stalled by delaying tactics for a full month, could be stalled no longer. He would have to send the Finnish delegation back to Moscow at once, and he anticipated "strong Russian pressure." He hoped that the German government would now use its influence on Finland's behalf and send Schulenburg instructions to that effect at once. In his report to Berlin, Blücher expressed the opinion that the Finns were likely to yield to the Soviet demands "on essential points unless this German support is given them in Moscow,"[45] and his opinion was reinforced by a conversation he had with Fieandt later the same day.[46] As usual, Blücher tried to prod Berlin to move in the desired direction by adding a warning. He reminded the Foreign Ministry that the Arctic Ocean Highway, the indispensable life line of the German transit traffic to and from Kirkenes, happened to cut right through the Petsamo mining facilities. Therefore, should Finland be forced to surrender control of the Kolosjoki mining operation to the Soviet Union, Germany risked serious impairment of its military as well as its economic interests in Finland.[47]

The warning was not lost on the German Foreign Ministry, although Wiehl, whose sudden fit of boldness had been taken amiss a few days before, was not prepared to stick his neck out again. He wrote another policy proposal, in the form of a draft telegram for Blücher, and passed it on to Schnurre who was with Ribbentrop in Salzburg. What he proposed was, in a nutshell, that the Finns should be left to fend for themselves. In the first three points of his draft he maintained that the attitude of the English government did not really prevent the Finns from making continued use of the alleged British refusal to accept a transfer of the concession; that it was premature to believe that "further dilatory conduct of the negotiations was impossible;" and that the Finns could resist the Soviet demand for a majority of the stock in the projected mixed concession company on the grounds that Finland was a sovereign state. In point four, Wiehl suggested that it was not "opportune for us to intervene in the Finnish-Russian negotiations in Moscow at this time," but the Finns should keep Germany "continually informed through our embassy in Moscow." The fifth and last point was even more discouraging from the Finnish point of view: "If the Finns yield to Russian pressure in Moscow beyond the limit mentioned in point 3 above, then it seems better to us that this happens without our approval and not with our agreement." Wiehl was even prepared to accept a concession company dominated by the Russians provided Germany's interests were protected.[48]

But again the director of the Economic Policy Department and his lord and master failed to see eye to eye. This time it was Ribbentrop's turn to take a strong stand. When Wiehl's draft telegram came back from Salzburg the next day,[49] it had been drastically altered, probably on the advice of Schnurre, and certainly after consultation with Hitler, with whom Ribbentrop and Schnurre had discussed the Petsamo question at the Berghof on January 26. In a subsequent letter to Schulenburg, Schnurre described the final version of the telegram as the outcome of the talk with Hitler.[50] The first three points in Wiehl's draft were left intact, but the last two were completely discarded and replaced by a new point four. "In order to make it easier for the Finns in their negotiations in Moscow to maintain the German-Finnish agreements in force," began the final version, Schulenburg had received instructions to say the following to Molotov:

Reports on the progress of the Soviet-Finnish negotiations regarding Petsamo have made it apparent to us that the Finns are having difficulties in securing recognition by the Soviet government of the German nickel interests based on the German-Finnish agreements.

We are therefore taking occasion to remind the Soviet government *once more* that we could agree to modification of the concession arrangement only on condition that the German-Finnish agreements regarding delivery of nickel and nickel ore to Germany would be fully recognized by the Soviet government and by the future concession company. We could not consent to any impairment of our nickel interests based on these agreements because of the importance of this metal for Germany, and all the more because we had entered our claims with the Finnish government and made the appropriate arrangements long before the Soviet government had indicated its interest in the nickel mines.[51]

From the German point of view, this represented a major gesture of support for the Finnish position in the Petsamo negotiations in Moscow, although this purpose was naturally not made explicit in the instructions issued to Schulenburg. His appeal to Molotov was to be based exclusively on German interests. This was what the Finns regarded as the most significant aspect of the telegram. They failed to see in it any basic improvement of their bargaining position, since it was quite conceivable that the Russians would simply agree to accept all of the German conditions and then proceed to force a Soviet-dominated concession company on Finland anyway. Thus, though Witting was mildly pleased when Blücher informed him about the démarche which Schulenburg was to make, he could restrain his enthusiasm. It would have been much better, he told Blücher, if Germany had decided to enter into the Moscow negotiations directly. Fieandt's reaction to the news has not been recorded, but he was told not to let the Russians find out that he knew of the démarche.[52]

Kivimäki's reaction was probably typical of how informed Finns felt about the démarche. When Wiehl brought the Ribbentrop telegram to his attention on January 28, Kivimäki remarked dryly that "this was after all something." Like Witting he pointed out that the Russians might well decide to accept the German demands, whereupon the Finnish negotiators in Moscow would probably stand entirely alone against the Russians as far as the other demands on Finland were concerned. Wiehl reminded him of the first three points in the telegram, in which possibilities for delaying the negotiations were enumerated. Kivimäki, who knew that there was nothing in those points which the Finns had not already tried, took "scant comfort from that" and asked what was going to happen if another crisis occurred. "I said that I could not give him an answer to that now," was Wiehl's reply. At the end of the conversation he requested that the Finns sign the long delayed nickel matte agreement as quickly as possible, lest the Russians accept the Finnish-German agreements already concluded without it. Kivimäki refused to commit himself. He merely suggested that the matter must await Ramsay's return from London, since it was Ramsay who had originally objected to the draft.[53]

It is tempting at this point to read something more into the Finnish reluctance to sign the nickel matte agreement than just dissatisfaction with the price offered by I.G. Farbenindustrie. Price was obviously an important factor, but it is quite possible that a political factor had also entered into the picture. So far, German support of Finland in the Petsamo question had been based, as far as the Finns knew, on purely selfish German economic considerations, since the Germans were vitally interested in getting Petsamo nickel and insisted that the Russians recognize the existing Finnish-German agreements. Now Wiehl was urging the immediate conclusion of the one remaining unsigned delivery contract. It must have occurred to the Finns that the unsigned nickel matte agreement might be their only ace in the diplomatic card game with the Germans—provided it remained unsigned. While it did, the Germans stood to lose the nickel matte deliveries from Petsamo, which were expected to become considerable by the end of 1941, should the Soviet Union get control of the mining operation. As soon as the nickel matte agreement was signed and the Russians guaranteed to honor it along with the other Finnish-German agreements, Germany's economic interests would presumably be safe regardless of who owned the concession. The Germans might then turn out to be quite willing to let the Russians dictate their terms to the Finns, provided Germany had no other vitally important reasons for keeping Finland out of the embrace of the Russian bear.

Although the Finns had deliberately tried to stimulate German interest in their country in various ways as a means of balancing the Soviet pressure, and although they had reasons to think that their labors had not been in vain, they could not be certain that Germany was sufficiently interested in Finland to let it become a stumbling block for German-Soviet relations. But they were certain that the Germans wanted the nickel matte and were afraid they might lose it should the Finns yield to the Russians too soon.

On January 30, Wiehl sent the draft of the nickel matte agreement to Blücher and instructed him to "please impress upon the Finnish government the need for conclusion of this agreement, which is an essential part of the total complex of agreements."[54] By that time, however, the Finnish-Soviet mixed commission had already resumed its negotiations in Moscow, and Ramsay was in Lisbon on the way home from his frustrating trip to London. The nickel matte agreement remained unsigned.

The Finns did not know that the German economic interest in Finland was by this time already matched by an even greater military interest. Hitler's decision of the previous August to secure the Petsamo area for Germany in all circumstances had been based on economic considerations. His decision in November to prevent another Soviet attack on Finland was connected with his resolve to go to war against the Soviet Union in the spring of 1941, but it was a decision which he was in no position to implement at the time should a Soviet invasion of Finland actually materialize. However, following the issuance of Directive No. 21 on December 18, the German planning for the coming war with the Soviet Union progressed rapidly.

Germany's growing military interest in Finland was reflected in the monthly activities reports by the chief of staff of the German Army in Norway. In his report for November 1940, Colonel Buschenhagen wrote that the "preparations for an offensive operation with limited objective from the Kirkenes area for the securing of Petsamo and the nickel works at Kolosjoki, planned under the code name of 'Reindeer,' were continued."[55] The report for December included the following information: "Because of new instructions given orally to the commander in chief by OKW and OKH, the theoretical preparations for 'Reindeer' are being expanded." The expansion involved a drive to the White Sea with four divisions with the objective of cutting off the Kola Peninsula. Buschenhagen also noted that the planning for this operation, which was given the code name of "Silver Fox," was hampered by the lack of information as a result of the need to maintain absolute secrecy. The "attitude of Sweden and Finland in this situation can not yet be clarified," he pointed out.[56]

The German military attaché in Helsinki and his staff had been asked to gather information for Buschenhagen's planning at an early stage of the "Reindeer" project. In early October, Colonel Rössing drew attention to the complete lack of Finnish preparations for the defense of the Petsamo area in a future war. No military construction was going on there, he noted, and old trenches and barbed wire obstacles used during the Winter War were completely neglected and quickly dilapidating. Rössing summed up what he considered to be Finland's operational intentions in the far north in two telling sentences: "Surrender of the territory north of Rovaniemi-Kemijärvi. Attempt to maintain land bridge with Sweden."[57]

Rössing was able to confirm these statements in early January in a conversation with Major General Aksel F. Airo, the Finnish quartermaster general, about the plans of the Finnish General Staff with respect to the Petsamo area. It was "*not* of any Finnish military interest," said Airo. As a peacetime outlet for trade it was of considerable value, but a war would automatically put an end to the trade. Because Finland did not have sufficient manpower to defend the whole length of its eastern border, the entire Petsamo area would have to be abandoned without a fight. The port facilities in Liinahamari and the bridges along the Arctic Ocean Highway would be demolished, said Airo, but he would not say whether the facilities of the Petsamo Nickel Company would also be blown up.[58]

The Germans now knew that all operations in the Petsamo area would be entirely up to them, and they proceeded with their planning for "Silver Fox" on that assumption. On January 23, Colonel Buschenhagen, who as chief of staff was responsible for the training of general staff officers, gave the current crop of senior trainees a remarkably realistic theoretical test. He put together a 26-page examination paper which included most of the information he had collected for "Silver Fox," complete with data on terrain and communications in the projected area of operations, the known strength of Finnish, Russian, Swedish, and German forces in the Northern Cap area, and up-to-date information on the political and military situation there. The trainees were told to prepare detailed operational plans for a joint Finnish-German response to a Soviet attack on Finland and North Norway. They were also to take the possibility of Swedish participation on their side into account.[59]

Four days later, Buschenhagen completed his own solution of the problem in the first operational plan for "Silver Fox." The plan assumed "at least the passive *participation of Sweden*" and "the active *participation of Finland* with an army capable of waging the war offensively according to operational directives given by Germany." The possibility of a Soviet preventive war against Finland was considered, and the question of how long the Finns could resist such an attack was raised. That they would not defend the Petsamo area was stated as a matter of fact and seen as a potential source of trouble for the Germans.[60] Buschenhagen took the operational study to Berlin for discussions with OKW and OKH,[61] and while he was there the first deployment directive for the attack on the Soviet Union was issued. It counted on "the active participation of *Rumania and Finland*" on the flanks of the attack, although the details would have to be determined later because of the strict secrecy which had to be observed. The primary assignment of the German Army in Norway remained the defense of Norway, but beyond that it would also "at the outset of the operations, if necessary even earlier, move into the *Petsamo area* and secure it together with Finnish forces against attacks on land, from the sea, and from the air, whereby special significance is assigned to the nickel mines which are important for the German armaments (Operation Reindeer)."[62]

By February 13, the German Army in Norway had worked out revised plans based on the general deployment directive of January 31. The first operational task listed in this document was the following: *"Securing the ore mines of the Petsamo area and the Arctic Ocean Highway."*[63] In other words, even within the scope of the expanded operation across the Petsamo area into the Soviet Union, no single target was of greater value than the nickel area. This was also underscored by the operational timetable for "Reindeer" appended to the revised plans for "Silver Fox." While it was already clear that "Silver Fox" could not be launched simultaneously with "Barbarossa," operation "Reindeer" would be.[64]

Thus, as the Finns faced the stormy month of February, decisions and plans were made in Berlin which made it increasingly unlikely that another Soviet aggression against Finland would occur. The Finns, however, did not know this yet. It has been claimed by some postwar writers that there was an exhaustive exchange of information and that a general agreement on a coordinated Finnish-German attack was reached between Colonel General Halder and Lieutenant General Erik Heinrichs, the Finnish chief of staff, when the latter visited Berlin to give a lecture on the Winter War at the end of January.[65] This has been emphatically denied by both Halder and Heinrichs. Although Halder in his conversation with Heinrichs found out that it would take the Finns nine days from the start of a mobilization to deploy eight divisions for operations on both sides of Lake Ladoga,[66] this was information which happened to come out of the small talk between two old acquaintances who, rather naturally, shared a mutual professional interest in military matters. Heinrichs was in no position to know that Halder had orders from the OKW to pump his Finnish friend for military information to the extent that it could be done without tipping Heinrichs off to Halder's purpose. Halder found this "deceitful" procedure "embarrassing," but he was convinced that Heinrichs never suspected just how interesting Halder considered the few pieces of information which he extracted in this fashion.[67]

That the Finns, including General Heinrichs, could not yet be told about the German military plans was an obvious consequence of the absolute necessity of preventing any part of the plans from leaking out and perhaps coming to the attention of the Russians. Hitler himself acted with extreme caution to maintain secrecy.[68] Even when he told Prime Minister Benito Mussolini of Italy at the Berghof on January 20 that Finland must "not be touched any more," he gave as his reason the "great importance of Finland for us because of its nickel resources, the only ones in Europe."[69] Thus it was an accurate report which Halder received from Colonel Rössing on January 27, a report cryptically noted in his war diary as follows: "Uncertainty in Finnish political circles about Germany's attitude."[70]

CHAPTER VII

No Supine Accommodation

Toward the end of January, 1941, the Fieandt delegation, reinforced by Dr. Castrén, finally returned to Moscow, and between
January 29 and February 11 the Finnish-Soviet mixed commission
met seven times without coming any closer to an agreement on
the Petsamo question. The first session did not get beyond preliminary generalities and was a friendly affair,[1] but the second
session, held on January 31, was not equally painless. Fieandt
opened the proceedings by stating the Finnish position. The Finnish
government's contract with Mond Nickel made it possible to take
over the mining concession for the duration of the war. For the
same period a joint Finnish-Soviet concession company could be
set up, provided that the management of the operations remained
in the hands of Petsamo Nickel, since it was legally impossible to
transfer the management to a third party. Fieandt submitted this
proposal as one which represented a concession by Finland to the
wishes of the Soviet Union, but Krutikov dismissed it as completely
unacceptable. It brought the two sides no closer to a solution than
they had been before, he said, and he insisted that the Finns accept
the demands he had put forward in December. The Soviet government was not interested in any kind of a holding company. It
insisted on the formation of a concession company with complete
control of all operations from mining to sales. If the Finns
wished to make use of the relevant provision in the contract with
Mond Nickel to form such a company on a temporary basis, that
would be quite acceptable, but they should also enact a special
law which would in effect make the temporary company a permanent one. Nothing short of a permanent arrangement which

gave the Soviet Union control of the operations would do, said Krutikov.[2]

When the two sides met again the next day, the Finns declared that they could not accept the Soviet demand. According to the account which Fieandt gave to Schulenburg after the session, he told Krutikov categorically that the requirement of a purely Finnish management of the interim company was a *"conditio sine qua non"* for the Finns, and he would have to leave Moscow if this condition was rejected. There could be no Russian managing director, and there could be no Soviet control of the company's stock. Krutikov seemed so taken aback by this and so unsure of himself for the rest of the meeting that Fieandt got the impression that Krutikov's instructions did not cover the possibility of such a negative Finnish attitude. Perhaps for that reason, and in order to avoid an immediate rupture of the negotiations, the remainder of the third session was conducted in an informal fashion with each side making compromise suggestions off the record in the hope of stumbling over something promising. While Krutikov hinted that the Soviet side might be prepared to go along with a division of the stock which the Finns could accept, Fieandt suggested that Finland might find a way to annul the Anglo-Canadian concession permanently and accept the formation of an all-inclusive Finnish-Soviet concession company. But Krutikov could not see how the Soviet Union could retreat from its demand for a Russian managing director, and Fieandt did not think that Finland could surrender control of the company's management to foreigners. The discussion ended after four hours, and the Finns promised to request new instructions from Helsinki.[3]

The fourth session took place on February 5 and lasted only ten minutes. All it accomplished was to formalize some of the ideas debated off the record five days before. The Finns expressed their acceptance of the Soviet demand for an all-inclusive concession company on the condition that Finland retain control of the management and of the majority of the stock. Krutikov allowed that the latter point was open to discussion, but on the question of Soviet control of the management there could be no compromise. Nevertheless, Fieandt advised the Finnish government to reject the demand for Soviet control, since it was likely to lead to "the Russification of the area."[4]

At its fifth session, held on February 7, the mixed commission

finally got down to details and discussed a draft agreement prepared by Witting and Fieandt and endorsed by the Finnish government.[5] The Finns proposed a joint stock company with a capital
of 700 million Finmarks ($14,000,000), of which almost 80
per cent would be expended at once to buy out the Anglo-Canadian
trust ($7,000,000) and pay off debts to I.G. Farbenindustrie
($4,000,000),[6] leaving the rest for anticipated price increases and
operating capital ($3,000,000). Finland was to have 51 per cent
of the shares in the new company and the Soviet Union 49 per cent.
Also, since Germany and the Soviet Union were to split the entire
nickel ore output, and since the Finns were already getting what little
nickel ore they needed out of the German allotment, the Russians
should provide Finland with a small portion of their share as well.

Krutikov proceeded to spell out a number of changes that the
Soviet Union would have to call for in the Finnish draft proposal.
The share capital would have to be split between the two governments on a fifty-fifty basis, and the company must be free of any
obligations to I.G. Farbenindustrie from the outset. The Soviet
Union must have equality with Finland in the company's management, and the managing director must be a Russian. One-fifth of
all engineers, foremen, and office personnel must also be Russians,
but it was quite all right if all of the laborers were Finns. The
Jäniskoski power station which supplied electricity to the mine
must be a part of the concession company. The entire organization
must be completed within one month of the signing of the final
agreement. Fieandt retorted that he was unable to accept the
demand for a Russian managing director. Krutikov reasserted that
the Soviet side was unable to yield on that point. Thus a clear
deadlock had been reached on a basic issue. Fieandt stated that
he would have to get new instructions from Helsinki, and the
session came to an end.[7]

Witting sent Fieandt the new instructions two days later. The
Finnish government still insisted on 51 per cent of the stock in
the joint company, and the power station had to be run by an
independent Finnish management since it supplied power to cus-
tomers outside the mining area, notably the port of Liinahamari.
The Russians could have two of the six members of the board of
directors, and both of these would have to reside in Helsinki, not
the Petsamo area, although two Russian auditors would be per-

mitted to reside there. Both the chairman and the vice-chairman of the board had to be Finns. The organization of the new company could be completed in six months after the signing of the agreement, "if at all possible." No agitation against Finnish company regulations would be tolerated. Fieandt was also to remind Krutikov that Finland was contractually committed to I.G. Farbenindustrie, which made the provision for full repayment necessary if the new company were to start its operations without any encumbrances. Also, German payments for nickel ore deliveries would have to be made through the Finnish-German clearing. Witting realized that this proposal would not release the negotiations from the "dead-center" position in which they were stuck, and he therefore instructed Kivimäki to implore the German government to "help strengthen the Finnish position in Moscow."[8]

Armed with these instructions, the Finnish delegates arrived for the sixth session of the mixed commission on February 10. As they had expected, the meeting turned into a tug of war as both sides adhered stubbornly to their respective positions. Krutikov insisted that Finland buy out I.G. Farbenindustrie, and Fieandt finally said he would find out whether the German firm might be willing to give up its rights. The Soviet side also insisted on the unconditional merger of the power station with the new concession company, and that the Finns get their own nickel for domestic consumption from some source other than the Soviet share of the Petsamo output. Finnish worries about the possibility of being denied further navicerts by the British if the Soviet demands were accepted were dismissed by the Soviet negotiators as a minor matter. Neither side budged an inch on the question of the company management. Exasperated, Krutikov finally declared that the negotiations would have to be turned over to higher authorities, but then he suddenly reversed himself and proposed another session for the following evening.[9]

If the Finns had taken Krutikov's decision to continue the negotiations as a promising sign, they were badly disappointed when the two delegations met again on February 11 for the seventh and last time. Fieandt and his colleagues told the Russians that they had taken preliminary steps to speed up the formation of the joint company, that they were prepared to accept a solution on the compensation question by third party arbitration, and that they would also accept the Soviet demand that the mining property be turned over to the new company unencumbered, except for the claims of I.G. Farbenindustrie should it refuse to be bought out. There could be no Finnish retreat in the matter of the control of the management, however. If the Russians would yield on that point, then Fieandt offered to advise his government to make concessions with regard to the power station and the division of the stock. Beyond that it was impossible for Finland to compromise, he asserted.

Again Krutikov appeared to be unsure of himself momentarily. Having heard the new Finnish proposal, he first suggested that the Finnish delegation request new instructions from Helsinki. Then, before the Finns had time to react to this suggestion, Krutikov declared that the Soviet government was not going to reduce any of its demands. The negotiations in the mixed commission had produced no positive results, he noted, and he would so report to his government. On that somber note the work of the Finnish-Soviet mixed commission ended. Fieandt subsequently told Schulenburg that the Russians had broken off the talks, without explicitly saying so, and he feared that the Russians would now "resort to reprisals against Finland" in order to force their demands through. In a report to Witting, Fieandt suggested that the Soviet Union was taking a strong and rigid position on the Petsamo question in order to impress upon Germany that "Russian influence in Finland was stronger than German."[10]

Considering the negotiations terminated, or at least temporarily interrupted, Fieandt prepared to return to Helsinki,[11] but he received instructions to remain in Moscow "for the time being."[12] To his surprise, he was summoned to Krutikov in the evening of February 15 and treated to a rather typical demonstration of a tactic frequently employed by Soviet negotiators. Krutikov welcomed him in a very friendly manner and launched into an expansive monologue, the gist of which was that all the problems dividing the Finns and the Russians in the Petsamo question had now been solved with the single exception of the appointment of the managing director of the joint company. The approach did not confuse Fieandt, however. He reminded Krutikov of all the unsolved problems and repeated that the Finnish government could never permit a Soviet management of the concession company.

Krutikov still tried to minimize the importance of the matter, but he soon realized that his blandishments were making no impact on his visitor. Reverting to form, he then demanded that the Finnish state must pave the way for a complete acceptance of the Soviet requirements by discharging all of its obligations to I.G. Farbenindustrie through compensation payments. Fieandt again reminded him that the German firm was not willing to go along with such an arrangement, whereupon Krutikov became visibly angered and denounced the "stubbornness" of I.G. Farbenindustrie. But he did not vent his anger on the Finns, and he even scheduled a new meeting of the mixed commission for February 17.[13]

There was to be no eighth session of the commission, however. The day it was supposed to take place, Fieandt was informed that Krutikov was ill, and the scheduled session would be postponed for two days.[14] It was clearly a case of diplomatic illness. On February 18, Vyshinsky summoned Paasikivi and informed him angrily that there was no good reason to continue the negotiations in the mixed commission, for Finland was only trying to drag out the affair anyway.[15]

Again Fieandt tried to return to Helsinki, and again he was ordered by Witting to stand by in Moscow, thereby proving, supposedly, that Finland was always ready to negotiate further. This procedure, which seemed pointless to Fieandt, judging by the number of times he had to be told not to go home, was urged upon Witting by Germany.[16] Grönblom did go to Helsinki to report, but he too was subsequently sent back to Moscow to cool his heels there along with Fieandt.[17] At the end of February, Grönblom and Castrén finally left when the Soviet government refused to renew their expired visas,[18] while Fieandt remained in Moscow until March 8, when he was called home to advise the Finnish government on the Petsamo question.[19]

Throughout this period there were constant consultations between the Finnish and German officials involved in the Petsamo question. In Berlin, Helsinki, and Moscow they exchanged information and conferred with each other as the crisis continued to deepen. On January 30, Germany intervened in Moscow again, as Schulenburg conveyed to Molotov the statements contained in Ribbentrop's telegram of January 27. The Finns, knowing how slippery Molotov could be, had not expected much from this

German gesture of support, and they were right. Schulenburg was unable to extract from Molotov the guarantees which Ribbentrop sought. Molotov had nothing to offer but generalities. The Soviet government was prepared to assume contractual obligations toward Germany for the delivery of 60 per cent of the Petsamo nickel ore production for the duration of the war, he said, and postwar arrangements could be made any time the Germans wanted, although Germany then ought to be satisfied with 50 per cent. He asserted that "Germany had not the least cause for fearing any encroachment upon its interest in the nickel ore deliveries." When Schulenburg repeatedly and emphatically pointed out that Germany was not interested in making any new arrangements with the Soviet Union, only in a Soviet guarantee that the existing Finnish-German agreements would be fully respected, Molotov again assured him that Germany had nothing to worry about. He refused, as always, to acknowledge the priority of the German claim, and he suggested that the German government should "signify its positive desire" to reach a settlement with the Soviet government in the matter. Schulenburg subsequently advised Berlin that such a settlement might well prove satisfactory, since the Soviet government "has always hitherto fulfilled its contractual obligations."[20]

The German Foreign Ministry was not inclined to put Schulenburg's faith in Soviet promises to the test. On February 5, Weizsäcker instructed him instead to insist in his continued talks with Molotov that the Finnish-German agreements, which went "back to April, 1940," be honored by the Soviet government. Schulenburg should say that Germany expected to pay for its share of the Petsamo nickel ore through the Finnish-German clearing, because payments through the German-Soviet clearing "would be considerably more difficult for us;" that Germany must be sure of getting 60 per cent of the nickel ore output without any time limit, since "a departure from this would mean an impairment of our interests;" and that Germany must be guaranteed that its share of the output would quickly reach the volume required for the war effort, which "can be achieved only if the management and the plans for development which have been worked out are not interfered with," that is, if "the existing German-Finnish agreements are recognized by the Soviet side."

In other words, Schulenburg was to give implicit support to the Finnish negotiators then in Moscow by taking a position which paralleled theirs. For his own private information he was told that the German Foreign Ministry agreed absolutely with the position taken so far by Fieandt and his colleagues in the mixed commission. "The most essential thing for him," read the telegram, "will be to see to it that the management of the technical operations remains in Finnish hands and that Finnish influence continues to be decisive in the business management of the future company."[21] Significantly, this telegram was relayed to Blücher with instructions to "make good use of the contents" in Helsinki.[22] For the Finns this was very encouraging news, even though nothing was said in the instructions to Schulenburg, or by anyone connected with the German Foreign Ministry, about what Germany might be prepared to do should the Soviet Union decide to disregard the German wishes and proceed to take more concrete measures against Finland. The Finns were left guessing on that crucial point.

From the outset of the renewed Finnish-Soviet Petsamo negotiations in Moscow the German government was attempting to impress upon the Finnish government that there was no great cause for concern. Kivimäki was told in the German Foreign Ministry that the nickel matter "was on the right track and he should not worry." His report had a "very soothing effect" on Witting, who informed President Ryti and Prime Minister Rangell at once.[23] The effect was quickly undone, however, when it was learned that Molotov had told Schulenburg on January 30 that the Soviet interest in the Petsamo area was "not merely economic, but predominantly political." This was not really news, of course, since Molotov had said as much before to both Finns[24] and Germans,[25] and Schulenburg had advised Berlin on November 1 that he considered the Soviet interest to be purely political and tied up with the security of Murmansk.[26]

The Finns themselves were quite aware of the obvious fact that political considerations were involved, but to have that fact pressed home so forcefully by Molotov to the Germans at a time when the Russians were assuring the Finns that nothing but economic considerations were behind the Soviet demands was disconcerting. Paasikivi, who was told about Molotov's remark by Schulenburg on February 1,[27] succumbed to pessimism, a pessimism partly mixed with the bitter satisfaction of having said so all the time. As he wrote in his diary on February 4: "It is good that special negotiators have been selected for the nickel matter. Had I handled the matter alone, I should have been accused of being compliant. Now they can see for themselves what can be done here."[28] And for a brief while he did indeed suffer in good company. Witting appeared rather depressed himself, and he remarked to Blücher that "it seems that for the Russians the goal is to penetrate the Petsamo area."[29] His mood led Blücher to warn Berlin that the Finns might yield to the Russians on all important points unless they were given German support. Should they yield, the entire Petsamo area was bound to fall under Soviet control.

The instant reaction of the German Foreign Ministry was to dispatch the following telegram to Helsinki: "We regard it as necessary that the matte agreement be signed as quickly as possible and turned over to the Russians by Fieandt." Kivimäki and Ramsay—the latter had at long last reached Berlin on his way home from London—had been so advised already, continued the telegram, and Blücher was urged to have the Finnish government issue the desired directive to Fieandt.[30] If the Finns were indeed using the unsigned nickel matte agreement as a means of pressuring the Germans into supporting them, this would tend to confirm the accuracy of the underlying assumption. Witting was quick to promise Blücher that he would get in touch with Petsamo Nickel at once and suggest that the nickel matte agreement be signed, at least provisionally, and he also promised to have Fieandt submit the text of the agreement to the Russians as soon as he received it.[31] But the agreement remained unsigned.

Reports received by the Finnish Foreign Ministry of the talks Kivimäki and Ramsay had with Wiehl and Schnurre in Berlin were apparently encouraging, and the Finnish government accepted Witting's proposal to issue relatively uncompromising instructions to the negotiators on the mixed commission in Moscow.[32] These were the instructions presented to the Russians in the form of a draft agreement at the fifth session on February 7. Further encouragement came swiftly as Blücher notified Witting of Schulenburg's instructions to support Fieandt's position in talks with Molotov. Witting also learned that the Germans "would not like to see Fieandt retreat beyond the line suggested by us for the negotiations." He should "stand especially firm" on the Finnish position regarding the management of the company.[33]

It was perhaps not so surprising that the American minister on February 7 found Witting unusually confident. A settlement was in sight in the Petsamo question, said Witting, a quite incomprehensible statement if based on the news of the Finnish-Soviet negotiations in Moscow. Obviously it was based on the encouraging news which Witting had received from Berlin, for he proceeded to outline to Schoenfeld a settlement in line with the instructions which had just been forwarded to Fieandt.[34] His subsequent monologue reflected none of the pessimism which he had felt only four days before. His people were quite used to living with the constant threat of Russian aggression, he explained; after all, they had been at war with Russia for a total of ninety-two years out of the last nine hundred, and they could cope with another Russian attack even now, "provided Russian resources were not concentrated exclusively on Finland." If Finland had followed "a policy of supine accommodation" after the Winter War, its situation would now have been "the same as that of the Baltic States."[35] Clearly, there would be no supine accommodation forthcoming from Finland.

No such buoyancy was evident among the Finnish negotiators in Moscow. Paasikivi thought that the situation was "delicate," and as he pondered the matter in search of a compromise solution he "hit upon the idea of proposing, if worst came to worst, an exchange of the nickel area for some other area."[36] His idea was not well received by Witting, who feared that it might appeal to some of his colleagues in the cabinet.[37] Blücher considered the proposed cure to be worse than the disease,[38] and van Scherpenberg telephoned Helsinki to tell Blücher that the Foreign Ministry regarded the idea as "a bad joke" and absolutely "undebatable."[39] Wiehl informed the embassy in Moscow that the sort of territorial swap suggested by Paasikivi was contrary to German interests and would make a mockery out of the Finnish commitments to Germany.[40]

The flurry of excitement Paasikivi's idea stirred in German diplomatic circles was hardly warranted, as indicated by the completely indifferent response to it in Helsinki. Nobody ever mentioned the idea again except Paasikivi himself, who revived it as a last resort proposal after his return to Helsinki in March.[41] By then, not even the Germans could be moved to comment on it, one way or the other.

Following the crucial fifth session of the mixed commission in Moscow on February 7, the Finns grew concerned again about the scope of the Soviet demands and the intransigent fashion in which they were maintained by Krutikov and Kurotsev. During a conversation with Weizsäcker the following day, Kivimäki described the negotiations as being "rather critical again," although he thought that the Finnish negotiators tended to view things much too pessimistically. But it would be helpful, he said, if Schulenburg were instructed to impress upon Molotov that Germany preferred to see the management of the projected Finnish-Soviet company in Finnish hands. Better still, Schulenburg might be told to "prophylactically warn Molotov against an act of violence." Wiehl, who sat in on most of the conversation, informed Kivimäki that the instructions sent to Schulenburg a couple of days earlier had practically met these wishes already.[42]

But three days later Kivimäki was back in the German Foreign Ministry again on Witting's instructions[43] to seek further support for the negotiators in Moscow. Woermann cheerfully greeted him with the remark that he hoped the Finnish minister had not come about the Petsamo matter again. Kivimäki, who must have begun to feel like a spinning phonograph record with the needle stuck in a groove, said no, but he got around to it anyway as the conversation progressed. He noted that the Russians were now "especially insistent" in demanding that the Finns abrogate their credit agreement with I.G. Farbenindustrie. Only the day before, van Scherpenberg had told him that Finland must remain firm on that point, said Kivimäki. "Because a matter of interest to Germany" was therefore involved, the German government should let it be known in Moscow that it wanted the credit agreement to remain in force. Woermann would not commit himself, but he promised to take the matter up with his colleagues.[44]

On February 10, Schulenburg carried out his instructions of five days before in a meeting with Molotov. The Soviet commissar turned out to be just as evasive as previously, generous in generalities and elusive in specifics. The German economic interests would be "unconditionally protected," of course. He could find no provision in the Finnish-German agreements of which he had been given copies for indefinite deliveries of 60 per cent of the Petsamo nickel ore production to Germany, however, at least not beyond 1947. When Schulenburg reminded him that the delivery agreement was anchored in a special exchange of letters, Molotov professed to know nothing about that correspondence. He also refused to admit that the Russians had announced their interest in Petsamo nickel "so much later" than the Germans and maintained instead that the Soviet claim had in fact been submitted to the Finns one month before the Finnish-German agreement was concluded. However, he promised to explain his government's attitude to the German demands more precisely in writing in the near future. In an attempt to sweeten the pill, perhaps, Schulenburg noted in his report to Berlin that Fieandt was continuing his negotiations "in accordance with our desires."[45]

The German Foreign Ministry found it "astonishing" that Molotov disclaimed any knowledge of the Finnish-German exchange of letters. "Everything else . . . was concluded merely in fulfillment of these government agreements," said Wiehl in his response to Schulenburg's report. The German government would await the written statement promised by Molotov, "but we are, and this should be emphasized once again, not prepared to yield on our demand for recognition of the German-Finnish agreements." It was also disturbing to note that Krutikov had demanded of the Finns that they buy out I.G. Farbenindustrie's interest in Petsamo, since that demand was in sharp contrast to Molotov's glib assurances to Schulenburg. Once more Schulenburg was instructed to remind Molotov of the exact dates of every important step in the chronology of the Finnish-German agreements,[46] and Blücher was instructed to find out whether the disputed exchange of letters had actually been submitted to the Russians by the Finns.[47] Blücher confirmed that this had been done on December 19.[48]

The German Foreign Ministry also kept pressuring the Finns to sign the nickel matte agreement. Blücher returned to the question in a conversation with Witting on February 8. He was told that Petsamo Nickel refused to sign because of the unreasonably low price offered by I.G. Farbenindustrie. Not only did the offer amount to a mere one-half of the normal peacetime price, but the German firm had reinserted into the draft a provision which had previously been eliminated by Petsamo Nickel. Anyway, said Witting, it was a simple business matter which the two firms ought to be allowed to work out by themselves. Blücher objected to this point of view and insisted that the nickel matte agreement was part and parcel of the whole complex of agreements bearing on the German interest in the Petsamo nickel. Witting then promised to get in touch with Ramsay and Söderhjelm about it,[49] and two days later he reported that his talks with the two directors of the Petsamo Nickel Company would begin the same day.[50]

Probably as an upshot of these talks, Ramsay and Baron Gustaf Woldemar Wrede, the new managing director of Petsamo Nickel, came to see Blücher on February 12 and explained that the delay was entirely the fault of I.G. Farbenindustrie, which had let all of January go by without making any new proposals after the Finns had rejected the proffered draft. The Finns agreed, however, that a speedy conclusion of the matter was desirable, and Wrede and Söderhjelm, whose combined signatures were binding on Petsamo Nickel, were prepared to go to Berlin for further negotiations with the German firm.[51]

The proposed negotiations in Berlin were promptly arranged. No information about them has been found, but the nickel matte agreement was finally signed on February 19. The Finns did not submit the text of it to the Russians, however, whatever the reasons for such a further delay may have been. In a draft telegram which would have Schulenburg make a démarche in Moscow, prepared in the name of Weizsäcker on March 6, it was noted that the Finns "had been asked" to turn the text over to the Russians.[52] But that request was actually made the same day in a telegram to Helsinki, and it was coupled with the reservation that the submission of the text be delayed until Schulenburg had made his démarche. The Finns would be notified as soon as the moment arrived.[53] Witting agreed with the procedure,[54] and he was duly notified on March 12.[55] Three days later he gave the text of the nickel matte agreement to the unofficial Soviet minister in Helsinki, Pavel G. Orlov,[56] who was a bit taken aback by the realization that another agreement had been concluded by the Finns with the Germans at a time when the Finns refused to sign anything at all with the Russians.[57]

Meanwhile the Finnish-Soviet negotiations were continuing on the political level. On February 12, the day after the talks in the mixed commission in reality ended, Paasikivi was called to Vyshinsky. The deputy commissar for foreign affairs was friendly but firm as the two men spent an hour discussing the Petsamo question in all its aspects. The failure of the mixed commission's work was regrettable, said Vyshinsky, but he thought that he and Paasikivi could find a solution if they tackled the problem "personally." Paasikivi retorted that anything which he might say "personally" would be of scant significance, since he had no other instructions than those issued to Fieandt. Vyshinsky then proceeded to present his own ideas and arguments, assuring Paasikivi that the Soviet government had no ulterior motives and no political interest in the Petsamo area, but merely an economic interest. That disingenuous assertion set the tone for Vyshinsky's smooth presentation of the problem.

There were at least three good reasons why the Soviet government had to insist on control of the management of the proposed joint company, explained Vyshinsky. For one thing, the Soviet Union was a great power and Finland was a very small state, and therefore Soviet prestige required "equality." No possible violation of Finland's sovereignty was involved, he said when Paasikivi objected to that type of logic. Paasikivi's remark that England had seen no need to demand similar "equality" when Mond Nickel was granted the concession was brushed aside as irrelevant. Secondly, Vyshinsky continued, the fact that Finland had the Petsamo territory and the political power in it also meant that the Soviet Union could achieve "parity" only by controlling the management of the company.

The arrangement would actually be of economic benefit to Finland, Vyshinsky explained, for the existing agreements with Germany were "disadvantageous" and would lead to an exploitation of the nickel ore deposit which really amounted to "despoiling" it. The Russians, on the other hand, intended to invest a "large amount" in the undertaking and place "first-rate experts" at the company's disposal. Therefore they had to insist on an equal division of the share capital, equality on the board of directors with the chairmanship rotating annually, one-fifth of the engineers, foremen, and office staff, and a Soviet managing director. As far as the last point was concerned, the Soviet government had already made its decision, Vyshinsky revealed. The Soviet Union "would not merely be the one who financed the whole thing and whose representative was present only on festive occasions; the Russians would also direct the undertaking." When Paasikivi remarked, half in jest, that the position of managing director "is too small a matter for you to begin a war against us on that score," Vyshinsky's chilling reply was: "We are already engaged in a commercial war with each other."[58]

Paasikivi's report on the conversation, as subsequently published in the *Blue-White Book* of 1941, said very little about what he had contributed to the exchange. The published version of the telegram recorded only this: "Regarding the post of managing director, I stuck to our position." That leaves considerable room for speculation about what he said on the other points. In his memoirs he claimed to have suggested to Vyshinsky that there might still be some ways in which the two sides could compromise, "for instance special determination of the composition of the personnel," but he gave no details.[59] He did, however, request Vyshinsky to present his compromise proposal, whatever it was, to the Soviet government.[60]

A report to the German Foreign Ministry from Schulenburg sheds additional light on Paasikivi's proposal. Schulenburg learned from Fieandt that Paasikivi had in fact made a proposal to Vyshinsky, and that it would have given the Soviet Union parity in management positions, the chairmanship of the board of directors in alternate years, and one-fifth of the engineers, but Finland would have the managing director.[61] This report was confirmed by the German Foreign Ministry in a telegram to Blücher, who was told to notify the Finnish government that parts of Paasikivi's compromise proposal endangered German interests.[62] A further confirmation was implicit in a report from Blücher to Berlin a few days later. Witting, he said, had reprimanded Paasikivi for having promised the Russians "to recommend that the Finnish government accept 20 per cent Russian engineers."[63]

In his memoirs, Paasikivi implied that the compromise proposal which he had asked Vyshinsky to submit to the Soviet government included merely a couple of general and relatively harmless suggestions; his detailed recommendation had been submitted, appropriately enough, only to Helsinki. The details of that recommendation, however, as described in Paasikivi's memoirs,[64] tally with the proposal which Fieandt, in his conversation with Schulenburg, claimed that Paasikivi had made to Vyshinsky. Paasikivi had thus gone beyond his instructions and had embarrassed his government.

It seems obvious that Paasikivi's "nerves"—as some of his Finnish and German colleagues rather unkindly put it at times—were failing him again at this juncture. Both contemporary sources and his own memoirs prove beyond any doubt that he was much more pessimistic about Finland's prospects than anyone else involved in the Petsamo question. He was convinced that Germany could not help Finland now, and nothing was therefore more important than the business of preventing another conflict with the Soviet Union.[65] He advised Witting that he considered his own compromise proposal the very least that Finland could offer, and he would consider the matter to have turned out "as well as it possibly could have" should the Soviet government accept it. Without German help, he said in a telegram to Witting, "we must, in order to avoid conflict, retreat in the nickel question, which after all is not of vital importance to us."[66] Years later, while writing his memoirs, he was still insisting that his view had been the correct one at the time and that a settlement might well have been reached with the Soviet Union on the basis of it. He lamented bitterly that he had instead been instructed to present to Vyshinsky "general views which I had already done several times." In his own mind he knew, even after the war, that the question "could not be solved" that way.[67]

Paasikivi's tragedy—and those days in mid-February 1941 were days of tragedy for him—was in some measure rooted in his own difficult nature. In even greater measure, however, blame must be put on Foreign Minister Witting, the man who withheld his full confidence from his envoy in Moscow and failed to keep him adequately informed about vital developments. Witting knew a good deal more about the tacit support given to Finland by Germany in the Petsamo question than he told Paasikivi. The foreign minister knew enough to base his policy on German support. The fact that the consistent German advice to negotiate "dilatorily" had so far worked indicated strongly that the policy was viable. That Finland had already come through several crises which it could hardly have hoped to survive if there were nothing more between Finland and the Soviet Union than the Finnish armed forces was still another indication that the German interest in Finland had somehow made itself felt where it counted—in Moscow. That the Germans did not tell the Finns everything about Berlin's motives, attitudes, and diplomatic maneuvers tended to be rough on Finnish nervous systems, but so far there had been no other damage done. Whether Paasikivi, with his ingrained distrust of all great powers, would in fact have been convinced by what Witting could have told him about the many indications of reliable German support is quite another matter, of course. But he should nevertheless have been kept informed.

When Paasikivi again urged the Finnish government to "keep in mind" his proposals for a Russian managing director every other year and "if absolutely necessary an exchange of the nickel area," Witting told Blücher that the proposal would have "no influence." The Finnish government might be prepared to let the Russians appoint half of the members of the board of directors, but a Finn would always preside.[68]

It is small wonder that Paasikivi was dejected as he went to see Vyshinsky again on February 18 to deliver the Finnish answer. He was to write later that the conversation was "one of the most difficult of my entire period in Moscow."[69] Vyshinsky, who was "very curt from the start," observed that the Finnish reply was a negative one, that the Soviet Union was a great power, and that its demands were therefore "categorical and definitive." Paasikivi could do no better than to deliver himself of the remarkable opinion that the work of the mixed commission was progressing well— presumably a desperate effort to get something beneficial out of Krutikov's spurious statements to Fieandt three days before, and he suggested that it ought to be left up to the commission to find a way out. Vyshinsky saw no reason at all for continuing the mixed commission. The Soviet government had now turned the whole matter over to him, he announced, and since Paasikivi obviously was not authorized to accept the Soviet demands, he had to conclude that those demands had been rejected by Finland. He protested against such an affront, declared Vyshinsky, and he was going to report it to his government. Nothing more could be done, "and the matter will now take its course, with all its consequences." At that point the deputy commissar terminated the interview "abruptly and was angrier than ever before."[70]

February 18, then, represented for all practical purposes the lowest point of the Finnish-Soviet Petsamo negotiations. They were in fact not to be pursued seriously again by either side, although both parties—and also Germany—continued to go through the motions appropriate to the situation for a while longer. And the shadow of crisis was to linger over Finland, to be interpreted in different ways according to the lights and information of each individual observer. Paasikivi did not take the rupture of the negotiations lightly. In his report to Helsinki on his conversation with Vyshinsky he noted that the negotiations were deadlocked and the situation menacing. "One now required guarantees of other kinds of adequate assistance from Germany also, not only diplomatic, in the event that this aid should prove to be necessary."[71] The matter had gone too far and had become "a prestige issue for the Kremlin," and Paasikivi did not think that the Russians were going to leave it as it stood.[72]

The nickel affair was after all of secondary importance to Finland, wrote Paasikivi to Witting. "We have assumed the risk exclusively for the sake of Germany," he declared. The Russians, in turn, had forced the Finns to take illegal measures directed against English interests in Finland, while the British themselves were too concerned with the problem of maintaining good relations with the Russians to give any support to the Finns. If one considered the matter thoroughly, wrote Paasikivi, it would become obvious that Germany was in no position to act any more resolutely vis-à-vis the Soviet Union in the present situation than in the past. In other words, it would be sheer folly to count on the Germans to provide adequate support for Finland. Paasikivi also gave vent to a central tenet of his political philosophy in an exceedingly bitter outburst, duplicated with frequent regularity in the two volumes of his wartime memoirs: "All great powers are the same, equally selfish, and we small nations are caught between them. We small states are the only respectable ones."[73]

Witting as usual related Paasikivi's sentiments and suggestions to Blücher. Personally he was "inclined to take the matter calmly," he said. "It is just another crisis. For the Russians, Petsamo is a touchstone for testing Finnish nerves and Finnish-German relations." Some "timid souls" in the Finnish government might regard the Soviet Union's behavior as the introduction to a declaration of war, however, and Witting would be grateful, he told Blücher, "if

Germany now would exercise influence on the negotiations in Moscow."[74] Having received Blücher's report on Witting's statements, the German Foreign Ministry replied at once: "We judge the situation just as calmly as the Finnish foreign minister. We are therefore of the opinion that no cause exists for a new German intervention in Moscow, but that we can wait for the written answer promised by the Russians."[75] This view seemed to be confirmed by intelligence reports from the Finnish General Staff that no Soviet military preparations could be discerned in the snowbound border regions.[76] On February 24, Witting told Blücher that "in the nickel question there is no sign of life from the Russians." He did think, however, that Fieandt should continue to make an *"acte de présence"* in Moscow, a view which Blücher again "reinforced."[77]

For Paasikivi, a veteran of the Moscow negotiations prior to the outbreak of the Winter War, the stormy meeting with Vyshinsky on February 18 and the ensuing silence may have been reminiscent of November, 1939. After Vyshinsky's threatening parting words, the silence must have been deafening for someone with Paasikivi's memories. His conviction that the worst was again about to happen, and his realization that Witting was not taking his advice seriously, combined to plunge him into a state of frustration and despondency. On February 24, Schulenburg reported to Berlin that the Finnish minister in Moscow was toying with the idea of quitting his post. Paasikivi had told at least two of his colleagues in the Moscow diplomatic corps that "because of his advanced age (he is 70 years old) he is not equal to the demands of the Moscow post, which is so exceedingly important and difficult for Finland." Schulenburg believed that "the negotiations with the Soviet government about the Petsamo question exceeded the strength of the minister's nerves," and he added that "certain remarks by colleagues friendly to Paasikivi tie directly into this."[78] One of those colleagues was probably Paasikivi's closest friend in Moscow, the Swedish minister, who told the American ambassador on February 26 that Paasikivi had spoken to him about his fears that the Soviet government might simply seize the Petsamo area since negotiations had led nowhere. Paasikivi "did not wish to be held responsible for such a development," said Assarsson to Steinhardt, and "he was seriously considering resigning his post."

Assarsson had "advised him strongly against such a course," since it "might merely encourage" the Russians.[79]

Assarsson's account, as reported by Schulenburg and Steinhardt, was essentially correct. Whether Paasikivi was motivated by a case of failing nerves is not really relevant. The fact is that his position as Finland's envoy in Moscow had become untenable and incompatible with his self-respect. The direct cause of his decision to resign was obviously the reprimand cabled to him by Witting. Paasikivi did not say so in his memoirs, but the wording of the telegram which contained his offer to resign indicated a direct relationship betwen the two events, and so do the dates of the two telegrams. Without saying exactly when he cabled his reprimand to Paasikivi, Witting informed Blücher on February 21 that he had done so.[80] Paasikivi cabled his resignation to Witting on February 20, which would indicate that Witting kept the matter under his hat until he had Paasikivi's resignation in his pocket. It was a bitter telegram:

Noting that our views concerning Finland's foreign policy are not sufficiently compatible, and since you do not appear to have faith in my political judgment and my experience, and since I do not want to be in any way involved in a policy which can lead to catastrophe, I am sending my resignation to Witting with the next courier, even though I do not wish to give the government unnecessary difficulties.

He believed he had noticed, continued Paasikivi, that the government no longer "regarded my services for the country to be so important that I needed to sacrifice myself by remaining in Moscow." His resignation would therefore settle the matter "to the satisfaction of both parties." He planned to make his resignation effective as of the end of May.[81]

Witting promptly obliged him. Paasikivi was recalled from Moscow in early March, ostensibly for consultations, but actually for good, even though his appointment was not terminated formally until the end of May as he had requested.

Although there was no sign of life from the Russians in the Petsamo question for a while after the Vyshinsky-Paasikivi confrontation on February 18, there was considerable activity on the Finnish-German front. The German Foreign Ministry had suggested that one could afford to just sit tight and wait for the Russians to make their next move, but Fieandt did not think this would be wise. If Schulenburg did not remind Molotov of his promise to submit a written statement of the Soviet position, then the Russians might well "conclude from that that the German interest in nickel is secondary," suggested Fieandt.[82] The German Foreign Ministry replied that "we still see no reason for reminding Molotov of the promised written statement," since the German position had been stated to the Russians repeatedly and in such forceful terms that they could not possibly be in doubt about "the genuine nature of our interests." The Russians also knew the Finnish position. Hence the next move was up to them.[83]

On February 27, Witting again remarked to Blücher that the Russians had still not returned to the Petsamo question, but there had been no ominous signs either of any intentions on their part to shift the game to a more sinister arena. All was quiet in the border regions, and Communist activity in Finland was no greater than usual. Witting thought that the Russians might be turning their attention to the Balkans.[84] The next day he seemed to find his optimism confirmed by a Soviet proposal to resume previously interrupted negotiations about a telegraph and telephone communications agreement, starting the first week of March in Moscow. This surprise initiative indicated to Witting that the Soviet government had not yet abandoned "the road of negotiations."[85]

But the Germans were tired of waiting for Molotov to make his move. Ribbentrop instructed Schulenburg to remind Molotov of his promise and at the same time "again emphasize our interest in the guarantees of our agreements with Finland."[86] However, before Schulenburg could carry out the instruction, he was called to Vyshinsky on February 28 and given the long awaited written statement. It turned out to be no more satisfactory than Molotov's glib assurances of two weeks earlier. The Soviet government was quite prepared to recognize Germany's right to receive nickel from Petsamo in the amount of 60 per cent of the total output until December 1, 1947, as provided for by the Finnish-German agreements, but nowhere in the statement was that recognition based on those agreements. The Soviet government "advocates," said the statement, that Germany "receive the right to obtain nickel ore that is produced from the mines of the Soviet-Finnish corporation" in the same quantity as specified in the Finnish-German agreements. Although the statement did say that the question of the "future

validity" of the provisions included in the Finnish-German agreements was to be "subject to a direct settlement between Germany
and Finland," that did in no way imply recognition of them. It was
no longer a question of a Soviet and a German share of the nickel
output, but of a Soviet and a Finnish share. What the Finns did
with their share was their own business. However, since the two
shares would be equal, and since this meant that Finland would not
be able to provide Germany with the anticipated quantity, the Soviet
government was willing to conclude a "special agreement" with the
German government for up to 10 per cent of the total production. As
for continued deliveries to Germany after December 1, 1947, that
would have to be studied separately, said the statement. The Soviet
government could "naturally not guarantee to Germany 'the right of
procurement of 60 per cent of the nickel ore for an unlimited
period'," but it was prepared to give "sympathetic consideration"
to the German wishes "within a definite period of time." The Soviet
government was just as interested as the German government in the
greatest possible volume of production, but it was "naturally not in
a position to judge of the quantity of nickel ore that may guarantee
satisfactorily the requirements of the German economy."[87]

While the German Foreign Ministry spent a busy week studying
Molotov's statement and working out new instructions for Schulenburg, the Russians returned to the offensive vis-à-vis the Finns.
Paasikivi faced Molotov in another difficult meeting on March 4.
He was told in "a serious tone" that the Petsamo question "now
finally had to be settled once and for all" on the terms proposed
by the Soviet government. In an effort to convince Paasikivi that
Finland was diplomatically isolated in the matter, Molotov handed
him copies of the German démarche of February 10 and the Soviet
statement of February 28, "so that you may be fully aware of
Germany's attitude and not rely on rumors." Paasikivi interjected
that he had received no new instructions and could make no commitments, but Fieandt was still in Moscow, he suggested hopefully.
Molotov dismissed the implied suggestion. There would be no
further meetings of the mixed commission, at least not until the
Soviet government had solved certain questions which had to be
clarified before any progress could be made. Again Paasikivi was
reminded that the Soviet Union had actually made "the greatest
concession by giving Petsamo to Finland," and the Finns ought to

keep that in mind. The Russians had none but economic objectives, declared Molotov, and they insisted on controlling the management of the Finnish-Soviet company only because they wanted to make sure that the mining operations were "efficiently conducted, and because they had experienced men." Paasikivi dryly informed him that "we had specialists too," and he pointed out that the mine was located on Finnish territory "and therefore the management belongs to us." A lengthy discussion ensued about that until Molotov closed the debate by stating that all matters involved could be discussed except the post of managing director. As usual he demanded that the Finnish government submit its final reply at the earliest opportunity. He was "very resolute," wrote Paasikivi in his report to Helsinki.[88]

Molotov's forceful return to the Petsamo question awakened new fears and confirmed existing ones in some hearts. Paasikivi advised the Finnish government to come up with a compromise proposal, because not to do so involved "much too great a risk."[89] Schulenburg reported to Berlin that Paasikivi had been strengthened in his inclination to urge his government to yield.[90] Steinhardt, after a talk with Paasikivi, reported to Washington that the Finnish minister, who was about to go to Helsinki, intended to propose a compromise which would give the Soviet government "substantially what it wants."[91] Even Fieandt appeared to have become uncertain, reported Schulenburg, to whom Fieandt had said that "the Finnish side was now urgently in need of German advice as to how it should proceed."[92] But Foreign Minister Witting calmly told Blücher that he would like to know the opinion of the German government before he took up the matter in the cabinet.[93] The same day, Kivimäki suggested to Wiehl that the Germans take up the management question themselves with the Soviet government "to the effect that a Soviet management could not function well on foreign soil." Wiehl had no encouragement to offer. He merely said that this was a question "which concerned only Finland and Russia," and no grounds for a German intervention existed.[94]

Wiehl was an exceptionally tight-lipped diplomat who never spoke out of turn. He did not tell Kivimäki that he was at that very moment at work on the German response to Molotov's written statement of February 28, and that he was in that connection giving full consideration to the crisis created by Molotov's statements to Paasikivi on March 4. In a covering memorandum to Ribbentrop, Wiehl did write that he considered it unwise to make the sort of representation in Moscow which Kivimäki had asked for. "Still," he added, "it seems prudent to correct, in a suitable form," the Soviet assertion that "Russia must have the management because it has assumed delivery obligations to us."[95] He put it even more strongly in a draft telegram intended for Schulenburg which he sent to Ribbentrop along with the memorandum. He would have Schulenburg tell Molotov that, since Germany was going to buy its nickel from the Finns and not from the Russians, the reason given by Vyshinsky on February 28 "why the Soviet government must insist on Soviet management is therefore not accurate."[96]

The following day, when the Swedish minister asked Weizsäcker about the progress of the Petsamo negotiations, the German state secretary was just as cautious as Wiehl had been the day before. "I told Mr. Richert," he reported later, "that we were not involved in these negotiations, though certainly considerably interested economically."[97] His reply must have caused some amusement in the Swedish Foreign Ministry, which had already accomplished the dual feat of breaking the secret German code and building a replica of the intricate decoding machine required to translate the coded messages into ordinary language. The Swedes were regularly deciphering "thousands and more thousands" of German telegrams transmitted by radio or by Swedish telegraph lines.[98]

Although the Finns continued to request direct intervention by Germany in Moscow in the Petsamo question, the best informed among them were not much worried any more. In addition to a rising German military interest in Finland, rather explicit assurances had finally come even through the German Foreign Ministry. On March 5, for instance, Kivimäki was told by Weizsäcker that the German position had been "definitively determined," and Finland could face "with complete assurance all surprises even in the nickel question." He had this from a reliable source, said Weizsäcker, and Kivimäki presumed it must have been Hitler himself. Two days later, Kivimäki learned from both the Foreign Ministry and the Propaganda Ministry that a turn of events "very advantageous for Finland" had occurred, and Finland should make no concessions to the Soviet Union involving territorial questions.[99] On March 13, Schoenfeld noted in a report to Washington that Witting was not "especially concerned" and that he had said that the Finnish government was "not now disposed to change its position regarding control of nickel mines."[100]

With one minor change, Wiehl's lengthy draft telegram of March 6 was approved by Ribbentrop on March 8 and dispatched to Schulenburg the next morning.[101] A copy was sent to Blücher on March 10 with instructions to notify the Finnish government of the contents.[102] The German note rejected Molotov's statement of February 28 on all points where it differed from the German position. "It is important to the German government that its interests, as now embodied in agreements, should suffer no restrictions through the contemplated changes in the mining company," said the note. Any deviation from the line prescribed in the Finnish-German agreements would undoubtedly cause "interruptions and interferences" detrimental to Germany's interests. Molotov's suggestion that Germany would be dealing with the Soviet Union after the new company went into operation was rejected outright. Germany intended to get all of its nickel from Finland and through the Finnish-German clearing.

Schulenburg submitted the note to the Soviet government on March 11 after having outlined its contents orally to Molotov on March 10.[103] The commissar for foreign affairs was clearly displeased. He emphasized that "the Soviet government was prepared to accommodate Germany in every way in the nickel matter and did not intend to contest the validity of the German-Finnish agreements." In view of the cooperation which the Soviet government had been demonstrating in its relations with Germany, also in the Petsamo question, he regretted to have to note that "the settlement of this question had run into more and more difficulties from the German side." The question had gone unsolved for much too long, he said, and any further delay of it would be intolerable for the Soviet government. Schulenburg retorted that the German government "valued the continued validity of the German-Finnish agreements above all," and it was not asking for more than an official confirmation by the Soviet government that these agreements would remain unimpaired after the projected reorganization of the concession company.

The official written Soviet reply to the German note was delivered to Schulenburg by Vyshinsky on March 24. It was brief and to the point. No guarantee of the sort requested by Germany was offered. The Soviet government merely declared itself prepared to consider the Finnish-German governmental agreements of July 24 and September 16, 1940, "when studying the question." The German complaint that the creation of a new concession company would hamper the fulfillment of the obligations assumed by Petsamo Nickel to I.G. Farbenindustrie was brushed aside as unfounded. The nickel matte agreement of February 19, 1941, would receive separate consideration by the Soviet government when the time came for determining what obligations to the German firm were to be taken over by the joint Finnish-Soviet company.[104]

The Petsamo question had now run into a dead end on both the Finnish-Soviet and the German-Soviet fronts. Between the Finnish and the Soviet governments there had been no new contact in the matter since the run-in on March 4, except that Witting submitted the text of the nickel matte agreement to Orlov on March 15. There were, in fact, to be no further confrontations with the Soviet Union for either of the two interested parties. For all practical purposes, March 24 represented the conclusion of the Petsamo question as a diplomatic problem. Few Finnish leaders were sufficiently optimistic to regard the question as closed yet, however, and the Finnish government launched another investigation of the whole matter in order to be prepared for the next Soviet move.

CHAPTER VIII

The Coming of the Good Season

D URING the second week of March, the Finnish government at last brought Fieandt back from Moscow, and it summoned both Paasikivi and Kivimäki to Helsinki for consultations. Kivimäki returned to his post in Berlin after a busy week of discussions with government officials and the German minister. Paasikivi, who departed from Moscow on March 11, stayed in Helsinki for two months, and his eventual return to Moscow in May had no other purpose than that of fulfilling the customary obligation to take formal leave of his host government and of his colleagues in the diplomatic corps. Nor did his recall to Helsinki seem to be for any particular purpose other than to remove an envoy who no longer enjoyed the confidence of his foreign minister. In his memoirs he referred to his "lengthy discussions in Helsinki" in a manner which suggested that he had not been much involved in them. He did note that he had at one point asked the Soviet minister in Helsinki what the current situation was in the nickel question, to which Orlov replied that it was the "same as when you left Moscow."[1] Unofficially, Paasikivi had already been succeeded in Moscow by Minister Hynninen.

Fieandt's recall, after his lengthy and reluctant *acte de présence* in the Soviet capital, had a practical purpose connected with the Petsamo question, however. He was named chairman of a new committee set up by the Finnish government for the purpose of working out a proposal for the reply to Molotov's demands of March 4. Appointed to serve with him on this committee were his two colleagues from the mixed commission, Grönblom and Castrén, and Aaro Pakaslahti, who had just been promoted from chief of the Political Department in the Finnish Foreign Ministry to secretary general of the Ministry. The first draft of the committee's proposal was quickly completed, and Kivimäki returned to Berlin on March 14 to submit it to the German Foreign Ministry for its comments.[2]

The committee's draft proposal reflected the greater sense of security which Finland's informed leaders now felt against the Soviet Union. In its draft reply, the Fieandt committee claimed that Finland had shown a spirit of "very far-reaching cooperation" at all times "in order to satisfy the economic interests" of the Soviet government in the Kolosjoki nickel resources. Even though Finland had "no treaty-based obligations to reserve for the Soviet Union special privileges with respect to the production of the mine in question," it had "nevertheless been well disposed" toward the Soviet wishes as demonstrated by its willingness to extend to the Soviet Union "the privilege of participating in the operation of the mine." But this did not mean, the draft proposal continued, that Finland's position as the sovereign possessor of the area in which the mine was located could be disregarded when organizing the projected Finnish-Soviet company, and the Soviet demand for control of the management "can therefore not be regarded as justified and not even as expedient." Both the chairman of the board of directors and the managing director would obviously have to be Finnish citizens. To accept the Soviet demand for additional management positions must also be rejected, since it would render the business management of the company "rather cumbersome." However, two posts already promised to the Soviet government were to be "reserved" for Russians. On the basis of this proposal, concluded the draft reply, the Finnish government stood ready to resume negotiations with the Soviet government, preferably in Helsinki.[3]

The nickel committee's draft could hardly be described as an attempt to accommodate the Soviet Union, and no accommodation was intended. As Kivimäki put it when he submitted a copy of the draft to Weizsäcker on March 17, "the Finnish negotiators expect a definitive rupture of the negotiations if they submit the projected answer." Paasikivi, who had seen the draft, declared flatly that it would "lead to another war in a few months" unless a firm guarantee of German support was given to Finland, related Kivimäki. Without such a guarantee, Paasikivi urged a compromise proposal of a sort which the Russians could be expected to accept. Should no compromise at all be possible, then Paasikivi would even suggest the cession of the Petsamo area against territorial compensation, said Kivimäki. Should Germany recommend a compromise, then representatives of I.G. Farbenindustrie and Petsamo Nickel ought to work out a proposal, perhaps "with suitable political counseling by the Foreign Ministry." Personally, Kivimäki would prefer an outright German guarantee of support, since that would "change the complexion of things entirely." It was also the hope of the Finnish government that it be given "clear advice" by the German government.[4]

There is nothing in the record of this conversation to indicate that Kivimäki received an answer to his restatement of the standard Finnish request. In view of the regularity with which they asked for explicit German promises of support against the Soviet Union, it should not have surprised the Finns if the officials of the German Foreign Ministry grew somewhat weary of it. As one of them said, with a trace of resignation, when Counselor Lundström also brought up the question on March 17: "But we have told you that you do not need to worry; that is after all something."[5]

To the Germans, the hints of support they were dropping from time to time must have seemed sufficient for the Finns to stake their security on them. They had indeed done that. But they were haunted by the thought of what they stood to lose should their faith in German support turn out to be misplaced. They had to keep fishing for more concrete assurances, as they did in the memorandum which Kivimäki gave Weizsäcker when they met on March 17. The memorandum, a summary of the Fieandt committee's proposal with comments, assumed that the Soviet Union would not let war come about over Petsamo if its interest were purely economic, but the issue would serve as an excuse for war if the Russians wanted one. In a concluding sentence, inserted by Kivimäki after consultation with Ryti, it was pointed out that to risk a definitive rupture of the Finnish-Soviet negotiations "involves such a major element of danger that Finland hardly dares to carry it alone."[6] Weizsäcker refused to comment.

The next day, Pakaslahti conveyed to Blücher the draft proposal of the reply to the Soviet Union as revised and approved by the Finnish government.[7] Blücher's summary demonstrates that it was based closely on the recommendation of the Fieandt committee: "1) No concessions in question of management and officials. 2) In control question the appointment of two Russian auditors can be considered. 3) Readiness to resume negotiations on this basis."[8]

The German response, as formulated, after close study,[9] in a memorandum by Schnurre dated March 21, which was endorsed without changes by Ribbentrop, was forwarded to Helsinki six days later and, simultaneously, presented to Kivimäki in Berlin. Germany expressed its full agreement with point one, but it wanted point two made stronger. This, it was suggested, could be done either by striking out the reference to the two Russian auditors altogether, or by making it clear that these auditors would have no authority other than that of ordinary "liaison personnel" between the Finnish management and the two Russian members of the board of directors. The Finnish government was advised, furthermore, that the German government was "not inclined to believe that any particular danger for Finland is involved in the projected answer . . . , not even if the negotiations should be broken off again." The Finns were also reminded that Petsamo talks were still in progress between Germany and the Soviet Union, which meant that a rupture of the Finnish-Soviet negotiations would have no decisive significance. It was noted that "the wishes of the Finnish government go beyond this,"[10] but Schnurre was confident that no additional statement of German support was required. At any rate, if the Finns believed the proposal they had formulated might strand the Finnish-Soviet negotiations, the proposal formulated by Schnurre would make it a certainty.

In the meantime the latest Soviet statement in the Petsamo question had been submitted to Germany on March 24,[11] confirming the failure of the German-Soviet discussions to produce a meeting of minds.

While Ribbentrop was considering Schnurre's memorandum of March 21, the Fieandt committee was at work on a study of some practical problems regarding the management and general organization of the projected Finnish-Soviet concession company. As

Schnurre forwarded his approved memorandum to Blücher on March 27, Witting was handing the Fieandt committee's report to Blücher. The document suggested an even stricter circumscription of the Soviet officials who might be involved in the concession company than the draft reply of March 14 had done. Only the most minimal supervisory powers should be granted to them, and none of them should have the right "to bring other employees or workers into the company." A number of specific reasons were advanced to explain why the Soviet Union ought not to be given any substantial influence in the management. Such an arrangement would "obviously cause disturbances, economic and political," in Finland. Russians, being used to a different economic system and different methods of operating an industrial enterprise, "would have trouble adjusting to local conditions." As a result one had to expect all sorts of differences of opinion which could easily lead to conflicts, "especially if the Soviet Union—which is to be anticipated—were to strive to widen its right of decision and its influence in the company and, from there, in Finland in other ways." Consequently any sort of rotation arrangement with respect to the position of chairman of the board of directors would also have to be dismissed as "impossible,"[12] declared the statement of the Fieandt committee.

Nothing was done by the Finnish government to submit its reply to the Soviet government. It was probably assumed that the international situation as it was developing during late March was keeping the Russians sufficiently busy with problems of greater importance than the Petsamo question. But the Finns did not yet dare to believe that their troubles with the Soviet Union were over, and continued to worry about the possibility that the Russians might not yet be finished with Petsamo. Kivimäki brought the matter up with Weizsäcker again on April 2. Referring to the German comments on the Finnish draft reply to the Soviet government, he pointed out "the great risk involved in following the German advice to be inflexible." Finland could only run such a risk if German support could be counted on with certainty, said Kivimäki. The tendency in Finland was to interpret the proffered German advice to mean that Germany would not "leave Finland in the lurch" in the event of trouble with the Soviet Union, but so far the Finnish government had received no "binding official confirmation of this interpretation," he complained. Weizsäcker's reply did not offer such a confirmation, but it was the closest that any German diplomat had ever come to doing so:

> I told the Minister that his worries did not seem quite justified to me. The Russian government knows, and this is also known in Helsinki, that we have given Moscow to understand that we do not want a new Finnish-Russian conflict at this time. This plain hint, *coupled with the good season which is now beginning,* ought surely to serve as sufficient warning to Moscow that it should not now let it come to a break between Russia and Finland.[13]

This time the hint was apparently strong enough for Kivimäki. Obviously the state secretary of the German Foreign Ministry would not, in such an important political context, speak in riddles merely to announce the imminent burgeoning of green leaves and spring flowers. What he was telling the Finnish minister was that a new campaigning season was approaching as the snow and mud of winter gave way to the hardening ground of spring and summer. In fact, before the week was over, German armies were to march in the Balkans. Kivimäki must have understood what Weizsäcker was hinting at, and he must have been satisfied at last that Finland had no further cause to worry, for the German records reveal no more attempts by him to obtain "binding official confirmation" of German support over Petsamo.

Europe had been buzzing with rumors of an impending German-Soviet armed conflict during the late winter of 1940–41. German activities in the Balkans during early 1941 and the shift of massive German forces to Poland and East Prussia had not gone unnoticed and fed the rumors. When Kivimäki returned to Berlin from Helsinki in mid-March, he mentioned to Weizsäcker that both Finland and Sweden were inundated by rumors of a planned German attack on the Soviet Union. "Naturally," he added, "these rumors were spread in Finnish circles with a certain undertone of satisfaction." While he had consistently denied them himself at home, he was interested in Weizsäcker's comment. To say that Weizsäcker in his reply did not deny the rumors is perhaps to infer too much. At any rate, as he himself recorded his answer, he "could not at all confirm these rumors."[14] The formulation was unusually vague.

The conspicuous increase of high-ranking German military visitors to Finland, starting in February, was not lost on Finnish observers either. When two such figures as the quartermaster gen-

eral of the German air force, Lieutenant General Hans Georg von
Seidel, and the chief of staff of the German Army in Norway,
Colonel Buschenhagen, showed up in the second half of February
and demonstrated a particular interest in north Finland, their
Finnish military hosts were bound to draw certain tentative conclusions. That the visit was concerned with more than merely the
supply organization of the German transit through Finland, the
official pretext, was quite obvious. Supply considerations would
hardly seem to have played much of a role, for instance, in Buschenhagen's cautious question on whether the Finns would be ready to
undertake the protection of a German troop concentration in north
Finland in the event of a war with the Soviet Union, *if ever such
a case were once to arise.* The Finns replied in the affirmative.
Buschenhagen stressed that the question was strictly hypothetical,
and the Finns would be "entirely wrong to draw conclusions" from
it.[15] But when he asked to be taken on a tour of north Finland and
in the course of it crisscrossed the area from the Swedish to the
Soviet border and from Rovaniemi to Petsamo, the Finnish officers
involved could hardly be blamed if they did have their thoughts
about it. At least Buschenhagen himself found it difficult to believe
that his Finnish escort on the trip, the chief of operations in the
General Staff, Colonel Kustaa A. Tapola, should not "have formed
his own ideas about it," even though Buschenhagen made no explicit revelations about German intentions.[16]

Following Buschenhagen's visit to Finland, the planning for the
German operations in north Finland progressed rapidly. Always the
primary objective remained the nickel area, and always the Finns
were to be left guessing. When the OKH on March 2 approved the
plans for "Silver Fox" submitted by the German Army in Norway
on February 13, it was emphasized that "all preparations which
extend to other states can only begin after authorization from the
political leadership, insofar as this has not already been given."[17] In
Finland's case, it was not to be given until the end of May. But the
German forces earmarked for the two operations involving Finland,
"Reindeer" and "Silver Fox," were already on the move during the
month of March as the concentration in the Kirkenes area of North
Norway commenced.[18] And on April 7, the OKW issued its order
covering the assignment of the German Army in Norway within the
general context of the attack on the Soviet Union. While the pri-

mary task remained the defense of Norway against possible attacks by England, the primary offensive task was to take and hold the Petsamo area because of "the special significance of its important nickel mines for the German arms industry." When Hitler gave his permission to begin talks with the Finns about the operation, it was also to be emphasized that the Petsamo area "must under no circumstances be given up" because of its nickel mines.[19] On the basis of the OKW directive, the General Staff of the German Army in Norway issued its final operational order to Mountain Corps Norway on April 18,[20] and on May 6 the commanding general of the forces in Arctic Norway issued detailed operational orders to his commanders, again with special emphasis on the importance of securing the nickel area.[21] Finally, on May 26, the OKW informed the German Army in Norway that Operation "Reindeer" would be triggered automatically in the event of a Soviet preventive attack.[22]

The Finns were not to learn the extent of the German military plans until the end of May, and even then the plans were revealed to them only as they directly involved Finland and as normal theoretical general staff studies for a war which it was hoped would never materialize. But by then the Finns had long since ceased to be much worried about any immediate danger from the Soviet Union. The center of gravity in European affairs had shifted to southeastern Europe, and as German and Soviet interests clashed sharply in that area, Soviet pressure on Finland eased up and soon ended altogether.

Germany had been extending its political and military influence in Rumania, Hungary, and Bulgaria since the beginning of 1941. During the month of March, Yugoslavia also began to move toward the Axis Powers and ultimately joined the Tripartite Pact on March 25. Two days later the pro-German government was overthrown, and on March 30 Yugoslavia declared itself neutral, although it did not formally renounce its ties with the Tripartite Pact. Germany reacted by ordering all German citizens out of Yugoslavia at once. Still, with a war expected momentarily, the Soviet Union on April 5 concluded a treaty of friendship and non-aggression with Yugoslavia. The next morning Germany attacked both Yugoslavia and Greece and defeated them in a short campaign.[23]

The previous fall, the Soviet Union might have considered such a moment of German military involvement elsewhere opportune for an invasion of Finland. But now, with German forces concentrated largely in the east rather than the west, the Russians were not inclined to take any chances. Instead, as the display of German power unfolded in the Balkans, the Soviet leaders clearly decided to avoid doing anything that could conceivably displease Germany. A striking demonstration of this radical change was provided when the Japanese Foreign Minister Yosuke Matsuoka left Moscow on April 13 after signing the Soviet-Japanese Neutrality Pact. To the great surprise of even the Russian dignitaries present, Stalin put in a personal appearance. After having extended his wishes for a pleasant journey to the Japanese officials, Stalin asked loudly for the German ambassador. When he found him in the crowd of foreign diplomats, Stalin threw his arms around Schulenburg and said for all to hear: "We must remain friends and you must now do everything to that end!"[24] The point of this unique and deliberate public display was lost on no one at the station.

Additional indications of the eagerness of the Soviet government to curry favor with Germany could be observed during the ensuing days and weeks. Stalin's personal assumption of open political leadership as the chairman of the Council of People's Commissars on May 6 was seen in this light. Another sign was the zeal with which the Soviet Union began to fulfill its delivery obligations to Germany under existing trade agreements in spite of the fact that Germany itself had fallen into serious arrears. The flow of Soviet goods quickly reached such gigantic proportions that the German transportation system, already heavily taxed by the troops and war equipment being carried east in preparation for the attack on the Soviet Union, was unable to handle it all.

The effects of these developments on Finnish-Soviet relations gradually began to manifest themselves. The Soviet government was no longer pressing for a settlement of the Petsamo question or any other outstanding issue. On the contrary, the Russians were beginning to initiate certain proposals which, if made a year earlier, could have led to a genuine improvement of relations with Finland and have prevented much of the coming, and already unavoidable, misfortune. As early as the middle of March, the Finns were informed that the Soviet Union was ready to permit Finnish exports to the Western Hemisphere by way of Murmansk, Arkhangelsk, and Vladivostok, for instance. The offer, which introduced an alternative to the Petsamo traffic, puzzled Witting.[25] It was the first of several positive indications that a change of heart had occurred in the Soviet Union as far as relations with Finland were concerned. Witting was hard to convince, which was perhaps not surprising. On March 26, he told Minister Schoenfeld that there had been some improvement lately in Finnish-Soviet trade relations, but the status of the Petsamo question remained "substantially unchanged."[26]

The German Foreign Ministry gave some further attention to the Petsamo question after the invasion of Yugoslavia and Greece. On April 7, Schnurre drafted an instruction for the embassy in Moscow and passed it on to Ribbentrop for decision.[27] In it, and in an accompanying memorandum,[28] he noted that "we gave the Finnish government the advice not to yield" in the management question, and he believed that the Finnish-Soviet talks were likely to be broken off if Finland assumed this stand "which has been jointly determined." He did not think there was anything Germany could do for the time being other than simply to handle the matter in a dilatory fashion and await the next stage of the Finnish-Soviet negotiations, since Germany had no material counter-arguments with which to delay the German-Soviet talks further. Schulenburg should be told to say nothing about the Petsamo question until Molotov raised it again himself. Whenever that happened, Schulenburg should make whatever oral use he considered suitable of whatever arguments might seem appropriate, but he should avoid taking any clear stand and say that he would discuss the matter during his pending visit to Berlin. This instruction was cabled to Schulenburg on April 10 after Ribbentrop had endorsed it.[29] However, since Molotov never brought the Petsamo question up again, Schulenburg did not have to carry out this particular delaying maneuver.

On their side, the Finns were also proceeding in a leisurely fashion. On April 18, the Finnish government completed a new version of its projected reply to the Soviet government's representations of March 4. Following the example of the German Foreign Ministry, the Finns left it up to the Russians to take the first step. Minister Hynninen, chargé d'affaires in Moscow in Paasikivi's absence, was sent a copy of the reply and instructed not to submit it unless asked by the Russians to do so. Even then he was to state the Finnish reply orally and not in the form of a written note. But first the opinion of the German Foreign Ministry was requested.[30] It came at the end of the month in a brief telegram from Weizsäcker: "No objections here against content of instruction to Finnish chargé d'affaires in Moscow."[31] Like Schulenburg, Hynninen was never called upon to carry out his instruction.

Around the middle of April, Blücher had several conversations about the new political climate with Finland's top leaders, including President Ryti, Prime Minister Rangell, and Foreign Minister Witting. All of them, he reported to Berlin, were especially interested in the various signs of relaxation which had become evident in Finnish-Soviet relations. They had pointed to the absence of any further Soviet pressure in the Petsamo question, the equally remarkable absence of any anti-Finnish broadcasts from Petrozavodsk during the past couple of weeks, and the conspicuously positive and obliging attitude of Soviet legation personnel in their recent contacts with Finns. Orlov, Zotov's still unofficial replacement as Soviet minister in Helsinki, was making a favorable impression on everybody as a reasonable man to deal with, something which could never be said of Zotov. The three Finnish leaders professed to be puzzled by this development. They had no clear notions as to why this apparent thaw in Finnish-Soviet relations had set in, they told Blücher, and he suggested to the Foreign Ministry in Berlin that it check with the embassy in Moscow for an explanation.[32] Responding to this request, Minister Tippelskirch reported that, as far as could be observed in Moscow, Finnish-Soviet relations had indeed become "more serene" lately. He attributed this to the recent developments in the Balkans.[33]

There was to be still another chapter in the chronicle of the Finnish-Soviet Petsamo dispute, but it was a strangely unreal and anticlimactic epilogue to an otherwise stormy story. When Orlov on April 24 finally presented his credentials as Soviet minister in Helsinki during a diplomatic reception at the presidential residence, he mentioned that he would like to make an appointment with Witting for the purpose of discussing the Petsamo question. Witting consented to the interview, but he confided to Blücher that it was his intention, when Orlov came to see him, to proceed "from the point where the negotiations stood at the outset ten months ago."[34] Orlov seemed to be in no hurry to set a time for the appointment, however, even though he was reported to have said in private conversations that the Petsamo question was "one of the most pressing tasks for him."[35]

Not until May 5 did Orlov bring up the Petsamo question during a general discussion with Witting. What he had to say has not been recorded. Judging by the memorandum of the conversation which Witting subsequently sent to Hynninen in Moscow, Witting did all the talking himself, and he spoke expansively and with confidence. He reminded Orlov of all the demands made upon Finland by the Soviet government since the Moscow treaty of 1940, demands which for the most part had no basis in the treaty. He complained that the Soviet Union, in addition to these demands, had failed to fulfill its own treaty obligation to ship grain to Finland.[36] All of this had created a "psychologically unfavorable effect here," said Witting. The Finns never knew what the Russians might demand next, and the Finnish attitude in the Petsamo question was a consequence of that uncertainty. Finland was quite prepared to continue the negotiations, but it could not retreat from the position it had taken in the mixed commission. The simplest solution would of course be to leave the concession matter as it was. If the Soviet government would abandon the idea of a joint Finnish-Soviet concession company and negotiate a normal commercial delivery agreement with Petsamo Nickel, "that would have a psychologically beneficial effect at this time," concluded Witting.[37]

What Orlov's reaction was to these statements cannot be ascertained, but three days later Blücher informed Berlin that Orlov had indicated to the Swedish minister in Helsinki that all differences between Finland and the Soviet Union would be settled shortly. On the strength of that information, if one is to believe Blücher, Witting instructed Hynninen to tell the Soviet government that if it genuinely desired good relations with Finland, "it might come to an understanding with Finland in the nickel question in the same elegant fashion as Germany did."[38] When Hynninen objected to reopening the matter on the basis of such instructions, the substance of which had been rejected by the Russians two months earlier, he was told that he should simply convey the current Finnish proposal orally. Should the Russians then request a written confirmation, he could give it to them. He could also suggest to them, as Witting had done to Orlov, that the easiest way to settle the Petsamo question would be to have the Soviet government sign a purchasing contract with Petsamo Nickel. That would make all the contemplated legal measures superfluous, he could say.[39]

Minister Hynninen presented the Finnish proposal to Vyshinsky on May 10. Vyshinsky listened patiently to the end, and then he observed that this point had been reached three months ago. He "considered himself able to say in advance," he said politely, "that the reply does not satisfy the USSR government." If Hynninen would give him the Finnish proposal in writing, he would nevertheless communicate it to his government.[40] Hynninen complied the same day. The written statement contained the essence of the reply worked out previously by the Fieandt committee and agreed upon between the Finnish and German Foreign Ministries, with additional passages repeating the suggestions made by Witting to Orlov on May 5.[41]

There was no Soviet reply. As Fieandt said to Blücher three days later, the Finns were hopeful that the Russians "because of other demands on their time will let the nickel question lie."[42] So they did. When Paasikivi on May 30 was received by Stalin in one of the rare audiences granted by the Soviet leader to foreign diplomats, Petsamo was not among the many questions they discussed. In the course of their friendly exchange of pleasantries, they assured each other that the interests of their two nations required the maintenance of good relations. Stalin remarked that Finland was carrying out its obligations under the 1940 peace treaty in a "correct way." Paasikivi, on the strength of assurances given by Witting before he returned to Moscow to take his official leave as Finland's minister there, assured Stalin that the Finnish government was firmly committed to a policy of neutrality. As a parting gesture to Paasikivi, Stalin promised that the Soviet Union would deliver 20,000 tons of grain to Finland.[43] It was a "very friendly" visit, said Paasikivi to Schulenburg the next day.[44] Less than four weeks later, Finland and the Soviet Union were at war again.

CHAPTER IX

"On Snow-Covered Tundras
Under the Midnight Sun"

THE thaw in Finnish-Soviet relations during the spring of 1941 was to an extent offset by a deepening crisis in Anglo-Finnish relations. Two separate developments combined to produce that situation, namely the growing impact of the German submarine warfare on British and neutral shipping in the North Atlantic and the mounting evidence of greater Finnish involvement with Germany. As the storm signals indicating an approaching German-Soviet armed conflict began to go up in May and June, the velvet gloves with which the British had so far handled Finland began to come off. It was only natural that the Petsamo traffic, the one point where Finland was seriously vulnerable to British pressure, should act as the barometer on which the deterioration of Anglo-Finnish relations could be most clearly registered.

The Petsamo traffic represented only a minor leak in the British economic blockade of Germany, of course. On the advice of its envoys in Helsinki and Stockholm, and under mild American pressure, the British government had allowed this traffic to continue on a limited scale during the winter of 1940–41 on the condition that Germany derive no benefits from it. In October, 1940, the British government had decided that navicerts would continue to be issued to Finnish vessels engaged in overseas trade through Petsamo. In November, an Anglo-Finnish agreement was reached whereby Finland permitted Great Britain to establish a system of trade inspectors in strategically located centers in north Finland, including Petsamo, Liinahamari, Salmijärvi, Ivalo, Sodankylä, Rovaniemi, and Tornio.[1] The British subsequently built up a considerable staff of consular officials and trade inspectors who, in addition to checking on the Petsamo trade, also gathered information about German transit across Finnish territory.[2]

More important to Great Britain than the Petsamo trade as such were the Finnish vessels engaged in it. England's survival depended in large measure on its ability to import food and other necessities from overseas, which in turn depended on the availability of a sufficient quantity of shipping to carry these goods to the British Isles. But German submarines, surface raiders, and long-range aircraft were constantly and mercilessly pounding away at Allied and neutral shipping in the North Atlantic. Ships were sunk at an alarming rate, threatening to reduce British imports to less than the minimum requirements. During the month of June, 1940, the darkest month for Atlantic shipping that year, a total of 585,496 tons of shipping was lost, most of it in the Atlantic Ocean. In April, 1941, a new peak was reached with a total loss of 687,901 tons, including 260,451 in the North Atlantic. At no time during that period did the monthly loss fall below 320,000 tons.[3]

In desperation, the British revived a device which had served them well in a similar crisis situation during World War I, namely that of pressuring neutral nations into transferring parts of their merchant marine tonnage to British time charter for the duration of the war. Several neutral nations, including Sweden, had already concluded such agreements with England by the time the first approach, for approximately 50,000 tons of shipping, was made to Finland in the fall of 1940. Although Minister Gripenberg urged acceptance, the Finnish government rejected the British demand. Eventually, in late February, 1941, Gripenberg was authorized to offer the British 37,000 tons, to be increased to 40,000 tons in August of that year.[4]

The British price had gone up, however. In December, 1940, the British government had raised its demand to 75,000 tons and coupled it with a threat to deny further navicerts to ships of Finnish registry. The demand, which amounted to nearly 40 per cent of all Finnish tonnage outside the Skagerrak mine barrier (and more than 80 per cent of that tonnage was employed in the Petsamo trade), was repeated in January, 1941, and again in February.[5] By early March, the sharpness of the British pressure had the Finns seriously worried. Finnish officials and shipping leaders, most notably Ramsay, took the matter up with a number of German officials in various government departments in Berlin, and Witting brought it to Blücher's attention in Helsinki. It was a clear case of either yielding to the British pressure or suffering the inevitable consequence, namely the stoppage of the Petsamo traffic, said Witting. Ramsay had suggested that it would be necessary to transfer at least 40 per cent of Finland's oceangoing tonnage to British time charter in order to keep the Petsamo trade alive, and Witting could see no way of avoiding it. Blücher warned that it would be a very dangerous step to take and urged him to consult with the proper officials in Berlin before he made a decision.[6]

In the middle of March, Ramsay informed German shipping authorities in Berlin, through the shipping expert in the German legation in Helsinki, that Finland could no longer afford to endanger its difficult negotiations with England by continuing the practice of letting Finnish vessels carry ore from Kirkenes to German Baltic ports. The British had agreed to permit traffic between Petsamo and Finnish Baltic ports only on the condition that the vessels involved carry no ore. Ramsay assumed that the British had torpedoed the S.S. "Oscar Midling" in December because it had ore aboard. He also assumed that three Finnish vessels, which had been brought in to Kirkwall by the Royal Navy in spite of their possession of navicerts, would be used by the British to pressure Finland in the charter question. He promised to keep the Germans informed about the progress of the negotiations with the British.[7]

As Ramsay was making his explanations to the German legation in Helsinki, the Finnish legation in Berlin did the same in the form of a verbal note. The implicit plea for German understanding and tolerance met with no positive response, however. The German government could not let a transfer of Finnish tonnage to Great Britain pass without registering its serious opposition, said the German reply of March 22. Since such an act amounted to giving active support to a power with which Germany was at war, it could not be reconciled with Finland's status as a neutral state. The German Foreign Ministry therefore expected that the Finnish government reject the British demands, and it felt compelled to point out that "submission by the Finnish government to Great Britain cannot be without consequences for the further execution of the German-Finnish agreements which have been concluded regarding the regulation of Finnish shipping through Petsamo."[8]

Thus, the Petsamo traffic faced elimination regardless of what the Finns might decide to do. Should they yield to the British demands, the Germans would put an end to it, and if they gave in to the Germans, the British would stop it. The Finns decided to deal dilatorily with both sides, and somehow they managed to get away with it for more than one month before the British pressure again became critical.

In late March, the British received evidence of increased German infiltration in Finland. This led the Ministry of Economic Warfare to withhold the provisional schedule of Finnish import quotas for the April-June quarter.[9] It was an effective warning which soon brought the Finns to Berlin pleading for relief. On April 28, Kivimäki and Ramsay called on State Secretary Weizsäcker and handed him a memorandum in which the latest developments in the Anglo-Finnish negotiations and their effects on the Finnish economy were outlined. It was noted that 55 ships (out of a total of 66 currently outside the Skagerrak mine barrier) were engaged in the Petsamo trade, by which Finland was receiving commodities of vital importance from the United States and South America. Cargoes estimated at some 85,000 tons were expected to reach Petsamo during the second quarter of 1941, including indispensable grain, flour, sugar, and mineral oils. If no agreement was reached with the British government in the very near future regarding the tonnage transfer matter, most of those cargoes would probably be lost, since the point had been reached where the Finns would have to offer the British something or else lose everything by "forcible seizure." The latest British demand, said the memorandum, was over 40,000 tons of shipping by August 1 and another 25,000 tons by October 1. Finland intended to approve the first of these transfers but not the second. It would propose that the transfer of 40,000 tons should include those Finnish vessels which were already chartered to Great Britain, and it would ask for a British guarantee that no further transfers of Finnish shipping be requested by the British for the remainder of the war. "It will naturally be attempted to conduct the negotiations as dilatorily as possible," concluded the memorandum. Weizsäcker promised to reexamine the whole problem "in a spirit of good will and with Finland's supply situation in mind." Meanwhile the Finns ought to explore the possibility of purchasing grain from the Soviet Union. Kivimäki informed him that negotiations with the Russians were already underway.[10]

The Anglo-Finnish crisis of April was temporarily eased, however, when the British decided that "for the moment the increase of German influence [in Finland] did not justify any reduction in the quotas." The import quotas for the second quarter of 1941 were eventually presented to Minister Gripenberg, "but with the warning that further signs of submission to Germany would lead to their reduction or suspension."[11]

Although the Germans were primarily concerned with keeping Finnish shipping from falling under British control, the idea of playing the time charter game apparently held its appeal for them too. On April 30, Veltjens stopped by to see Ambassador Ritter in the Foreign Ministry. He was on his way to Finland again on another assignment for Göring, he said. The trip was connected with his current pet scheme of finding ways to run the British blockade. He would like to try to charter three or four Finnish vessels to carry rubber and other vital materials for Germany from South America to Portugal and Spain. If the Foreign Ministry agreed, his efforts to that end might stand a better chance of success, especially if he could officially promise the Finns in return that the German government was prepared to give its consent to an Anglo-Finnish agreement on the charter question. Perhaps, he inquired of Ritter, he could suggest that the Germans would let the Finns charter one ship to the British for every two ships chartered to the Germans. Ritter approved of the scheme, but no records have been found showing how this latest Veltjens mission turned out.[12] Presumably the Finns stalled him just as effectively as they were stalling the British.

The "further signs of submission to Germany" of which the British had warned Gripenberg in April began to appear in May, when the British learned that petroleum products imported by Finland through British controls were being sold, contrary to Finnish promises, to the Petsamo Nickel Company, thus directly benefitting Germany.[13] What finally broke the camel's back, however, was something more than a brittle straw; it was the rapid and conspicuous increase of German troops in north Finland in early June. For the first time the Finns were presented with an ultimatum in the charter question, as the British gave them until June 5 to come up with a definitive reply. The Finnish government complied. It agreed to increase Finnish shipping sailing under British time charter to 40,000 tons by August 1, including the 18,000 tons of shipping already chartered to the British by individual Finnish shipping lines. It was hoped that this step would suffice to keep the Petsamo traffic going long enough to bring home the valuable Finnish cargoes then on the high seas headed for Petsamo.[14] It nearly worked. Finland by this device won some ten days of grace before the British finally closed down all trade through Petsamo.

In the light of what was going on in north Finland during the first three weeks of June, events which indicated the strong likelihood of Finnish involvement in the rapidly approaching German-Soviet conflict, it has to be admitted that the British displayed an astonishing degree of good will and patience toward Finland. Regardless of Finland's motives, and regardless of the causes of its apparent involvement in the German plans for what seemed to be an imminent attack on the Soviet Union, Great Britain could hardly have been blamed had it decided to take even sterner measures, and at an earlier time, against a country which seemed to be on the verge of taking up arms side by side with the enemy. The British possessed more than sufficient evidence to justify a tougher line in their relations with Finland. As a matter of fact, had they known the full extent of Finland's involvement, they would have had to crack down on it at every vulnerable point earlier than they actually did.

The German military planning during the first four months of 1941 for the occupation of the Petsamo area and for operations through north Finland into Soviet territory has been briefly outlined in previous chapters. Although the Finns had not participated in that planning and had not been initiated into those aspects of the plans which concerned them directly, they had been obliquely warned from time to time about the possibility of a German-Soviet conflict. The Germans simply assumed that Finland would be a participant when the time came.[15] There was not even a plan for how and when to initiate the Finns until April 28, when General Warlimont of the OKW prepared one for submission to Hitler. Warlimont proposed that "military conferences must be preceded by *political contacts.*" There should be two military conferences between top Finnish and German officers. During the first of these, to be held in Germany, the chief of the OKW Operations Staff, General Alfred Jodl, was to reveal "the mission with which the Finns will be charged." After the Finns had had a few days to consider this information, they should be given an opportunity to "clarify any possible dubious problems" in a second conference. In both conferences, German intentions could be camouflaged by "(a) the overall plan not being mentioned at all and (b) the intentions from the Finnish area being represented as possible necessary offensive-defensive measures."[16]

Two days later, Hitler approved Warlimont's proposal. At the same time he announced that Operation "Barbarossa" would commence on June 22.[17] The formula to be used in all conversations with the Finns was outlined as follows: "Major developments possible in the west. Hence protection in the east necessary. Russia has occasionally treated us in an unfriendly fashion, so we had better prepare ourselves for surprises."[18] That formula was subsequently observed faithfully by German civilian and military officials involved in the talks with the Finns.

The political contact which was to precede and pave the way for the military conferences was made on May 20, when Minister Schnurre was received by President Ryti in Helsinki. According to Ryti's postwar testimony at the war guilt trials in Helsinki, Schnurre explained to him that German-Soviet relations had been deteriorating lately, mainly because of the developments in the Balkans. Both sides had therefore taken "certain security measures of a military nature." It was not Hitler's wish or intention to start a war, but the possibility of an armed conflict had to be taken into account, since the Russians "might direct an attack against Finland and the Balkans." Schnurre revealed, thereby confirming officially for the first time what the Finns had long suspected, that Molotov during his visit to Berlin in November had requested a free hand for the Soviet Union to move against Finland and that Hitler had refused. Having made this telling point, Schnurre suggested that the Finnish government send one or more general staff officers to

Germany "to discuss how military measures should be coordinated" in the event of a Soviet attack on Finland. Ryti replied that Finland would never participate in an aggressive war against the Soviet Union and wished to remain outside all great power conflicts. However, should it be attacked, Finland would of course defend itself. "We would naturally be happy," said Ryti, "if in such a defensive war we received assistance from the outside."[19]

Later the same day, Ryti discussed the German proposal with Prime Minister Rangell, Foreign Minister Witting, Defense Minister Waldén, and Field Marshal Mannerheim. It was quickly agreed that the invitation to send staff officers to Germany for a military orientation must be accepted,[20] and Schnurre could report to Ribbentrop that his Helsinki talks had been "successfully concluded."[21] The "Finnish guests" would arrive in Berlin by special plane on May 24, he announced.[22]

It was a high-powered group of staff officers which gathered for the first Finnish-German military conference at the temporary OKW headquarters in Salzburg on Sunday, May 25. The German delegation was headed by General Jodl (Field Marshal Keitel put in a brief appearance to welcome the Finnish visitors) and included Colonel Buschenhagen of the Army in Norway, Captain Bürkner of the OKW Foreign Intelligence Department, and Lieutenant Colonel Bernhard von Lossberg of the OKW Operations Department (standing in for his chief, General Warlimont). The Finnish delegation was equally representative. It was headed by General Heinrichs as chief of the General Staff and included the chiefs of three of his departments, namely Colonel Tapola of Operations, Colonel Einar N. Mäkinen of Mobilization, and Colonel Harald V. Roos of Supply. Also included was the chief of the Finnish Naval Staff, Commodore Svante A. Sundman.

The purpose of the Salzburg conference was merely to put the Finns in the picture to the extent required for carrying out the German plans, not to reach an agreement about military cooperation. The Finnish delegation was in any case not authorized to make commitments, and none was made.[23] But the Finnish officers must have listened with undivided attention and rising astonishment to what Jodl told them about Germany's intentions in the event of a war with the Soviet Union and what it was hoped that the Finns would do. Jodl never mentioned the "Barbarossa" plan, nor any other plan by its code name or with complete candor. Of the three main operations involved in the "Barbarossa" plan (into north, central, and south Russia), Jodl referred only to the northern drive against Leningrad through the Baltic states, and he provided no details. It was hoped, he said, that the Finns, in conjunction with the German assault on Leningrad, would launch a main attack of their own in the region around Lake Ladoga. He would also like them to take limited defensive measures in the Petsamo area in connection with a German drive from North Norway against Murmansk, contribute one army corps to a German drive from the Salla area against Kandalaksha, and attack the Soviet base at Hanko with German air and possibly ground support. Also brought up in the course of his discourse were the Åland Islands, problems of air and naval operations, and mobilization schedules. On each point the Finns were asked to comment, and ideas were exchanged, but the whole discussion remained hypothetical—at least in form. According to the German protocol of the conference, however, General Heinrichs remarked in conclusion that "the presence of the Finnish representatives indicates the Finnish attitude, even though the political authorization does not yet exist." The protocol also noted that the Finns agreed with the suggested division of the command structure on the Finnish front (Falkenhorst in the north, Mannerheim on the "Ladoga front"), and that they promised to mobilize their coastal artillery in Petsamo and lay down a mine barrier there.

It is also worthy of note that Jodl opened his briefing by stressing—as the drafts and final versions of the German operational plans had always done—the *"Occupation of Petsamo* (nickel mines)."[24]

During the following three days, the Finnish staff officers engaged in detailed discussions in Berlin with a large number of top officers of the German army, navy, and air force. That both sides obtained a considerable amount of useful technical and tactical information in the course of those exchanges emerges clearly from several German reports on the meetings.[25] But again no agreements were made. As he left for Finland on May 28, General Heinrichs reiterated to Captain Bürkner that a military collaboration of the kind suggested by the Germans for the possible conflict with the Soviet Union could only take place if authorized by the Finnish government. Having made his statement of constitutional principle, Heinrichs proceeded, however, to ask Bürkner whether that authorization should be communicated to Germany through military or diplomatic channels. As the question was recorded by Bürkner in a memorandum, it implied that Heinrichs took it for granted that such a political decision by the Finnish government would readily be forthcoming.[26]

Be that as it may, in spite of the positive attitude shown by the Finnish officers during their visit to Germany, the absence of any political decision by the Finnish authorities in favor of military cooperation with Germany bothered the German military leaders. Buschenhagen, in his report to his own staff in Oslo, wrote that the results of the discussions were "not yet satisfactory, since the political authorization was lacking." He expected to be informed of the Finnish government's decision in Helsinki on June 3, he wrote.[27]

The second Finnish-German military conference took place in Helsinki on June 3–5.[28] The German delegates were Colonel Buschenhagen, representing the OKW, and Colonel Eberhard Kinzel, chief of the Eastern Intelligence Department of the OKH. They came well prepared,[29] and the results of their talks were gratifying, as their subsequent written reports demonstrated.[30] At the outset, Buschenhagen was presented with an encouraging memorandum[31] written by General Heinrichs after close consultation with Field Marshal Mannerheim.[32] It began by stating that "the measures previously recommended" could be carried out as soon as "the political side of the question has been clarified." In the meantime, Mannerheim wished to say, continued the memorandum, "that the interest which has been aroused by these recommendations is not at all confined to operational or purely military-technical matters. The idea which underlies the expositions made by the highest German military authorities can not but inspire joy in Finland's martial soul [*Soldatenherz*] and is understood here as a historic portent of a great epoch." The remainder of the memorandum dealt with the projected utilization of the Finnish forces in the prospective war, operations against Soviet targets desired of the German air force by the Finns, Finnish facilities to be turned over to the Germans for their use, and the questions of the Åland Islands and Hanko.

Even with the introductory reference to the political proviso, it is extremely difficult to interpret this Finnish answer to the recommendations the Germans had made in Salzburg and Berlin as a "negative" one.[33] That the Germans regarded the memorandum as a positive answer and the outcome of the Helsinki talks as successful is clear enough. "Finland now ready for full participation within the framework of the Salzburg and Berlin talks," reported Buschenhagen as early as June 4.[34] Slightly reworded, the same sentence appeared in Buschenhagen's written report of June 7, a copy of which he personally gave to Heinrichs upon his return to Helsinki one week later.[35] The sentence upset Heinrichs so much that he marched right into Mannerheim's office and read it to him. Mannerheim became very angry and was about to demand a correction, but on second thought he decided that such an official protest might cause unnecessary friction with the Germans. Instead he satisfied his indignation by refusing to take the offensive document in his hands.[36] It would appear that the only thing that was wrong with the sentence was that it stated the hard truth of Finland's commitment much too bluntly for the sensitive Finns, who were obsessed with avoiding the appearance of being involved with the Germans in the planning of an aggressive war. Both Buschenhagen and Kinzel took note of this obsession in their written reports. Buschenhagen put it this way: "In view of the constitutional restriction binding on the president, Finland considers it to be important that the opening of the hostilities against Russia should not originate with the Finns or from Finnish territory."[37] Kinzel mentioned in his report that Heinrichs had explained how the Finnish political situation tended to make aggressive war unpalatable and unwise. "Finland would therefore welcome it if the German operations were begun first and hopes that it will then be provoked into an attack by the Russians."[38]

Although the political authorization was still lacking, the Finns had in fact already committed themselves, and they had no illusions regarding the possible diplomatic solution of the German-Soviet differences which the Germans kept referring to. The wheels of war began to roll even as the Helsinki conference broke up. On June 5, the first of numerous German troop ships began to leave Stettin and Oslo for Finnish ports on the Gulf of Bothnia. For ten days troops kept coming, entraining as they arrived for

Rovaniemi, where some camped just outside of town while others marched north on the Arctic Ocean Highway. On June 7, German units in North Norway also headed for the Arctic Ocean Highway and began to march south. Officially these troop movements were parts of a massive operation to relieve German forces in North Norway, and for purposes of camouflage that fiction was kept alive until June 18, when all of the forces converging on the Arctic Ocean Highway from both ends suddenly turned east and marched on the Soviet border. The timetable further called for the occupation of the Petsamo area on June 22 and attacks across the Soviet border on June 29 in the northernmost sector and on July 1 in the central sector.[39]

Finnish preparations were also proceeding according to plan. General Heinrichs confirmed to the German military attaché on June 10 that the mobilization of all Finnish forces would take place in stages during the next seven days.[40] On the same day, Colonel General von Falkenhorst issued his first field order to the Finnish V Army Corps, which was to come under his command on June 15 after being renamed the III Army Corps.[41] On June 12, Colonel Rössing could report to Berlin, on the strength of information received from General Heinrichs, that the Finns would be ready to commence operations by June 28.[42] They wanted to know, however, and in plain language, whether there would actually be war or whether a peaceful solution might still be possible.[43] General Jodl at once authorized Buschenhagen to inform the Finns that they could count on war "with certainty."[44] That afternoon, June 14, President Ryti met with the Foreign Relations Committee of the cabinet, and at that meeting the Finnish-German military arrangements were approved.[45] The political authorization had at last been given. The next day, the High Command of the German Army in Norway took over command in north Finland according to plan.[46] On June 17, the day and exact hour of the imminent German invasion of the Soviet Union were indirectly revealed to the Finnish forces through a field order issued by the German headquarters in Rovaniemi. One sentence read as follows: "Air reconnaissance over Russian territory is permitted as of June 22 at 2:30 A.M."[47] Two days later, another German order issued to all forces under Falkenhorst's command referred explicitly to June 22 as the "day of attack."[48]

This summary account of the joint Finnish-German preparations for an attack on the Soviet Union during the four weeks leading up to June 22 has ignored the political aspect of the question as the Finnish political leadership saw it at the time. A full discussion of that aspect would take us outside the scope of the present study, but it should be clear from materials presented in the previous chapters that the Finns had been conditioned by continuous Soviet pressures since the summer of 1940 for the role they were to play in June, 1941. The purpose of this summary of the military preparations is not to indict Finland's leaders for the course they felt compelled to follow—no such indictment could be wholly justified—but merely to provide information vital for an understanding of the deterioration of Anglo-Finnish relations and its impact on the Petsamo question.[49]

Clearly, such massive movements of German forces onto Finnish territory could not pass unobserved or be explained away as an exchange of forces between North Norway and Germany. Given the political atmosphere then prevalent in Europe, an atmosphere teeming with wild rumors and firm proof of an imminent German-Soviet armed conflict, an entirely sinister complexion was necessarily added to the German troop movements in north Finland. When the Finns simultaneously set in motion the expensive machinery of a general mobilization, foreign observers must be forgiven if they suspected collusion between the Finns and the Germans. That British suspicions were aroused at an early stage of these developments is known. The British had got wind of the visit of the Finnish military delegation to Germany in late May, and the British military attaché, Lieutenant Colonel J. H. Magill, had inquired about it in the Finnish General Staff. He was told that "General Heinrichs sits in his office and has not flown [to Berlin]."[50] Minister Vereker went straight to President Ryti and asked the same question. Ryti told him that a few high-ranking officers had indeed been to Berlin "to discuss questions arising from the German transit rights."[51] Since these two versions differed radically, somebody was not telling the truth, and the British were entitled to draw their own conclusions. That a British ultimatum involving the Petsamo traffic followed is hardly surprising.

As soon as the Finns had complied with the British ultimatum by promising to turn over a specified amount of tonnage to British time charter, the British found an opportunity to tighten the pressure again. The delicate question of what to do about the Polish legation in Helsinki had for some time been a minor source of friction between Finland and Germany. Now the Germans were pressing for a quick decision. In early June, Vereker handed Witting a note in which it was stated that the expulsion of the Polish legation from Finland would be regarded by the British government as an unfriendly act and as a sign of Finnish submission to Germany. Gripenberg was told in the Foreign Office and in the Ministry of Economic Warfare that such a step on the part of Finland must necessarily have an unfavorable effect on the Petsamo traffic. After consulting with Blücher, Witting told Vereker that the contemplated closing of the Polish legation in Helsinki did not reflect a Finnish submission to German orders. "If Finland must starve," he instructed Gripenberg to tell the Foreign Office, "it would not feel any sweeter if it were to be caused by English measures." To Blücher he said that he expected to close the Dutch, Belgian, and Norwegian legations soon also.[52]

The breakdown of all but formal diplomatic relations between Finland and Great Britain came immediately after the Finnish mobilization began. The presence of British trade inspectors in all of the centers of north Finland from Rovaniemi to Petsamo, the route along which the German troop concentration was taking place, was highly inopportune, and Field Marshal Mannerheim urged that the Foreign Ministry take immediate steps to remove them. Witting summoned Vereker on June 12 and requested that eleven British inspectors be temporarily moved to south Finland while the troop movements lasted. Vereker agreed to cable London for instructions, but he pointed out that the Finnish request would make a bad impression there. Witting would also have liked to get the British consuls out of Petsamo and Rovaniemi, but Vereker insisted that such a demand would mean the rupture of diplomatic relations. As Witting subsequently reported to Blücher, he could not afford to take that risk, since fourteen Finnish ships with 55,000 tons of "particularly valuable goods" were still at sea bound for Petsamo from the United States.[53]

It was too late in the game for the Finns to postpone the inevitable British crackdown on the Petsamo traffic by making minor concessions. Even Blücher realized that Minister Vereker, and therefore also the British government, was fully and accurately informed of what was going on in Finland. The only thing which puzzled Blücher was that the British had not yet taken retaliatory measures.[54] He did not have to wait long. On June 14, the British made their long-awaited decision to deny further navicerts to Finnish vessels engaged in the Petsamo trade. The measure was to go into effect the following day and was announced publicly on June 19.[55] The Finnish government was informed through a note delivered by Vereker to President Ryti. Witting gave a copy of it to Blücher, who transmitted it to Berlin in the English original:

> Since Germany is our enemy we shall oppose her and those fighting with her wherever we can. If, therefore, Finland joins a Russo-German war on the side of Germany she will forfeit British support and sympathy and we shall have to subject her to every form of economic pressure in our power.
>
> Owing to the uncertainty of the present political situation we are detaining ships now on their way to Petsamo. Immediately the attitude of the Finnisch [sic] Government becomes clear to His Majesty's Government, they will be prepared to examine the question of the continued detention of these ships in the light of the political military situation then prevailing.[56]

In its written reply, the Finnish government declared that it was "compelled to protest against unjustified step."[57] Then it took prompt advantage of the opportunity to remove three British consuls and all trade inspectors from north Finland. Vereker was informed that the personnel in question had been rendered effectively unemployed by the British closure of the Petsamo traffic, and they had twenty-four hours to get out.[58] When they refused to comply with this order,[59] Vice-Consul J. D. Robinson in Rovaniemi and five trade inspectors stationed in Salmijärvi, Ivalo, Sodankylä, Rovaniemi, and Tornio were picked up by the Finnish State Police and transported to Helsinki (three of them were actually placed in a camp for Winter War foreign volunteers still in Finland). Consul E. E. M. Nielsen in Petsamo and Consul C. Roseberry in Tornio were asked to leave at once since their safety could no longer be guaranteed. Two Norwegians who had worked for the British were arrested and sent to Kirkenes by the Germans.[60] When Consul Nielsen showed no inclination to leave Petsamo, it was decided to let him stay until 2:30 A.M. on June 22, when he would be taken into custody along with the Soviet consular personnel and taken across the Norwegian border.[61] Consul Roseberry in Tornio was picked up by a German officer at 3:00 A.M. on June 22 and sent across the Swedish border to Haparanda by horse-and-buggy the next evening.[62]

The Germans were anxious to have the Finnish government go beyond these measures and break off diplomatic relations with Great Britain. On June 18, Blücher advised Ribbentrop that an immediate and complete Finnish break with England was in Germany's interest. A "dangerous espionage center" would be destroyed, and one would move one step closer to the goal of ridding the European continent of the British.[63] Ribbentrop agreed and instructed Blücher to put pressure on Witting.[64] However, not until July 28 did the Finnish government announce its decision to close its legation in London and invite the British to do the same with their legation in Helsinki.[65]

As long as Anglo-Finnish diplomatic relations continued to function, the question of surrendering Finnish tonnage to British time charter also remained alive. Expecting immediate British seizure of Finnish ships at sea after June 15, the Finnish government tried to evade such a calamity by ordering all Finnish ships in North America to head for Brazilian ports.[66] Apparently this order met with some resistance on the part of Finnish shipowners. Urged on by Blücher, Witting made every effort to get the desired cooperation from the shipowners (or so he told Blücher), but in vain.[67] Orders were also issued to place Finnish ships overseas under Panamanian flag, and this was actually done in many cases.[68] Both Great Britain and the United States apparently respected the Panamanian flag flown by Finnish ships until early September.[69] More surprisingly, the British government did not follow through on its decision to detain all Finnish ships at sea. A few ships on the way to Petsamo were brought into British ports, but beyond that no seizures were made.[70]

For some reason the British did not seem to relish the idea of simply seizing Finnish ships. Gripenberg was told by the minister of war transport that such a procedure would be both "unpleasant" and "complicated." Amicable negotiations would be better.[71] The Finns continued to argue that because of a shortage of tonnage, they were unable to turn over more than 40,000 tons. The British argued that Finland's need for tonnage had been reduced since the Petsamo traffic was ended, and the shortage argument was therefore no longer valid. And all the while the Germans kept insisting that they could in no circumstances accept the surrender of any Finnish tonnage to the British.[72] The Germans won out in the end. On July 21, Gripenberg was instructed by Witting to inform the British government that Finland could make available no more than 33,500 tons of shipping. The minister was to communicate this offer to the British authorities "in categorical, unmistakable language and to report immediately their reaction."[73] In view of the earlier agreement to surrender 40,000 tons, and in view of the fact that the British had since decided not to count the ships already confiscated among the tonnage demanded for time charter, this reduction of the Finnish offer amounted to an outright rejection, or at best an invitation to the British to break off the negotiations. A week later, that was in fact effectively accomplished when Witting initiated the proceedings which culminated in the rupture of diplomatic relations.

Two days before Operation "Barbarossa" was launched, a curious exchange took place in the Finnish Foreign Ministry. Since it offers a clue to Witting's thinking, and probably also to the philosophy which underlay the fateful foreign policy that took Finland into the war on Germany's side, it should be recounted. Vereker had come to see Witting about the removal of the British trade inspectors from north Finland, a measure which he protested with a display of great anger. He demanded that Finland observe its obligations as a neutral power. For a moment, the Finnish foreign minister reverted to his professorial status and lectured his British visitor on the realities of international politics. At sea, he discoursed, the Finnish government obeyed the rules laid down by England and did not permit its warships to fire on British ships. By the same token, the Finnish government offered no resistance to German soldiers on land and did not permit them to be shot at. His anger gone, Vereker announced that Finland should only wait. England would win the war, and British ships would then arrive in Finland "with flags waving." Witting did not dispute the possibility of a British victory, but he could not imagine that it could occur before the fall of 1943. And he repeated his lesson in power realities: if the Finns were to start resisting the Germans now, "then no Finn would be alive when the flag-bedecked English ships arrived." The conversation ended on a friendly note, reported Witting to Blücher later the same day, adding that the British were apparently burning the archives in their legation.[74]

All the while the wheels of war continued to roll. Shortly after midnight on Sunday, June 22, the military resources of Germany were turned against the Soviet Union along a front stretching from Hungary to the Baltic. At 2:30 A.M., Mountain Corps Norway under General Dietl crossed the border into the Petsamo area.[75] By 11:05 it could report that Operation "Reindeer," the occupation and securing of Petsamo, had been successfully carried out without incidents.[76] The deployment of the Finnish III Army Corps was continuing "according to plan."[77] And Hitler sent a message to President Ryti, assuring him that *come what may, Germany will never leave Finland in the lurch. . . . With these lines I confirm also the agreements which have been concluded between our military authorities.*[78]

While the Finnish and German forces continued their deployment along the Soviet border, Finland's political leadership proclaimed the country's neutrality while waiting for the Soviet provocation which would relieve them of the onus of aggression. The Russians obliged them. Incursions into Finnish air space by Soviet planes grew to a full-fledged air offensive by June 25. As a consequence, the Finnish parliament on that day endorsed by unanimous vote a government proclamation which stated that Finland, as a result of Soviet aggression, found itself in a state of war.[79]

It has been claimed that it is "impossible to come up with anything but uncertain conjectures about how things might have turned out had the Soviet Union not attacked Finland from the air on June 25."[80] The evidence, however, supports the conclusion that regardless of whether the Soviet air attacks had taken place, "the course of events would have been substantially unaltered."[81] That the Finnish preparations for an invasion of the Soviet Union would or could have been halted short of the invasion itself had the provocation not been forthcoming is extremely unlikely. The Finns were in too deeply to get out after June 22, and all of the prearranged preparations proceeded according to plan until they culminated in aggression on the appointed dates.

Announcing the beginning of the German invasion on June 22,

Colonel General von Falkenhorst noted quite correctly that "The German-Finnish army under my command joins in this attack," and he ordered the Finnish III Army Corps to commence operations on its sector at 2:30 A.M. on July 1.[82] At 4:05 A.M. on July 1, the following message was dispatched from General Siilasvuo's command post to Falkenhorst's headquarters in Rovaniemi: "Attack by Finnish III Army Corps commenced as ordered."[83] Equally indicative of Finland's commitment was a dispatch forwarded to Falkenhorst by the German liaison officer at Mannerheim's field headquarters in Mikkeli in the afternoon of June 24, *the day before* the Russians provided the Finns with the desired provocation. The dispatch stated that Finland had authorized the commencement of German air strikes from Finnish bases against Soviet territory as of that midnight. Simultaneously, ground reconnaissance across the border could begin.[84] It would appear that the Russian air offensive early the next morning came in the nick of time.

During the week before the first Finnish forces went into action in conjunction with the German drive against Murmansk and Kandalaksha, several German reports each day testified to the relentless progress of the Finnish preparations "according to plan." The relevant German field orders and war diaries tell the same story. There was nothing about those preparations which could be described as coincidental, tentative, or defensive. The die had been cast before June 25; indeed, it had been cast well before June 22. The rest was practically automatic and very much "according to plan."

What would have happened had Finland decided to remain neutral—or had tried to resist the Germans in cooperation with the Russians? Since it has been suggested that a policy of neutrality was still a possibility for Finland in the spring of 1941,[85] and that the Finnish leaders made "an appalling mistake in June 1941,"[86] it is of interest to note the postwar reflections of General Warlimont. Had the Finns opted for a different policy, Warlimont would have been prominently involved in formulating the German operational response to it. A Finnish declaration of neutrality would not have been respected by Hitler, says Warlimont, "because the Petsamo nickel area was indispensable to the German war economy." In addition, since Finnish neutrality would represent an intolerable menace to the German position in Norway, "it would at all events have been a military necessity to occupy Finland with German troops north of a line running roughly from the Rybachi Peninsula to the northern end of the Gulf of Bothnia." After that, Finland would probably have had no choice but to accept the partial German occupation under protest or join with Germany. In either case Finland could expect to be attacked by the Soviet Union.[87]

Should the Finns have decided to make common cause with the Russians and fight the Germans, an unthinkable course of action to the Finns and therefore of strictly academic interest, the Germans would have been forced to take up defensive positions in north Finland and North Norway for the time being—"but in all circumstances including Petsamo." That could have been accomplished, according to Warlimont, without any unfavorable effects on Operation "Barbarossa." It is probably a fair guess, however, that Hitler would not for long have tolerated the existence of a neutral space south of the German-occupied area of Finland. He would probably have placed still greater emphasis on taking Leningrad quickly. Then he would have placed strong German forces along the southern coastline of the Gulf of Finland and put an economic stranglehold on Finland which would eventually have starved the Finns into submission.[88] To have bowled the Finns over by a massive attack would have been impossible for lack of the necessary forces. The blitz campaign against Yugoslavia had been possible in April, and even then it had caused a delay in the "Barbarossa" timetable. After "Barbarossa" got underway, a full-fledged attack on Finland was out of the question.[89] But the economic strangulation suggested by Warlimont would indeed have stood a very good chance of success.

That the initial onslaught against the Soviet Union from Finnish territory should have emanated from the Petsamo area was perhaps a logical climax to the 1940–41 chapter of the Petsamo question, a tragic climax with an element of poetic justice mixed in. For the Finns it was the beginning of three years of successful warfare against the Russians, followed by sudden and costly defeat. The costs of the adventure included the loss of the Petsamo area. Paasikivi's bitter comment that the "Petsamo nickel was much too large and dangerous a mouthful for Finland to swallow"[90] was in the end proved accurate.

But on the day of the invasion, Sunday, June 29, a warm (71°F) day without a cloud in the sky, Finnish apprehensions were balanced by hope. The crusade against "sub-culture [*Unkultur*] and Bolshevism" had begun, announced Falkenhorst to his Finnish-German army.[91] A few days later, as the attack of the bulk of the Finnish army commenced on the Ladoga front, Mannerheim proclaimed a holy war to "destroy the Bolshevik menace for all times."[92] There was something awe-inspiring and romantic about the great clash of arms. In Falkenhorst's headquarters in Rovaniemi, one excited officer waxed poetic as he sat down in the evening of June 29 to compose the German Army in Norway's invasion day report to the OKW: "On snow-covered tundras under the midnight sun, Mountain Corps Norway crossed the Russian border, broke through the Russian border fortifications, and forded the Titovka River."[93]

That was about as close to Murmansk as General Dietl's Mountain Corps Norway would ever come.

CHAPTER X

Epilogue: Mining the Precious Nickel, 1941–1944

FOR fifteen months, the nickel deposit in Petsamo had drawn three great powers into a diplomatic contest, a contest which had afforded Finland an opportunity to resist heavy Soviet pressure and gain a precarious security in the form of German protection. The price which Finland eventually had to pay for that security was active involvement as a cobelligerent of Germany in the war against the Soviet Union. The outbreak of that war terminated the diplomatic tug of war over the Petsamo nickel, and during the ensuing three years the Petsamo question was to be a purely economic one. Located in that part of Finland which during the war was under German military control, the Petsamo area would be overrun by the Red Army in the fall of 1944 and subsequently annexed by the Soviet Union. June, 1941, therefore, in effect marked the end of the Petsamo question as a Finnish problem. Henceforth, for a little over three years, it was to be a German problem.

Paragraph 12 of the 1934 contract with Mond Nickel entitled the Finnish government to confiscate the Kolosjoki mine and all of its property in the event of Finland's becoming involved in a war. It was further provided that the property would be restored to Mond Nickel when the emergency situation was over, and the duration of the contract would be extended commensurately.[1] On August 5, 1941, the Finnish government decided to invoke this clause in the contract. The same day, the Petsamo Nickel Company was notified that it had been placed under government jurisdiction.

Its affairs would henceforth be handled by a government-appointed administrative commission headed by the minister of trade and industry, Väinö Tanner. Rounding out the three-man commission were Petsamo Nickel's own veteran directors, Dr. Söderhjelm and Dr. Ramsay.[2]

On August 16, the entire output of the Kolosjoki nickel mine was committed to Germany under the provisions of a new credit agreement between I.G. Farbenindustrie and Petsamo Nickel.[3] During the brief negotiations in Helsinki, the question of the mining concession itself was not raised by I.G. Farbenindustrie's spokesmen, Paul Haefliger and Dr. G. Frank-Fahle. At the time there seemed to be no urgent need to tamper with the existing arrangements.[4] The important thing was to secure the nickel production for Germany as quickly as possible, and to raise the concession issue in that connection might well have a retarding influence on the business at hand.

But the Germans were in fact strongly inclined to take advantage of their political and military position to acquire possession of the legal rights to the concession as well. During a quick visit to Stockholm, Minister Schnurre discussed the question with Fieandt and discovered that a certain amount of resistance could be expected among government officials in Helsinki. The Finns, he learned, were not anxious to aggravate further their already strained relations with Great Britain and the United States by going beyond the measures already taken. They were entitled to confiscate the concession for the duration of the war, but to cancel it would be a clear violation of the rights of the Anglo-Canadian trust. Nevertheless, at a meeting in Berlin on October 7, Schnurre recommended that Germany request the transfer of the Petsamo concession to a joint Finnish-German company controlled by German interests. The German industrial syndicate composed of I.G. Farbenindustrie, Krupp, and Metallgesellschaft would provide 70 per cent of the company's capital and exercise a commensurate influence over its operations. This new company, in turn, would replace Petsamo Nickel in the agreements between that firm and I.G. Farbenindustrie. In effect, the latter company would control both ends of the operation—the Finnish as well as the German. Even so, Schnurre optimistically thought that the Finns would welcome such an arrangement for political reasons, since it would strengthen

Finland's good relations with Germany and have the advantage of manifesting the solidarity between the two states to the outside world.[5]

Schnurre could hardly have been more mistaken. What the Finns above all wished to avoid was a clear manifestation of solidarity with Germany. They claimed that theirs was a separate war, provoked by the Soviet Union, and that they were merely cobelligerents of Germany by an accident of circumstances. They meant to do whatever they could to persuade the Allied world that this myth was reality. Collaboration with Germany in practice was one thing, but to enshrine it in legal documents was quite another.

Schnurre was to discover the error of his assumption when he went to Helsinki in late October accompanied by Counselor Ludwig of the Ministry of Economics. They brought with them the drafts of a series of agreements which they hoped to conclude with the Finnish government, including a "Draft of a Statute for Nordland Nickel O.Y.,"[6] a "Standing Orders for the Board of Directors of Nordland Nickel O.Y.,"[7] and a draft of a "Syndicate Agreement regarding Nordland Nickel O.Y."[8] These documents called for sweeping Finnish concessions. The Germans expected to have two out of three members of the proposed executive board and four out of six members of the board of directors. With 70 per cent or more of the share capital, they would also control the annual shareholders' meeting, where each share was worth one vote. Furthermore, the draft agreements did not limit the rights of the proposed new company to Petsamo, but entitled it to exploit "nickel ore deposits located in Finland." The Germans also intended to obtain the concession for a fifty-year period, with an option to renew it for another fifty years.[9] About the only concession which the Germans seemed willing to make to the Finns was to let the company's name be rendered in Finnish translation, presumably Pohjoismaan Nikkeli O.Y. That, however, could not conceal the fact that the Germans were demanding more of the Finns than the Russians had in 1940. That they were no more successful than the Russians had been should not have surprised them.

When Schnurre and Ludwig presented their draft agreements to the Finnish leaders in late October, they met with a frustrating reception. Even though Schnurre raised the proposed German share of the company's capital to 80 per cent, he found President Ryti very accommodating. The president expressed immediate agreement in principle and said that he would have Fieandt work out the details. Fieandt refused to do so, and Schnurre went back to Ryti and again found him favorably disposed. Yet no action resulted. Schnurre complained to the Foreign Ministry in Berlin that the resistance seemed to come from Finnish political and industrial circles, and he singled out Minister Tanner as the chief obstacle.[10] Tanner was of the opinion that it would be best to leave the administration of the mine in Finnish hands till the end of the war. He alleged that "broad circles of the Finnish people" would be "displeased" if Germany were to take advantage of the existing situation of wartime emergency to win control of a Finnish enterprise, and he was nasty enough to point out that the Finns would be quick to compare Germany's behavior with the Soviet Union's behavior in the Petsamo question.[11]

Foreign Minister Witting used precisely the same argument in a conversation with Blücher on November 14, adding that an agreement such as Germany proposed would provide grist for the British propaganda mill. He reminded Blücher that the Finns had taken over the management of the mine as trustees, and they had assured Germany of 90 per cent of its output. He had been under the impression, he said, that this arrangement was perfectly satisfactory to I.G. Farbenindustrie.[12]

The directors of I.G. Farbenindustrie were not satisfied, however. Since the early 1930's, they had been engaged in an intensive campaign to free themselves from their dependence on International Nickel by getting control of a European source of nickel ore supplies. They were not about to let the Petsamo concession slip through their fingers if there was a way of preventing it. What they had in mind was stated with all possible clarity in a memorandum dated October 17, in which the proposed Nordland Nickel O.Y. was discussed: "The financing of the new company must be kept within the limits of sound economics, since it must be capable of competing with Inco-Mond after the war."[13] A month later, in a preface to another draft of a concession agreement, I.G. Farbenindustrie argued that it had always been the policy of the Anglo-Canadian trust to maintain a world monopoly of nickel production.

Specifically, Mond Nickel had been intent on preventing outsiders from "acquiring a base for themselves on the nickel market with the aid of the Petsamo deposit." The political situation had now changed so completely, however, that this monopoly could be broken.[14]

I.G. Farbenindustrie failed to achieve its goal. Neither the company's own representatives nor the German Foreign Ministry could break down the passive resistance of the Finns in the concession matter. It seemed as if the Germans were falling victims to the very strategy of procrastination which they had prescribed for the Finns when the Russians were pressing their demands in 1940–41. In December, 1941, Haefliger informed officials of the Ministry of Economics that negotiations between his firm and the Finnish government were still going on, but he was unable to predict the outcome.[15] Even as Haefliger spoke, however, the Foreign Ministry received a cable from Blücher, who had learned from a reliable source that the Finnish decision had been made: Kivimäki had already received instructions to inform the German government that Finland rejected the German request for a transfer of the mining concession to the proposed German-Finnish company.[16]

Shortly thereafter the Ministry of Economics deserted the cause of I.G. Farbenindustrie. A memorandum circulated in the ministry in early January, 1942, suggested that an intervention in the concession matter by the German government could have nothing but undesirable consequences. So long as it was obviously important to the Finnish government that the nickel question be handled as an ordinary business relationship between two private companies, and so long as the Finns were satisfied with the technical performance of I.G. Farbenindustrie, it seemed wise to let sleeping dogs lie.[17] The only thing that really mattered, after all, was to obtain the nickel ore so desperately needed for the German war industry, and Germany was already in a position to exercise effective control over the exploitation of the Kolosjoki mine. The long-range business interests of I.G. Farbenindustrie would have to be put on ice for the duration of the wartime emergency. Its immediate assignment was to produce nickel for the German steel mills.

The story of how the Petsamo nickel was extracted, transported, and refined during the Continuation War is the story of a truly improbable mining venture. Undertaken in an active theater of war, it was pursued to the bitter end in spite of a host of unfavorable conditions. The bulging files of the German Ministry of Economics and I.G. Farbenindustrie present a picture of constant frustration, of high hopes regularly dashed. There were perennial construction delays, unending transportation problems, unfulfilled production goals, a constant labor shortage, loaded ore vessels lost at sea, and brainstorming sessions without number in Berlin to seek solutions to the crises which cropped up with uncanny regularity. From a business point of view, the venture was an unqualified disaster. The combined expenditures of the German government and I.G. Farbenindustrie must have made the nickel worth its weight in gold. Only a national emergency could justify such a venture, and it was indeed such an emergency. According to a report prepared in July, 1944, by an official of the Ministry of Armaments and War Production, Germany depended at that time on Petsamo for up to 80 per cent of its nickel requirements. If that source were to be lost, the reopening of long abandoned German mines, which would take considerable time to accomplish, would still provide no more than 50 per cent of the nickel required for the war effort.[18]

As the war against the Soviet Union got underway in the summer of 1941, few of these problems were anticipated. Taking into account the "barren nature of the land and the absence of communications" in the Petsamo area, a spokesman for I.G. Farbenindustrie nonetheless advised the Ministry of Economics on July 3 that the smelting plant at Kolosjoki would be ready for production of nickel matte by the end of the year with an initial capacity of 10,000 metric tons annually.[19] Two weeks later, Haefliger told General Hermann von Hanneken, under state secretary in the Ministry of Economics, that the Jäniskoski power station would be able to supply electric power at half of its planned capacity by autumn, enough to operate one of the two electric furnaces in the Kolosjoki smelting plant. The second furnace would start up in March, 1942, when the power station would reach full capacity. Haefliger also indicated that the ore body at Kaulatunturi was much richer than previously believed. He was about to lead a group of experts to Petsamo in the near future for another look at the mine, he added, and he offered to investigate the Soviet nickel ore deposits on the Kola Peninsula while he was in the vicinity.[20] The offer was accepted "in principle," but he was advised to wait until the combat activities in the area were over.[21]

Almost at once difficulties cropped up, setting the pattern for the future. A military dispatch from Kolosjoki in early July reported that most of the construction and mine workers in Petsamo had been drafted by the Finnish army on June 22 and that all work had stopped. The most alarming consequence of this was that the dam across the rapids at Jäniskoski could not be built before the onset of winter, when work on it must be suspended until spring, which in turn meant that the smelting furnaces in Kolosjoki would remain idle for another year.[22] Haefliger discovered for himself how serious the situation was when he visited Helsinki in mid-August. Ninety per cent of the labor force at Jäniskoski and Kolosjoki had been drafted, he was told by officials of Petsamo Nickel, who hoped to obtain six hundred Russian prisoners of war as replacements. Haefliger's most optimistic estimate now was that one smelting furnace might go into operation by March 1, 1942.[23]

Even that proved to be an overly optimistic estimate. Re-scheduled for June, 1942, the starting up of smelting furnace number one had to be postponed again when Outokumpu failed to deliver seventy tons of copper for the power cables.[24] The copper was eventually supplied by Germany, the cables were strung, and on July 24 the time-consuming process of heating up the first furnace was begun.[25] In late August, a full year behind schedule, the production of nickel matte at Kolosjoki was finally begun.[26] But again trouble intervened to force still another delay. The Finnish engineers, unaccustomed to working the furnace, caused extensive damage to it and had to shut it down for repairs.[27] Restarted in mid-November, the furnace promptly broke down again and did not resume operations until Christmas, slowly working up to its capacity.[28]

The Germans were exasperated. Spokesmen for I.G. Farben-industrie blamed the failure of the furnace squarely on Petsamo Nickel, whose management and engineers allegedly had refused to listen to the advice proffered by German experts. I.G. Farben-industrie insisted on taking a direct hand in the technical operations at Kolosjoki, but the Ministry of Economics cautioned restraint and tact lest "the well-known national pride of the Finns" be offended. Haefliger nevertheless spoke his mind rather plainly at a meeting with Petsamo Nickel's managing director, Baron Wrede, in Berlin on November 24. He went through a long list of German complaints, concluding with the declaration that the failure of the smelting furnace could not be dismissed as a simple case of growing pains. The problem was not the furnace, but the technical management, and it should be replaced, Haefliger suggested.[29]

The Finns were indeed offended. Dr. Ramsay was "astonished," according to a report from the German legation in Helsinki,[30] and Baron Wrede found Haefliger's criticism incomprehensible and unacceptable. It was apparent, he suggested, in a broadside which matched the offending German criticism, that Haefliger was expressing conclusions formed on the basis of simplified and distorted versions of isolated occurrences presumably reported without much understanding by I.G. Farbenindustrie's liaison man with Petsamo Nickel, Dr. Otto Buddenberg. Wrede alleged that Buddenberg was not getting on very well with his Finnish colleagues anyway, and he ought to be replaced.[31] Having disposed of the acrimonious formalities which the situation seemed to call for, however, the Finns quickly acted on the German complaints. Professor Otto Barth, a German national with a long-standing affiliation with Petsamo Nickel, was removed from his post as technical manager of the Kolosjoki smelting plant on the grounds of incompetence. Although his theoretical knowledge of the science of metallurgy was generally recognized, he lacked—according to his many German critics—the necessary practical experience. His place was taken by Dr. W. Schubardt, an I.G. Farbenindustrie engineer.[32] Shortly thereafter the production of nickel matte at Kolosjoki was finally begun in earnest. In February, 1943, I.G. Farbenindustrie began to include nickel matte in its monthly production statistics.[33]

The Germans had every reason to be exasperated. Except for the smelting plant, everything was ready for production at Kolosjoki, but so long as the furnaces remained idle or unfinished, production could not proceed. Ore excavation had been started as early as December, 1940, and the crusher was ready to receive it the following year. The Germans had expected an annual output of 10,000 tons of nickel matte by the end of 1941, yet they had to wait until February, 1943, for the production to reach half of capacity, and another six months before full capacity was finally achieved. While they were waiting, they had shipped some 11,000

tons of raw ore to Hamburg for reduction to nickel matte by
Norddeutsche Affinerie and to nickel by I.G. Farbenindustrie's
Oppau Works. But this was little more than an experiment, intended to discover the exact mineral properties of the Kolosjoki
ore and to learn how best to treat it.[34] The remainder of the ore
produced during the more than two years since excavation began
was stored in Kolosjoki, where the ore dump by January, 1943,
contained more than 20,000 tons.[35] In 1942, the mining had
practically come to a standstill because the ore could not be
processed locally and transportation of raw ore all the way to
Germany would be a grossly uneconomical venture.

In view of the indispensable requirement of supplying nickel to
the German war industry, however, I.G. Farbenindustrie early in
1942 began to argue that the transportation of raw ore to Germany
would, nonetheless, have to be undertaken. The German government was asked to consider two possible routes: by sea via
Kirkenes and overland through north Finland to the Gulf of
Bothnia for transfer to ships there.[36] It was a drastic proposal,
regardless of which route might be selected. The distance by either
route to Hamburg or German Baltic ports was forbidding. While
the Baltic route was the shorter of the two, it involved trucking
from Kolosjoki along some 300 miles of the Arctic Ocean Highway—a poor road in the best of circumstances; reloading in
Rovaniemi for transport by rail to Kemi or Oulu; and finally reloading again both in Finnish and German ports. The other route
was much longer, but it involved only about 30 miles of overland
trucking to the docks in Kirkenes, where ore vessels could carry
the cargo directly to the plant in Hamburg. On the other hand,
the voyage from Kirkenes to Hamburg would be fraught with
danger of enemy interference and could lead to serious losses.

But the greatest problem involved in such a venture was to
obtain the necessary trucks, ships, auxiliary services, and manpower. In view of the fact that the raw ore was almost fifteen times
bulkier than its matte concentrate, the transportation apparatus
required would be commensurately larger also. The war in Russia
was placing increasingly heavy demands on German equipment,
including trucks, and Finland had none to spare. Ships were always
in short supply. Nevertheless, the growing urgency of replenishing
the dwindling German nickel reserves seemed to justify even the

most drastic measures, as officials of I.G. Farbenindustrie repeatedly pointed out to various government agencies in the course
of the summer of 1942.

It was Göring, in his capacity as commissioner of the Four
Year Plan, who finally cut the Gordian knot of bureaucratic red
tape. In a communication issued to all concerned through a
division of the Four Year Plan on September 9, the matter was
definitively settled: "The speedy transportation here of the ore
for the German armaments industry is of decisive importance for
the outcome of the war [*kriegsentscheidend*]." At the same time an
order for fifty-five 4.5-ton trucks scheduled for the armed forces
was summarily diverted to Petsamo Nickel for the ore transport.[37]
In December, a military transport unit consisting of thirty 3.5-ton
Citroen trucks was transferred by the OKW from Paris to Petsamo
on full-time assignment to the Kolosjoki to Kirkenes ore transport.[38]

At long last things were starting to move for the Germans in
Petsamo. In January, 1943, I.G. Farbenindustrie began to issue
regular monthly reports on the production and transportation
figures.[39] The following month, nickel matte was included in the
statistics for the first time, and the first trickle of it—90 tons—was
shipped to Germany.[40] By March, the statistics included 16,300
tons of ore and 470 tons of matte produced at Kolosjoki and
4,870 tons of ore and 473 tons of matte shipped to Germany for
processing.[41]

But once again difficulties sprang up. As the excavation of ore
went into higher gears, the ore storage dump at Kolosjoki continued
to swell. With the smelter still running only at half capacity, the
ore transport apparatus proved unequal to the task. Month after
month the ore dump grew bigger. At the end of September, 1943,
it held 44,214 tons waiting to be processed or moved to Kirkenes,
and another 5,995 tons had piled up in the port of Kirkenes waiting
to be loaded.[42] The problem was solved in part when the second
smelting furnace in Kolosjoki finally could start production in early
July;[43] now twice the previous amount of ore could be reduced to
matte locally, thereby easing the strain on the truck convoys.

The real bottleneck, however, was Kirkenes. Its ore harbor,
built and owned by the Norwegian iron ore mining company A/S
Sydvaranger, had a monthly loading capacity of only 5,000 tons,
much less than required for the Petsamo transports. In April,

I.G. Farbenindustrie sent an urgent request to the Todt Organization in Norway to do everything possible to expand the loading
facilities in Kirkenes.[44] The request received instant response, and
within a month the Kirkenes ore harbor could handle 15,000 tons
monthly. By then, however, there was a new complication: the
Reich commissar for Norway and the commanding general in the
area decided that the temporarily idled A/S Sydvaranger should
resume operations, which meant that its iron ore transports would
soon compete for loading space with the nickel ore. The Todt
Organization proposed that a brand new ore harbor be constructed
for the Petsamo ore at Jakobsnes, located just across the fjord
from Kirkenes to the east.[45] Against the opposition of I.G. Farbenindustrie, whose officials were deeply discouraged by the prospect
of still more delays, the Jakobsnes project was authorized. Planned
to handle 15,000 tons a month, it was given top construction
priority. All the time and effort expended on the project in the
ensuing fifteen months were wasted, however. On September 6,
1944, the last of numerous progress reports noted that most of
the required equipment had arrived at Jakobsnes, the rest was on
the way, and everything would be assembled and ready for use on
schedule.[46] Two weeks later, Finland quit the war. Then came the
successful Russian invasion of the Petsamo area. Kirkenes was to
remain the transshipment port for Petsamo nickel ore till the end,
and it proved adequate for the task once the problems of the first
half of 1943 had been straightened out.

The loss of the S.S. "Bygdöy," which hit a mine in May, 1943,
and sank with 1,740 tons of nickel ore and 51 tons of matte, pointed
up the danger of the Kirkenes to Hamburg route and led to a
reconsideration of the Baltic route. Comparing the carrying capacity of the two routes if all the available trucks were to go to
either Kirkenes or Rovaniemi, the Ministry of Economics and
I.G. Farbenindustrie both determined, independently of each other,
that Kirkenes offered the more profitable alternative. The Ministry
of Economics concluded that losses at sea would have to exceed
35 per cent before Rovaniemi could be considered preferable to
Kirkenes. It was accordingly decided to continue using Kirkenes
as long as losses stayed within the 35 per cent range.[47] Rovaniemi
was to be used only for nickel matte transports, and roughly one-
third of all matte shipped to Germany in 1943 went by way of

Rovaniemi. Thereafter Kirkenes alone was used for all transports.[48]

By July of 1943, all of the various troubles which for two years had prevented the commencement of regular operations in Petsamo had finally been worked out. The two electric furnaces in the Kolosjoki smelter were both functioning smoothly, reducing the bulk of the ore to matte as it came out of the mine, and easing the great strain on the fleet of company and military trucks. Although the Germans never ceased their continuous and massive effort to expand the local smelting capacity for as long as they remained in Petsamo, none of their many plans and concrete preparations to that end could be translated into higher production figures in the short time left before the Germans were driven out. The production level reached by the Kolosjoki smelter in August, 1943, would remain remarkably stable through August, 1944, the last month of normal work at the mine.

But in the twenty months that the Petsamo nickel mine was an active producer for its German client, there was considerable cause for satisfaction. A total of 387,615 metric tons of nickel-copper ore was brought out of the mine during that period. Of that total, 289,520 tons were converted into matte in Kolosjoki, and 113,568 tons were shipped to Germany. The Finns received the grand total of 209 tons, and the remainder had to be left behind when the Russians came. The smelter produced 16,990 tons of nickel-copper matte, of which 15,661 tons were shipped to Germany. Finland's share amounted to 1,328 tons. The nickel content of the matte was roughly 55 per cent. (See Table 1 for production and transport statistics.)

Not all of the ore and matte shipped to Germany arrived in Hamburg. Mines and enemy attacks took their toll of the small ore vessels plying the treacherous waters around Norway's vast coastline, but the losses were surprisingly light, far short of the 35 per cent which the Ministry of Economics had established as the tolerance limit. The sinking of the S.S. "Westerwald," which had taken aboard the last shipment of 88.9 tons of matte in Kirkenes on October 19, 1944, was little more than a nuisance, a final insult delivered by the enemy.[49] Petsamo had already served its purpose by providing Germany with four-fifths of its nickel supplies in 1943 and 1944. According to a report submitted to Armaments and Munitions Minister Albert Speer by the Ministry of

TABLE 1

PRODUCTION IN PETSAMO AND TRANSPORTS TO GERMANY,
1943-44[50]

Year and month	Nickel ore (in metric tons)		Nickel matte (in metric tons)	
	Total production	Sent to Germany	Total production	Sent to Germany
1943				
January	4,224	900	78.20	—
February	12,317	—	411.30	90.00
March	16,300	4,870	470.50	473.40
April	12,858	3,440	370.00	449.90
May	16,261	8,550	487.80	378.00
June	20,913	9,375	365.00	402.73
July	22,844	4,845	766.70	328.64
August	26,573	10,067	1,000.43	697.35
September	26,378	11,280	910.27	1,183.37
October	22,360	8,735	1,127.59	949.92
November	19,721	6,452	903.18	964.87
December	21,748	4,647	1,041.19	489.01
1944				
January	18,598	2,000	911.38	1,153.58
February	17,754	4,970	1,013.18	594.78
March	14,207	6,080	1,084.61	1,448.47
April	18,842	7,631	1,113.49	615.77
May	18,794	2,500	1,046.75	1,396.84
June	21,664	2,575	1,087.05	1,011.39
July	25,213	5,523	1,579.93	1,196.42
August	24,639	9,128	1,080.75	1,542.49
September	5,407	—	140.48	205.29
October	—	—	—	88.90
Totals 1943-44:	387,615	113,568	16,989.78	15,661.12

Economics, Germany's stockpile of nickel at the end of August, 1944, plus stepped-up domestic mining efforts, would meet the demands of industry until June 1, 1946.[51]

The judgment of the German military authorities, first made in August, 1940, had been vindicated: the Petsamo nickel mine had indeed been indispensable to the German war industry. For the

German Army in Norway—as well as for the Army of Lapland, which assumed jurisdiction in north Finland in January, 1942—the defense of the nickel area held highest priority at all times. In March, 1942, when Hitler feared that the Allied powers might attempt to open a second front in Europe to relieve the pressure on the Soviet Union, he concluded that "the nickel mines in north Finland, which are vitally important for Germany, present what for us is the most dangerous and therefore the most probable enemy target."[52] His constant concern was reflected again in his Directive No. 44, issued on July 21, 1942, and in Directive No. 50, of September 28, 1943. In both, the defense of the Petsamo nickel area was particularly stressed. In the former, Hitler expressed the conviction that the outcome of the war might rest on whether Germany could hold the nickel area.[53]

Until the area was lost to the Russian attackers, this concern was also reflected in the extreme measures taken to protect the facilities of Petsamo Nickel against Soviet air raids. The area reputedly had stronger anti-aircraft defenses than "any other spot on the eastern front."[54] And efforts were made to place as many of the Kolosjoki facilities as possible underground. At Jäniskoski, the power house was provided with a massive overhead cover of reinforced concrete, a major construction job which, ironically, was completed just as Finland was about to quit the war and the facilities served by the power station were being idled by the total evacuation of Finnish personnel.[55] Like the Jakobsnes ore harbor, the Jäniskoski air raid bunker was an exercise in futility.

Finland's exit from the war came as no great surprise to the Germans, who knew that the Finns had considered two sets of Soviet peace terms between February and April, 1944, and that Paasikivi had flown to Moscow on one occasion to discuss the terms. After that the Germans no longer considered the Finns to be reliable allies, and they doubted that the Finns would have the ability—even if they should prove to have the will—to withstand a major Soviet assault on their main front. That assault came on June 10, after the Finnish front on the Karelian Isthmus had been softened up by air strikes and massive artillery shelling. The artillery barrage may have been the most concentrated in the history of war: reportedly the Russians had lined up 300 to 400 guns per kilometer of front. Within a week, the Russians had broken through the Finns' first and second lines of defense, and Viipuri fell on June 21. By the middle of July, the front was finally stabilized, largely because the Russians pulled out their best units and transferred their complete attention to the task of driving the main German forces back into Germany. But it was clear that the Russians could finish off Finland whenever they chose to do so, and the Finns quickly made the necessary moves to get out of the war while they could still do so of their own volition. On August 4, Marshal Mannerheim succeeded Ryti as president on the strength of a unanimous parliamentary vote, and it seemed clear that the special assignment of the man who had led the nation's forces in war would be to lead the nation out of that war. On August 25, the Soviet government was asked to receive a Finnish peace delegation. The Russians agreed, provided the Finns would break off relations with Germany and order all German troops out of Finland by September 15. Finland accepted these preconditions on September 2. On September 19, the Soviet-Finnish armistice agreement was signed in Moscow.[56]

On September 4, Dr. Schubardt reported from Kolosjoki to I.G. Farbenindustrie's office in Berlin that the Finns had started to evacuate all women and children from the area, and that the evacuation of the entire supervisory staff and labor force of Petsamo Nickel would follow within the week. All mining and smelting operations had been halted. Schubardt requested the immediate dispatch to Petsamo of more than one thousand replacements from Germany, including engineers, work foremen, skilled workers, and manual labor. He would try, he said, to keep the smelting furnaces from cooling down, so that matte production could be resumed as soon as the necessary manpower arrived.[57] He was advised that the continued production of nickel matte and its immediate shipment to Germany had top priority; whether any other activities could be resumed depended entirely on the availability of manpower.[58]

It would be difficult to imagine a more inauspicious time and place for mounting the sort of effort suggested by Schubardt. The Petsamo mine, abandoned by its owners, stripped of its labor force, and located in a theater of war which was momentarily expected to see vigorous combat, was not a likely prospect for a long and productive life. Yet Hitler again decided that every effort must be made to exploit the mine. Urgent directives to that effect were given on September 5 to the Ministry of Economics and the Ministry of Armaments and Munitions. Minister Speer at once dispatched ten skilled craftsmen by air to Kolosjoki to assist Schubardt in his attempt to keep the furnaces warm. Another forty men were to be sent as soon as possible to run the smelting plant, and it was hoped that the necessary manual labor could be obtained from the local army units until regular mining workers could be sent from Germany. The Todt Organization was advised to prepare to take over the Jäniskoski power station from the Finns, and the local army headquarters was asked to lend its full support to the task of transporting the remaining ore and matte from Kolosjoki to Kirkenes.[59] By September 8, a company of 150 miners stood ready to be flown to Petsamo, when Hitler suddenly decided to suspend all preparations for five days in view of new developments at the front.[60]

Not until September 18 did Hitler announce his decision that operations at the Kolosjoki mine would be continued.[61] The responsible governmental and military authorities were alerted to prepare for the transport to Petsamo of the skilled labor force which had been assembled during the previous ten days. Only the forty smelter workers actually were sent on their way, and they never reached Petsamo. The only ones to get there were the ten men flown there earlier on the orders of Speer, and the I.G. Farbenindustrie engineer who had been appointed head of the ore mining.[62] On October 11, I.G. Farbenindustrie was informed by the government that recent developments in the Petsamo area had made it impossible to assign more manpower to the mining project. Personnel already en route would be recalled, and all scheduled deliveries would be stopped.[63] The same day, the Department of War Economy in the OKW inquired of the Mining Section of the Ministry of Economics whether the Petsamo nickel works ought to be destroyed in the event of a German military withdrawal from the area. An affirmative reply was given the following day,[64] and on October 13 the OKW issued the following order to the Twentieth Mountain Army in Finland: "With the concurrence of the appropriate government department, the destruction of the mine, the smelter, and the power plant is considered necessary to the extent consistent with the military situation. The preparatory measures must be so conducted that production can continue until the last moment."[65]

It was a superfluous order. The expected Russian attack against the Petsamo area had commenced on October 7 and was making spectacular progress. On the 10th, as Russian units crossed the Arctic Ocean Highway to the east of Kolosjoki, the commanding general of the Twentieth Mountain Army ordered the nickel works demolished.[66] The job was carried out with the greatest thoroughness. The OKW was informed that in order to put the mine back in production, all facilities would have to be constructed from scratch.[67] In one day the work of ten years had been wiped out.

REFERENCE MATTER

Notes

Abbreviated titles of works frequently cited in the notes:
Blue-White Book II = Finland Reveals Her Secret Documents on Soviet Policy, March 1940–June 1941.
DGFP = Documents on German Foreign Policy 1918–1945, Series D.
FRUS = Foreign Relations of the United States, Diplomatic Papers.
TMWC = Trial of the Major War Criminals before the International Military Tribunal, Nuremberg.

CHAPTER I

1. For the text of the treaty, see John H. Wuorinen, *A History of Finland* (New York & London, 1965), pp. 485–91.
2. J. O. Söderhjelm, "Nickeldiplomati," *Hufvudstadsbladet,* November 2, 1966.
3. John F. Thompson and Norman Beasley, *For the Years to Come: A Story of International Nickel of Canada* (New York & Toronto, 1960), p. 254.
4. J. O. Söderhjelm, letter to the author, November 28, 1966. A German translation of the contract between the Finnish government and Mond Nickel is found in the files of the German Ministry of Economics, Section II Bg., *Akten betreffend Nachrichten über das Berg-, Hütten- und Salinenwesen in Finnland,* A.XII.1.152, vol. 2, part 3, July 1941–January 1943, T–84/99/1393067–81.
5. Thompson and Beasley, *For the Years to Come,* p. 256.
6. *Ibid.* For additional information on the development of the Petsamo Nickel Company and its facilities, see the technical articles by Paavo Haapala, K. Hanson, P. Ensiö, and Walter Nordin in *Vuoriteol- lisuus/Bergshanteringen,* Nos. 1–2 (1945), and Juho Kusti Paasikivi, *President Paasikivis minnen,* II, *Mellankrigstiden: Som sändebud i Moskva* (Helsinki, 1959), p. 164 (hereafter referred to as *Minnen,* II). "The Role Played by the Mond Nickel Company in the Petsamo

205

Venture," 8 pp., April 7, 1967, was generously prepared for the author's use by Mr. Frank B. Howard-White of International Nickel Ltd., Thames House, Millbank, London. A German translation of the contract of March 4, 1938, whereby the Finnish government granted the Petsamo Nickel Company the right to develop and use the hydroelectric power of the Jäniskoski Rapids, is found in the files of the Ministry of Economics cited in n. 4, above, T–84/99/1393104–110.

7. See, for instance, the threatening reference to Finland in a speech by Andrei A. Zhdanov, Leningrad Party Secretary, on November 29, 1936, quoted in Jane Degras, ed., *Soviet Documents on Foreign Policy,* III, *1933–1941* (London, New York, & Toronto, 1953), p. 226.

8. The best accounts of these proposals and of the discussions they precipitated are found in Väinö Tanner, *The Winter War: Finland against Russia, 1939–1940* (Stanford, 1957), pp. 3–16 (translated from the Finnish, *Olin ulkoministerinä talvisodan aikana* [Helsinki, 1950]); and Max Jakobson, *The Diplomacy of the Winter War: An Account of the Russo-Finnish War, 1939–1940* (Cambridge, 1961), pp. 7–65, *passim.* See also John H. Wuorinen, ed., *Finland and World War II, 1939–1944* (New York, 1948), pp. 44–47.

9. Juho Kusti Paasikivi, *President J. K. Paasikivis minnen 1939–1940* (Helsinki, 1958), p. 39 (hereafter referred to as *Minnen,* I).

10. *Ibid.,* p. 41.

11. *Ibid.,* pp. 47, 52–53.

12. *Ibid.,* p. 58, and Tanner, *The Winter War,* p. 41.

13. Paasikivi, *Minnen,* I, p. 60.

14. *Ibid.,* p. 63.

15. *Ibid.,* pp. 66, 76. The political parties, whose views were solicited by the government, tended to agree that the Petsamo was expendable provided its cession would save the Karelian Isthmus for Finland. Only Foreign Minister Eljas Erkko demurred. See Tanner, *The Winter War,* pp. 53–54, 58.

16. Paasikivi, *Minnen,* I, p. 74. See also Tanner, *The Winter War,* p. 66

17. For excellent accounts of the diplomacy of the Winter War and its preliminaries, see Jakobson, *The Diplomacy of the Winter War,* and Tanner, *The Winter War.*

18. The official British account of the Anglo-French strategic deliberations and plans involving Scandinavia during the Winter War is J. R. M. Butler, *Grand Strategy,* II, *September 1939–June 1941* (London, 1957), pp. 91–150. See also Thomas K. Derry, *The Campaign in Norway* (London, 1952).

19. Gustaf Mannerheim, *Minnen,* II, *1931–1946* (Helsinki, 1952), pp. 124, 127–29, 136–38, and Erik Heinrichs, *Mannerheimgestalten,* II, *Marskalken av Finland* (Helsinki, 1959), pp. 115, 127–28.

20. Mannerheim, *Minnen,* II, p. 152. Mannerheim did not describe how the Petsamo area was lost, only at what point the Finns dug in and halted the Soviet advance.

21. Paasikivi, *Minnen,* I, pp. 182–83, 186. An offer to evacuate the Petsamo area was included in the Soviet peace overture received in Helsinki on February 23, 1940. See Tanner, *The Winter War,* p. 172.
22. For the text of the Moscow treaty, see Wuorinen, *A History of Finland,* pp. 501–4, or *Blue-White Book II,* pp. 35–39.
23. Degras, ed., *Soviet Documents,* III, p. 445.
24. Paasikivi, *Minnen,* I, pp. 171, 172, 178, 187, 190.
25. Mannerheim, *Minnen,* II, p. 231.
26. Paasikivi, *Minnen,* I, p. 202.
27. See, for instance, telegram from Ambassador Steinhardt (Moscow) to Secretary Hull, March 9, 1940, in *FRUS,* 1940, I, p. 592.
28. J. O. Söderhjelm, letter to the author, November 28, 1966.
29. "Aufzeichnung über die Sitzung betr. Finnland am 28. März 1940. 18 Uhr," 2110H/456728–32 (also in *DGFP,* IX, No. 16), and memo by van Scherpenberg, e.o.W.V. 1130, April 2, 1940, 5382H/E361680–85.
30. *DGFP,* VIII, No. 411.
31. *Ibid.,* No. 429.
32. *Ibid.,* No. 471.
33. *Ibid.,* No. 418.
34. "Auszug aus einem Brief des Gesandten von Blücher, Helsinki, vom 11. Januar 1940 an VLR v. Grundherr," B18/B003362.
35. *DGFP,* VIII, No. 672.
36. *Ibid.*
37. *Ibid.,* No. 651.
38. Blücher to AA, No. 95, March 3, 1940, B19/B003510.
39. Wiehl to DGH, No. 144, March 21, 1940, 6434/H060041.
40. For the minutes of the conference, see above, n. 29.
41. *Ibid.*
42. Memo by van Scherpenberg, see above, n. 29.
43. Nr. e.o.W.V. 1129/40, 5382H/E361678–79. The document's number indicates that it was written on April 1 or 2, 1940.
44. Weizsäcker to DGH, No. 166, April 11, 1940, 6434/H060017–18.
45. Blücher to AA, No. 178, April 12, 1940, 6434/H059593.
46. Schnurre and Blücher to Ritter, No. 219, May 5, 1940, 6434/H059544–45.
47. Carl Clodius, "Sitzung des Handelspolitischen Ausschusses am 16. Mai 1940. Nr. 15. Streng vertraulich," W.H.A. 762, 5382H/E361672–73 and 77.
48. Memo by van Scherpenberg, e.o.W. 2711 g., May 21, 1940, 2110H/456735 (also in *DGFP,* IX, No. 293).
49. Blücher to AA, No. 185, April 18, 1940, 6434/H059580–81.
50. The authoritative German account of the Norwegian campaign is Walther Hubatsch, *"Weserübung." Die deutsche Besetzung von Dänemark und Norwegen 1940,* 2nd rev. ed. (Göttingen, 1960). See also Derry, *The Campaign in Norway.*

51. Blücher to AA, No. 187, April 19, 1940, 6434/H059577–78.
52. Memo by Weizsäcker, St.S. Nr. 323, April 26, 1940, 441/221272–73
53. Blücher to AA, No. 216, May 4, 1940, 6434/H059547.
54. Blücher to AA, No. 148, March 27, 1940, 6434/H059631–32.
55. Blücher to AA, No. 152, March 29, 1940, 6434/H059624–27.
56. Blücher to AA, No. 158, April 1, 1940, 6434/H059616–18.
57. Blücher to AA, No. 159, April 1, 1940, 6434/H059614–15.
58. On April 6, for instance, Blücher prudently advised the German Foreign Ministry to drop plans for a Finnish-German sports meet in Helsinki because of the prevailing "bitterness against Germany also in Finnish sports circles." Blücher to AA, No. 167, April 6, 1940, 6434/H059606.
59. Blücher to AA, No. 180, April 13, 1940, 6434/H059590–91.
60. Halem to DGH, No. 200, May 6, 1940, 6434/H059980.
61. See, for instance, the memo of May 20, 1940, by the Ministry of Economics' Wehrwirtschaftliche Forschungsstelle, "Änderungen der Versorgungslage Deutschlands und der Deutschland zugänglichen Neutralen infolge Besetzung Dänemarks, Norwegens, der Niederlande und Belgiens," geheim, T–84/143/1447304–307. Also indicative of Germany's intention to exploit its new economic opportunities in Scandinavia is a memo prepared by I.G. Farbenindustrie, Volkswirtschaftliche Abteilung, "Britische, belgische und amerikanische Kapitalbeteilungen an wichtigen Unternehmen der chemischen und Bergbauindustrie in Finnland," Vowi 4062, July 9, 1940, T–83/88/3460913–915. See also OKW/Wi VII f, "Die deutsche Aussenhandelslage, Nr. 7," July 6, 1940, T–77/101/825960–63, and "Die deutsche Aussenhandelslage, Nr. 8," August 2, 1940, T–77/101/825950–53.
62. Ritter to the Embassy in Moscow, the Legations in Copenhagen, Stockholm, Helsinki, Reval [Tallinn], Riga, and Kaunas [Kovno], and the Foreign Ministry's Representative to the Reich Commissar for the Occupied Norwegian Territories in Oslo, W.V. 1599/40, May 11, 1940, 441/221259–67 (the Moscow copy has been used here).
63. This is the clear implication of Blücher's telegram No. 300 of June 6, 1940 (6434/H059468–71): "Demand for Petsamo nickel not rejected any more."
64. Ritter to DGH, No. 221, May 21, 1940, 6434/H059956.
65. Blücher to AA, No. 268, May 25, 1940, 6434/H059497–98.
66. *Ibid*
67. Blücher to AA, No. 258, May 22, 1940, 6434/H059503.
68. Blücher to AA, No. 295, June 4, 1940, 6434/H059472–74.
69. Fieandt's statements were reported by Blücher in two lengthy telegrams to AA, No. 300, June 6, 1940, 6434/H059468–71, and No. 305, June 7, 1940, 6434/H059463–65.
70. The original sentence read: "Ryti also ready for a radical change of mind." Blücher toned it down in the account he cabled to AA, No. 300 (see above, n. 69).

71. Blücher to AA, No. 309, June 8, 1940, B19/B003608.
72. Blücher to AA, No. 316, June 10, 1940, 6434/H059456.
73. Gruppe XXI, Ia, Nr. 1216/40 geh., June 10, 1940, T–312/ 1033/9231314–16.
74. Blücher to AA, No. 320, June 11, 1940, 6434/H059454, and No. 321, June 11, 1940, 6434/H059451–52.
75. OKW, Heimatstab Nord, Ia, Tgb. Nr. 805/40 g.Kdos., June 11, 1940, T–312/989/9182057.
76. Buschenhagen to Major Neef, June 11, 1940, T–312/989/ 9182075
77. Gruppe XXI, Ia, lfd. Nr. 399, June 12, 1940, T–312/989/ 9182083.
78. Gruppe XXI, Ia, Nr. 1235/40 g.Kdos., June 12, 1940, T–312/ 989/9182056.
79. Gruppe XXI, Ia, Nr. 1237/40 g.Kdos., June 12, 1940, T–312/ 989/9182055.
80. Gruppe XXI, Ia (Dr.), 370/40 g.K., June 13, 1940, T–312/989/ 9182069.
81. Gruppe XXI, Ia, Nr. 1287/40 geh., June 15, 1940, T–312/989/ 9182054.
82. Blücher to AA, No. 329, June 14, 1940, 6434/H059433.
83. Gen.Kdo. Geb.Korps Norwegen, Ia, lfd. Nr. 117, July 22, 1940, T–312/989/9181853.
84. Gruppe XXI, Ia, "Morgenmeldung," July 24, 1940, T–312/989/ 9181850
85. Blücher to AA, No. 346, June 18, 1940, 6434/H059414–15.
86. Blücher to AA, No. 359, June 21, 1940, B19/B003625.
87. Blücher to AA, Tgb. Nr. 1821, "Innhalt: Demarche Sammlungs- partei und Gesinnung in Finnland," Abschrift Pol. VI 1868, June 25, 1940, L274/L085775–77.
88. Blücher to AA, No. 342, June 17, 1940, 6434/H059419–20.
89. Memo by Grundherr, Pol. VI 1709, June 18, 1940, B19/ B003613.
90. DNB, *Eigendienst,* Nr. 171, Mittags, June 19, 1940, p. 68, B19/B004123.
91. Blücher to AA, No. 352, June 20, 1940, 6434/H059408.
92. Memo by Weizsäcker, St.S. Nr. 453, June 19, 1940, B19/ B003615.
93. Fabricius to AA, No. 945, June 19, 1940, B19/B003614.
94. See, for instance, Schulenburg to AA, No. 1243, June 27, 1940, L274/L085770, and No. 1264, June 29, 1940, L274/L085769.
95. On this, see *Blue-White Book II* and Wuorinen, ed., *Finland and World War II,* pp. 81–91.
96. C. Leonard Lundin, *Finland in the Second World War* (Bloom- ington, 1957), pp. 13, 82–83.
97. See *DGFP,* X, No. 10, n. 2.
98. The account of I.G. Farbenindustrie's rise as a nickel producer

in the interwar period is based on two memoranda prepared by officers of the firm for the Ministry of Economics: Brendel and Schlecht, "Über die Aufnahme und Entwicklung der Nickelmetallgewinnung in der I.G.," January 29, 1942 (10 pp.), T–84/99/1392868–877, and Cl/Sch (presumably Cluss and Schlecht), "Notiz betreffend Nickel," December 12, 1941, T–84/99/1392777. See also F. B. Howard-White, *Nickel: An Historical Review* (Princeton & New York, 1963), pp. 187–88.

99. See the memo by Brendel and Schlecht (above, n. 98), p. 8, T–84/99/1392875.

100. Weber-Andreae diary, December 23, 1939, T–83/91/3465439.

101. *Ibid.*, April 1, 1940, T–83/91/3465739.

102. *Ibid.*, May 27, 1940, T–83/91/3465838.

103. *Ibid.*, June 15, 1940, T–83/91/3465899–901.

104. *Ibid.*, June 19, 1940, T–83/91/3465912.

105. See above, n. 99.

106. See, for instance, "Aktenvermerk" by Ritter, June 27, 1940, 4416H/E83850.

107. Weizsäcker to the Embassy in Moscow, No. 1088, June 27, 1940, B19/B003628.

108. Blücher to AA, No. 378, June 28, 1940, B19/B003630.

109. Schnurre to DGH, No. 292, June 29, 1940, 6434/H059882. The letter from Schnurre to Fieandt in its original incomplete form is microfilmed as 6509/H072850. The letter from Fieandt to Schnurre in its final form, as signed by Fieandt on July 24, 1940, is found in *DGFP*, X, No. 221.

110. Memo by Schnurre, W.V. 2458/40, July 1, 1940, 5382H/E361687–88 and –720 (also in *DGFP*, X, No. 74). The texts of the various agreements which comprised the trade treaty of June 29 have been filmed as 9208/H249624–76.

CHAPTER II

1. *Blue-White Book II*, No. 14.

2. Paasikivi, *Minnen*, II, p. 162.

3. DNB, *Eigendienst*, Nr. 125, Morgens, May 4, 1940, p. 2, L274/L085755.

4. On May 22, for instance, Blücher reported to the Foreign Ministry (No. 257, 6434/H059504) that his naval attaché had learned from a ranking officer in the Finnish General Staff that Russian officers on the Finnish-Soviet border commission had expressed to Finnish colleagues their fears of Germany and had "justified Russian measures in the Baltic area with that."

5. Paasikivi, *Minnen*, II, p. 164.

6. Arvi Korhonen, *Barbarossaplanen och Finland* (Tampere, 1963), p. 43.

7. *Blue-White Book II,* No. 14.

8. Memo from Witting to Blücher, "Inhalt: Petsamon Nikkeli OY, Abschrift, streng vertraulich," Tgb. Nr. 159 g., September 9, 1940, 6674/H090515–17.

9. Paasikivi, *Minnen,* II, p. 164.

10. *Blue-White Book II,* No. 15. For other accounts of the conversation, see Witting's memo of September 9, 1940 (above, n. 8); Blücher to AA, No. 376, June 28, 1940, 6509/H072849; *DGFP, X,* Nos. 62 and 77; *FRUS,* 1940, I, p. 332.

11. Anthony F. Upton, *Finland in Crisis, 1940–1941: A Study in Small-Power Politics* (Ithaca, 1965), p. 106.

12. *Ibid.*

13. *Ibid.,* p. 107.

14. See Butler, *Grand Strategy,* II, pp. 235–36. The official British account of the economic warfare and its methods is W. N. Medlicott, *The Economic Blockade,* I–II (London, 1952–59).

15. Paasikivi, *Minnen,* II, pp. 186–87.

16. Blücher to AA, No. 385, June 29, 1940, B19/B003633.

17. *DGFP, X,* No. 62.

18. Unsigned memo by Blücher, July 1, 1940, 6509/H072851–52, and Blücher to AA, No. 388, July 1, 1940, 4416H/E083851.

19. Below to AA, No. 1094, July 2, 1940 (designated "Militärattaché 592 g." for relay to OKW and OKH Attachégruppe), B19/B003636–37.

20. See, for instance, *DGFP, X,* No. 24.

21. Weizsäcker to the Embassy in Moscow, No. 1088, June 27, 1940, B19/B003628. See also Schnurre to DGH, No. 288, June 27, 1940, 6434/H059890.

22. *DGFP, X,* No. 77.

23. See *ibid.,* No. 182.

24. Ritter to the Embassy in Moscow, W.V. 2462/40 II, No. 1134, July 3, 1940, 4416H/E083852–53 (also in *DGFP, X,* No. 98).

25. Weizsäcker to "Bach", W.V. 2462/Ang. III, July 3, 1940, 4416H/E083854–55. Schulenburg's telegram of July 1 and Ritter's of July 3 were forwarded to DGH by Schnurre on July 4 (6434/H059873–74)

26. Upton, *Finland in Crisis,* p. 107, maintains that Germany, during the Berlin talks, "had asked for the concession herself and been refused." Neither part of that assertion is accurate.

27. Blücher to AA, No. 300, June 6, 1940, 6434/H059468–71.

28. *DGFP, IX,* No. 367.

29. *Ibid.,* X, No. 122.

30. Memo by Blücher (see above, n. 18).

31. Unsigned memo in Blücher's handwriting, July 1, 1940, 6509/H072975.

32. Blücher to AA, No. 388, July 1, 1940, 4416H/E083851.

33. See *DGFP, X,* Nos. 136, 182, 259.

34. There is no record of this conversation in *Blue-White Book II,* only a brief sentence about it on p. 23. The conversation was described, however, in Witting's memo of September 9, 1940 (see above, n. 8), and in Blücher to AA, No. 396, July 4, 1940, 6509/H072941.

35. Schulenburg to AA, No. 1305, July 5, 1940, B19/B003640.

36. Schnurre to DGH, No. 307, July 6, 1940, 6434/H059866.

37. Blücher to AA, No. 403, July 8, 1940, 6509/H072974.

38. Blücher to AA, No. 396, July 4, 1940, 6509/H072941.

39. *DGFP,* X, No. 122.

40. See above, n. 38

41. Unsigned memo in Blücher's handwriting, July 8, 1940, 6509/H072942.

42. The original memo (W.V. 2550) has not been found, but it was probably identical with the draft telegram of the same date signed by Wiehl and intended for DGH, which Wiehl passed on to Ritter (see below, n. 45)

43. Unsigned memo addressed to Ritter, probably by Wiehl as indicated by his initial and annotations, July 8, 1940, 4416H/E083857.

44. 4416H/E083858.

45. Zu W.V. 2550, 4416H/E083859. This is the document published in *DGFP,* X, No. 136, with a wrong date, an assumed number, and a footnote indicating that the editors had not found the actual telegram. That telegram is in the files of DGH (see below, n. 46).

46. Wiehl to DGH, No. 312, July 10, 1940, 6434/H059861.

47. Blücher to AA, No. 416, July 11, 1940, 6509/H072937-38. The translation of this telegram published in *DGFP,* X, No. 150, is based on an imperfect copy.

48. *Blue-White Book II,* No. 19.

49. See above, n. 47.

50. Weizsäcker to the Embassy in Moscow, No. 1200, July 13, 1940, B19/B003645-46. See also *DGFP,* X, No. 150, n. 1.

51. Schnurre to DGH, No. 318, July 13, 1940, B19/B003647-48.

52. Blücher to AA, No. 435, July 19, 1940, 4416H/E083868-69.

53. Blücher to AA, No. 429, July 16, 1940, B19/B003652.

54. See above, n. 52.

55. Letter from the Reich Minister of Economics, signed by Dr. Bergemann, to Wiehl, V.Ld. 8/47602/40 II, November 9, 1940, 4416H/E083889-90.

56. *DGFP,* X, No. 182.

57. Draft telegram by Schnurre intended for the Embassy in Moscow, zu W.V. 2710/40 Ang. II, July 18, 1940, 4416H/E083870.

58. Draft telegram by Schnurre intended for DGH, zu W.V. 2710/40, 4416H/E083871-73.

59. Schnurre to DGH, No. 327, July 19, 1940, 4416H/E083866.

60. Blücher to AA, No. 445, July 23, 1940, 4416H/E083865. Regarding the negotiations, see also the memo by Brendel and Schlecht (above, chapter I, n. 98), pp. 9-10, T-84/99/1392876-77.

61. See *DGFP*, X, No. 221, and 6509/H072850.
62. *DGFP*, X, No. 221, n. 4.
63. See above, n. 8.
64. Schnurre to the Embassy in Moscow, No. 1280, July 24, 1940, 4416H/E083863.
65. Blücher to AA, No. 435, July 19, 1940, 6509/H072933–34.
66. Draft telegram by Weizsäcker intended for the Embassy in Moscow, W.V. 2832/40, July 26, 1940, B19/B003666–67.
67. *DGFP*, X, No. 259.
68. Blücher to AA, No. 436, July 19, 1940, 6434/H059350.
69. Blücher to AA, No. 443, July 23, 1940, 6434/H059339–40.
70. Blücher to AA, No. 465, July 29, 1940, 6434/H059324.
71. Blücher to AA, No. 448, July 24, 1940, 4416H/E083864.
72. *FRUS*, 1940, I, pp. 334–35.
73. *Ibid.*, 1939, I, pp. 793–820, and 1940, II, pp. 2–49; Butler, *Grand Strategy*, II, pp. 75–79; Cordell Hull, *The Memoirs of Cordell Hull*, I (New York, 1948), pp. 679–81, 690, 734–36.
74. *FRUS*, 1940, II, pp. 50–53; Medlicott, *Economic Blockade*, II, p. 29.
75. See *FRUS*, 1940, II, pp. 53–54; Butler, *Grand Strategy*, II, p. 235. All German diplomatic missions in Europe and in the United States, Panama, Uruguay, Argentina, Brazil, Chile, and Japan were sent a summary of the British regulations along with instructions for combatting them in a circular telegram from Ritter, No. 190, August 3, 1940, 6434/H059308 (the Helsinki copy). See also *DGFP*, X, No. 283.
76. See Blücher to AA, No. 471, August 1, 1940, 6434/H059318.
77. Blücher to AA, No. 470, August 1, 1940, 6434/H059319.
78. See Ritter's telegram (above, n. 75).
79. Blücher to AA, No. 484, August 7, 1940, 6434/H059305–07.
80. Blücher to AA, No. 491, August 9, 1940, 6434/H059296–98.
81. Blücher to AA, No. 536, August 28, 1940, 6434/H060524.
82. See Blücher to AA, No. 539, August 29, 1940, 6434/H060520. See also Korhonen, *Barbarossaplanen och Finland*, pp. 98–99.
83. Leitner to DGH, No. 464, September 7, 1940, 6434/H059710; Kramarz to AA, No. 473, September 9, 1940, 6434/H059700.
84. Blücher to AA, No. 475, August 3, 1940, 6434/H059315.
85. See above, n. 80.
86. *FRUS*, 1940, II, pp. 55–60.

CHAPTER III

1. Blücher to AA, No. 469, August 1, 1940, 4416H/E083876.
2. *DGFP*, X, No. 301.
3. *Ibid.*, XI, No. 26.
4. Blücher to AA, No. 483, August 6, 1940, B19/B003682.
5. See above, chapter II, n. 8.

6. Blücher to AA, No. 488, August 8, 1940, 4416H/E083875.
7. Söderhjelm, "Nickeldiplomati," *Hufvudstadsbladet,* November 2, 1966, and letter to the author, November 28, 1966.
8. Söderhjelm, "Nickeldiplomati," *Hufvudstadsbladet,* November 2, 1966.
9. On the activities of the SNS, see Upton, *Finland in Crisis,* pp. 98–132 *passim,* 169–70, and 200; *Blue-White Book II,* Nos. 22, 23, and 26; Paasikivi, *Minnen,* II, pp. 77–87 and 90–101.
10. Paasikivi, *Minnen,* II, p. 87.
11. *Ibid.,* p. 98.
12. *Ibid.,* p. 101.
13. August Rei, comp., *Nazi-Soviet Conspiracy and the Baltic States. Diplomatic Documents and Other Evidence* (London, 1948), p. 53.
14. *Ibid.*
15. Report by Kreve-Mickevičius taken from the records of the Lithuanian legation in Washington, quoted in House of Representatives, 83rd Cong., 2nd Sess., Select Committee on Communist Aggression, *Report of the Select Committee to Investigate Communist Aggression and the Forced Incorporation of the Baltic States into the U.S.S.R.* (Washington, 1954), III, pp. 341–42. See also House of Representatives, 83rd Cong., 2nd Sess., *House Reports,* XIII, *Special Reports of Select Committee on Communist Aggression,* No. 2684, Part 13, *Communist Takeover and Occupation of Lithuania* (Washington, 1954–55), p. 12.
16. Upton, *Finland in Crisis,* p. 130.
17. See *Blue-White Book II,* pp. 19–22 and Nos. 16, 29, 30, 31, and 34; Paasikivi, *Minnen,* II, pp. 106–30. See also *DGFP,* X, Nos. 62 and 223, and XI, Nos. 27, 31, and 136; memos by Weizsäcker, St.S. Nr. 509, July 2, 1940, B19/B003726, St.S. Nr. 687, September 11, 1940, B19/B003731–33, and St.S. Nr. 706, September 17, 1940, B19/B003746–47; memos by Grundherr, Pol.VI 2517, September 20, 1940, B19/B003752, and Pol.VI 2551, September 28, 1940, 2110H/456746; Below to AA, No. 1094, July 2, 1940, B19/B003636–37; Schulenburg to AA, No. 1305, July 5, 1940, B19/B003640; Woermann to DGH, No. 298, July 3, 1940, 6434/H059876, and No. 309, July 6, 1940, 6434/H059864; Rintelen to DGH, No. 305, July 5, 1940, 6434/ H059868, and No. 335, July 25, 1940, 6434/H059839; Blücher to AA, No. 403, July 8, 1940, 6509/H072974, and No. 544, September 3, 1940, 6434/H060515–17; political reports by Blücher to AA, Tgb. Nr. 153 g., September 4, 1940, 6674/H090508 (with appendix: "Vorschlag der Sovietunion," 6674/H090513–14, and "Gegenvorschlag Finnlands," 6674/H090509–12), and Tgb. Nr. 160 g., September 11, 1940, 6674/H090518 (with appendix: "Vorschlag Nr. 2 der Sovietunion, gegeben 4.9.40," 6674/H090522–24); DNB, *Eigendienst,* Nr. 209, July 26, 1940, Abends, p. 93, B19/B004121.
18. *Blue-White Book II,* No. 22. Blücher believed that Molotov, by forcing the resignation of Tanner, hoped to accomplish three things: the Finnish government would be undermined; Tanner would be po-

litically ruined; and the Social Democratic Party, by losing its most powerful figure, would be more vulnerable than before to Communist influences. Blücher to AA, Tgb. Nr. 2258, "Inhalt: Vorstoss Molotows gegen Minister Tanner," July 27, 1940, L274/L085823.

19. *Blue-White Book II,* pp. 18–19 and Nos. 18 and 23.

20. Blücher to AA, No. 437, July 19, 1940, 6434/H059348–49.

21. Blücher to AA, No. 467, July 29, 1940, 6434/H059321, and No. 515, August 15, 1940, 6434/H060555.

22. Mannerheim, *Minnen,* II, p. 248.

23. Paasikivi, *Minnen,* II, pp. 131–39.

24. Upton, *Finland in Crisis,* pp. 117, 123–24.

25. Blücher to AA, No. 342, June 17, 1940, 6434/H059419–20, and No. 361, June 21, 1940, 6434/H059401; memo by Grundherr, Pol.VI 1709, June 18, 1940, B19/B003613; DNB, *Eigendienst,* Nr. 171, June 19, 1940, Mittags, p. 68, B19/B004123.

26. Blücher to AA, No. 430, July 16, 1940, 6434/H059358–60.

27. Blücher to AA, No. 447, July 24, 1940, 6434/H059334; Wied to AA, No. 1210, July 24, 1940, B19/B003660; Schulenburg to AA, No. 1462, July 24, 1940, B19/B003662; DNB, *Eigendienst,* Nr. 206, July 24, Abends, p. 100, L274/L085801.

28. Weizsäcker to the Embassy in Moscow, No. 1292, July 26, 1940, B19/B003663; Weizsäcker to DGH, No. 338, July 26, 1940, 6434/H059835; Weizsäcker to the Legations in Stockholm (No. 821), Kaunas (No. 225), Riga (No. 306), and Tallinn (No. 266), July 26, 1940, B19/B003665.

29. *DGFP,* X, No. 331

30. Blücher to AA, No. 461, July 27, 1940, B19/B003671.

31. Zechlin to AA, No. 170, July 24, 1940, B19/B003659.

32. Memo to Po.VI, July 25, 1940, L274/L085811.

33. Memo to Woermann, Po.VI 2124, July 29, 1940, L274/L085820.

34. Frohwein to AA, No. 290, July 31, 1940, B19/B003672.

35. Frohwein to AA, No. 298, August 2, 1940, L274/L085833.

36. Zechlin to AA, No. 182, August 3, 1940, L274/L085843.

37. Zechlin to AA, No. 187, August 7, 1940, B19/B003686.

38. Blücher to AA, No. 486, August 8, 1940, 6434/H059303–04.

39. Blücher to AA, No. 493, August 9, 1940, 6434/H059292.

40. Blücher to AA, No. 514, August 15, 1940, 6434/H060557.

41. *FRUS,* 1940, I, p. 338.

42. *Ibid.,* p. 340.

43. Schulenburg to AA, No. [?], August 29, 1940, relayed by Woermann to DGH, No. 446, August 30, 1940, 6434/H059730.

44. *FRUS,* 1940, I, p. 337.

45. *Ibid,* p. 338.

46. *Ibid.*

47. *Ibid.,* p. 340.

48. Wied to AA, No. 1239, July 31, 1940, L274/L085825.

49. *DGFP,* X, No. 279.

50. Wied to AA, No. 1275, August 12, 1940, B19/B003702.

51. Telegram from Wied, relayed by Woermann to DGH, No. 401, August 18, 1940, 6434/H059776.

52. Blücher to AA, No. 398, July 4, 1940, 6434/H059378–81.

53. Blücher to AA, No. 461, July 27, 1940, B19/B003671.

54. Memo by Blücher, August 16, 1940, 6674/H090495–97, sent to AA as Tgb. Nr. 132 g., "Inhalt: Unterredung mit dem Minister-präsidenten," 6674/H090491–94. Excerpts were sent to AA in Nos. 521 (6434/H060545–46) and 522 (6434/H060543–44) on August 16, 1940.

55. The full text of Ryti's address was published in *Hufvudstads-bladet*, August 19, 1940. For excerpts, see *Blue-White Book II*, No. 25.

56. Upton, *Finland in Crisis*, p. 128.

57. Paasikivi, *Minnen*, II, p. 88.

58. *Ibid.*, pp. 88–89.

59. Memo by Woermann, Pol.VI 2124, July 29, 1940, L274/ L085820.

60. Memo by Weizsäcker, St.S. Nr. 619, August 3, 1940, B19/ B003678

61. *DGFP*, X, No. 341.

62. *Ibid.*, No. 280.

63. Franz Halder, *Kriegstagebuch*, ed. by Hans-Adolf Jacobsen, II (Stuttgart, 1963), p. 33.

64. *Ibid.*, p. 50.

65. The best account of this and subsequent Veltjens trips to Finland is found in Martti V. Terä, *Tienhaarassa. Syksyn 1940 tapahtumat Barbarossasuunnitelman taustaa vasten* (Helsinki, 1962). See also Korhonen, *Barbarossaplanen och Finland*, pp. 87–93; Mannerheim, *Minnen*, II, pp. 251–53; Heinrichs, *Mannerheimgestalten*, II, pp. 228–30; *DGFP*, X, Nos. 330 and 336. A large number of unpublished German records shed further light on the development of the arms transaction and related matters.

66. Korhonen, *Barbarossaplanen och Finland*, pp. 87–89.

67. Rainer von Fieandt, letter to the author, April 30, 1965, appendix 2; *DGFP*, X, No. 366.

68. Memo by Schnurre on conversation with Veltjens, August 23, 1940, B19/B003718–20.

69. See Blücher to AA, No. 539, August 29, 1940, 6434/H060520, and Leitner to DGH, No. 464, September 7, 1940, 6434/H059710.

70. See Korhonen, *Barbarossaplanen och Finland*, pp. 108–12.

71. B19/B003763, B19/B003764–65, and 6509/H072910.

72. Memo by Grundherr, Pol.VI 2892 g., September 20, 1940, B19/B003753–55; Weizsäcker to Ribbentrop via the Embassy in Rome, No. 1317, September 20, 1940, B19/B003756–58; *DGFP*, XI, No. 86

73. *DGFP*, XI, No. 139.

74. Carl Olof Frietsch, *Finlands ödesår 1939–1943* (Helsinki, 1945), p. 243.

75. Lundin, *Finland in the Second World War*, p. 84.
76. *Ibid.*, pp. 86–88. For comparison, see Frietsch, *Finlands ödesår*, pp. 243–45, 252–57, 277–80, and 299–304.
77. Frietsch, *Finlands ödesår*, pp. 244–45. His third alternative, he wrote in his book, was neutrality in cooperation with Sweden. He neglected to mention that this alternative was tried twice by the Finnish government, only to be vetoed by the Soviet Union each time. See *Blue-White Book II*, Nos. 3, 5, 6, 7, 50, 53, and 56.
78. One example of this was his vitriolic attack on those whom he called the "apostles of chauvinism," namely those Finns who, after the outbreak of the Continuation War in 1941, called for the incorporation of Soviet areas into a "Greater Finland." Frietsch condemned them in unmerciful terms and recounted how he had always opposed them and all their works, and had warned against their ideas in public speeches. To prove his point he cited a speech made in Porvoo in November, 1941 (see *Finlands ödesår*, pp. 371–82). The press quoted him otherwise at the time, however. Among other things, he told his Porvoo audience the following: Finland was invading Soviet Karelia "in order to secure for our country a frontier which reflects more fully than any frontier we have ever had the demand for strategic security." Quoted by Torsten G. Aminoff, "Opinionerna under fortsättningskriget. Ett utkast," *Appell*, XIII:28 (September 5, 1957), p. 8. Frietsch, it seems, possessed certain chameleonic qualities.
79. See *FRUS*, 1940, I, p. 611.
80. See Butler, *Grand Strategy*, II, pp. 267–94. The best account of the German invasion plan is Karl Klee, *Das Unternehmen "Seelöwe." Die geplante deutsche Landung in England 1940* (Göttingen, 1958), which should be read in conjunction with Karl Klee, ed., *Dokumente zum Unternehmen "Seelöwe." Die geplante deutsche Landung in England 1940* (Göttingen, 1959). See also Peter Fleming, *Operation Sea Lion: The Projected Invasion of England in 1940—An Account of the German Preparations and the British Countermeasures* (New York, 1957).
81. *DGFP*, X, No. 280.
82. *Ibid.*, No. 297.
83. *Ibid.*, No. 325.
84. *Ibid.*, No. 330.
85. Halder, *Kriegstagebuch*, II, p. 62.
86. See *DGFP*, X, No. 330, n. 2.
87. Wi.Rü.Amt/Wi., "Bedeutung Finnlands für die deutsche Wehrwirtschaft," August 19, 1940, T–312/1010/9205486–87.
88. Halder, *Kriegstagebuch*, II, p. 78.
89. *Ibid.*, p. 71.
90. AOK 20, Ia, *Kriegstagebuch Nr. 4*, entries for August 12, 13, and 14, 1940, T–312/989/9181540.
91. OKW, WFSt/Abt. L Nr. 33230/40 g.K.Chefs., *"Betr.:* Norwegen," August 16, 1940, T–312/1010/9205478–79.

92. Letter from Warlimont to Buschenhagen, OKW, Chef der Abt. Landesverteidigung, Nr. 00646/40 g.K., August 20, 1940, T–312/1010/9205467–68.

93. "Mil.Geo.-Stellungnahme zu der Frage Wie und wo könnte Russland das nördliche Norwegen abschneiden?" August 23, 1940, T–312/1010/9205480.

94. Gruppe XXI/Ia g.K.Chefs., Aktennotiz, "Aufstellung eines Operationsentwurfes 'Renntier'," August 23, 1940, T–312/1010/9205481. The document carried the annotation that it had been translated from Norwegian, a device used early in the planning stage to mislead uninitiated readers by implying that such documents came from the captured archives of the Norwegian General Staff.

95. Gruppe XXI, Aktennotiz, "Betr. Renntier," Chefs., August 23, 1940, T–312/1010/9205482–83

96. See also Earl F. Ziemke, *The German Northern Theater of Operations, 1940–1945* (Washington, 1960), pp. 113–15, 121–22.

97. General d.Artl. a.D. Walter Warlimont, letter to the author, October 11, 1965.

98. General d.Inf. a.D. Erich Buschenhagen, letter to the author, September 29, 1965.

99. *Ibid.*

CHAPTER IV

1. Witting's memo of September 9, 1940 (see above, chapter II, n. 8); *Blue-White Book II*, p. 23; Paasikivi, *Minnen*, II, p. 166.

2. Witting's memo of September 9, 1950 (see above, chapter II, n. 8).

3. Blücher to AA, No. 544, September 3, 1940, 6509/H072923.

4. This telegram, referred to in Schulenburg's report of September 6 as No. 1592, has not been found.

5. *DGFP, XI,* No. 26.

6. *Ibid.,* No. 34.

7. Draft telegram by Wiehl intended for the Embassy in Moscow, September 10, 1940, 4545H/E146176–77; Wiehl to the Embassy in Moscow, No. 1659, September 11, 1940, 4416H/E083878, relayed to DGH the same day as No. 476, 4416H/E083877.

8. See above, chapter II, n. 8.

9. Blücher to AA, No. 553, September 9, 1940, 6509/H072922.

10. Blücher to AA, No. 557, September 10, 1940, B19/B003730. The credit agreement was signed on September 16.

11. Memo by Weizsäcker, St.S. Nr. 688, September 11, 1940, B19/B003739.

12. Undated telegram from the Finnish Foreign Ministry to its legation in Berlin, B19/B003740. The telegram included the information that its contents had been sent to Paasikivi "the day before yesterday," which could not have been later than September 9, the day Witting

gave Blücher a comprehensive memo about the Petsamo question.

13. See *DGFP*, X, No. 150, part 3.

14. Accounts of the conversation are found in *Blue-White Book II*, No. 27; Paasikivi, *Minnen*, II, pp. 166–67; Schulenburg to AA, No. 1962, September 16, 1940, B19/B003745; Blücher to AA, No. 567, September 16, 1940, 6509/H072921.

15. *FRUS*, 1940, I, pp. 341–42.

16. *Ibid.*, pp. 342–43.

17. *DGFP*, XI, No. 69.

18. Blücher to AA, No. 571, September 20, 1940, 6509/H072917.

19. Blücher to AA, No. 586, September 23, 1940, 6509/H072919.

20. Paasikivi, *Minnen*, II, p. 168.

21. Blücher to AA, No. 618, October 4, 1940, 6434/H060443.

22. Paasikivi, *Minnen*, II, p. 34.

23. Blücher to AA, No. 597, September 27, 1940, 6434/H060467.

24. Blücher to AA, No. 602, September 30, 1940, 6434/H060456.

25. See above, n. 21.

26. Blücher to AA, No. 631, October 7, 1940, 6434/H060420.

27. Blücher to AA, No. 641, October 9, 1940, 6434/H060406.

28. *Blue-White Book II*, p. 23.

29. *Ibid.;* Paasikivi, *Minnen*, II, p. 168; Blücher to AA, No. 651, October 12, 1940, 6509/H072912.

30. Blücher to AA, No. 441, July 22, 1940, 6434/H059343.

31. Memo by Blücher of telephone conversation with Schnurre on September 19, 1940, 6509/H072920.

32. *DGFP*, XI, No. 139.

33. *Ibid.*, No. 140.

34. See letter from Wiehl to Ribbentrop, e.o.W. 5003 g.Rs., November 4, 1940, B19/B003838–40. The letter contained a report by Veltjens on his statements to Finnish leaders.

35. Memo by Weizsäcker to Ribbentrop's Secretariat, W 4646/40 g., October 8, 1940, 2110H/456750–51, relayed to Ribbentrop in Fuschl the same evening by teletype as No. 34, B19/B003788–89 (also in *DGFP*, XI, No. 162).

36. *DGFP*, XI, No. 196.

37. *Ibid.*, No. 232.

38. Memo by Weizsäcker, St.S. Nr. 787, October 29, 1940, B19/B003807.

39. *DGFP*, XI, No. 253

40. *Ibid.*, No. 258.

41. *Ibid.*, No. 274.

42. *Blue-White Book II*, No. 37, and *FRUS*, 1940, I, pp. 352–53.

43. *Blue-White Book II*, No. 38.

44. *Ibid.*, No. 41.

45. *Ibid.*, No. 42.

46. *Ibid.*, No. 43.

47. *Ibid.*, No. 44.

48. Memo by van Scherpenberg, e.o.W. 5230 g., November 16, 1940, 2111H/456787.
49. *FRUS,* 1940, I, p. 354.
50. *Blue-White Book II,* No. 46.
51. *Ibid.*
52. Paasikivi, *Minnen,* II, pp. 171–72.
53. See, for instance, *FRUS,* 1940, II, pp. 57–60.
54. *Ibid.,* pp. 58–59.
55. See, for instance, Kreutzwald to AA, No. 691, November 1, 1940, B19/B003825; Schnurre and Schulenburg to AA, No. 2308, November 1, 1940, B19/B003829; *DGFP,* XI, No. 274.
56. *DGFP,* XI, No. 258.
57. Memo by Blücher, October 31, 1940, B19/B003812.
58. Memo by Blücher, November 1, 1940, B19/B003832–33.
59. Memo by Weizsäcker, November 2, 1940, B19/B003831.
60. Schnurre and Schulenburg to AA, No. 2308, November 1, 1940, B19/B003829–30. Underscored in the original.
61. The telegram to Moscow has not been found, but the text was relayed to DGH by Wiehl, No. 633, November 2, 1940, B19/B003826–27.
62. The letter itself has not been found, but the text was included in a teletype message to Ribbentrop from Wiehl, e.o.W. 5003 g.Rs., November 4, 1940, B19/B003838–40.
63. Letter from the Reich Minister of Economics, signed by Dr. Landfried, to Wiehl, *"Betr.:* Nickelvorkommen Petsamo," V.Ld. 8/47602/40, November 5, 1940, 2111H/456778–80.
64. Wiehl to Ribbentrop (see above, n. 34).
65. See *ibid.,* and memo by Wiehl, November 5, 1940, B19/B003845–46.
66. Wiehl to the Embassy in Moscow, No. 1998, November 5, 1940, B19/B003847–48.
67. Wiehl to DGH, No. 640, November 6, 1940, 6437/H063709–10.
68. Schulenburg to AA, No. 2363, November 8, 1940, B19/B003851.
69. Wiehl to DGH, No. 651, November 8, 1940, 6437/H063696–97.
70. *"Aufzeichnung* betreffend Petsamo-Nickel," unsigned, but apparently by Wiehl, W. 5099 g., November 9, 1940, 2111H/456784–86 (also in *DGFP,* XI, No. 308).
71. Letter from the Reich Minister of Economics, signed by Dr. Bergemann, to Wiehl, V.Ld. 8/47602/40 II, November 9, 1940, 4416H/E083889–90.
72. The records of these conversations, prepared by Minister Schmidt of Ribbentrop's secretariat and Counselor Hilger of the embassy in Moscow, are published in *DGFP,* XI, Nos. 325, 326, 328, and 329.
73. *Ibid.,* pp. 547, 548, 555, and 556.

74. See Gustav Hilger and Alfred G. Meyer, *The Incompatible Allies: A Memoir-History of German-Soviet Relations, 1918–1941* (New York, 1953), p. 323. In an earlier telegram to the State Department, Steinhardt noted that his informant "accompanied the German Ambassador to Berlin with Molotov." *FRUS,* 1940, I, p. 575.

75. *FRUS,* 1940, I, p. 584.

76. *DGFP,* XI, pp. 551 and 555.

77. Weizsäcker to the Embassy in Moscow (from Fuschl via AA), No. 2087, November 16 (sent Nov. 17), 1940, 4416H/E083887–88. See also *DGFP,* XI, No. 344.

78. Schnurre and Schulenburg to AA, No. 2482, November 18, 1940, B19/B003867–68.

79. *DGFP,* XI, No. 355.

80. Blücher to AA, No. 736, November 22, 1940, 6434/H060261–64.

81. *DGFP,* XI, No. 405.

82. Wiehl to DGH, No. 697, November 27, 1940, 6437/H063634–35.

83. Blücher to AA, No. 746, November 28, 1940, 6434/H060244–46.

84. Blücher to AA, No. 752, November 30, 1940, 6434/H060234–35; memo by Weizsäcker of conversation with Kivimäki, St.S. Nr. 868, November 30, 1940, B19/B003892; Ribbentrop to DGH, No. 704, November 29, 1940, B19/B003889 and 6509/H072888; Wiehl to the Embassy in Moscow, No. [?], e.o.W. 5541 g.Rs., December 2, 1940, B19/B003893.

85. Memo by Grundherr, Pol.VI 3531 g., November 12, 1940, B19/B003854 (also in *DGFP,* XI, No. 322); memo by Woermann, November 12, 1940, B19/B003855.

86. Memo by the Finnish Legation in Berlin, November 12, 1940, B19/B003856.

87. Memo by van Scherpenberg, e.o.W. 5230 g., November 16, 1940, 2111H/456787, relayed by Wiehl to DGH, No. 677, November 19, 1940, 4416H/E083891.

88. Memo by Weizsäcker, St.S. Nr. 837, November 18, 1940, B19/B003866.

89. Blücher to AA, No. 725, November 20, 1940, 6434/H060285.

90. Wipert von Blücher, *Gesandter zwischen Diktatur und Demokratie. Erinnerungen aus den Jahren 1935–1944* (Wiesbaden, 1951), p. 207.

91. *Ibid.,* p. 205

92. Unsigned memo of conversation with Ribbentrop, found in Wiehl's files, November 22, 1940, 4416H/E083896.

93. *DGFP,* XI, No. 411; Wiehl to DGH, No. 699, November 28, 1940, 4416H/E083902–03. See also the instructions for Veltjens, who was back in Helsinki, forwarded by Wiehl to DGH, No. 689, November 24, 1940, 4416H/E083899–900, and given to Veltjens by Blücher on November 25, 1940 (see 6509/H072905).

94. Halder, *Kriegstagebuch,* II, p. 183.

95. *Ibid.,* p. 210.

96. *TMWC,* XXVI, p. 48.

97. During the Nuremberg trials, two key witnesses for the Soviet prosecution in the High Command case, namely General Buschenhagen and Field Marshal Friedrich Paulus, both of whom were brought to Nuremberg from Soviet prisons and returned there subsequently, testified that the Finnish General Staff was informed about Directive No. 21 at the time it was issued on December 18, 1940. According to these two witnesses (and a third witness who had no first-hand knowledge of the things he testified about) the Finnish chief of staff was present at the OKW headquarters at the time and was fully initiated as far as Finland's assigned role was concerned. One of the witnesses stated that the Finns had participated in the planning itself since September, 1940. Buschenhagen and Paulus also claimed to have met the Finnish chief of staff in Berlin in mid-December (see *ibid.,* VII, pp. 161, 258, 309–10, 328, 337). Paulus, who acted as a spokesman for Soviet anti-German propaganda after his capture at Stalingrad in 1943, and who spent his post-POW days in East Germany where he died in 1957, never retracted his Nuremberg testimony, which was perhaps understandable. See *"Ich stehe hier auf Befehl!" Lebensweg des Generalfeldmarschalls Friedrich Paulus,* edited by Walter Görlitz (Frankfurt am Main, 1960), pp. 127–28. His biographer, Dr. Görlitz, repeated Paulus' false testimony regarding this incident in his book *Der Zweite Weltkrieg 1939–1945,* I (Stuttgart, 1951), p. 218. Paulus and Buschenhagen actually met the Finnish chief of staff in Berlin at the end of January, 1941, as the contemporary German military records make clear. Buschenhagen, who was released by the Russians in 1955 and returned to his home in Bavaria, has since corrected his Nuremberg testimony on this point. Specifically, he has stated that the prolonged Soviet interrogation caused him to misdate his meeting with the Finnish chief of staff (Buschenhagen himself was in Berlin both in mid-December, 1940, and at the end of January, 1941). Buschenhagen, letters to the author, November 25, 1963, February 18, 1964, and January 5, 1966. See also Heinrich's *Mannerheimgestalten,* II, p. 231, n. 2.

98. "Vereinbarung zwischen der deutschen Wehrmacht und dem finnischen Generalstab betr. den Urlauberverkehr aus Kirkenes durch Finnland nach Deutschland und zurück und die dazu notwendigen Transporte," Helsinki, November 22, 1940, T–312/992/9185565–73.

CHAPTER V

1. The *Blue-White Book II* for 1941 contained less than one page of text (p. 25), and no documents for the period November 19, 1940, through January 14, 1941.

2. *DGFP,* XI, No. 405.

3. Blücher to AA, No. 741, November 27, 1940, 6509/H072892–95.
4. See *DGFP,* XI, Nos. 411 and 474; Korhonen, *Barbarossaplanen och Finland,* pp. 158–61; Upton, *Finland in Crisis,* pp. 181–82; Wiehl to DGH, No. 688, November 23, 1940, 6437/H063644, No. 689, November 24, 1940, 6437/H063643, and No. 699, November 28, 1940, 6437/H063632; memo by Blücher to Veltjens, November 25, 1940, 6437/H063645; Blücher to AA, No. 740, November 25, 1940, 6434/H060254, and No. 749, November 29, 1940, 6434/H060240.
5. *DGFP,* XI, No. 474.
6. Wiehl to DGH, No. 700, November 28, 1940, 4416H/E083904.
7. Blücher to AA, No. 752, November 30, 1940, 6434/H060234–35.
8. Paasikivi, *Minnen,* II, pp. 172–74; Blücher to AA, No. 760, December 4, 1940, 6434/H060219 (an imperfect copy was published in *DGFP,* XI, No. 447).
9. Paasikivi, *Minnen,* II, p. 173.
10. Blücher to AA, No. 766, December 7, 1940, 6434/H060210–12. Grönblom's name was incorrectly given as "Grönwald."
11. Blücher to AA, No. 769, December 9, 1940, 6434/H060205.
12. Schnurre's telegram has not been found, but the text was sent to DGH by Wiehl in No. 724, December 11, 1940, 4416H/E083911. There is no mention of it in Paasikivi's memoirs.
13. Blücher to AA, No. 782, December 12, 1940, 6434/H060174.
14. Blücher to AA, No. 785, December 14, 1940, 6434/H060169.
15. Wiehl to the Embassy in Moscow, No. 2278, e.o.W.V. 4502, December 11, 1940, B19/B003905–07, relayed by Wiehl of DGH, No. 726, December 12, 1940, 6437/H063603–04. The Petsamo Nickel Company was represented in the negotiations by Henrik Ramsay and Baron Gustaf Woldemar Wrede. The latter had recently succeeded Söderhjelm as managing director.
16. The agreement between I.G. Farbenindustrie and Petsamo Nickel was submitted to AA in the form of a memo from I.G. Farbenindustrie. A copy was found in the "Petsamo" file of DGH (6509/H072887).
17. According to an annotation found in *ibid.*
18. See Wiehl to DGH, No. 741, December 17, 1940, 6509/H072883.
19. Schnurre and Schulenburg to AA, No. 2731, December 14, 1940, B19/B003921–22, relayed by van Scherpenberg to DGH, No. 739, December 17, 1940, 6509/H072879–80.
20. Wiehl to DGH, No. 742, December 17, 1940, 4416H/E083909–10.
21. A delivery contract was actually signed on November 29/30, 1940, but the Soviet government ignored its existence. Söderhjelm, "Nickeldiplomati," *Hufvudstadsbladet,* November 2, 1966.
22. *FRUS,* 1940, I, p. 355.
23. Blücher to AA, No. 797, December 19, 1940, 6434/H060142.

24. Blücher to AA, No. 806, December 23, 1940, 6434/H060122.

25. Blücher to AA, No. 801, December 20, 1940, 6434/H060133–36.

26. *Ibid.;* Clodius to DGH, No. 745, December 19, 1940, 6509/H072870.

27. Blücher to AA, No. 190, March 22, 1941, 6440/H066661.

28. See, for instance, Blücher to AA, No. 632, October 7, 1940, 6434/H060419, No. 649, October 12, 1940, 6434/H060386–88, No. 652, October 12, 1940, 6434/H060382–83, No. 721, November 19, 1940, 6434/H060293, and No. 750, November 30, 1940, 6434/H060239; Blücher to AA, Tgb. Nr. 3191, "Inhalt: Äusserungen von Mitgliedern der hiesigen Englischen Gesandtschaft," October 12, 1940, 441/221251. See also Der Chef des Sicherheitspolizei und des SD to Ribbentrop, *"Betr.:* Finnische Befürchtungen bezüglich einer Sperrung des Petsamo-Schiffsverkehrs durch England," VI G 3 Gh/Ki AZ: 5851/40, October 26, 1940, 1397/360386–88, and *"Betr.:* Lagebericht Finnland," VI G 3 Gh/Ki AZ: 6034, November 2, 1940, 1397/360393–96.

29. Blücher to AA, No. 766, December 7, 1940, 6434/H060210–12.

30. *Ibid.*

31. *Ibid.*

32. A copy of the instruction to the Finnish delegation was given to Blücher by the Finnish Foreign Ministry and forwarded by him to Berlin on December 21, 1940, as No. 803, 6434/H060128–29.

33. *DGFP*, XI, No. 562.

34. Paasikivi, *Minnen,* II, pp. 174–75.

35. Schnurre to AA, No. 2801, December 23, 1940, relayed by Clodius to DGH, No. 748, December 24, 1940, 6437/H063580–81.

36. Fieandt, letter to the author, April 30, 1965, appendix 1.

37. Paasikivi, *Minnen,* II, p. 72.

38. See above, n. 35.

39. *DGFP,* XI, No. 562.

40. Blücher to AA, No. 808, December 27, 1940, 6434/H060116–20.

41. *Ibid*

42. Blücher to AA, No. 4, January 3, 1941, 6440/H067057–58.

43. Blücher to AA, No. 810, December 30, 1940, 6434/H060113.

CHAPTER VI

1. Schnurre and Schulenburg to AA, No. 10, January 3, 1941, B19/B003946.

2. Clodius to DGH, No. 4, January 4, 1941, 6441/H070015.

3. Blücher to AA, No. 6, January 7, 1941, 6440/H067051–52.

4. See *DGFP*, XI, No. 637.

5. *FRUS*, 1941, I, p. 1.

6. *Ibid.,* pp. 1–2.

7. Memo by Press Attaché Hans Metzger of the DGH, January 14, 1941, 6440/H067029, relayed by Blücher to AA, No. 17, January 14, 1941, 6440/H067028.

8. Blücher to AA, No. 13, January 13, 1941, 6440/H067035–36.

9. *DGFP,* XI, No. 676; *FRUS,* 1941, I, pp. 4–5.

10. *DGFP,* XI, No. 676.

11. Schulenburg to AA, No. 154, January 22, 1941, B19/B003962.

12. *FRUS,* 1941, I, p. 4.

13. *Ibid.,* No. 675.

14. See above, n. 8.

15. "Aktenvermerk" by van Scherpenberg, e.o.Ha.Pol. 123, January 14, 1941, 2111H/456802.

16. Wiehl to DGH, No. 19, January 15, 1941, 6441/H070009.

17. Blücher to AA, No. 19, January 15, 1941, 6440/H067021.

18. Wiehl to DGH, No. 26, January 17, 1941, 6440/H067018.

19. Blücher to AA, No. 22, January 18, 1941, 6440/H067017.

20. Schulenburg to AA, No. 117, January 16, 1941, B19/B003953.

21. Wiehl to DGH, No. 25, January 17, 1941, 6441/H070006.

22. See above, n. 19.

23. *DGFP,* XI, No. 675.

24. Wiehl to DGH, No. 35, January 21, 1941, 6441/H070001.

25. *DGFP,* XI, No. 687.

26. Ribbentrop from Fuschl to AA, No. 36, January 24, 1941, B19/B003964, relayed by AA to DGH, No. 49, January 25, 1941, 6441/H069993 (also in *DGFP,* XI, No. 703).

27. Blücher, "Unterhaltung mit Aussenminister am 15. Januar 1941," 6509/H073126–27; Blücher to AA, No. 18, January 15, 1941, 6440/H067023–25; *FRUS,* 1941, I, p. 5.

28. Blücher to AA, No. 40, January 23, 1941, 6440/H066983–84.

29. Blücher to AA, No. 42, January 24, 1941, 6440/H066977–78.

30. In his report to AA, Blücher referred to the English official as a Mr. "Food," which was probably an error. Presumably the official in question was Dingle Foot, secretary of state for economic warfare.

31. Blücher to AA, No. 46, January 25, 1941, 6440/H066965–70.

32. *Blue-White Book II,* No. 60.

33. See above, n. 27.

34. Wiehl to DGH, No. 35, January 21, 1941, 6441/H070001; Blücher to AA, No. 35, January 22, 1941, 6440/H066991–93.

35. Blücher to AA, No. 26, January 20, 1941, 6440/H067006–07.

36. Blücher to AA, No. 35, January 22, 1941, 6440/H066991–93.

37. Upton, *Finland in Crisis,* pp. 205–6.

38. Halder, *Kriegstagebuch,* II, p. 247.

39. Schnurre to DGH, No. 32, January 20, 1941, 6441/H070003.

40. Blücher to AA, No. 33, January 21, 1941, 6440/H066998.

41. Blücher to AA, No. 63, January 29, 1941, 6440/H066921.

42. *Blue-White Book II,* No. 61; Paasikivi, *Minnen,* II, p. 176;

Blücher to AA, No. 35, January 22, 1941, 6440/H066991–93; Schulenburg to AA, No. 153, January 22, 1941, B19/B003961. Witting's instruction to Paasikivi was also relayed to Berlin and submitted by
Kivimäki to AA; see Wiehl, "Aufzeichnung betr. Petsamo-Nickelfrage,"
Ha.Pol.VI 234/41, B19/B003958–59 (also in *DGFP*, XI, No. 687).
   43. Paasikivi, *Minnen*, II, pp. 176–77; Blücher to AA, No. 41, January 24, 1941, 6440/H066980–81; Schulenburg to AA, No. [163?], January 24, 1941 (not found), relayed by van Scherpenberg to DGH, No.
51, January 25, 1941, 6441/H069991.
   44. Blücher to AA, No. 41, January 24, 1941, 6440/H066980–81.
   45. See above, n. 31.
   46. Blücher to AA, No. 48, January 25, 1941, 6440/H066957–60.
   47. *DGFP*, XI, No. 711.
   48. The draft telegram is unsigned, but its file number (zu Ha.Pol.VI
289/41) and a handwritten marginal note point to Wiehl as the author.
B19/B003972–73.
   49. Ribbentrop from Sonderzug Heinrich to AA, No. 48, January
27, 1941, B19/B003974–75
   50. *DGFP*, XII, No. 4.
   51. Ribbentrop to DGH, No. 58, January 27, 1941, 6441/H069986–
87 (also in *DGFP*, XI, No. 717). The telegram to the embassy in
Moscow (No. 164) was sent the same day (see *DGFP*, XI, No. 717,
n. 4).
   52. Blücher to AA, No. 56, January 28, 1941, 6440/H066940–42
(also in *DGFP*, XI, No. 720). The original German copy says that
it was Fieandt who was not to reveal to the Russians that he knew of
the instruction to Schulenburg; the published English translation in
DGFP erroneously says it was Witting.
   53. Memo by Wiehl, Dir.Ha.Pol. 16, January 28, 1941, B19/
B003980–81, relayed by Wiehl to DGH, No. 62, January 29, 1941,
6441/H069983–84.
   54. Wiehl to DGH, No. 62 (see foregoing note).
   55. "Tätigkeitsbericht der Gruppe XXI/Abt. Ia in der Zeit vom
1.–30.11. 1940," g.Kdos.Chefs., T–312/992/9185547–54.
   56. "Tätigkeitsbericht des Armee-Oberkommandos Norwegen/Abt.
Ia in der Zeit vom 1.12.–31.12.40," g.Kdos.Chefs., T–312/992/
9185675–81.
   57. Gruppe XXI, Ia 80/40 g.Kdos., "Ergebnis der Besprechung mit
Oberst Rössing," October 11, 1940, T–312/1010/9206144–47.
   58. Rössing to Generalstab des Heeres and Gruppe XXI, *"Betr.:*
Finnland—Kampfführungsabsichten des finnischen Generalstabes im
Petsamogebiet," Tgb.Nr. 3/41 g.Kdos., January 10, 1941, T–312/
1010/9206136–39.
   59. AOK Norwegen, Chef des Generalstabes, Nr. 136/41 g.Kdos.,
January 23, 1941, T–312/993/9185884–909. See also "Tätigkeitsbericht des Armee-Oberkommandos Norwegen/Abteilung Ia in der
Zeit vom 1.1.–31.1.1941," g.Kdos.Chefs., T–312/993/9185810–16.

60. AOK Norwegen, Ia Nr. 3/31 g.Kdos.Chefs. (Silberfuchs), Entwurf, January 27, 1941, T–312/1010/9206092–106. Underscored in the original.

61. See Halder, *Kriegstagebuch*, II, pp. 264–65.

62. OKH, Gen.St.d.H. Op.Abt.(I) Nr. 050/41 g.Kdos., "Aufmarschanweisung Barbarossa," January 31, 1941, T–312/1010/9205566–85. Underscored in the original.

63. AOK Norwegen, Ia Nr. 10/41 g.K.Chefs. 'Silberfuchs', *"Betr.:* Barbarossa," February 13, 1941, T–312/1010/9206058–62. Underscored in the original.

64. "Sicherung von Petsamo, der Erzgruben und der Eismeerstrasse," Anlage 2a zu AOK Norwegen, Ia Nr. 10/41 g.K.Chefs. 'Silberfuchs', February 13, 1941, T–312/1010/9206066.

65. See Helmuth Greiner, *Die Oberste Wehrmachtführung 1939–1943* (Wiesbaden, 1951), p. 357, n. 50. See also Halder, *Kriegstagebuch*, II, p. 264, n. 2 to entry for January 30, 1941.

66. Halder, *Kriegstagebuch*, II, p. 264.

67. Halder, letter to the author, November 24, 1964. Halder's letter confirms the account given by Heinrichs (*Mannerheimgestalten*, II, p. 233). Greiner (see above, n. 65), whose statement about this meeting was based on a memo by one of General Jodl's adjutants which gave a misleading version of the Halder-Heinrichs conversation, is contradicted by his immediate superior, General Warlimont, who recalls that Halder protested at the time against the version given in the memo. For some unexplained reason no correction was made, and Greiner used the memo for his postwar account (Warlimont, letter to the author, November 28, 1964). See also Mannerheim, *Minnen*, II, p. 261, and Waldemar Erfurth, *Der finnische Krieg 1941–1944* (Wiesbaden, 1950), p. 27. For a detailed discussion of the meeting between Halder and Heinrichs, see H. Peter Krosby, *Suomen valinta 1941* (Helsinki, 1967), pp. 124–30.

68. See Greiner, *Die Oberste Wehrmachtführung*, p. 346.

69. *Ibid.*, p. 347; *TMWC*, XXXIV, p. 467.

70. Halder, *Kriegstagebuch*, II, p. 255.

CHAPTER VII

1. Blücher to AA, No. 66, January 31, 1941, 6440/H066916–17.

2. Blücher to AA, No. 68, February 1, 1941, 6440/H066909–11; memo by Wiehl, Dir.Ha.Pol. 20, February 1, 1941, 2111H/456810–11; Paasikivi, *Minnen*, II, pp. 177–78. Paasikivi actually described the Finnish proposal as it emerged after several sessions of the mixed commission, not in its original form as one is led to believe.

3. Schulenburg to AA, No. 244, February 3, 1941, B19/B003986–87; Blücher to AA, No. 71, February 3, 1941, 6440/H066896–901; memo by Wiehl, Dir.Ha.Pol. 21, February 3, 1941, 2111H/456812–13.

4. *Blue-White Book II,* No. 63; Blücher to AA, No. 79, February 6, 1941, 6440/H066877–78.

5. This description of the Finnish draft is based on Witting's account as reported by Blücher to AA, No. 77, February 5, 1941, 6440/H066883–84.

6. Witting remarked to Blücher that "payment of German claims was naturally not expected" (*ibid.*). In other words, the Finnish draft was not a sincere proposal. Provisions for buying out the German and Anglo-Canadian interests were included in order to give the draft a semblance of sincerity. On balance, the draft was designed to be unacceptable to the Russians, not a genuine effort to reach a compromise. The dollar amounts were given in the original Finnish proposal and thus represent the 1941 rate of exchange.

7. Blücher to AA, No. 81, February 8, 1941, 6440/H066870–74.

8. Blücher to AA, No. 83, February 10, 1941, 6440/H066864–66.

9. Blücher to AA, No. 84, February 11, 1941, 6440/H066861–62; memo by Woermann, U.St.S.Pol. Nr. 93, February 11, 1941, B19/B004009; *DGFP,* XII, No. 42.

10. *Blue-White Book II,* No. 64; Blücher to AA, No. 87, February 12, 1941, 6440/H066853–55, No. 90, February 13, 1941, 6440/H066847–49, and No. 91, February 14, 1941, 6440/H066844–45; Schulenburg to AA, No. 296, February 11, 1941, B19/B004015, relayed by Schnurre to DGH, No. 107, February 12, 1941, 6441/H069956.

11. Schulenburg to AA, No. 303, February 13, 1941, B19/B004018–19.

12. Blücher to AA, No. 91, February 14, 1941, 6440/H066844–45.

13. Schulenburg to AA, No. 323, February 16, 1941, B19/B004028, relayed by Wiehl to DGH, No. 133, February 17, 1941, 6441/H069933–34; Blücher to AA, No. 96, February 17, 1941, 6440/H066833–34.

14. Blücher to AA, No. 102, February 18, 1941, 6509/H073053.

15. *Blue-White Book II,* No. 67. The copy of this document that Kivimäki gave to Woermann on February 20 (B19/B004034) contained two sentences not found in the version published in the *Blue-White Book II.* In those sentences Paasikivi said that additional German guarantees, and "not only diplomatic," were required.

16. Blücher to AA, No. 108, February 20, 1941, 6440/H066812, No. 117, February 24, 1941, 6440/H066794, and No. 126, February 28, 1941, 6440/H066778–79; Schulenburg to AA, No. 482, March 5, 1941, B19/B004049 (also in *DGFP,* XII, No. 123), relayed by Wiehl to DGH, No. 174, March 6, 1941, 6441/H069906–07.

17. Blücher to AA, No. 108, February 20, 1941, 6440/H066812, and No. 111, February 21, 1941, 6440/H066807–08.

18. Blücher to AA, No. 121, February 27, 1941, 6440/H066786–87.

19. Blücher, "Unterhaltung mit Aussenminister am 8. März 1941,"

6509/H072177–78; Blücher to AA, No. 147, March 8, 1941, 6440/
H066748; Schulenburg to AA, No. 539, March 11, 1941, B19/
B004070–71, relayed by van Scherpenberg to DGH, No. 191, March
12, 1941, 6509/H073021–22; *Blue-White Book II*, p. 27.
  20. Schulenburg to AA, No. 209, January 31, 1941, B19/B003982–
83 (also in *DGFP*, XI, No. 737), relayed by Schnurre to DGH, No.
82, February 4, 1941, 6441/H069971–73.
  21. *DGFP*, XII, No. 16.
  22. Schnurre to DGH, No. 86, February 5, 1941, 6441/H069968–
70.
  23. Blücher to AA, No. 66, January 31, 1941, 6440/H066916–17.
  24. *Blue-White Book II*, No. 15.
  25. *DGFP*, X, No. 182.
  26. Schnurre and Schulenburg to AA, No. 2308, November 1, 1940,
B19/B003829–30.
  27. Blücher to AA, No. 71, February 3, 1941, 6440/H066896–901;
memo by Wiehl, Dir.Ha.Pol. 21, February 3, 1941, 2111H/456812–13.
  28. Paasikivi, *Minnen*, II, p. 179.
  29. Blücher to AA, No. 71 (see above, n. 27).
  30. Schnurre to DGH, No. 81, February 4, 1941, 6441/H069974.
  31. Blücher to AA, No. 77, February 5, 1941, 6440/H066883–84.
  32. *Ibid.;* Blücher to AA, No. 72, February 4, 1941, 6440/
H066892–94.
  33. Schnurre to DGH, No. 86 (see above, n. 22).
  34. *FRUS*, 1941, I, p. 9.
  35. *Ibid.*, pp. 10–11.
  36. Paasikivi, *Minnen*, II, p. 179.
  37. Blücher to AA, No. 79, February 6, 1941, 6440/H066877–78.
  38. See above, n. 7.
  39. Memo by van Scherpenberg, included as part 1 of a document
designated "Zu Ha.Pol.VI458," February 8, 1941, 2111H/456819.
  40. The draft of this telegram is part 2 of *ibid.*
  41. Memo by Weizsäcker, St.S. Nr. 179, March 17, 1941, B19/
B004083–84.
  42. Memo by Weizsäcker, St.S. Nr. 98, February 8, 1941, B19/
B004001.
  43. See above, n. 8.
  44. Memo by Woermann, U.St.S.Pol. Nr. 93, February 11, 1941,
B19/B004009.
  45. *DGFP*, XII, No. 42.
  46. Wiehl to the Embassy in Moscow, No. 273, February 12, 1941,
B19/B004006–07.
  47. Schnurre to DGH, No. 108, February 12, 1941, 6441/H069955.
  48. See above, n. 12.
  49. See above, n. 7.
  50. See above, n. 8.

51. Blücher to AA, No. 85, February 12, 1941, 6509/H073066.
52. Zu Ha.Pol. 1192 g. Ang. II, B19/B004057–62.
53. Wiehl to DGH, No. 174, March 6, 1941, 6441/H069906–07.
54. Blücher, "Unterhaltung mit Aussenminister am 7. März 1941," 6509/H073035; Blücher to AA, No. 145, March 7, 1941, 6440/H066751.
55. Clodius to DGH, No. 187, March 10, 1941, 6441/H069893–96; Blücher to AA, No. 157, March 12, 1941, 6440/H066736.
56. Orlov, who had taken Zotov's place in a somewhat irregular manner, did not formally present his credentials to President Ryti until April 24.
57. Blücher to AA, No. 190, March 22, 1941, 6440/H066661.
58. *Blue-White Book II*, Nos. 65 and 66; Paasikivi, *Minnen*, II, pp. 179–81; Blücher to AA, No. 90, February 13, 1941, 6440/H066847–49, and No. 95, February 15, 1941, 6440/H066836–38; Schulenburg to AA, No. 303, February 13, 1941, B19/B004018–19, relayed by van Scherpenberg to DGH, No. 122, February 15, 1941, 6441/H069946–47.
59. Paasikivi, *Minnen*, II, p. 180.
60. *Ibid.*, p. 181.
61. Schulenburg to AA, No. 303 (see above, n. 58).
62. Wiehl to DGH, No. 128 [incorrectly numbered 118], February 15, 1941, 6441/H069949.
63. Blücher to AA, No. 111, February 21, 1941, 6440/H066807–08.
64. Paasikivi, *Minnen*, II, p. 181.
65. Schulenburg to AA, No. 303 (see above, n. 58).
66. Paasikivi, *Minnen*, II, pp. 181–82.
67. *Ibid.*, p. 182.
68. Blücher to AA, No. 95 (see above, n. 58).
69. Paasikivi, *Minnen*, II, p. 182.
70. *Ibid.*; *Blue-White Book II*, No. 67; Schulenburg to AA, No. 342, February 19, 1941, B19/B004038; Blücher to AA, No. 106, February 19, 1941, 6440/H066815–18; memo by Woermann, U.St.S.Pol. Nr. 129, February 20, 1941, B19/B004033.
71. See above, n. 15.
72. Paasikivi, *Minnen*, II, p. 183.
73. *Ibid.*
74. Blücher to AA, No. 106 (see above, n. 70).
75. Moraht to DGH, No. 142, February 20, 1941, 6441/H069929. See also Wiehl, "Aufzeichnung über den Stand der Petsamo-Verhandlungen," Dir.Ha.Pol. 44/41, February 22, 1941, B19/B004041–42.
76. See above, n. 63.
77. Blücher to AA, No. 117, February 24, 1941, 6440/H066794–95.
78. Schulenburg to AA, Tgb. Nr. A/631/41, February 24, 1941. A copy of this report (Pol.VI 922 g.) was sent to Grundherr by DGH on March 1, 1941 (6674/H090660).

79. *FRUS,* 1941, I, pp. 12–13.
80. See above, n. 63.
81. Paasikivi, *Minnen,* II, pp. 230–231.
82. See above, n. 77.
83. Wiehl to DGH, No. 151, February 25, 1941, 6441/H069927. The telegram was actually sent on February 27.
84. See above, n. 18.
85. Blücher to AA, No. 126, February 28, 1941, 6440/H066778–79.
86. Ribbentrop from Fuschl to AA, No. 109, February 27, 1941, B19/B004043, relayed by Clodius to DGH, No. 155, February 28, 1941, 6441/H069922 (and relayed to the embassy in Moscow as No. 395 of February 27).
87. Schulenburg to AA, No. 443, February 28, 1941, B19/B004045–46 (also in *DGFP,* XII, No. 109), relayed by Wiehl to DGH, No. 161, March 3, 1941, 6441/H069916–17.
88. *Blue-White Book II,* No. 68. A fuller version of Paasikivi's telegram was given to Wiehl by Kivimäki on March 6 (B19/B004054–55). Other accounts of the interview are found in Paasikivi, *Minnen,* II, p. 184; Schulenburg to AA, No. 482 (see above, n. 16); Blücher to AA, No. 142, March 6, 1941, 6440/H066753–56; Wiehl, "Aufzeichnung betreffend Petsamo," Dir.Ha.Pol. 57/41, March 6, 1941, 2111H/456832; *FRUS,* 1941, I, pp. 13–14.
89. Paasikivi, *Minnen,* II, p. 184.
90. *DGFP,* XII, No. 123.
91. *FRUS,* 1941, I, p. 14.
92. *DGFP,* XII, No. 123.
93. Blücher to AA, No. 142 (see above, n. 88).
94. Wiehl, "Aufzeichnung betreffend Petsamo" (see above, n. 88).
95. Wiehl, "Aufzeichnung betreffend Petsamo," Dir.Ha.Pol. 58/41, March 6, 1941, 2111H/456833–34.
96. Draft telegram prepared by Wiehl for Weizsäcker's signature, zu Ha. Pol. 1192 g. Ang. II, B19/B004057–62. Though undated, the draft was obviously written on March 6.
97. Memo by Weizsäcker, St.S. Nr. 160, March 7, 1941, B19/B004063.
98. Erik Boheman, *På vakt. Kabinettssekreterare under andra världskriget* (Stockholm, 1964), pp. 152–54.
99. Korhonen, *Barbarossaplanen och Finland,* pp. 218–19.
100. *FRUS,* 1941, I, p. 14.
101. No. 155 (from Fuschl), March 8, 1941, B19/B004064; *DGFP,* XII, No. 139.
102. Clodius to DGH, No. 187 (see above, n. 55).
103. Schulenburg to AA, No. 539 (see above, n. 19).
104. The Soviet note in German translation was sent by Counselor Hilger to AA as Tgb.Dg. 48/41 g. (zu Ha.Pol. 2019/41 g.), March 25, 1941, 260/169942–44; a copy was relayed to DGH (6674/

H090783–84). Schulenburg summarized the main points of the note in his telegram No. 685 to AA, March 25, 1941, B19/B004101 (also in *DGFP*, XII, No. 204), relayed by Schnurre to DGH, No. 239, March 26, 1941, 6434/H059273.

CHAPTER VIII

1. Paasikivi, *Minnen*, II, p. 185.
2. Blücher to AA, No. 159, March 14, 1941, 6440/H066733–34.
3. "Entwurf zur Antwort an die Sowietunion [*sic*] in der Nickelfrage. Vertraulich," 6 pp., 6509/H072994–99.
4. Memo by Weizsäcker, St.S. Nr. 179, March 17, 1941, B19/B004083–84, relayed by Schnurre to DGH as Ha.Pol. 1742 g. I, March 28, 1941, 6674/H090739–41.
5. Korhonen, *Barbarossaplanen och Finland,* p. 219.
6. Memo by the Finnish Legation, March 17, 1941, B19/B004085–87.
7. The draft was sent to Blücher with Pakaslahti's calling card, on which was scribbled: "At the request of Minister Witting I submit this draft to Your Excellency." 6509/H073019.
8. Blücher to AA, No. 180, March 18, 1941, 6440/H066681.
9. Schnurre to DGH, No. 221, March 21, 1941, 6509/H073017.
10. Memo by Schnurre, zu St.S. Nr. 179, March 21, 1941, B19/B004093–95, relayed by Schnurre to DGH, No. 245, March 27, 1941, 6434/H059269–70.
11. *DGFP,* XII, No. 204.
12. "Ausschuss zur Klarlegung der Angelegenheit betreffend die Aktiengesellschaft 'Petsamon Nikkeli O.Y.': Praktische Gesichtspunkte betreffend die Leitung und die Organisation der vorgesehenen finnisch-sowjetrussischen Aktiengesellschaft. Streng vertraulich," 5 pp. Undated and unsigned. 6509/H073010–14.
13. Memo by Weizsäcker, St.S. Nr. 200, April 2, 1941, 260/169931, relayed by Schnurre to DGH, No. 262, April 4, 1941, 6434/H059266. Emphasis added.
14. Memo by Weizsäcker, St.S. Nr. 181, March 17, 1941, B19/B004088.
15. *DGFP,* XII, No. 69.
16. Buschenhagen, letter to the author, May 21, 1964.
17. OKH, Gen.St.d.H. Op.Abt. (IN) Nr. 188/41 g.Kdos.Chefs., *"Betr.:* Silberfuchs," March 2, 1941, T–312/1010/9206024–26.
18. "Tätigkeitsbericht der Armee-Oberkommandos Norwegen/Abteilung Ia in der Zeit vom 1.3.–31.3.1941," g.Kdos.Chefs., T–312/993/9186144–52.
19. OKW, WFSt/Abt.L. (I Op.) Nr. 44355/41 g.K.Chefs., "Weisung an den Wehrmachtbefehlshaber Norwegen über seine Aufgaben im Fall 'Barbarossa'," April 7, 1941, T–312/1010/9205930–35.
20. AOK Norwegen, Ia Nr. 14/41 g.Kdos.Chefs. (Silberfuchs),

"Operations-anweisung des Geb.Korps Norwegen," April 18, 1941, T–312/993/9186543–53.

21. Befehlshaber im Polarbereich, Ia Nr. 14/41 g.K.Chefs., Silber-fuchs, "Befehl für das Unternehmen 'Silberfuchs'," May 6, 1941, T–312/1011/9206579–84; Anlage "R" zu Befehlshaber im Polarbe-reich, Ia Nr. 14/41 g.Kdos.Chefs., "Befehl zur Besetzung des Petsamo-gebietes in Finnisch-Lappland (Fall "A" Renntier)," May 6, 1941, T–312/1011/9206585–92.

22. AOK Norwegen, Ia Nr. 91/41 g.Kdos.Chefs., May 26, 1941, T–312/1011/9206515; OKW/WFSt/Abt. L (I Op) Nr. 44803/41 g.Kdos.Chefs., May 26, 1941, T–312/1011/9206514. For a detailed account of the progress of the German planning for the Finnish theater of war and the development of the military cooperation with the Finns from February to mid-May, 1941, see Krosby, *Suomen valinta 1941*, pp. 84–146.

23. See the numerous German records about these developments in *DGFP*, XII, *passim*.

24. *Ibid.,* No. 333.

25. See above, n. 2.

26. *FRUS*, 1941, I, p. 16.

27. Schnurre, "Entwurf einer telegrafischen Instruktion an Moskau," zu Ha.Pol. 2019/41 g. [incorrectly numbered 2018], prepared for Weizsäcker's signature and submitted to Ribbentrop on April 8, 1941, 260/169939–41.

28. Memo by Schnurre, zu Ha.Pol. 2019/41 g., April 7, 1941, 260/169937–38.

29. *DGFP*, XII, No. 305. The instruction was relayed to DGH for information (6674/H090780–82) with a covering letter by van Scherpenberg (6674/H090779) on April 21, 1941.

30. Blücher to AA, No. 252, April 19, 1941, 6440/H067070–71.

31. Weizsäcker to DGH, No. 323, April 29, 1941, 6434/H059257.

32. Blücher to AA, No. 249, April 19, 1941, 6440/H066565–66.

33. *DGFP*, XII, No. 402, relayed by Woermann to DGH, No. 316, April 26, 1941, 6434/H059260.

34. Blücher to AA, No. 269, April 24, 1941, 6440/H067095–96.

35. Blücher to AA, No. 277, April 26, 1941, 6440/H067109; AOK Norwegen, Ic Nr. 62/41 g.Kdos.Chefs., "Nachrichtenblatt Nr. 2," May 8, 1941, T–312/993/9186923.

36. Apparently Witting neglected to mention that Finland was in serious arrears with respect to its own deliveries to the Soviet Union, which was the official Soviet explanation for halting further grain shipments to Finland.

37. *Blue-White Book II,* No. 69.

38. Blücher to AA, No. 312, May 8, 1941, 6440/H067170–71.

39. Blücher to AA, No. 324, May 10, 1941, 6440/H067189–90.

40. *Blue-White Book II,* No. 70.

41. *Ibid.,* No. 71.

42. Blücher to AA, No. 329, May 13, 1941, 6440/H067197.

43. The grain was actually delivered to Finland before the Continuation War broke out on June 25.

44. Paasikivi, *Minnen*, II, pp. 239, 248–49; Schulenburg to AA, No. 1280, June 1, 1941, 260/170000.

CHAPTER IX

1. Medlicott, *Economic Blockade*, I, p. 628.

2. In mid-June, 1941, Witting informed Blücher that there were three British consuls and eleven trade inspectors in north Finland (Blücher to AA, No. 438, June 16, 1941, 6440/H067353–55). In early August, 1941, a list submitted by the British legation to the Finnish Foreign Ministry in connection with the evacuation from Finland of all British personnel included the names of six persons with consular status and seven trade inspectors. See *"British Legation, Helsingfors. List A. List of members of the Legation who require facilities to leave Finland and a German safe-conduct for the journey to the United Kingdom."* Conveyed by Witting to Blücher on August 12, 1941, 6440/H067819–23.

3. See Butler, *Grand Strategy*, II, pp. 571–73.

4. Georg A. Gripenberg, *Finland and the Great Powers: Memoirs of a Diplomat*, translated from the Swedish with an introduction by Albin T. Anderson (Lincoln, 1965), pp. 177–78.

5. Memo by the Finnish Legation, April 27, 1941, 260/169961–64 (given to Weizsäcker on April 28 by Kivimäki and Ramsay).

6. Blücher, "Unterhaltung mit Aussenminister am 8. März 1941," 6509/H072177–78; Blücher to AA, No. 149, March 8, 1941, 6440/H066694–95.

7. Report from the shipping expert of the German legation in Helsinki to the Merchant Shipping Office in the German Ministry of Commerce, *"Betr.:* Austausch finnischer Schiffe. Vorgang: Erlass SI/RS 1244/41 g.," March 15, 1941, 6440/H066692–93. See also Blücher to AA, No. 174, March 17, 1941, 6440/H066691.

8. Leitner to DGH, No. 224, March 22, 1941, 6434/H059276–77.

9. Medlicott, *Economic Blockade*, I, p. 631.

10. Memo by Finnish Legation (see above, n. 5); memo by Weizsäcker, St.S. Nr. 284, April 28, 1941, 260/169960.

11. Medlicott, *Economic Blockade*, I, p. 631.

12. Ritter, "Aktenvermerk," e.o.Ha.Pol. 261 g.Rs., April 30, 1941, 260/169970–71.

13. Medlicott, *Economic Blockade*, I, p. 632.

14. Blücher to AA, No. 378, June 3, 1941, 6440/H067261, and No. 387, June 5, 1941, 6440/H067269–70.

15. On March 17, Hitler told his top generals that the participation

of Finnish forces could be counted on "with certainty" only for operations against the Soviet naval base at Hanko. Halder, *Kriegstagebuch*, II, p. 319.

16. *Trials of War Criminals before the Nuernberg Military Tribunals under Control Council Law No. 10, Nuernberg, October 1946–April 1949*, X (Washington, 1951), pp. 982–84.

17. *Ibid.*, pp. 984–85, and *TMWC*, XXVI, pp. 399–401.

18. Halder, *Kriegstagebuch*, II, p. 387.

19. Hjalmar J. Procopé, *Fällande Dom som friar. Dokument ur Finlands krigsansvarighetsprocess* (Stockholm, 1946), p. 117; Mannerheim, *Minnen*, II, pp. 263–64; Korhonen, *Barbarossaplanen och Finland*, pp. 249–50.

20. Mannerheim, *Minnen*, II, p. 264.

21. Schnurre and Blücher to AA, No. 353, May 22, 1941, 6440/ H067225.

22. Schnurre and Blücher to AA, No. 354, May 22, 1941, 6440/ H067226.

23. Heinrichs, *Mannerheimgestalten*, II, pp. 235–38; Greiner, *Die Oberste Wehrmachtführung*, p. 387. Bernhard von Lossberg, *Im Wehrmachtführungsstab: Bericht eines Generalstabsoffiziers* (Hamburg, 1950), p. 114, claimed that Jodl's detailed exposition was given only *after* the Finns had committed themselves to participate in a German preventive war against the Soviet Union. The contemporary records do not support this claim, and it is flatly contradicted by Greiner.

24. OKW, WFSt/Abt. L (I Op.) Nr. 44794/41 g.K.Chefs., *"Protokoll der Besprechungen mit den Vertretern der finnischen Wehrmacht am 25.5.41 in Salzburg,"* May 25, 1941, T–312/1011/9206447–56. Underscored in the original.

25. See, for instance, "Wünsche auf taktischem Gebiet," Chefs., May 26, 1941, T–312/1011/9206469 (a marginal note by Buschenhagen says that he gave the document to Colonel Tapola on May 26); "Unterlagen für Besprechungen in Berlin. Qu.1—Gebiet," undated, T–312/ 1011/9206474; OKH, Gen.St. d.H.–Op.Abt. IN Nr. 991/41 g.Kdos.Chefs., *"Protokoll über die deutsch/finnischen Besprechungen am 26.5.41,"* May 26, 1941, T–78/458/6435360–63; Halder, *Kriegstagebuch*, II, p. 429.

26. Memo by Bürkner, OKW, Abt. Ausland, Nr. 183/41 g.Kdos.Chefs., Ausl. III Org., May 28, 1941, T–312/1011/9206430–32.

27. Buschenhagen to Lieut.-Col. von Buttlar, AOK Norwegen, May 28, 1941, T–312/1011/9206445. For a detailed discussion of the Finnish-German staff talks in Salzburg and Berlin, see Krosby, *Suomen valinta 1941*, pp. 147–73. See also Korhonen, *Barbarossaplanen och Finland*, pp. 253–68.

28. According to Korhonen, *Barbarossaplanen och Finland*, pp. 269, 272, and 276, the Helsinki conference began several days before June

3 and lasted a full week. This is not correct. Korhonen's assumption was based on a note in Halder's *Kriegstagebuch*, II, p. 435, recording a visit by Kinzel on May 29 "prior to taking off for Finland," and on the faulty recollection of Heinrichs, whom Korhonen interviewed. Heinrichs thought he recalled that Buschenhagen came to Helsinki at least as early as May 30 (letter to the author, December 30, 1964). There is documentary proof, however, that Buschenhagen was still in Berlin as late as June 1, when he sent a message to Oslo from Heimatstab Nord, the Berlin liaison staff of AOK Norwegen (see Heimatstab Nord, Ic Nr. 63/41 g.Kdos.Chefs., June 1, 1941, T–312/1011/9206413). Buschenhagen recalls clearly that the talks in Helsinki began on June 3 and ended on June 5, that he travelled to Helsinki in the company of Kinzel (probably on June 2), and that he was back in Germany on June 6 (letters to the author, November 25, 1963, and April 20, 1964). Halder recorded in his *Kriegstagebuch*, II, p. 446, that Kinzel reported back to him on June 6.

29. For some of their instructions and lists of desiderata, see OKW, WFSt/Abt. L (I Op.) Nr. 44813/41 g.Kdos.Chefs., "*Betr.:* Barbarossa," May 28, 1941, T–312/1011/9206433–34; "*Zusammenstellung der deutschen Wünsche für den Fall einer militärischen Zusammenarbeit mit Finnland auf den Quartiermeistergebiet*," g.Kdos.Chefs., T–312/1010/9205495–98 (this document was actually given to the Finns in Salzburg); OKW, WFSt/Abt. L (I Op.) Nr. 44832/41 g.Kdos.Chefs., June 2, 1941, T–312/1011/9206439–40.

30. Buschenhagen, "Ergebnis der deutsch-finnischen Besprechungen in Helsinki 3.–5.6.1941," AOK Norwegen, Der Chef des Generalstabes, Nr. 140/41 g.Kdos.Chefs., June 7, 1941, T–312/1011/9206338–42; Kinzel, "*Protokoll über die Besprechungen in Finnland vom 3.–6. Juni 1941*," OKH, Fremde Heere Ost, Chef, Nr. 74/41 g.Kdos.Chefs., June 10, 1941, T–78/458/6435456–59; Halder, *Kriegstagebuch*, II, p. 447.

31. Yleiesikunnen Päällikkö, "P[ro] M[emoria]," June 2, 1941, T–312/1011/9206345–47.

32. Heinrichs, letters to the author, September 3, 1964; September 21, 1964; December 30, 1964.

33. Korhonen, *Barbarossaplanen och Finland*, p. 274, does so, however.

34. Buschenhagen to OKH Attachéabteilung, Berlin, for relay to General Jodl, OKW W.F.St., Chefs., June 4, 1941, T–312/1011/9206427; Buschenhagen to Wehrmachtbefehlshaber Norwegen, Chefs., June 4, 1941, T–312/1011/9206428. The words "and Berlin" are missing from the latter telegram.

35. Buschenhagen, letter to the author, April 20, 1964.

36. Heinrichs, letter to the author, December 30, 1964. Buschenhagen recalls that Heinrichs objected to the sentence, but that he agreed with the contents of the report generally (letter to the author, April 20, 1964).

37. Article 33 of Finland's constitution states: "Decisions of war and peace shall be taken by the President with the consent of Parliament." Article 76, however, authorizes the president to mobilize the armed forces by a simple order-in-council.

38. For a detailed discussion of the Finnish-German staff talks in Helsinki, see Krosby, *Suomen valinta 1941*, pp. 174–95.

39. AOK Norwegen, Ia Nr. 68/41 g.Kdos.Chefs., V. Ang., "Zeittafel 'Silberfuchs'. Stand vom 10.6.41," June 10, 1941, T-312/1011/ 9206327–31.

40. Heimatstab Nord, Ia Nr. 78/41 g.Kdos.Chefs., June 10, 1941, T-312/1011/9206303.

41. AOK Norwegen, Ia Nr. 148/41 g.Kdos.Chefs. (Silberfuchs), "Operationsanweisung für das V. finnische Armee-Korps," June 10, 1941, T-312/1011/9206332–34.

42. OKH, Attachéabteilung (zbV) Gen.St.d.H. Nr. 114/41 g.K.Chefs., June 12, 1941, T-312/1052/9252764.

43. Buschenhagen and Rössing to OKH Attachéabteilung, AOK Norwegen, 1. Staffel, Abt. Ia Nr. 36/41 g.K.Chefs., June 14, 1941, T-312/1010/9205502.

44. Memo by Ritter about conversation with Jodl on June 14, e.o.Pol.I.M. 1843 g.Rs., June 16, 1941, 260/170017.

45. Rössing to the relevant OKH and OKW departments, Nr. 78/41 g.Kdos.Chefs., June 15, 1941, T-78/458/6435424.

46. Buschenhagen to AOK Norwegen (Oslo) for relay to OKW and OKH, Nr. 23/41 g.Kdos.Chefs., June 15, 1941, T-312/1011/9206210.

47. AOK Norwegen (Befehlsstelle Finnland), Abt. Ia Nr., 39/41 g.Kdos.Chefs., "Armeebefehl," June 17, 1941, T-312/1011/9206828–29. Copy No. 3 was issued to the Finnish III Army Corps. An order issued to that unit the same day by its commander, Major General Hjalmar Siilasvuo, included all of the relevant deployment details agreed upon with the Germans without making it plain that war was imminent. The reason for the "extraordinary maneuvers" was the presence of foreign troops in Finland and the threat of attack from "other states." However, the jurisdictional boundaries of the corps were extended eastward to the White Sea. *"Entfaltungsbefehl des AK,"* III. Armeekorps, Stab, Nr. 2/III/2 b/L 5616 geh., June 17, 1941, T-312/1000/9194719–21 (translated from Finnish).

48. AOK Norwegen (Befehlsstelle Finnland), Abt. Ia Nr. 65/41 g.Kdos., "Besondere Anordnungen für die Aufklärung," June 19, 1941, T-312/1011/9206890–93. Copies 4–6 were issued to the Finnish III Army Corps.

49. For a detailed discussion of Finland's military and political preparations for the attack on the Soviet Union in June, 1941, see Krosby, *Suomen valinta 1941*, pp. 196–231.

50. Blücher to AA, No. 367, May 30, 1941, 6440/H067246.

51. Blücher to AA, No. 425, June 12, 1941, 6440/H067333–34.

52. Blücher to AA, No. 395, June 6, 1941, 6440/H067288–90.

53. Blücher to AA, No. 423, June 12, 1941, 6440/H067326–28. See also Blücher to AA, No. 422, June 12, 1941, 6440/H067323–24.

54. Blücher to AA, No. 427, June 13, 1941, 6440/H067336. Two British trade inspectors were arrested by the Finnish State Police on June 14 for observing German troop movements through the port and railway station in Oulu. Two others were given twenty-four hours to leave town. See counterintelligence report by Major Warzecha, A.O. III Nr. 6/41 g., June 15 (and 19), 1941, T–312/1013/9208444–45.

55. Medlicott, *Economic Blockade*, I, p. 632; Gripenberg, *Finland and the Great Powers*, pp. 179–80.

56. Blücher to AA, No. 438, June 16, 1941, 6440/H067353–55.

57. Quoted in the original English in *ibid*.

58. *Ibid*.

59. Blücher to AA, No. 452, June 17, 1941, 6440/H067373.

60. Warzecha, A. O. III Nr. 8/41 g., June 17, 1941, T–312/1013/9208448.

61. Warzecha, Befehlsstelle Finnland, A.O. III Nr. 19/41 g.Kdos., June 19, 1941, T–312/1013/9208443. See also Blücher to AA, No. 460, June 18, 1941, 6440/H067385.

62. A detailed and rather amusing report on this significant operation was submitted by the German officer involved, Sonderführer Kurt von Löbbecke, *"Bericht über die vorläufige Sicherstellung des britischen Konsuls in Tornio, Roseberry, am 22.6.1941,"* AOK Norwegen (Befehlsstelle Finnland), Abt. Ic, June 23, 1941, T–312/1013/9208439–41. Löbbecke, an interpreter with an obvious sense of humor, seemed to enjoy the sarcastic and imperturbable Englishman. The security officer who subsequently escorted Roseberry to the Swedish border was all business, however. He recorded in all seriousness that he waited for the driver of the horse-and-buggy to return from the Swedish side of the border in order to interrogate him about "possible intelligence materials obtained from Roseberry." See Feldpolizei-Sekretär, Geheime Feldpolizei 629, Sonderkommando b. AOK Norwegen (Befehlsstelle Finnland), *"Betrifft:* Abtransport des engl. Konsuls Roseberry nach Schweden," June 23, 1941, T–312/1013/9208438.

63. Blücher to AA, No. 457, June 18, 1941, 6440/H067380.

64. Ribbentrop to DGH, No. 511, June 19, 1941, 260/170023.

65. Wuorinen, ed., *Finland and World War II*, pp. 131–32.

66. Blücher to AA, No. 442, June 16, 1941, 6440/H067360.

67. Blücher to AA, No. 544, July 1, 1941, 6440/H067512.

68. Blücher to AA, No. 522, June 27, 1941, 6440/H067474, No. 544 (see above, n. 67), and No. 547, July 1, 1941, 6440/H067517.

69. Blücher to AA, No. 950, September 14, 1941, 6440/H067579.

70. Witting told Blücher on June 28 that the British had recently confiscated more than 40,000 tons of Finnish shipping, a figure which seems somewhat exaggerated (Blücher to AA, No. 531, June 28, 1941, 6440/H067485–87).

71. Gripenberg, *Finland and the Great Powers*, p. 192.

72. See above, n. 70.

73. Gripenberg, *Finland and the Great Powers*, p. 192.

74. Blücher to AA, No. 473, June 20, 1941, 6440/H067400–03.

75. AOK Norwegen, Ia Nr. 2194/41 g.Kdos., "Morgenmeldung," June 22, 1941, T–312/994/9187190.

76. AOK Norwegen (Befehlsstelle Finnland), Abt. Ia Nr. 109/41 g.Kdos., June 22, 1941, T–312/994/9187197.

77. See above, n. 75.

78. Sent to Blücher by Ribbentrop as No. 529, June 23, 1941, 6434/H059213–14. Underscored in the original.

79. See Krosby, *Suomen valinta 1941*, pp. 215–21; Korhonen, *Barbarossaplanen och Finland*, pp. 311–28; Wuorinen, ed., *Finland and World War II*, pp. 105–11; Upton, *Finland in Crisis*, pp. 282–94; Mannerheim, *Minnen*, II, pp. 272–76.

80. Korhonen, *Barbarossaplanen och Finland*, p. 324.

81. Upton, *Finland in Crisis*, p. 293.

82. AOK Norwegen (Befehlsstelle Finnland), Abt. Ia Nr. 111/41 g.Kdos.Chefs., "Armeebefehl," June 22, 1941, T–312/1052/9252745–46.

83. Captain Karhunen to AOK Norwegen [Befehlsstelle Finnland] Ia, July 1, 1941, T–312/1004/9198663. See also AOK Norwegen (Befehlsstelle Finnland), Abt. Ia Nr. 280/41 g.Kdos., "Zwischenmeldung 1.7.1941," July 1, 1941, T–312/1000/9194638.

84. Verbindungsstab Nord, Ia Nr. 77/41 g.Kdos., June 24, 1941, T–312/1000/9194683. See also AOK Norwegen (Befehlsstelle Finnland), Ia, *Kriegstagebuch*, entry for June 24, 1941, T–312/1000/9193968. The entry for June 25 (T–312/1000/9193969–70) shows that air attacks were not ordered until 11 A.M. and the first German dive bombers flew their missions against the Murmansk railroad that afternoon. In other words, the Soviet air offensive began before the German.

85. See the chapter entitled "Lost Opportunities" in Upton, *Finland in Crisis*, pp. 235–60.

86. *Ibid.*, p. 293.

87. Warlimont, letter to the author, November 9, 1964.

88. Warlimont, letter to the author, November 28, 1964.

89. See above, n. 87.

90. Paasikivi, *Minnen*, II, p. 186.

91. Falkenhorst, "Armeetagesbefehl," June 29, 1941, T–312/1000/9194665.

92. Mannerheim, "Tagesbefehl des Oberbefehlshabers N:o 4," July 7, 1941, T–312/1000/9194609. The holy war theme was even more strongly stated in Mannerheim's Order of the Day No. 3 (see Heinrichs, *Mannerheimgestalten*, II, p. 278).

93. AOK Norwegen (Befehlsstelle Finnland), Abt. Ia Nr. 257/41 g.Kdos., "Tagesmeldung 29.6.1941," T–312/1000/9194666.

CHAPTER X

1. See T–84/99/1393077.
2. Letter to Petsamon Nikkeli O.Y. from Vilho Annala, Deputy Minister of Trade and Industry, No. 2412, August 5, 1941, T–83/88/3460901.
3. T–83/88/3460902–905.
4. "Vermerk über Nickelerz aus Petsamo," [August 25, 1941], T–84/99/1393087.
5. Schnurre, "Aufzeichnung über die Sitzung im Auswärtigen Amt am 7. Oktober 1941 betr. Nickelvorkommen Petsamo/Finnland," October 9, 1941, T–84/99/1393089–93.
6. "Entwurf einer Satzung der Nordland Nickel O.Y.," T–84/99/1393096–98.
7. "Geschäftsordnung für den Aufsichtsrat der Nordland Nickel O.Y.," T–84/99/1393099.
8. "Entwurf. Konsortialvertrag betr. Nordland Nickel O.Y.," T–84/99/1393100–102.
9. I.G. Farbenindustrie, "Notiz betr. Konzessionsvertrag Petsamo," geh. October 17, 1941, T–84/99/1393111–16.
10. Blücher to AA, No. 1202, g.Rs., October 27, 1941, 2111H/456853–54 (also in DGFP, XIII, No. 429). The telegram was obviously a report composed by Schnurre, not Blücher. Standard procedure required that Schnurre dispatch his report through the legation.
11. Zechlin to AA, No. 1285, November 10, 1941, 260/170335 (see also DGFP, XIII, No. 429, n. 3).
12. Blücher to AA, No. 1316, November 14, 1941, 260/170357–58 (also in DGFP, XIII, No. 469).
13. See above, n. 9.
14. "Vorbemerkung," [November 20, 1941], T–84/99/1393120–22.
15. Hausbrand, "Aktenvermerk," Der Reichswirtschaftminister, II Bg 16007/41, December 22, 1941, T–84/99/1392819–21.
16. Blücher to AA, No. 1504, December 11, 1941, 261/170434 (see also DGFP, XIII, No. 469, n. 2).
17. Memo from V Ld. 8 [Mühlbach?] to Section II Bg. 3 (both in Ministry of Economics), zu II Bg 16007/41, January 2, 1942, T–84/99/1392818.
18. Schüring, "Vermerk für Herrn Ministerialdirektor Borsch," [Reichsministerium für Rüstung und Kriegsproduktion,] Amtsgruppe I, Az.: Tgb. Nr. 47, I–V–D, Sch/Pw., July 11, 1944, geheime Reichssache, T–84/99/1392404–405. See also Der Reichswirtschaftsminister, OBH. 1366/44 geheime Reichssache, "Niederschrift aus der Besprechung vom 10. Juli 1944 über Fortführung der Luftschutzbauten von Petsamo," July 28, 1944, T–84/99/1392407–411.
19. Der Reichswirtschaftsminister, II EM 8151/41, "Vermerk. Betr.: Nickelvorkommen Petsamo (Finnland)," July 4, 1941, T–84/99/1393050–052.

20. Haefliger to under state secretary von Hanneken, Ministry of Economics, July 15, 1941, geh., T–84/99/1393059–062 (or T–84/99/1392729–733).

21. Dr. Balzer to Haefliger, "*Betr.:* Petsamo-Nickel," Reichswirtschaftsministerium, II EM 1665/41 g., July 29, 1941, T–84/99/1392762. In late August, spokesmen for I.G. Farbenindustrie again expressed their interest in inspecting the Kola nickel deposits, but they were told by General Hanneken that such a trip would have to await developments at the front (see above, n. 4). As things turned out, the Kola nickel areas were not captured by the German forces.

22. OKW/WiRüAmt, Stab Ia, Abschrift für die Akten, geh., July 10, 1941, T–84/99/1392734.

23. Haefliger and Frank-Fahle, *Bericht über die Reise der Herren Haefliger und Dr. Frank-Fahle nach Helsingfors in der Zeit vom 13. bis 19.8.1941 zu Verhandlungen wegen Petsamon Nikkeli O.Y.*, geheim, August 21, 1941, pp. 8–11, T–83/88/3460895–898.

24. Letter from I.G. Farbenindustrie to Reichswirtschaftsministerium, Bergbau-Abteilung, May 22, 1942, T–84/99/1392968; memo by Ritter and Henze of I.G. Farbenindustrie, Finanz-Sekretariat/Geh. 971, "Versand von Nickelerz aus Petsamo nach Deutschland," May 29, 1942, T–84/99/1392971; I.G. Farbenindustrie to Reichswirtschaftsministerium, Bergbau-Abteilung, June 29, 1942, T–84/99/1392148.

25. I.G. Farbenindustrie to Reichswirtschaftsministerium, Bergbau-Abteilung, "Nickelgewinnung im Petsamo-Gebiet," August 1, 1942, T–84/99/1392884.

26. "Besprechung mit Unterstaatssekretär von Hanneken am 26.8.1942 im Reichswirtschaftsministerium," II Bg. 10442/42, August 26, 1942, T–84/99/1392942–946.

27. Walter Nordin, "Petsamon Nikkeli OY:s kraftsörjning och elektriska anläggningar," *Vuoriteollisuus/Bergshanteringen*, No. 1–2 (1945), pp. 56–57.

28. DGH to AA, December 21, 1942 (copy in files of Ministry of Economics), T–84/99/1393225.

29. Der Reichswirtschaftsminister, Nr. II Bg. 10912/42, "*Vermerk:* Programm der Arbeiten in Petsamo," November 21, 1942, T–84/99/1393040–042; Der Reichswirtschaftsminister, Nr. II Bg, 10868/42, "*Vermerk* über Ferngespräche mit General Mummenthey von der IG. vom 6. und 12. November 1942," November 13, 1942, T–84/99/1393033–034; I.G. Farbenindustrie A/G, Vermittlungsstelle W., "*Niederschrift über eine Nickel-Besprechung in Berlin am 24. November 1942*," geheim, T–84/99/1393154–157.

30. DGH to AA, November 30, 1942 (copy in files of Ministry of Economics), T–84/99/1393184.

31. Letter from Petsamon Nikkeli O.Y. (signed by Söderhjelm and Wrede) to I.G. Farbenindustrie, December 5, 1942, T–84/99/

1393171–173. For Haefliger's rejoinder, see his letter of December 19, 1942, T–84/99/1393221–222.

32. See above, n. 28.

33. See, for instance, *Petsamo Produktions-Tabelle*, T–84/99/1392711, covering the period from January, 1943, to March, 1944.

34. See *Nickelvorkommen und Nickelgewinnung in Petsamo/Finnland*, July 28, 1942, T–84/99/1393149–152.

35. See above, n. 33.

36. See above, n. 24 and n. 34. See also letter from I.G. Farbenindustrie to Reichswirtschaftsministerium, Abteilung Bergbau, II Bg. 07558/42, June 8, 1942, T–84/99/1392965–67; *Ergebnis der Reise nach Petsamo vom 30.7. bis 12.8.1942*, T–84/99/1392919–923.

37. Der Beauftragte für den Vierjahresplan, Der Generalbevollmächtigte für das Kraftfahrwesen, Az. 76a 0024–IIc, *"Betr.:* Lkw für Nickelerztransporte von Petsamo nach Deutschland," September 9, 1942, T–84/99/1392991.

38. Oberkommando der Wehrmacht, Wi Amt/Amtsgruppe Wi Ausl III a^2 Nr. 41586/42 g., *"Betr.:* Nickelwerk Petsamo," December 24, 1942, T–84/99/1393212.

39. See above, n. 33.

40. I.G. Farbenindustrie, Vermittlungsstelle W, "Petsamo/Nickel-Meldung für Monat Februar 1943," geheim, March 9, 1943, T–84/98/1391696.

41. I.G. Farbenindustrie, Vermittlungsstelle W, "Petsamo Nickel-Meldung für Monat März 1943," geheim, April 12, 1943, T–84/98/1391745.

42. I.G. Farbenindustrie, Vermittlungsstelle W, "Petsamo-Nickelmeldung für den Monat September 1943," October 12, 1943, T–84/99/1392081.

43. See "Übersicht über Förderung und Erzeugung an Nickelerzen und Nickelmatte Petsamo im I. and II. Halbjahr 1943," zu Bg 2074/43 g., T–84/98/1392026.

44. I.G. Farbenindustrie, Vermittlungsstelle W, to Gebietsbeauftragten Norwegen der Organisation Todt, April 22, 1943, T–84/98/1391714.

45. I.G. Farbenindustrie, Vermittlungsstelle W, to Oberkommando der Wehrmacht, Wi Stab-Inland, May 5, 1943, T–84/98/1391751; I.G. Farbenindustrie, Vermittlungsstelle W, to Reichswirtschaftsministerium, Bergbauabteilung, May 24, 1943, T–84/98/1391831; WeWiStb. Norw. T I 7154/43 geh., May 29, 1943, T–84/98/1391783; Schoerner, General der Gebirgstruppe u. kar. General des XIX Geb.AK. Qu. Nr. 1127/43 geh., June 1, 1943, T–84/98/1391835; Reichskommissar Norwegen to Oberberghauptmann Gabel, Reichswirtschaftsministerium, "Betr.: Nickelverladungen von Petsamo," June 5, 1943, T–84/98/1391780–781.

46. I.G. Farbenindustrie, Vermittlungsstelle W, to Reichswirtschafts-

ministerium, Bergbauabteilung, "Erzverladeanlage Jakobsnes," September 13, 1943, T–84/99/1392615.

47. I.G. Farbenindustrie, Vermittlungsstelle W, to Reichswirtschaftsministerium, Abteilung Bergbau, May 21, 1943, T–84/98/1391798; I.G. Farbenindustrie, Vemittlungsstelle W, *"Zahlen-Unterlagen betr.* Erz- und Mattetransporte für die Besprechung im Reichswirtschaftsministerium am 28. Mai 1943, vormittags 11 Uhr, V. Stock Saal 7," May 27, 1943, T–84/98/1391801–803; Der Reichswirtschaftsminister, Vermerk zu II Bg 8b–1095/43 g., *"Betr.*: Erz- und Mattetransport von Petsamo nach Deutschland," May 27, 1943, T–84/98/1391804–807; Der Reichswirtschaftsminister, II Bg. 8b/1095/43 g–A.22.1.152 Bei, *"Niederschrift* aus der Besprechung vom 28.5.1943 betr. Erz- und Metall-Transport von Petsamo," May 28, 1943, T–84/98/1391808–809.

48. See *Petsamo-Produktionstabelle,* T–84/99/1392620.

49. Oberkommando der Wehrmacht, Fwi Amt Inl 2/I Nr. 010322/44 g, October 26, 1944, T–84/99/1392623; I.G. Farbenindustrie, Vermittlungsstelle W, "Restsendung Petsamo-Matte," December 15, 1944, T–84/99/1392655.

50. The table is based on the monthly reports of I.G. Farbenindustrie, as well as certain corrective and supplementary reports, filmed as T–84/98/1391407, 1391696, 1391745, 1391764, 1391784, 1391887, 1391960, 1391980, and T–84/99/1392081, 1392090, 1392150, 1392153, 1392180, 1392210, 1392253, 1392283, 1392317, 1392348, 1392401, 1392433, 1392499, 1392586, 1392599.

51. Reichswirtschaftsministerium, Der Oberberghauptmann, to Reichminister Professor Albert Speer, August 25, 1944, with enclosure: *Vermerk über die Deckung des deutschen Nickelbedarfs*, geheim, T–84/145/1449432–435.

52. Wehrmachtbefehlshaber Norwegen, Ia Nr. 17/42 g.Kdos./ Chefsache, March 14, 1942, *Abschrift! Fernschreiben OKW/WFST/ OP (M) NR. 55493/42 GK Chefs.* (signed by Hitler), T–312/1648/32–34.

53. *Blitzkrieg to Defeat: Hitler's War Directives 1939–1945,* edited, with an Introduction and Commentary, by H. R. Trevor-Roper (New York, Chicago & San Francisco, 1964), pp. 127–28 and 147–48.

54. Ziemke, *The German Northern Theater of Operations,* p. 246.

55. See Der Reichswirtschaftsminister, OBH. 1366/44 g.Rs., "Niederschrift aus der Besprechung vom 10. Juli 1944 über Fortführung der Luftschutzbauten von Petsamo," July 28, 1944, T–84/99/1392407–411; Dr. Ing. Wilhelm Witte, "Bericht über meinen Besuch bei der Petsamon Nikkeli O.Y. in Kolosjoki (Finnland) vom 19.–26.VII.1944," T–84/99/1392469–474; I.G. Farbenindustrie, Vermittlungsstelle W, "Petsamo / Sicherung der Grube," August 21, 1944, T–84/99/1392604 and –606.

56. See Ziemke, *The German Northern Theater of Operations,* pp. 273–91.

57. Dr. Schubardt, Nickelwerk Kolosjoki, Telegramm über OKW

an IG Farben, Berlin NW 7, Vermittlungsstelle W, General Mum-
menthey, SSD – LEBD 04 4.9. 1315 (DG HOSF 833) geheim, T–84/
99/1392669; Dr. Schubardt, Nickelwerk Kolosjoki, Telegramm über
OKW an IG Farben, Berlin NW 7, Vermittlungsstelle W, General
Mummenthey, SSD LEBD 05 4/9 2330 – Qem – Qed, geheim,
"Lagebericht vom 4.9.44," T–84/99/1392670.

58. Mummenthey, I.G. Vermittlungsstelle W, Telegramm über
Wehrmachtfernschreiber, Dr. Schubardt, Petsamonnikkeli, Kolosjoki,
September 5, 1944, T–84/99/1392671.

59. Ministerialrat Henne, "Betrifft: Besprechung mit Reichsminister
Speer am 6.9.1944," geheim, September 6, 1944, T–84/99/1392678–
679; "Vermerk Betr.: Nickelerzgrube Petsamo," geheim, September 6,
1944, T–84/99/1392676.

60. "Vermerk über ein Ferngespräch mit Min.Rat Henne vom
8.9.1944," September 8, 1944, T–84/99/1392680–681.

61. Der Reichswirtschaftsminister, OBH. 5, "Vermerk über Ferngespräche am 18. September 1944," September 19, 1944, T–84/99/
1392701–703.

62. See, for instance, Der Reichswirtschaftsminister, OBH 5, to OT,
Einsatzgruppe Wiking, Fsa. Nr. 3854/mue geheim, September 9, 1944,
T–84/99/1392686; "Aktenvermerk Betr.: Fachleute für Bergbau,
Hütte und elektrische Zentrale in Petsamo," September 12, 1944,
T–84/99/1392691–692; Dr. Hans Jahns, "Aktenvermerk über eine
Besprechung mit Herrn Dipl. Ing. Bodinus, Einsatzgruppe Wiking und
über ein Ferngespräch mit Herrn RR Schwarz," September 18, 1944,
T–84/99/1392698–699; ORR. Dr. Jahns to Diplom-Ingenieur Red-
dehase, "Betrifft: Leitung des Bergwerks Petsamo," Der Reichswirtschaftsminister, OBH. 5 – 1883/44 – A.22.1.152 Bei, September 21,
1944, T–84/99/1392522–525; Dr. Schubardt, Nickelwerk Kolosjoki,
an IG Farben, Berlin, Vermittlungsstelle W, General Mummenthey,
aus dem Felde 39 28.9. 1800, September 28, 1944, T–84/99/1392551;
Der Reichswirtschaftsminister, OBH. 5 02004/44 geheim, "Niederschrift aus der Besprechung vom 10. Oktober 1944. Betrifft: Weiter-
betrieb von Petsamo," October 10, 1944, T–84/99/1392571–573.

63. Mummenthey, Akten-Notiz, Mth/MH/10 Verm.St.W, October
11, 1944, T–84/99/1392574.

64. "Vermerk. Betr.: Nickelerzbergbau Petsamo," O.B.H. 02005/44
geheim, October 12, 1944, T–84/99/1392576.

65. OKW/Fwi Amt/Inland Nr. 2000/44 gK an Geb. AOK 20/Ia
(Finnland), October 13, 1944, T–84/99/1392579.

66. Ziemke, The German Northern Theater of Operations, pp. 303–
04. See also Der Reichswirtschaftsminister, OBH. 5 02168/44,
"Mündlicher Bericht von Betriebsführer Heimann über seinen Einsatz
in Petsamo (Kammi-Kivi)," November 15, 1944, T–84/99/
1392639–641.

67. Geb.AOK 20 Ia Nr. 3624/44 g., October 10, 1944 (copy sent
to the Ministry of Economics on October 20 by the OKW/Fwi Amt/
Inland), T–84/99/1392617.

Abbreviations

Ia = *Erster Generalstabsoffizier,* chief operations officer on a German military staff.

Ic = *Dritter Generalstabsoffizier,* chief intelligence officer on a German military staff.

AA = *Auswärtiges Amt,* the German Foreign Ministry.

Abt. = *Abteilung,* department, section, unit.

Abw. = *Abwehr,* the Counterintelligence Section of the *Ausl./Abw.* (see below).

AK (A.K.) = *Armeekorps,* army corps.

Ang. = *Angabe,* a designation given to follow-up documents in a particular case. Such items carry the file number of the original document plus Ang. I, Ang. II, etc.

AO = *Abwehroffizier,* counterintelligence officer.

AOK = *Armeeoberkommando,* headquarters of an army.

Artl. = *Artillerie,* artillery.

Att.Abt. = *Attaché-Abteilung,* the section of the *Gen.St.d.H.* (see below) which directed the work of German military attachés abroad.

Ausl. = *Ausland,* the Foreign Intelligence Section of the *Ausl./Abw.* (see below).

Ausl./Abw. = *Amt Ausland/Abwehr,* the Intelligence and Counterintelligence Department of the *OKW* (see below).

betr. = *betreffend* (or *betrifft*), concerning (or concerns), re.

Chefs. = *Chefsache,* top secret military (for commanding officer only).

D = *Abteilung Deutschland,* Department for German Internal Affairs in the German Foreign Ministry.

DGH = *Deutsche Gesandtschaft Helsinki,* the German Legation in Helsinki.

DNB = *Deutsches Nachrichtenbüro,* German News Agency, owned by the Ministry of Propaganda.

e.o. = *ex officio,* where this precedes a document file number, it indicates that there are no previous documents on the subject bearing that particular file number.

finn. = *finnisch*, Finnish.

Fr.H.Ost = *Fremde Heere Ost*, Eastern Intelligence Department of the *Gen.St.d.H.* (see below).

g., geh. = *geheim*, secret.

Geb.Korps = *Gebirgskorps*, mountain corps (corps or corps-level army unit trained in mountain warfare).

Gen.Kdo. = *Generalkommando*, headquarters of a corps or corps-level army unit.

Gen.St.d.H. = *Generalstab des Heeres*, the General Staff of the German Army.

g.K., g.Kdos. = *geheime Kommandosache*, top secret military.

g.Rs. = *geheime Reichssache*, top state secret.

Gr. = *Gruppe*, task force temporarily assembled for specific combined operations (e.g., Gruppe XXI, for the invasion of Denmark and Norway).

H. = *Heer*, the German Army.

Ha.Pol. = *Handelspolitisch*, symbol for the Economic Policy Department of the German Foreign Ministry.

H.Qu. = *Hauptquartier*, headquarters.

Inf. = *Infanterie*, infantry.

KTB = *Kriegstagebuch*, war diary.

L = *Abteilung Landesverteidigung*, the National Defense Department of the *WFSt.* (see below).

lfd.Nr. = *laufende Nummer*, serial number.

Lkw. = *Lastkraftwagen*, truck, lorry.

Mil.Att. = *Militärattaché*, military attaché.

Ob.d.H. = *Oberbefehlshaber des Heeres*, Commander in Chief of the German Army.

Ob.d.L. = *Oberbefehlshaber der Luftwaffe*, Commander in Chief of the German Air Force.

Ob.d.M. = *Oberbefehlshaber der Kriegsmarine*, Commander in Chief of the German Navy.

OKH = *Oberkommando des Heeres*, the High Command of the German Army.

OKL = *Oberkommando der Luftwaffe*, the High Command of the German Air Force.

OKM = *Oberkommando der Kriegsmarine*, the High Command of the German Navy.

OKW = *Oberkommando der Wehrmacht*, the High Command of the German Armed Forces (Hitler's supreme headquarters).

Op.Abt. = *Operationsabteilung*, the Operations Section of the *Gen.St.d.H.* (see above).

ORR = *Oberregierungsrat*, a grade in the German civil service.

Pol. = *Politisch*, symbol for the Political Department of the German Foreign Ministry, subdivided according to geographical areas designated by Roman numerals (e.g., Pol. VI for Scandinavia and the Baltic States).

Qu. = *Quartiermeister,* quartermaster.

RAM = *Reichsaussenminister,* the German Foreign Minister.

RR = *Regierungsrat,* a grade in the German civil service.

SD = *Sicherheitsdienst,* intelligence and counterintelligence agency of the *SS* (see below).

Skl. = *Seekriegsleitung,* the German Naval War Staff (*viz.,* the operations staff of the OKM).

SS = *Schutzstaffeln,* the para-military elite corps of the German National Socialist Party, used for police and military purposes.

St.S. = *Staatssekretär,* state secretary, the permanent civil service head of a German government department.

Tgb. = (1) *Tätigkeitsbericht,* activity report; (2) *Tagebuch,* diary, log, journal.

U.St.S. = *Unterstaatssekretär,* under state secretary, the second highest civil service rank within a German government department, usually held by heads of the primary departmental divisions.

VO = *Verbindungsoffizier,* liaison officer.

W = (1) *Wehrmacht,* the German Armed Forces; (2) *Wirtschaftspolitisch,* symbol for the Economic Policy Department of the German Foreign Ministry, subdivided according to geographical areas designated by Roman numerals (e.g., W V for Northern Europe).

WB = *Wehrmachtbefehlshaber,* designation of a general officer commanding all German armed forces within a specified area (e.g., *Wehrmachtbefehlshaber Norwegen*).

WFSt. = *Wehrmachtführungsstab,* the Operations Staff of the *OKW* (see above).

Wi.Rü = *Wehrwirtschafts- und Rüstungsamt,* the War Economy and Armaments Office of the *OKW* (see above).

z.b.V. = *zur besonderen Verwendung,* for special assignments.

zu = where this precedes a document file number, it indicates that the previous items on the same subject have that number.

Bibliography

I. UNPUBLISHED GERMAN DOCUMENTARY SOURCES

As a space-saving device, only individual documents were identified fully in the source notes, followed always by microfilm references. By matching these references with the corresponding microfilm numbers below, the source folder of each document can be found. In order to facilitate the matching process, the microfilm references have been placed ahead of the folder descriptions and the list has been arranged according to a rising progression of microfilm numbers (66–6674, B18–L287, T–71/92—T–312/1651).

66/46108–731: Auswärtiges Amt, *Aufzeichnungen des Ger.Dr. Paul Schmidt (Dolmetscher)*, geheim, vol. 1, August, 1924–December, 1940.

260/169924–170363: Auswärtiges Amt, Büro des Staatssekretärs, *Akten betreffend Finnland*, geheime Reichssache, vol. 3, April 1–November 15, 1941.

261/170364–659: Auswärtiges Amt, Büro des Staatssekretärs, *Akten betreffend Finnland*, geheime Reichssache, vol. 4, November 16, 1941–June 25, 1942.

441/221241–360: Deutsche Botschaft Moskau, *Politik (Deutschland). Politische Beziehungen zwischen Deutschland und den nordischen Staaten, Schweden, Norwegen, Finnland und auch Dänemark*, D Pol 2 Nord, vol. 1, January 27, 1939–May 13, 1941. Item 9/2.

1397/360368–460: Auswärtiges Amt, Inland II, *Sicherheitspolizei: Finnland*, geheim, D II—Aktenheft 8–3/78, August 12, 1940–December 10, 1942. Item 93.

2110H/456699–761: Auswärtiges Amt, Handelspolitische Abteilung, *Handakten Wiehl: Finnland*, vol. 5, March, 1938–October, 1940. Item 11/4.

2111H/456764–854: Auswärtiges Amt, Handelspolitische Abteilung,

Handakten Wiehl: Finnland, vol. 6, November 1, 1940–October 30, 1941. Item 11/5.

4416H/E083849–878: Auswärtiges Amt, Handelspolitische Abteilung, *Handakten Wiehl: Finnland,* vol. 5, March, 1938–October, 1940. Item 11/4.

4416H/E083879–911: Auswärtiges Amt, Handelspolitische Abteilung, *Handakten Wiehl: Finnland,* vol. 6, November 1, 1940–October 30, 1941. Item 11/5.

4545H/E146175–180: Auswärtiges Amt, Handelspolitische Abteilung, *Handakten Wiehl: Finnland,* vol. 5, March, 1938–October, 1940. Item 11/4.

5382H/E361671–761: Auswärtiges Amt, Handelspolitische Abteilung, *Handakten Wiehl: Finnland,* vol. 5, March, 1938–October, 1940. Item 11/4.

6434/H059186–282: Deutsche Gesandtschaft Helsinki, *Erlasse,* Nos. 201–600, March 18–July 1, 1941. Item 1/1.

6434/H059283–665: Deutsche Gesandtschaft Helsinki, *Berichte,* Nos. 121–499, March 13–August 12, 1940. Item 1/2.

6434/H059666–60104: Deutsche Gesandtschaft Helsinki, *Erlasse,* Nos. 70–500, February 14–September 24, 1940. Item 1/3.

6434/H060105–574: Deutsche Gesandtschaft Helsinki, *Berichte,* Nos. 501–813, August 13–December 30, 1940. Item 1/4.

6434/H060575–955: Deutsche Gesandtschaft Helsinki, *Erlasse,* Nos. 601–1100, July 1–September 4, 1941. Item 1/5.

6434/H061727–744: Deutsche Gesandtschaft Helsinki, *Drahterlasse und Drahtberichte,* December 4, 1939–March 13, 1940. Item 3/1.

6437/H063562–844: Deutsche Gesandtschaft Helsinki, *Drahterlasse,* Nos. 501–761, September 24–December 31, 1940. Item 4/1.

6440/H066561–67063: Deutsche Gesandtschaft Helsinki, *Berichte,* Nos. 1–250, January 1–April 19, 1941. Item 6/1.

6440/H067064–522: Deutsche Gesandtschaft Helsinki, *Berichte,* Nos. 251–550, April 19–July 1, 1941. Item 6/2.

6440/H067523–68125: Deutsche Gesandtschaft Helsinki, *Berichte,* Nos. 551–1000, July 1–September 24, 1941. Item 6/3.

6441/H069370–623: Deutsche Gesandtschaft Helsinki, *Drahterlasse,* April 24, 1939–March 13, 1940. Item 7/3.

6441/H069624–886: Deutsche Gesandtschaft Helsinki, *Drahtberichte,* April 27, 1939–March 13, 1940. Item 7/4.

6441/H069887–70020: Deutsche Gesandtschaft Helsinki, *Drahterlasse,* Nos. 1–200, January 2–March 3, 1941. Item 7/5.

6505/H070023–294: Deutsche Gesandtschaft Helsinki, *Multex-Telegramme,* Nos. 1–900, January 8–November 4, 1941. Item 8/1.

6507/H070861–71044: Deutsche Gesandtschaft Helsinki, *Multex-Telegramme,* Nos. 1–512, March 21–December 31, 1940. Item 9/1.

6509/H072101–107: Deutsche Gesandtschaft Helsinki, *Telegramme,* Nos. 482 and 485, June 22, 1941. Item 11/4.

6509/H072108–180: Deutsche Gesandtschaft Helsinki, *Freiwilligen-frage,* 1941. Item 11/5.

6509/H072206–442: Deutsche Gesandtschaft Helsinki, *Schriftwechsel der Schiffahrtssachverständigen beim deutschen Konsulat in Petsamo,* September, 1940–July, 1941.

6509/H072443–847: Deutsche Gesandtschaft Helsinki, *Schriftwechsel der Schiffahrtssachverständigen beim deutschen Konsulat in Petsamo,* September 15, 1940–February 10, 1941.

6509/H072848–992: Deutsche Gesandtschaft Helsinki, *Petsamo,* 1940. Item 11/7.

6509/H072993–73144: Deutsche Gesandtschaft Helsinki, *Petsamo,* 1941. Item 11/8.

6674/H090462–866: Deutsche Gesandtschaft Helsinki, *Geheimer Schriftwechsel,* Nos. 13–187/1940 and 1–92/1941 (March, 1940–April, 1941). Item 24/1.

6674/H090867–91280: Deutsche Gesandtschaft Helsinki, *Geheimer Schriftwechsel,* Nos. 99–252/1941 (April–September, 1941). Item 24/2.

6674/H091953–92217: Deutsche Gesandtschaft Helsinki, *Geheimer Schriftwechsel. Verschiedenes: Geheimberichte des Oberkommandos der Kriegsmarine betr. Handelsschiffahrt. Geheimberichte der Wehrmacht,* 1940–1943. Item 24/5.

B18/B003020–497: Auswärtiges Amt, Büro des Staatssekretärs, *Akten betreffend Finnland,* vol. 1, July, 1939–February 29, 1940.

B19/B003499–4191: Auswärtiges Amt, Büro des Staatssekretärs, *Akten betreffend Finnland,* vol. 2, March 1, 1940–March 31, 1941.

L271/L085467–490: Auswärtiges Amt, Büro des Staatssekretärs, *Akten betreffend Finnland,* geheime Reichssache, vol. 3, April 1–November 15, 1941. Item 16/2.

L274/L085686–767: Auswärtiges Amt, Politische Abteilung, *Akten betreffend finnisch-russischer Krieg,* Po 3 A Fin./Rus., vol. 5, Pol. VI Nos. 581–1775, March 4–June 24, 1940. Item 4/3.

L274/L085768–958: Auswärtiges Amt, Politische Abteilung, *Akten betreffend finnisch-russischer Krieg,* Po 3 A Fin./Rus., vol. 6, Pol. VI Nos. 1829–3018, June 30–December 31, 1940. Item 4/4.

L275/L086026–089: Auswärtiges Amt, Politische Abteilung, *Akten betreffend finnisch-russischer Krieg: Stellungnahme der Neutralen und Feindmächte,* Po 3 B Fin./Rus., vol. 4, Pol. VI Nos. 477–714, February 21–March 18, 1940. Item 5/3.

L275/L086090–197: Auswärtiges Amt, Politische Abteilung, *Akten betreffend finnisch-russischer Krieg: Stellungnahme der Neutralen und Feindmächte,* Po 3 B Fin./Rus., vol. 5, Pol. VI Nos. 721–1192, March 19–April 29, 1940. Item 5/4.

L277/L086261–324: Auswärtiges Amt, Politische Abteilung, *Akten betreffend innere Politik, Parlaments- und Parteiwesen,* Po 5

Finnland, vol. 1, Pol. VI Nos. 659/1936–1159/1940 (July 6, 1936–May 3, 1940). Item 6/1.

L287/L087553–620: Deutsche Botschaft Moskau, *Politik (Deutschland): Politische Beziehungen zwischen Deutschland und den nordischen Staaten, Schweden, Norwegen, Finnland und auch Dänemark,* D Pol 2 Nord, vol. 1, January 27, 1939–May 13, 1941. Item 9/2.

T–71/92/594611–645: Statistisches Reichsamt, Abteilung Ausland, *Zeitungsausschnitte sowie div. and. Artikel u. Berichte über Finnland.* Item RWM/20/2.

T–77/101/825878–6237: Oberkommando der Wehrmacht, Wehrwirtschafts- und Rüstungsamt, *Akten 66 k l a-d, Beiträge der Abteilungen und Gruppen zum Wirtschaftsbericht WStb. Schriftwechsel,* 1938–1940. Item Wi/IF 5.434.

T–78/458/6435243–532: Generalstab des Heeres, Abteilung Fremde Heere Ost, *Chefsachen Fremde Heere Ost,* vol. 1, April 24, 1939–September 2, 1941. Item H3/1.

T–78/458/6435690–918: Generalstab des Heeres, Abteilung Fremde Heere Ost, *Kriegsstellenbesetzung Diensteinteilung,* November 6, 1939–March 7, 1945. Item H3/4.

T–83/88/3460888–910: I.G. Farbenindustrie, *Bericht über die Reise der Herren Haefliger und Dr. Frank-Fahle nach Helsingfors in der Zeit vom 13. bis 19.8.1941 zu Verhandlungen wegen Petsamon Nikkeli O.Y.,* August 21, 1941 (seven *Anlagen*). Item 37.

T–83/88/3460913–915: I.G. Farbenindustrie, Volkswirtschaftliche Abteilung, *Britische, belgische und amerikanische Kapitalbeteiligungen an wichtigen Unternehmen der chemischen und Bergbauindustrie in Finnland,* Vowie 4062, July 9, 1940. Item 143.

T–83/91/3464607–6029: I.G. Farbenindustrie, Direktor Eduard Weber-Andreae, *Tagebuch,* December 1, 1938–July 20, 1940. Items 52–59.

T–83/92/3466030–7261: I.G. Farbenindustrie, Direktor Eduard Weber-Andreae, *Tagebuch,* July 23, 1940–December 31, 1941. Items 60–66.

T–83/93/3467262–8222: I.G. Farbenindustrie, Direktor Eduard Weber-Andreae, *Tagebuch,* January 2, 1942–October 14, 1943. Items 67–73.

T–84/88/1379354–357: *Die Nickelerzvorkommen und Nickelverarbeitung Norwegens und Finnlands* [provenance and authorship uncertain]. Item EAP 66–c–12–5/1.

T–84/88/1379358–428 and T–84/89/1379429–489: Statistisches Reichsamt, Auslandsforschung, *Die Wirtschaftsstruktur Finnlands,* 1942. Item EAP 66–c–12–5/2a.

T–84/89/1379490–494: Statistisches Reichsamt, Auslandsforschung, *Die ernährungswirtschaftliche Versorgungslage Finnlands* (1943?). Item EAP 66–c–12–5/3a.

T–84/89/1379495–504: Reichswirtschaftsministerium, *Finnland, Statistisches Material* (1944). Item EAP 66–c–12–5/5a.

T–84/89/1379780–951: Oberkommando der Wehrmacht, Wehrwirtschafts- und Rüstungsamt, Geheim-Archiv, *Skandinavien. Betrachtung der Wirtschaft der drei nordischen Staaten nach der Besetzung Norwegens und Dänemarks durch deutsche Truppen,* geheim, April 10, 1940. Item EAP 66–c–12–5/8.

T–84/89/1380067–684: Reichswirtschaftsministerium, Hauptabteilung II Bergbau, *Akten betreffend: Nachrichten von dem Berg-, Hütten- pp. Wesen in Schweden und Norwegen, auch Spitzbergen. A.XXII.1.110,* vol. 8, October 1, 1942–March 31, 1943. Item EAP 66–c–12–5/5b.

T–84/98/1391291–680: Reichswirtschaftsministerium, Hauptabteilung II Bergbau, *Das Berg-, Hütten- und Salinenwesen in Finnland. Beiakten: Nickelerzbergwerk Petsamo (geheim). A.XXII.1.152,* vol. 3, February, 1943. Item EAP 66–c–12–20/16.

T–84/98/1391681–2080 and T–84/99/1392081–271: Reichswirtschaftsministerium, Hauptabteilung II Bergbau, *Das Berg-, Hütten- und Salinenwesen in Finnland, insbesondere das Nickelerzbergwerk Petsamo. A.XXII.1.152, Beiakten,* vol. 1, 1943–March 31, 1944. Item EAP 66–c–12–20/8.

T–84/99/1392272–711: Reichswirtschaftsministerium, Hauptabteilung II Bergbau, *Berg-, Hütten- u. Salinenwesen in Finnland. Nickelerzbergwerk Petsamo. A.XXII.1.152 Bei.,* vol. 2, April 1, 1944. Item EAP 66–c–12–20/9.

T–84/99/1392712–3283: Reichswirtschaftministerium, Hauptabteilung II Bergbau, *Akten betreffend: Nachrichten über das Berg-, Hütten- und Salinenwesen in Finnland. A.XXII.1.152,* vol. 2, July, 1941–January, 1943. Item EAP 66–c–12–20/20.

T–84/143/1447302–307: Oberkommando der Wehrmacht, Wehrwirtschafts- und Rüstungsamt, Geheim-Archiv, *Änderungen der Versorgungslage Deutschlands und der Deutschland zugänglichen Neutralen infolge Besetzung Dänemarks, Norwegens, der Niederlande und Belgiens,* geheim, May, 1940. Item EAP 66–c–12–62/37.

T–84/145/1449344–746: Reichswirtschaftsministerium, Hauptabteilung II Bergbau, *Nickel* (1944). Item 66–c–12–62/81. (Of special interest are frames 1449426–468: *Nickel Berichte, Statistiken.*)

T–312/989/9181510–570: Gruppe XXI, *Kriegstagebuch Nr. 4,* June 11–October 31, 1940. AOK 20, E 280.

T–312/989/9181573–2098: Gruppe XXI, *Anlagenband 1 zum Kriegstagebuch Nr. 4,* Anlagen 1–170, geheim, June 11–September 21, 1940. AOK 20, E 280/1.

T–312/989/9182101–236: Gruppe XXI, *Anlagenband 2 zum Kriegstagebuch Nr. 4,* Anlagen 171–212, geheim, September 21–October 31, 1940. AOK 20, E 280/2.

T–312/989/9182312–363: Gruppe XXI, *Anlagenband 4 zum Kriegs-*

tagebuch Nr. 4: Umgliederung Geb.-Korps Norwegen, Ia Nr. 1995/41 g.K. AOK 20, E 280/4.

T–312/989/9182366–397: Gruppe XXI, *Anlagenband 5 zum Kriegstagebuch Nr. 4,* Anlage 1, *Artillerieregiment,* Ia Nr. 1995/41 g.K. AOK 20, E 280/5.

T–312/992/9184700–807: Gruppe XXI, O.Qu./Qu.2, *Kriegstagebuch,* vol. 2, August 11–October 31, 1940, geheime Kommandosache. AOK 20, W 6500/b.

T–312/992/9185545–669: Gruppe XXI, Ia, Ic, IIa, *Tätigkeitsberichte,* November, 1940. AOK 20, 12564/1.

T–312/992/9185672–804: Armee-Oberkommando Norwegen, Ia, Ic, IIa, *Tätigkeitsberichte,* December, 1940, Chefsache. AOK 20, 12564/2.

T–312/993/9185807–6011: Armee-Oberkommando Norwegen, Ia, Ic, IIa, Tätigkeitsberichte, January, 1941, Chefsache. AOK 20, 12564/3.

T–312/993/9186014–138: Armee-Oberkommando Norwegen, Ia, Ic, IIa, *Tätigkeitsberichte,* February, 1941, Chefsache. AOK 20, 12564/4.

T–312/993/9186141–502: Armee-Oberkommando Norwegen, Ia, Ic, IIa, *Tätigkeitsberichte,* March, 1941, Chefsache. AOK 20, 12564/5.

T–312/993/9186505–741: Armee-Oberkommando Norwegen, Ia, Ic, IIa, *Tätigkeitsberichte,* April, 1941, Chefsache. AOK 20, 12564/6.

T–312/993/9186744–982: Armee-Oberkommando Norwegen, Ia, Ic, IIa, *Tätigkeitsberichte,* May, 1941, Chefsache. AOK 20, 12564/7.

T–312/994/9187077–335: Armee-Oberkommando Norwegen, Ia, Ic, IIa, *Tätigkeitsberichte,* June, 1941, Chefsache. AOK 20, 13386/1.

T–312/999/9193337–493: Armee-Oberkommando Norwegen, Ic, *Tätigkeitsbericht,* June 11–October 2, 1941, geheim. AOK 20, 18207/1.

T–312/1000/9193953–4258: Armee-Oberkommando Norwegen (Befehlsstelle Finnland), *Kriegstagebuch,* June 3, 1941–January 13, 1942. AOK 20, 19070/1.

T–312/1000/9194261–748: Armee-Oberkommando Norwegen (Befehlsstelle Finnland), *Anlagen zum Kriegstagebuch,* vol. 1, June 10–August 31, 1941. AOK 20, 19070/2.

T–312/1004/9198431–970: Armee-Oberkommando Norwegen (Befehlsstelle Finnland), *Anlagen zum Kriegstagebuch, I, Tagesmeldungen,* June 20–July 10, 1941. AOK 20, 19070/12.

T–312/1010/9205466–488: Gruppe XXI, Chef/Ia, *Anlagen zum Kriegstagebuch: Renntier,* August 16–September 7, 1940. AOK 20, 20844/1.

T–312/1010/9205491–550: Armee-Oberkommando Norwegen (Befehlsstelle Finnland), Ia, *Anlagen zum Kriegstagebuch: Chefsachen* [*zu deutsch-finnischen Generalstabsbesprechungen*], June 2–November 18, 1941. AOK 20, 20844/2.

T–312/1010/9205553–675: Armee-Oberkommando Norwegen, Ia, *Akte "Barbarossa,"* January 31–July 23, 1941, geheime Kommandosache Chefsache. AOK 20, 20844/3.

T–312/1010/9205678–6183: Armee-Oberkommando Norwegen, Chef/ Ia, *Anlagen zum Kriegstagebuch: "Silberfuchs,"* vol. 1, January 10–May 8, 1941, Chefsache. AOK 20, 20844/4.

T–312/1011/9206186–601: Armee-Oberkommando Norwegen, Chef/ Ia, *Anlagen zum Kriegstagebuch: "Silberfuchs,"* vol. 2, May 4– June 18, 1941, Chefsache, AOK 20, 20844/5.

T–312/1011/9206604–934: Armee-Oberkommando Norwegen, Chef/ Ia, *Anlagen zum Kriegstagebuch: "Silberfuchs,"* vol. 3, June 12, 1941–January 10, 1942, Chefsache. AOK 20, 20844/6.

T–312/1013/9208025–452: Armee-Oberkommando Norwegen (Befehlsstelle Finnland), Ic, *Anlagen zum Kriegstagebuch, II, Verschiedenes, Feindliche Propaganda, Eigene Propaganda beim Feinde, Luftaufklärung, Feindnachrichten, Gefangenaussagen,* June 17, 1941–January 5, 1942. AOK 20, 25353/2.

T–312/1013/9208819–9383 (cont. on T–312/1014): Armee-Oberkommando Norwegen (Befehlsstelle Finnland), Ia/Ic, *Anlagen zum Kriegstagebuch, IVa, Tagesmeldungen unterstellter Einheiten,* June 20–October 31, 1941. AOK 20, 25353/4.

T–312/1028/9225169–347: Armee-Oberkommando Norwegen, Ia, *Tätigkeitsberichte für den Monat Januar 1942,* Chefs. AOK 20, 29362/1.

T–312/1029/9226436–651: Armee-Oberkommando Norwegen (Befehlsstelle Finnland), O.Qu./Qu.2, *Kriegstagebuch,* June 5, 1941– January 10, 1942. AOK 20, 33166/1.

T–312/1029/9226656–7013: Armee-Oberkommando Norwegen (Befehlsstelle Finnland), O.Qu./Qu.2, *Anlagen zum Kriegstagebuch, II, Zusammenarbeit mit Finnland auf dem Quartiermeister Gebiet,* May 19, 1941–January 9, 1942. AOK 20, 33166/2/I.

T–312/1032/9229687–989: Armee-Oberkommando Norwegen (Befehlsstelle Finnland), Ia, *Kriegstagebuch,* June 3, 1941–January 13, 1942. AOK 20, 35198/1.

T–312/1032/9230558–653: Gruppe XXI, Ia, *Anlagen zum Kriegstagebuch: Sonderakte Norwegen-Kirkenes,* June 22–October 16, 1940. AOK 20, 35198/6.

T–312/1033/9230956–1351: Armee-Oberkommando Norwegen, Chef/ Ia, *Anlagen zum Kriegstagebuch: Allgemein [Weisungen für die Verteidigung Norwegens],* September 21, 1940–May 1, 1942, Chefsachen. AOK 20, 35641.

T–312/1033/9231561–2007 (cont. on T–312/1034): Armee-Oberkommando Norwegen, O.Qu., *Anlagen zum Kriegstagebuch: Beurteilungen der Versorgungslage–Norwegen und Finnland,* May 1–November 30, 1941. AOK 20, 36037/1.

T–312/1041/9240309–510: Armee-Oberkommando Norwegen, Ia, *Tätigkeitsberichte für den Monat Juni 1943*, g.Kdos.Chefs. AOK 20, 40216/1.
T–312/1052/9252440–789: Armee-Oberkommando Norwegen, Ia, *Anlage 1 zu (Geb.)A.O.K. 20 Ia Nr. 290/44 g.Kdos.Chefs. v. 21.7.44*, g.Kdos.Chefs., June 2–December 31, 1941. AOK 20, 58628/1.
T–312/1648/4–183: Armee-Oberkommando Norwegen, Ia, *Tätigkeitsberichte für den Monat März 1942*, Chefs. AOK 20, 29362/3.
T–312/1651/207–522: Armee-Oberkommando Norwegen, Ia, *Tätigkeitsberichte für den Monat April 1944*, g.Kdos.Chefs. AOK 20, 52519/1.

II. PUBLISHED DOCUMENTARY SOURCES

Degras, Jane, ed. *Soviet Documents on Foreign Policy*, vol. 3, *1933–1941*. London, New York & Toronto: Oxford University Press for the Royal Institute of International Affairs, 1953.
Documents on German Foreign Policy 1918–1945, Series D (1937–1945), VIII, *The War Years, September 4, 1939–March 18, 1940*. Washington, D.C.: U.S. Government Printing Office, 1954. Department of State Publication 5436.
———, IX, *The War Years, March 19–June 22, 1940*. Washington, D.C.: U.S. Government Printing Office, 1956. Department of State Publication 6312.
———, X, *The War Years, June 23–August 31, 1940*. Washington, D.C.: U.S. Government Printing Office, 1957. Department of State Publication 6491.
———, XI, *The War Years, September 1, 1940–January 31, 1941*. Washington, D.C.: U.S. Government Printing Office, 1960. Department of State Publication 7083.
———, XII, *The War Years, February 1–June 22, 1941*. Washington, D.C.: U.S. Government Printing Office, 1962. Department of State Publication 7384.
———, XIII, *The War Years, June 23–December 11, 1941*. Washington, D.C.: U.S. Government Printing Office, 1964. Department of State Publication 7682.
Finland Reveals Her Secret Documents on Soviet Policy, March 1940–June 1941: The Attitude of the USSR to Finland after the Peace of Moscow, with a preface by Hjalmar J. Procopé, minister of Finland to the United States. New York: Wilfred Funk, 1941. Official Blue-White Book of Finland.
Foreign Relations of the United States, Diplomatic Papers, 1939, I, *General*. Washington, D.C.: U.S. Government Printing Office, 1956. Department of State Publication 6242.

————, 1940, I. *General.* Washington, D.C.: U.S. Government Printing Office, 1959. Department of State Publication 6818.

————, 1940, II, *General and Europe.* Washington, D.C.: U.S. Government Printing Office, 1957. Department of State Publication 6496.

————, 1940, III, *The British Commonwealth, The Soviet Union, The Near East and Africa.* Washington, D.C.: U.S. Government Printing Office, 1958. Department of State Publication 6638.

————, 1941, I, *General, The Soviet Union.* Washington, D.C.: U.S. Government Printing Office, 1958. Department of State Publication 6642.

Halder, Franz. *Kriegstagebuch. Tägliche Aufzeichnungen des Chefs des Generalstabes des Heeres, 1939–1942,* issued by Arbeitskreis für Wehrforschung, ed. by Hans-Adolf Jacobsen. Stuttgart: W. Kohlhammer Verlag, 1963–64, 3 vols.

House of Representatives, 83rd Congress, 2nd Session, *House Reports,* vol. XIII, *Special Reports of Select Committee on Communist Aggression,* No. 2684, Part 13, *Communist Takeover and Occupation of Lithuania.* Washington, D.C.: U.S. Government Printing Office, 1954–55.

House of Representatives, 83rd Congress, 2nd Session, Select Committee on Communist Aggression. *Report of the Select Committee to Investigate Communist Aggression and the Forced Incorporation of the Baltic States into the U.S.S.R.,* vol. 3. Washington, D.C.: U.S. Government Printing Office, 1954.

Klee, Karl, ed. *Dokumente zum Unternehmen "Seelöwe". Die geplante deutsche Landung in England 1940.* Göttingen, Berlin & Frankfurt: Musterschmidt Verlag, 1959. Vol. 4b of *Studien und Dokumente zur Geschichte des Zweiten Weltkrieges,* issued by Arbeitskreis für Wehrforschung in Frankfurt a.M.

Nazi Conspiracy and Aggression. Washington, D.C.: U.S. Government Printing Office, 1946, 8 vols. and Supplements A and B.

Nazi-Soviet Relations 1939–1941: Documents from the Archives of the German Foreign Office, ed. by Raymond James Sontag and James Stuart Beddie. Washington, D.C.: U.S. Government Printing Office, 1948. Department of State Publication 3023.

Rei, August, comp. *Nazi-Soviet Conspiracy and the Baltic States. Diplomatic Documents and other Evidence,* issued under the auspices of the Estonian National Council and the Estonian Information Centre. London: Boreas Publishing Company, 1948.

Seidl, Alfred, ed. *Die Beziehungen zwischen Deutschland und der Sowjetunion 1939–1941. Dokumente des Auswärtigen Amtes.* Tübingen: H. Laupp'sche Buchhandlung, 1949.

Select Committee on Communist Aggression. *See* House of Representatives. . . .

Trevor-Roper, H. R., ed. *Blitzkrieg to Defeat: Hitler's War Directives*

1939–1945, with Introduction and Commentary. New York, Chicago, & San Francisco: Holt, Rinehart and Winston, 1964.
Trial of the Major War Criminals before the International Military Tribunal, Nuremberg, 14 November 1945–1 October 1946. Proceedings Documents and other Material in Evidence. Official Text. English Edition. Nuremberg: Secretariat of the Tribunal, 1947–49, 42 vols.
Trials of War Criminals before the Nuernberg Military Tribunals under Control Council Law No. 10, Nuernberg, October 1946–April 1949. Washington, D.C.: U.S. Government Printing Office, 1949–53, 15 vols.

III. LETTERS AND INTERVIEWS

Buschenhagen, Erich. General of the Infantry, Oberstdorf, Federal Republic of Germany.
Fieandt, Rainer von. Former Prime Minister of Finland, Helsinki.
Halder, Franz. Colonel General and former chief of staff of the German Army, Aschau, Federal Republic of Germany.
Heinrichs, Erik. General of the Infantry, former chief of staff and commander in chief of the Finnish Armed Forces, Helsinki (deceased 1965).
Howard-White, Frank B. International Nickel Ltd., Thames House, Millbank, London.
Ivalo, Asko. Ambassador of Finland to India, New Delhi.
Jacobsen, Hans-Adolf. Historian and editor of Halder's diary, Buschdorf bei Bonn, Federal Republic of Germany.
Korhonen, Arvi. Professor of History at Helsinki University (deceased 1967).
Maczek, Max, Engineer, technical director, and member of the Board of Directors of Kupferbergbau Mitterberg Gesellschaft m.b.H., Mühlbach am Hochkönig, Salzburg, Austria.
Pakaslahti, Aaro. Ambassador of Finland to Spain, Madrid.
Söderhjelm, Johan Otto. Former managing director of the Petsamo Nickel Company, former member of Finland's parliament and minister of justice, Helsinki.
Talvela, Paavo. General of the Infantry (Res.), Helsinki, Finland.
Tapola, Kustaa A. General of the Infantry, Helsinki, Finland.
Warlimont, Walter. General of the Artillery, Gmund am Tegernsee, Federal Republic of Germany.
Wuorinen, John H. Emeritus Professor of History at Columbia University, Gardner, Mass.
Ziemke, Earl F. Professor of History at the University of Georgia, Athens, Ga.

IV. MEMOIR LITERATURE

Blücher, Wipert von. *Gesandter zwischen Diktatur und Demokratie. Erinnerungen aus den Jahren 1935–1944.* Wiesbaden: Limes Verlag, 1951.

Boheman, Erik. *På vakt. Kabinettssekreterare under andra världskriget.* Stockholm: P. A. Norstedt & Söners Förlag, 1964.

Born, Ernst von. *Levnadsminnen.* Helsinki: Söderström, 1954.

Churchill, Winston S. *The Second World War.* Boston: Houghton Mifflin, 1948–53, 6 vols.

Erfurth, Waldemar. *Der finnische Krieg 1941–1944.* Wiesbaden: Limes Verlag, 1951.

Frietsch, Carl Olof. *Finland ödesår 1939–1943.* Helsinki: Söderström, 1945.

Greiner, Helmuth. *Die Oberste Wehrmachtführung 1939–1943.* Wiesbaden: Limes Verlag, 1951.

Gripenberg, Georg A. *Finland and the Great Powers: Memoirs of a Diplomat,* trans. from the Swedish with an introduction by Albin T. Anderson. Lincoln: University of Nebraska Press, 1965.

Hägglöf, Gunnar. *Svensk krigshandelspolitik under andra världskriget.* Stockholm: P. A. Norstedt & Söners Förlag, 1958.

Hedin, Sven. *Utan uppdrag i Berlin.* Stockholm: Fahlcrantz & Gumælius, 1949. English translation by Joan Bulman, *Sven Hedin's German Diary, 1935–1942.* Dublin: Euphorion Books, 1951.

Hess, Wilhelm. *Eismeerfront 1941. Aufmarsch und Kämpfe des Gebirgskorps Norwegen in den Tundren vor Murmansk.* Heidelberg: Scharnhorst Buchkameradschaft, 1956. Vol. 9 of *Die Wehrmacht im Kampf.*

Hilger, Gustav, and Alfred G. Meyer. *The Incompatible Allies: A Memoir-History of German-Soviet Relations, 1918–1941* (New York: Macmillan, 1953).

Hölter, Hermann. *Armee in der Arktis. Die Operationen der deutschen Lappland-Armee.* Bad Nauheim: Verlag Hans-Henning Podzun, 1953.

Hull, Cordell. *The Memoirs of Cordell Hull.* New York: Macmillan, 1948, 2 vols.

Kordt, Erich. *Nicht aus den Akten. Die Wilhelmstrasse in Frieden und Krieg. Erlebnisse, Begegnungen und Eindrücke, 1928–1945.* Stuttgart: Union Deutsche Verlagsgesellschaft, 1950.

————. *Wahn und Wirklichkeit. Die Aussenpolitik der Dritten Reiches. Versuch einer Darstellung.* Stuttgart: Union Deutsche Verlagsgesellschaft, 1948.

Lossberg, Bernhard von. *Im Wehrmachtführungsstab. Bericht eines Generalstabsoffiziers.* Hamburg: H. H. Nölke Verlag, 1950.

Mannerheim, Carl Gustaf Emil. *Minnen.* Helsinki: Holger Schildts Förlag, 1952, 2 vols. English translation by Count Eric Lewenhaupt, *The Memoirs of Marshal Mannerheim.* London: Cassell, 1953.

Paasikivi, Juho Kusti. *President J. K. Paasikivis minnen 1939–1940.* Helsinki: Söderström, 1958.

—————. *President J. K. Paasikivis minnen, II, Mellankrigstiden: Som sändebud i Moskva.* Helsinki: Söderström, 1959.

Paulus, Friedrich. *"Ich stehe hier auf Befehl!" Lebensweg des Generalfeldmarschalls Friedrich Paulus mit den Aufzeichnungen aus dem Nachlass, Briefen und Dokumenten,* herausgegeben von Walter Görlitz. Frankfurt a.M.: Verlag für Wehrwesen Bernard & Graefe, 1960. English translation by Col. R. H. Stevens, *Paulus and Stalingrad.* London: Methuen, 1963.

Raeder, Erich. *Struggle for the Sea.* London: William Kimber, 1959.

Schmidt, Paul. *Statist auf diplomatischer Bühne 1923–45.* Bonn: Athenäum-Verlag, 1949.

Tanner, Väinö. *The Winter War: Finland Against Russia, 1939–1940.* Stanford: Stanford University Press, 1957. Translated from the Finnish, *Olin ulkoministerinä talvisodan aikana.* Helsinki, 1950.

Warlimont, Walter. *Im Hauptquartier der deutschen Wehrmacht 1939–1945. Grundlagen, Formen, Gestalten.* Frankfurt a.M.: Bernard & Graefe Verlag für Wehrwesen, 1962. English translation by R. H. Barry, *Inside Hitler's Headquarters, 1939–45* (New York: Frederick A. Praeger, 1964).

Weizsäcker, Ernst von. *Erinnerungen.* München: Paul List Verlag, 1950. English translation by John Andrews, *Memoirs of Ernst von Weizsäcker.* Chicago: Henry Regnery, 1951.

Wigforss, Ernst. *Minnen, III, 1932–1949.* Stockholm: Tidens Förlag, 1954.

V. HISTORICAL STUDIES

Assman, Kurt. *Deutsche Schicksalsjahre. Historische Bilder aus dem Zweiten Weltkrieg und seiner Vorgeschichte.* Wiesbaden: Eberhard Brockhaus, 1950.

Beloff, Max. *The Foreign Policy of Soviet Russia, II, 1936–1941.* London: Oxford University Press, 1949.

Butler, J. R. M. *Grand Strategy, II, September 1939–June 1941.* London: HMSO, 1957. History of the Second World War. United Kingdom Military Series.

Dallinn, David J. *Soviet Russia's Foreign Policy, 1939–1942.* New Haven: Yale University Press, 1942.

Derry, Thomas K. *The Campaign in Norway.* London: HMSO, 1952. History of the Second World War. United Kingdom Military Series.

Enander, Bo F. *Finland och det andra världskriget. En återblick på finländsk utrikespolitik, 1939–1944.* Stockholm: A. Bonnier, 1944.

Erfurth, Waldemar. *Die Geschichte des deutschen Generalstabes von 1918 bis 1945.* Göttingen: Musterschmidt-Verlag, 1957. Vol. 1 of *Studien zur Geschichte des Zweiten Weltkrieges,* issued by Arbeitskreis für Wehrforschung in Frankfurt a.M.

Fleming, Peter. *Operation Sea Lion: The Projected Invasion of England in 1940—An Account of the German Preparations and the British Countermeasures.* New York: Simon & Schuster, 1957.

Görlitz, Walter. *Der Zweite Weltkrieg 1939–1945,* vol. 1. Stuttgart: Steingrüben-Verlag, 1951.

Heideman, Bert R. M. "A Study of the Causes of Finland's Involvement in World War II at Three Separate Times: November, 1939; June, 1941; September, 1944." Ann Arbor: University of Michigan, University Microfilms, Doctoral Dissertation Series, Publication 5676, 1952.

Heinrichs, Erik. *Mannerheimgestalten,* II, *Marskalken av Finland.* Helsinki: Holger Schildts Förlag, 1959.

Howard-White, F. B. *Nickel: An Historical Review.* Princeton & New York: D. Van Nostrand, 1963.

Hubatsch, Walther. *"Weserübung": Die deutsche Besetzung von Dänemark und Norwegen 1940. Nach amtlichen Unterlagen dargestellt, mit einem Anhang: Dokumente zum Norwegenfeldzug 1940,* 2nd rev. ed. Göttingen, Berlin & Frankfurt: Musterschmidt-Verlag, 1960. Vol. 7 of *Studien und Dokumente zur Geschichte des Zweiten Weltkrieges,* issued by Arbeitskreis für Wehrforschung in Stuttgart.

Jakobson, Max. *The Diplomacy of the Winter War. An Account of the Russo-Finnish War, 1939–1940.* Cambridge: Harvard University Press, 1961.

Klee, Karl. *Das Unternehmen "Seelöwe": Die geplante deutsche Landung in England 1940.* Göttingen, Berlin & Frankfurt: Musterschmidt-Verlag, 1958. Vol. 4a of *Studien und Dokumente zur Geschichte des Zweiten Weltkrieges,* issued by Arbeitskreis für Wehrforschung in Frankfurt a.M.

Korhonen, Arvi. *Barbarossaplanen och Finland.* Tampere: Söderström, 1963. Original Finnish edition: *Barbarossasuunnitelma ja Suomi: jatkosodan synty.* Porvoo & Helsinki: Söderström, 1961.

———. *Viisi sodan vuotta. Suomi toisen maailmansodan myrskyissä.* Porvoo: Söderström, 1958.

Krosby, H. Peter. *Suomen valinta 1941.* Helsinki: Kirjayhtymä, 1968 [copyright 1967].

Kuussaari, Eero, and Vilho Niitemaa. *Finlands krig 1941–1945. Lantstridskrafternas operationer.* Stockholm: Militärlitteraturföreningens Förlag, Nr. 198, 1949.

Langer, William L., and S. Everett Gleason. *The Challenge to Isolation, 1937–1940.* New York: Harper & Brothers, 1952.
———. *The Undeclared War, 1940–1941.* New York: Harper & Brothers, 1953.
Lundin, C. Leonard. *Finland in the Second World War.* Bloomington: Indiana University Press, 1957.
Mazour, Anatole G. *Finland between East and West.* Princeton: D. Van Nostrand, 1956.
Medlicott, William N. *The Economic Blockade.* London: HMSO, 1952–59, 2 vols. History of the Second World War. United Kingdom Civil Series.
Procopé, Hjalmar J. *Fällande dom som friar. Dokument ur Finlands krigsansvarighetsprocess.* Stockholm: Fahlcrantz & Gumælius, 1946.
Rossi, A. [pseud. for Angelo Tasca]. *The Russo-German Alliance, August 1939–June 1941.* Boston: The Beacon Press, 1951.
Soini, Yrjö. *Dömda—för vad? Krigsansvarighetsfrågan 1944–1949.* Helsinki: Holger Schildts Förlag, 1956.
Sturney, A. C. *The Story of Mond Nickel* (Plaistow: Privately printed, 1951).
Tarulis, Albert N. *Soviet Policy toward the Baltic States, 1918–1940.* Notre Dame: University of Notre Dame Press, 1959.
Terä, Martti V. *Tienhaarassa. Syksyn 1940 tapahtumat Barbarossa-suunnitelman taustaa vasten.* Helsinki: Otava, 1962.
Thompson, John F., and Norman Beasley. *For the Years to Come: A Story of International Nickel of Canada.* New York: G. P. Putnam's Sons; and Toronto: Longmans, Green, 1960.
Tippelskirch, Kurt von. *Geschichte des Zweiten Weltkriegs.* Bonn: Athenäum-Verlag, 1951.
Toynbee, Arnold and Veronica M., eds. *Survey of International Affairs 1939–1946: The Initial Triumph of the Axis.* London: Oxford University Press for the Royal Institute of International Affairs, 1958.
Upton, Anthony F. *Finland in Crisis, 1940–41: A Study in Small-Power Politics.* Ithaca: Cornell University Press, 1965.
Wahlbäck, Krister. *Finlandsfrågan i svensk politik 1937–1940.* Stockholm: P. A. Norstedt & Söners Förlag, 1964.
Weinberg, Gerhard L. *Germany and the Soviet Union, 1939–1941.* Leiden: E. J. Brill, 1954.
Wuorinen, John H. *A History of Finland.* New York & London: Columbia University Press for the American-Scandinavian Foundation, 1965.
———, ed. *Finland and World War II, 1939–1944.* New York: Ronald Press, 1948.
Ziemke, Earl F. *The German Northern Theater of Operations, 1940–1945.* Washington, D.C.: U.S. Government Printing Office, 1960. Department of the Army Pamphlet No. 20–271.

262   Bibliography

VI. PERIODICAL ARTICLES

Aminoff, Torsten G. "Mannerheimgestalten i klarare belysning," *Appell*, XIII:39 (November 22, 1957), 1, 8.

————. "Marskalkens memoarer som historisk källa," *Appell*, XIII:30 (September 20, 1957), 1, 8.

————. "Opinionerna under fortsättningskriget. Et utkast," *Appell*, XIII:28 (September 5, 1957), 1, 8.

————. "Risto Ryti och Storfinland. En källkritisk skiss," *Appell*, XIV: 11 (March 14, 1958), 4–5.

————. "Somaren 1940," *Appell*, XIV:4 (January 24, 1958), 1, 8.

Anthoni, Eric. "Ett försök att skildra Finlands andel i andra världskriget," *Historisk tidskrift för Finland*, XLII:3 (1957), 156–61.

Bonsdorff, Göran von. "Finland mellan öst och väst," *Statsvetenskaplig tidskrift*, LIV:5 (1951), 331–50.

Bonsdorff, Henrik von. "Våra krigsmål hösten 1941," *Appell*, XIV:13 (March 28, 1958), 4–5.

Bourcart, Général. "La guerre de Finlande," *Revue d'Histoire de la Deuxième Guerre Mondiale*, III:9 (January, 1953), 15–24.

Ensiö, P. "Kaulatunturin nikkelimalmin käsittely Petsamon Nikkeli O.Y.:n sulimossa," *Vuoriteollisuus/Bergshanteringen*, No. 1–2 (1945), 33–43.

Fieandt, Rainer von. "Finnland zwischen West und Ost," *Information der Internationalen Treuhand A.G.*, No. 16 (March, 1962), 1–12.

Grzybowski, Kazimierz. "The Soviet Doctrine of Mare Clausum and Politics in Black and Baltic Seas," *Journal of Central European Affairs*, XIV:4 (January, 1955), 339–53.

Haapala, Paavo. "Petsamon nikkelimalmialueen löytöhistoria, tutkimukset ja geologia," *Vuoriteollisuus/Bergshanteringen*, No. 1–2 (1945), 1–9.

————. "Kaulatunturin kaivos," *Vuoriteollisuus/Bergshanteringen*, No. 1–2 (1945), 10–18.

Hanson, K. "Petsamon Nikkeli OY:s gruvindustriella byggnadsverksamhet," *Vuoriteollisuus/Bergshanteringen*, No. 1–2 (1945), 19–32.

Herlitz, Nils. "Några notiser rörande krisen i juni 1941," *Statsvetenskaplig tidskrift*, LXII (1959), 318–19.

Klink, Ernst. "Deutsch-finnische Waffenbrüderschaft 1941–1944," *Wehrwissenschaftliche Rundschau*, VIII:7 (July, 1958), 389–412.

Korhonen, Arvi. "Amerikkalainen Suomen sodanaikaisen politiikan tuomarina," *Suomen kuvalehti*, No. 45 (November 9, 1957), 24–25, 54, 56.

————. "Rauhaton välirauhan aika," *Suomalainen Suomi*, XXXV:1 (1967), 23–29.

Krosby, H. Peter. "The Diplomacy of the Petsamo Question and Finnish-German Relations, March-December 1940," *Scandia*, XXXI:2 (1965), 291–330.

————. "The Diplomacy of the Petsamo Question and Finnish-German

Relations, January–June 1941," *Scandia,* XXXII:1 (1966), 169–211.

Nordin, Walter. "Petsamon Nikkeli OY:s kraftsörjning och elektriska anläggningar," *Vuoriteollisuus/Bergshanteringen,* No. 1–2 (1945), 44–61.

Olsson, Henrik A. "Två frågor rörande de svensk-finska förbindelserna 1939–1940," *Statsvetenskaplig tidskrift,* LVIII (1955), 124–41.

Skodvin, Magne. "Norges plass i Hitlers militære planar etter 7. juni 1940," *Historisk tidsskrift,* XXXV (1949–51), 429–58.

Stein, George H. and Krosby, H. Peter, "Das finnische Freiwilligen-Bataillon der Waffen-SS: eine Studie zur SS-Diplomatie und zur ausländischen Freiwilligen-Bewegung," *Vierteljahrshefte für Zeitgeschichte,* XIV:4 (October, 1966), 413–53.

VII. NEWSPAPER ARTICLES

Andreen, Per G. "Svensk-finska unionsplaner 1940–41," *Svenska Dagbladet* (Stockholm), August 8, 1961.

———. "Unionsplanens förlisning," *Svenska Dagbladet,* August 10, 1961.

Aström, Sven-Erik. "Beskt piller att svälja," *Hufvudstadsbladet* (Helsinki), August 22, 1957.

Bonsdorff, Henrik von. " 'Armen bör få tid för uppmarsch'. Blücherrapport om politiken i juni 1941," *Hufvudstadsbladet,* January 15, 1958.

———. "Berlin krävde brytning med London," *Hufvudstadsbladet,* January 29, 1958.

———. "Günther-besök -41 oroade Berlin," *Hufvudstadsbladet,* January 5, 1958.

———. "Hitlerbrev bekräftade avtal," *Hufvudstadsbladet,* January 19, 1958.

———. "Krigstida poker om Petsamo," *Hufvudstadsbladet,* December 15, 1957.

———. "När Finland drogs in i kriget på nytt," *Hufvudstadsbladet,* June 22, 1966.

———. "Trekampen om Petsamo oavgjord. Tyskt-finländskt spel under täcke om nickel 1940–41," *Hufvudstadsbladet,* December 22, 1957.

———. "Veltjens-rapport om transiteringen 1940: Mannerheim-Ryti godkände prompt," *Hufvudstadsbladet,* December 1, 1957.

Krosby, H. Peter. "Saksan Suomen-politiikka 1939 ja 1941," *Uusi Suomi* (Helsinki), August 15, 1967.

"Russisk angrepsplan mot Norge og Sverige i 1940," *Aftenposten* (Oslo), morning edition, February 21, 1964.

Söderhjelm, J. O. "Nickeldiplomati," *Hufvudstadsbladet,* November 2, 1966.

Steinby, Torsten. "Krigscensuren 1939–1945," *Hufvudstadsbladet,* October 31, 1962.

Index

Adlerkreutz, Colonel Carlos, 63
Airo, Major General Aksel F.: on defense of Petsamo, 123
Åland Islands: Soviet demand for, 32, 56, 57, 58; threat of Soviet occupation of, 63; mentioned, 173, 174
Aluminum, 49
Anglo-French Expeditionary Corps: abandons Narvik front, 18
Arctic Ocean: Finland needs outlet to, 3, 12
Arctic Ocean Highway: constructed, 4; for transit of German troops, 51, 118; abandoned by Finns, 123; Germans to secure, 124, 176; and transportation of ore, 194; Russians cross, 202
Arkhangelsk, 160
Armaments industry, German: nickel needed for, 35, 69, 71, 124, 190, 194, 198
Arms and munitions: German supplies to Finns, 11, 14, 16, 51, 65, 66; in Veltjens Agreement, 80, 81; British view of German supply to Finns, 104
A/S Sydvaranger, 195, 196
Assarsson, Vilhelm: reports Paasikivi considering resignation, 144–45; mentioned, 41
Australia, 27

Balkans: Germany marches on, 157; effect of military moves in, 162;

mentioned, 146, 160, 171
Baltic Sea: and overland trade route, 87
Baltic states: Soviet annexation of, 25, 26, 51, 55–56, 62, 68; German missions in, 59; information on Soviet troops from, 60; Finnish view of annexation, 63; German offensive through, 173; mentioned, 67, 135
Bank of Finland, 103
"Barbarossa," Operation, 96, 124, 171, 172–73, 181, 184
Barents Sea: fishing industry in, 4, 87
Barth, Professor Otto, 193
Belgium, 21
Below, Carl von, 36
Bessarabia: Soviet annexation of, 25, 26, 56; mentioned, 90
Blaufarbenwerke: nickel production of, 28
Blücher, Wipert von: urges German interest in Finland, 11–12, 69, 87, 118; and Finnish-German trade talks, 15, 16, 20, 21–22, 30; reports political climate in Finland, 17, 21, 25, 26, 63, 64, 162; on Witting, 17, 95; opinion of Kivimäki, 17–18; concern for security of Petsamo, 22–23; reports Russians at Petsamo border, 23, 60–61; advises German occupation of Kirkenes, 24; and Finnish-Soviet Petsamo talks, 36, 40,

265

73, 74, 108, 110–11, 113, 115, 134, 143–44, 163–64, 228n6; reports opinion of Ramsay, 40–41; instructions to Haefliger, 42; and Anglo-Finnish relations, 43, 167, 178–79, 180; reports on Sobolev proposal, 44; on German consul in Petsamo, 50; and Finnish fear of Russians, 59; lines of communication of, 98; reacts to Paasikivi's proposal, 135; on sports meet with Finns, 208n58; mentioned *passim*

Blue-White Book, 97, 140

Boheman, Erik, 62

Bolsheviks, 3

Botshkarev, 60

Brauchitsch, Field Marshal Walther von, 70

Brazil, 27

British Ministry of Economic Warfare, 35, 49, 168

British Reprisals Order, 49

Buddenberg, Dr. Otto, 193

Bukovina: Soviet annexation of, 25, 26, 56

Bulgaria, 117, 159

Bürkner, Captain Leopold: attends German-Finnish military conference, 172–74; mentioned, 69

Buschenhagen, Colonel Erich: orders Norwegian border battalions, 23–24; requests reinforcement in North Norway, 23–24, 70, 71, 72; reports preparations for "Reindeer," 122–23; prepares for "Silver Fox," 123–24; in Finland, 158, 236n28; attends German-Finnish military conference, 172, 174, 175; testimony of, at Nuremberg, 222n97

Butler, Richard A.: Gripenberg confers with, 104–5

Castrén, Dr. Erik: and legality of Anglo-Canadian contract, 109; on Fieandt delegation, 126, 131; on Fieandt committee, 153

Censorship: in Finland, 63

Coal, 15

Cobalt, 11

Commercial Policy Committee, 16

Communists: activity of, in Finland, 115, 146

Continuation War: and German transit agreement, 67; mentioned, 190

Copper: Germans purchase from Finns, 10, 11, 13, 16, 21; for power cables, 192

Cripps, Sir Stafford: in favor of Soviet-Finnish concession, 79, 84; and English position on Petsamo, 116; mentioned, 68

Denmark, 16, 18–19

Diesel oil, 43

Dietl, General Eduard, 71, 182, 185

East Prussia: German forces in, 157

Erkko, Eljas, 206n15

Estonia: annexed by Soviets, 25, 55; reports of Russian forces in, 59–60, 61

Fabricius, Wilhelm: reports Soviet moves against Finland, 26

Falkenhorst, Colonel General Nikolaus von: and forces in North Norway, 70; in command in north, 173; commands Finnish V Army Corps, 176, 183; and crusade against Bolshevism, 185; mentioned, 71

Fieandt, Rainer von: appointed to trade delegation, 20–21; on possible British invasion of Petsamo, 21–22; signs trade treaty, 30; his attitude toward trade negotiations, 30–31; on rights to nickel concession, 40; on time limit for German deliveries, 47; and financing of Kolosjoki construction, 54; and German arms deliveries, 65–66; reports Finnish position on Petsamo, 82; chosen for delegation to Moscow, 101; advises withholding nickel matte agreement, 102; contact of, with Schnurre, 103, 113, 187; negotiates for Soviet-Finnish concession, 106–9, 126–31, 134, 137, 142, 144, 145–46, 148, 152–57, 164; Germans agree with position of, 133; refuses to work out German-Finnish concession, 189; mentioned, 104, 118, 120, 140, 141, 147

Finnish V Army Corps (Finnish III Army Corps): Falkenhorst issues orders to, 176; deployment of, 182, 183, 237n47

Finnish Foreign Ministry: understanding of English position, 79. *See also* Witting, Foreign Minister

Finnish-Swedish union talks, 107

Finnmark: German occupation of, 23, 24

Fish flour plant, 87

Fisheries, German, 87

Fishing industry, 4, 87

Four Year Plan, German, 195

France: considers second front in Scandinavia, 8; Soviets avoid engaging, 10; German assault on, 18, 20, 21; collapse of, 24-25, 68

Frank-Fahle, Dr. G., 187

Frietsch, Carl Olof: on Finnish involvement with Germany, 67, 68; on Finnish invasion of Soviet Karelia, 217n78

Frohwein, Hans, 60

Frose: I.G. Farbenindustrie plant at, 28

Fuel: Finns need to import, 50

Gartz, Åke: suggested for delegation to Moscow, 101

Gasoline: shipping of, 49

Geological Commission of Finland, 4

German Foreign Ministry: attitude toward Winter War, 11; on importance of Petsamo nickel, 12, 13, 14; in trade negotiations, 13; on Finnish trade delegation, 20; and Molotov's response to Finnish-German trade treaty, 37; and Finnish Soviet Petsamo talks, 39, 41, 42, 45–46, 59, 87, 98, 136, 137, 147, 149, 154; reaction to British shipping blockade, 50; and rumor of Russian takeover of Finland, 59; presses for signing of nickel matte agreement, 134; and British time charter demands,

167–68. *See also* Ribbentrop, Joachim von

German Ministry of Armaments and War Production [*or* Munitions], 191, 201. *See also* Speer, Albert

German Ministry of Economics, 13, 28, 191, 197–98, 201. *See also* Ludwig, Waldemar

German News Bureau (DNB), 25–26

German-Norwegian armistice agreement, 23

German-Soviet Non-Agression Pact, 11, 55, 68, 75–76, 90

Göring, Marshal Hermann: and arms deliveries to Finns, 65, 66; on importance of nickel ore, 88–89, 195; mentioned, 81, 169

GPU (Soviet secret police), 106

Grain: Finns import, 163, 164, 168, 169, 233n36, 234n43

Great Britain: Soviets consider defense against, 8; Soviets avoid provoking, 10; possible Finnish turn to, 11; attitude toward, in Finland, 21; possible retaliation by, considered, 22, 35; Soviets want withdrawal from Petsamo, 34, 37–38; interference of, with Finnish shipping, 48–50, 116, 165–70, 177–79, 238n70; shipping blockade of, 51–52; anticipation of German offensive on, 62, 68; Russians refuse closer cooperation with, 68, 85, 108; speculations on activities of, 70; Paasikivi advises shut out of Petsamo, 79; attitude of, toward Petsamo concession, 83, 84, 85, 86, 100, 103, 104–5, 109, 119, 129; and Ramsay's negotiations, 115–16; possible attack on Norway, 159; negotiates for time charter, 166; good will of, toward Finland, 170; suspicion over Finnish involvement, 177; breakdown of Finnish relations with, 178–80; Finns avoid further aggravation of, 187; mentioned, 89, 143

Greece, 27, 70, 159, 161

Gripenberg, Georg A.: on shipping interference, 48, 180–81; checks on Cripps' statement, 84; and reports of anti-English feeling in Finland, 104; confers with Butler, 105; urges acceptance of time charter, 166; warned of retaliation by Britain, 178; mentioned, 79, 85, 116, 169

Grönblom, Berndt: chosen for delegation to Moscow, 101; in Finnish-Russian negotiations, 102, 106–9; returns to Helsinki, 131; serves on Fieandt committee, 153

Grundherr, Werner von: Kivimäki visits, 25; mentioned, 94

Gulf of Bothnia: German troops in ports of, 175–76; and overland trade route, 194

Gulf of Finland: Soviet military base proposed on, 6

Günther, Christian, 63

Hackzell, Antti, 12

Haefliger, Paul: on significance of Petsamo ore, 28–29; to be cautious in negotiations, 42; reports on possible division of concession, 44–45; spokesman for I.G. Farbenindustrie, 187, 190; on preparation for production at Kolosjoki, 191, 192; complains to Petsamo Nickel, 192–93

Halder, Colonel General Franz: on Hitler's intentions for Finland, 96; fears Russian invasion of Finland, 117; denies Finnish-German military collusion, 125; mentioned, 69, 70, 227n67

Hanko: Soviets demand base at, 6; Soviets offer to return to Finns, 32; transit agreement, 57, 58, 66; German offensive against, 173, 174

Hanneken, General Hermann von, 191, 241n21

Hanseatic League, 19

Harbor, ice free: Finnish need for, 4, 9. *See also* Liinahamari

Heinrichs, Lieutenant General Erik: denies knowledge of German plans, 125; attends Finnish-German military conference, 172,

173, 174, 175, 176; mentioned, 227n67, 236n28

Hilger, Gustav, 91

Hitler: and arms for Finland, 16, 51, 65, 66, 69; attitude of, toward Petsamo, 22, 70, 72, 122, 159, 199; decides to invade Soviet Union, 51, 65, 122, 125; Finnish interpretation of speech of, 64; concern over Russian threat to Finland, 69; talks with Molotov, 85, 90–91; implied protection of Finland, 95–96; Directive No. 21, 96, 122, 222n97; consultations on Petsamo negotiations, 119; approves Warlimont proposal, 171; confirms military agreements with Finns, 182; speculation on his reaction to different Finnish policy, 183–84; Directive No. 44, 199; Directive No. 50, 199; and continuation of Petsamo operations, 201; mentioned, 149

Holland, 21

Hungary, 159

Hynninen, Paavo J.: to assist Paasikivi, 78; and Finnish delegation in Moscow, 101; succeeds Paasikivi, 152; receives new instructions, 161–62; presents new proposal to Vyshinsky, 163–64

I.G. Farbenindustrie: new process for refining nickel, 27; expansion of, 28; negotiates with Krupp, 29; contract with Petsamo Nickel, 29, 30, 34, 42, 46–47, 53, 74, 92, 104, 121, 138, 151; on anticipated Petsamo production, 90; to show agreements to Molotov, 101–2; in Soviet-Finnish draft agreements, 128, 129, 130, 131, 136, 137; new agreement with Petsamo Nickel, 187; wants control of concession, 189; frustration of, in Petsamo, 191, 192–93; and transportation of raw ore, 194–95, 196; mentioned, 44, 77, 103, 154, 200, 201, 241n21. *See also* Oppau

The International Nickel Company of Canada: Mond Nickel subsidiary of, 4; monopoly of, 4, 27, 189; investment in Petsamo, 5; possible pull-out from Petsamo, 21, 75; agreement with I.G. Farbenindustrie, 28; restriction in selling Petsamo shares, 48. *See also* Mond Nickel Company of London; Nickel mining concession, Anglo-Canadian contract; Petsamo Nickel Company

Iron pyrites, 13, 16

Ivalo: British trade inspector in, 166, 179

Jakobsnes: new harbor at, 196, 199

Jäniskoski hydroelectric power station: planned, 5; military guards at, 117; Russians move to include in concession, 128, 129, 130; completion of, 191, 192; defense of, 199; Todt Organization to take over, 201; order destruction of, 201

Jodl, General Alfred: military conference with Finns, 171–73, 235n23

Kandalaksha: German offensive against, 173, 183

Karelia, Eastern, 3, 6, 217n78

Karelian Isthmus, 3, 6, 8, 117, 199–200, 206n15

Kattegat, 19

Kaulatunturi mountain range: nickel-copper ore in, 4, 5, 191

Keitel, Field Marshal Wilhelm, 69, 172

Kinzel, Colonel Eberhard: attends German-Finnish military conference, 174, 175; mentioned, 236n28

Kirkenes: possible Russian acquisition of, 23, 24; shipment of ore by way of, 45, 167, 194, 195–96, 201; German transit to, 51, 66, 118; in "Reindeer," 122; German concentration in, 158

Kivimäki, Professor Toivo M.: government of, 17; appointed envoy in Berlin, 18; reports Finnish attitude toward Russia, 25; in German-Finnish Petsamo talks, 36, 43–44, 74, 190; seeks German support, 64, 76–77, 82, 83, 94, 129, 133, 136, 154, 156–57; and German arms deliveries, 65–66 and German transit agreement, 66; lines of communication of, 98; and Soviet-Finnish Petsamo talks, 101–2, 112–13, 120–21, 148, 149, 153, 155; consultations in Helsinki, 152; and Fieandt proposal, 153, 155; appeals to Germany on shipping, 168, 169; rejects German proposal on concession, 190; mentioned, 60, 89, 114, 134

Kola Peninsula: nickel ore deposits at, 191, 241n21; mentioned, 33, 122

Kolosjoki: as facility for Petsamo mining, 5; untouched during Winter War, 10; German concern for security of, 22–23, 70, 71, 117, 118, 124, 173, 183–84, 199; prepare for production at, 44, 46; financing of construction at, 54, 191–92; begin mining operations at, 77; production at, 91, 187, 193, 197, 201; possible Soviet propaganda at, 94, 115; Germans plan advance on, 122–23; confiscated, 186, 187; German control of, 190; destruction of, ordered, 201–2. *See also* Nickel ore, Smelter plant

Korhonen, Arvi, 33

Kreutzwald, Reiner, 13

Kreve-Mickevičius, Professor Vincas 57

Krupp: nickel production of, 28; in planned industrial syndicate, 187

Krutikov, Alexei D.: in Soviet-Finnish Petsamo negotiations, 105, 107–8, 126–31, 136, 142

Kurotsev: in Soviet-Finnish Petsamo talks, 105, 136, 137

Labor at Petsamo mines: shortage of, 191; and Finnish draft of workers, 192; Finns withdraw after armistice, 200; Germans

seek to supply, 200–201
Lake Ladoga: area in Winter War, 8; "Ladoga front," 173, 185
Lapland: German Army of, 199
Latvia, 25, 29
League of Nations, 25
Leningrad: proposals for defense of, 6; German offensive against, 173, 184
Liinahamari: Finns acquire harbor at, 4; rail communications to, 4; protection of, 8; control of shipping in, 35; abandoned in war, 123; British trade inspector in, 166; mentioned, 22, 128
Lithuania, 25, 57, 59
Lossberg, Lieutenant Colonel Bernhard von: attends German-Finnish military conference, 172
Low Countries, 68
Ludwig, Waldemar: in German-Finnish trade talks, 14, 15; presents draft concession agreements to Finland, 188–89
Lundström, Edvin: seeks assurance of German support, 93–94, 154

Magill, Lieutenant Colonel J. H., 177
Mäkinen, Colonel Einar N.: attends German-Finnish military conference, 172
Mannerheim, Field Marshal Gustaf: on Hanko transit agreement, 58; and arms deliveries, 65; and dangers of Soviet concession, 94; asks for partial mobilization, 116–17; in command on Ladoga front, 173; response to German military proposals, 174, 175; urges removal of trade inspectors, 178; succeeds Ryti as president, 200; mentioned, 10, 51, 172, 185
Mätäsvaara molybdenum mine, 10
Matsuoka, Yosuke, 160
Metallgesellschaft, 29, 187
Mikoyan, Anastas I., 54, 73–74
Molotov, Vyacheslav M.: initiates discussion of Petsamo, 6; in 1940 peace negotiations, 9–10; demands nickel concession, 32, 33, 34, 73, 74, 75, 76–77, 99–101; his strategy in Petsamo dispute, 36, 37, 38; and German interest in Petsamo, 39, 45, 48, 53–54, 70, 92–93, 97, 98, 99, 113–14, 119–20, 131–32, 136, 137; and Anglo-Finnish contract, 41, 85–86, 89; protests arrest of SNS leaders, 56, 214–15n18; indicates intention to annex Finland, 57; in talks with Paasikivi, 77, 78, 79, 84, 107, 147–48; conversations with Hitler and Ribbentrop, 90–91, 94, 95, 171; his political interest in Petsamo, 133; his statement of Soviet position, 146–47, 148–49, 150; Fieandt's reply proposal to, 152–53; mentioned, 44, 161
Molybdenum: Finns supply to Germany, 10, 13, 21, 116
The Mond Nickel Company of London: Petsamo ore contract of, 4–5, 126, 186; agreement with I. G. Farbenindustrie, 28; Finns negotiate to recover concession from, 74–75; and talks with Ramsay, 109, 115; mentioned, 117, 139, 190. See also The International Nickel Company of Canada; Nickel mining concession, Anglo-Canadian contract; Petsamo Nickel Company
Mountain Corps Norway, 159, 182, 185
Murman Coast: Soviet defense of, 6; Russian troop movements on, 24
Murmansk: German offensive against, 72, 173, 183, 185, 239n84; security of, 133; mentioned, 88, 160
Mussolini, Benito: talks with Hitler, 125

Narvik, 16, 18, 22–23, 70
National Coalition Party, 25
Navicerts: British require, 35; for Finnish vessels, 48–49, 50, 52, 116, 165, 166, 179; mentioned, 129

Nickel mining concession: Soviet demand for, 29–30, 57, 73; negotiations for Soviet-Finnish, 33–34, 38, 95, 105–6; three-way agreement suggested, 36; German position on, 39, 48, 76, 81, 91, 114, 187–90; and Veltjens Agreement, 80; Finnish-English discussions of, 104–5, 115–16; management of Soviet-Finnish, 105–6, 126, 127, 128, 130, 133, 135, 139–40, 148, 149, 153, 155–56, 161; draft agreement for Soviet-Finnish, 128
——Anglo-Canadian contract: in 1939 Soviet-Finnish negotiations, 6; as factor in 1940 Soviet-Finnish settlement, 10, 12–13; in German-Finnish negotiations, 15; Germans seek annulment of, 28–29; Finns rely on legal rights of, 33–34, 76, 82, 86, 100, 109, 187; Soviets want annulment of, 37, 38; possible pull-out considered, 40–41, 127, 128; opposes delivery of ore to Germany, 41, 42–43; Finns suggest Russian dealing on, 79; compensation of, 108, 228n6; Ramsay seeks transfer of, 115–16. *See also* The International Nickel Company of Canada; The Mond Nickel Company of London
Nickel ore: production dominated by International Nickel, 4, 189; Germany to purchase Nivala output, 10–11; negotiations for delivery to Germany of Kolosjoki, 13–14, 20, 21, 27, 28, 29, 30–31, 37–38, 41–42, 47–48, 69, 88–89, 90, 102–4, 121–22, 129, 134, 137–38, 146–47, 150–51; new processing of, 27; matte sold to I. G. Farbenindustrie, 27–28; delivery to Soviets of, 34–35, 54, 78–79, 132; production of refined, 45; value of, at Kolosjoki, 45, 88–89, 90; production and transport of Kolosjoki matte, 95, 191–92, 193, 195, 197, 198, 201; Finnish traffic forbidden by British, 167; I. G. Farbenindustrie to

compete with International Nickel in, 189; mines in Germany abandoned, 191; excavation at Kolosjoki begun, 193; matte produced by Norddeutsche Affinerie, 194; storing of, 194, 195; transportation of raw, to Germany, 194–95, 198, 201
Nielsen, E. E. M., 179
Nivala: negotiations for ore at, 10–11, 28; output promised to Germany, 13–14, 29; mentioned, 15
Non-Agression Pact. *See* German-Soviet Non-Aggression Pact
Norddeutsche Affinerie, 28, 194
Nordland Nickel O. Y.: proposed German-controlled company, 188, 189
Northern Cap, 3, 10, 87, 123
Norway: German invasion of, 5, 16, 17, 18–19, 20, 21, 22; prefers Germany to Russia, 24; exiled government of, 25; nickel ore in, 27; Soviets fear German occupation of, 33; Finland considers alignment with, 76; German Army in Norway, 122, 124, 159, 176, 177, 183, 199; defense of, 159; iron ore in, 196
——North: Russian intentions in, 23; German transit to, 51; German army in, 70, 158; mentioned, 106, 124
Norwegian High Command, 23, 24
Nuremberg trials: testimony at, on Finnish participation, 222n97

Oppau: I. G. Farbenindustrie works at, 26–27, 28, 194
Orlov, Pavel G.: seen as reasonable man, 162; to discuss Petsamo, 162–63, 164; mentioned, 138, 151, 152
Outokumpu Company: and delivery of Nivala output, 29; fails to deliver copper, 192

Paasikivi, Dr. Juho Kusti: in 1939 Finnish-Soviet negotiations, 6, 8; on 1940 peace talks, 10; negotiates nickel agreement in Moscow, 32, 33–34, 41, 73, 74, 75, 77–78, 79, 91, 98–101; on Finland's dilemma, 35–36; reports more conciliatory Russian attitude, 43; on motives of SNS, 56; seeks accommodation with Soviets, 64, 77–78, 86, 106, 107, 133, 143; talks with Vyshinsky, 83, 84, 139–43, 144; reports English conditions, 85; lines of communication of, 98; and anti-Finnish radio campaign, 112; inadequately informed, 113; advises resumption of Soviet-Finnish Petsamo talks, 117; compromise solution of, 135–36, 141–42; resignation of, 145; meets with Molotov, 147–48; summoned to Helsinki, 152; view of Fieandt proposal, 153–54; meeting with Stalin, 164; to discuss peace terms, 199; mentioned, 45, 46, 53, 57, 61, 92, 97, 116, 184

Pakaslahti, Aaro: on Fieandt committee, 153, 155

Pam, Edgar, 5

Parkkina, 4

Pasvik River: guards at bridge, 117

Paulus, Field Marshal Friedrich, 222n97

Petroleum, 169

Petrozavodsk: broadcasts from, 111, 162

Petsamo Bay, 8

Petsamo Nickel Company: subsidiary of Mond Nickel, 5; proposed German takeover of, 21; negotiates with I.G. Farbenindustrie, 27, 29, 30, 42, 46–47, 134, 137–38, 151; Molotov demands elimination of, 34; ordered to start operation, 44; condition to sale of shares in, 48; contract with I.G. Farbenindustrie, 53, 74, 92, 102, 104; negotiates with Soviets, 54, 79, 102, 126; negotiates with Soyuzpromexport, 54, 103; imports petroleum products, 163, 164, 169; under government jurisdiction, 186–87; report draft of labor force, 192; and failure of

smelting furnace, 192–93; Finns withdraw from, 200; mentioned, 123, 154, 163. *See also* International Nickel Company of Canada: Mond Nickel Company of London; Nickel mining concession; Söderhjelm, Dr. Johan O.

Pielisjärvi: molybdenum mine at, 10

Poland, 157

Polish legation, 178

Portugal, 169

Power plant. *See* Jäniskoski hydroelectric power plant

Pravda, 56–57

Propaganda offensive: Soviet against Finland, 6, 61, 62, 111–12; Kolosjoki potential center of Communist, 94–95, 108, 115

Railroads: in Petsamo, 4; Soviets demand transit agreement for, 58

Ramsay, Dr. Henrik: on Petsamo Nickel board, 5; on Petsamo problem, 40; discusses threat to Finnish shipping, 50–51, 167, 168; efforts of, to preserve concession, 103; confers with British, 109, 115–16, 117, 118, 122; and Finnish-German exchange of views, 113; and nickel matte agreement, 121, 138; on government commission to operate mine, 187; mentioned, 134, 193

Rangell, Johan (Jukka) Wilhelm, 117, 133, 162, 172

"Reindeer," Operation, 71, 72, 122–23, 124, 158, 159, 182

Ribbentrop, Joachim von: and German attitude toward Winter War, 11; response to Soviet pressure on Petsamo, 39, 81, 88, 89, 95, 114–15, 118–20, 131–32; and arms deliveries to Finland, 65-66; talks to Molotov, 85, 90; instructs Schnurre, 91; and Fieandt, 107, 155; Wiehl's recommendations to, 113–14, 149, 150; pressures Molotov, 146; urges Finnish diplomatic break with Britain, 180; mentioned, 42, 46, 59, 87, 161, 172

Richert, Arvid, 26, 62, 149
Ritter, Dr. Karl: on Finnish trade delegation, 20; on Russian attitude in Petsamo, 38, 39, 40; on economic reorganization of Europe, 40; on German position in Petsamo, 40–41, 42, 45; mentioned, 15, 169
Robinson, J. D., 179
Roos, Colonel Harald V.: attends German-Finnish military conference, 172
Roseberry, C., 179, 180, 238n62
Rössing, Colonel Horst: on preparation for defense of Petsamo, 123; on German attitude toward Finns, 125
Rovaniemi: British trade inspector in, 166, 179; German troops at, 176; nickel matte transport through, 196–97; mentioned, 4, 158
Rubber, 169
Ruge, General Otto, 24
Rumania, 56, 91, 124, 159
Rumanian General Staff, 26
Russo-Finnish treaty of Tartu (Dorpat), 3
Russo-Finnish Winter War. *See* Winter War
Rybachi Peninsula: Finns acquire part of, 3; proposed exchange for Eastern Karelia, 6, 8; Russians take western littoral of, 9; Russian fortification of, 23
Ryti, Risto: in German-Finnish trade talks, 14, 15, 16, 21; foreign policy of government of, 17; hopes for quick German victory, 63; on Finnish-Soviet relations, 64, 75–76; and German delivery of arms, 65; and German mineral concession, 80; explains Finnish position, 83–84; elected president, 109; rejects mobilization request, 116–17; sets up German-Finnish military conference, 171–72; authorizes military involvement, 176; receives Hitler's assurances, 182; and Schnurre concession proposals, 189; succeeded by Mannerheim, 200; mentioned, 133, 154, 162, 177

Salmijärvi: trade inspector in, 166, 179
Salzburg conference: purpose of, 172–75
Scandinavia: economic position of, 18–19
Schnurre, Dr. Karl: in Finnish-German trade talks, 14, 15–16, 18, 20, 30–31; explains German position, 46; and Soviet-Finnish Petsamo talks, 80, 82, 87, 88, 91–93, 98, 102, 118–19; objects to Grönblom, 101; contact with Fieandt, 103, 106–8, 113, 187–89; negotiates German-Soviet trade treaty, 108–9, 110, 111; as spokesman for Wiehl's recommendations, 114; reponse to Fieandt proposal, 155–56; instructions of, to Schulenburg, 161; sets up Finnish-German military conferences, 171–72; mentioned, 13, 47, 48, 73, 74, 134
Schoenfeld, Arthur, 49, 62, 76, 103, 111, 112, 150, 161
Schubardt, Dr. W.: new technical manager at Petsamo, 193; requests German labor, 200; efforts of, to continue production, 201
Schulenburg, Count Friedrich W. von der: conversations with Molotov, 37, 38, 45, 46, 53–54, 73, 91, 131–32, 136, 137, 146, 149; accepts interim Petsamo solution, 44; and German-Finnish delivery contract, 48, 132–33; on Soviet intentions in Finland, 59; advises Finns in Soviet negotiations, 87, 88, 102, 118–20; lines of communication of, 98; opinion of trade embargo, 112; to press German position, 131–33, 136, 137, 149, 151; reports Paasikivi proposal, 140; and Molotov's statement of Russian position, 146; new instructions for, 146, 147, 150, 161–62; reports Paasikivi inclination to yield, 148; Stalin em-

braces, 160; mentioned, 30, 39, 40, 41, 53, 89, 92, 129, 130, 144, 145
Secret Protocol. *See* German-Soviet Non-Aggression Pact
Sederholm, Professor J. Johannes, 4
Seidel, Lieutenant General Hans Georg von, 158
Shipping: potential German control of Petsamo, 16, 22–23, 51, 66; controlled by British, 35; British interference with Finnish, 48–50, 51–52, 116, 238n70; Finnish-U.S., 86; Soviets permit Finns use of ports, 160; Finns negotiate with Britain on, 165–70, 177–78, 180–81; of ore, 191, 193–94, 195, 196, 197. *See also* Navicerts
Siilasvuo, Major General Hjalmar, 183, 237n47
"Silver Fox," Operation, 72, 122, 123–24, 158
Skagerrak mine barrier, 166, 168
Slovakia, 25
Smelter plant: for Petsamo mining, 5, 14; production scheduled for, 191; delay in operation of, 192–93, 195; new technical manager for, 193; efforts to increase capacity of, 197; Germans attempt to continue operation of, 200–201; destruction of, ordered, 201–2
SNS: Tanner opposition to, 58; Soviet support of, 61, 62; mentioned, 56, 94
Sobolev, Arkady A.: concession proposal of, 43, 44; conciliatory memo of, 53, 54
Social Democrat Party: and resignation of Tanner, 215n18
Society for Peace and Friendship between Finland and the Soviet Union (SNS). *See* SNS
Sodankylä: British trade inspector in, 166, 179
Söderhjelm, Dr. Johan O.: appointed to Petsamo Nickel board, 5; discusses possible German takeover of Petsamo, 21; negotiations with Soyuzpromexport, 54–55, 77, 78–

79; efforts of, to preserve concession, 103; and German nickel matte agreement, 138; on government commission to operate mines, 187
South Africa, 27
South America, 35, 51, 168, 169
Soviet-Finnish armistice agreement (1944), 67, 200
Soviet-Finnish negotiations (1939), 6
Soviet-Finnish Peace Treaty of 1920, 9, 75
Soviet-Finnish peace treaty of 1940. *See* Treaty of Moscow.
Soviet-Japanese Neutrality Pact, 160
Soyuzpromexport: negotiations with, 54, 79, 103
Spain, 169
Speer, Albert, 197, 201
S.S. "Bygdöy," 196
S.S. "Oscar Midling," 167
S.S. "Westerwald," 197
Stalin, Joseph: in negotiations over Rybachi Peninsula, 8; refuses closer cooperation with England, 68; and realities of geography, 78; conversation with Cripps, 79; displays friendship for Schulenburg, 160; meeting with Paasikivi, 164
Stanley, Robert C., 5
Steinhardt, Laurence A., 91, 144, 145, 148
Stewen, Lieutenant Colonel M. K., 51
Submarine warfare, German, 71, 165
Sundman, Commodore Svante A.: attends German-Finnish military conference, 172
Svinhufvud, Per Evind, 18
Sweden: shipping of, 51; German missions in, 59; and Soviet threat to Finland, 63; Finland considers alignment with, 76; in German military designs, 123, 124; time charter agreement with England, 166; mentioned, 157
Swedish Foreign Ministry: breaks German code, 149
Swedish People's Party, 67

Talvela, Major General Paavo, 51
Tanner, Väinö: replaced as foreign minister by Witting, 17; resignation of, 57, 58, 214–15n18; heads government commission to operate Kolosjoki mine, 187; urges Finnish control of concession, 189
Tapola, Colonel Kustaa A., 158, 172
Tass, 32
Telegraph and telephone communications agreement, Soviet-Finnish, 146
Thomas, General Georg, 69
Thurston, Walter, 61, 62
Time charter: British, of Finnish vessels, 166, 167, 168, 170, 178, 180–81; Germans attempt to use, 169
Tippelskirch, Werner von, 113, 162
Todt Organization, 196, 201
Tornio: British trade inspector at, 166, 179
Trade: Finnish, 19, 123; Finnish-Soviet relations, 112, 116, 118, 161; German-Soviet, 160. *See also* Trade negotiations
Trade inspectors: British, in Finland, 166, 178–81, 234n2, 238n54
Trade negotiations: German-Finnish, 10, 13–14, 15–16, 18, 24–25, 27, 29–30, 37, 50; Finnish-Soviet, 13, 54–55, 77; Soviet-German, 102, 108–9, 110, 111
Transit agreement: German-Finnish, 66, 67, 96, 104, 158, 166. *See also* Hanko; Veltjens Agreement
Treaty of Moscow, 9, 22, 45, 75, 163, 164
Trifona, 4
Tripartite Pact, 159
Tromsö, 23

United Press, 59
United States: interest in International Nickel, 10; Finnish shipping to, 48, 50, 51, 52, 168, 178, 180; British avoid offending, 49, 86; pressure of, to continue Petsamo traffic, 165; mentioned, 35, 187
U.S. State Department, 49

Van Scherpenberg, Hilger: in negotiations on Petsamo, 14–15, 38; statement on economic situation, 18; memorandum on German dilemma, 42; memorandum on Petsamo, 82–83; insists on interest of I.G. Farbenindustrie, 136; mentioned, 135
Veltjens, Lieutenant Colonel Joseph: in arms negotiations, 65; negotiates troop transit agreement, 66; does not promise aid, 81; on Helsinki negotiations, 89; attempts to obtain Finnish vessels, 169; mentioned, 99
Veltjens Agreement: signed, 66; as barrier to Soviets, 80; as indication of German interest, 82–83; political implications of, 88
Vereker, Gordon: on German-Finnish nickel delivery contract, 41–42, 49; requests British vice-consulate in Petsamo, 50; inquires about military conferences, 177; on Polish legation, 178; protests removal of trade inspectors, 181; mentioned, 84
Viipuri: offer to return to Finns, 32; fall of, 200
Vladivostok, 160
Vuoksenniska Company, 10
Vyshinsky, Andrei Y.: talks with Paasikivi, 83, 84, 85, 131, 139–43, 144; negotiates only with Finns, 89; demands resumption of Finnish-Soviet talks, 116, 117; and statement of Soviet position, 146; on management question, 149; replies to German demands, 151; hears new Finnish proposal, 164

Waldén, Major General Rudolf: informed of arms deliveries, 65; acting prime minister, 109; mentioned, 172
Warlimont, Major General Walter: on importance of Petsamo area, 70, 71; view of "Reindeer," 72; plan for Finnish submission to Germany, 171; on Finland's pol-

icy options, 183–84; mentioned, 227n67

Wasastjerna, Professor Jarl Axel, 36

Weber-Andreae, Eduard, 28–29

Weizsäcker, Ernst von: and German attitude on Russo-Finnish war, 11; on effect of invasion of Norway, 17; on importance of Petsamo ore, 30, 69; proposal for nickel concession, 39; on German position on nickel concession, 45, 76, 77, 82, 149; confirms German transit agreement, 66; reports Soviet pressure on Finns, 81; on Soviet-German talks, 94; reports Hitler's protection, 95; lines of communication of, 98; instructs Schulenburg, 132; Kivimäki confers with, 156–57; studies Finnish shipping problem, 168, 169; mentioned, 26, 39, 48, 62–63, 64, 74, 87, 138, 153, 154

Wied, Prince of, 62, 63

Wiehl, Emil: and German-Finnish Petsamo negotiations, 14; attitude toward Soviet-Finnish Petsamo discussions, 42–43, 87, 103, 112, 118–19; discusses Veltjens Agreement, 83; questions Göring, 88–89; and Finnish-German nickel matte agreements, 101–2, 122; on German-Finnish exchange of views, 112–13; recommendations to Ribbentrop, 113–14, 120–21; and German response to Molotov statement, 148–49, 150; mentioned, 91, 134, 135, 136, 137

Winter War: interrupts Petsamo construction schedule, 5; confirms Soviet disinterest in Petsamo, 8–9; and German-Finnish relations, 11; fear of Germany seen as cause, 32–33; and German delivery of arms, 65; Soviet gains in, 76; Heinrichs lectures on, 125; mentioned, 10, 26, 61, 123, 135

Witting, Foreign Minister Rolf: and German-Finnish trade talks, 16, 20; to improve relations with Germany, 17–18, 63, 76; in close contact with Blücher, 25; suggest

joint solution of Petsamo problem, 36; and German position in Petsamo, 40, 42, 120; response to German warnings, 43; and Soviet-Finnish concession talks, 43–44, 73, 79, 86, 107, 117–18, 128–29, 130, 131, 148, 228n6; and German-Finnish nickel contract, 47, 134, 137–38; and British shipping interference, 48–49, 167; Germans threaten Petsamo traffic, 50; attitude of, toward Russia, 59, 111, 146, 161; and German arms deliveries, 65; memo of, on history of nickel negotiations, 74; suggests beginning mining operations, 77; and Paasikivi, 78, 140–42, 145; seeks German support, 81, 86–87, 95, 120, 135, 136, 143–44, 148; and English position, 85, 105, 116; informed of German conditions, 92–93; lines of communications of, 98; and choice of delegation to Moscow, 101; on trade embargo, 112; establishes military guards at mines, 117; response of, to Schulenburg's démarche, 120; discussions with Orlov, 163, 164; on closing Polish legation, 178; and break with Britain, 180–81, 182; opposes German-Finnish concession, 189; mentioned, 33, 41, 48, 51, 52, 53, 56, 61, 64, 89, 100, 103, 109, 115, 150, 151, 156, 162, 172

Woermann, Ernst, 36, 60, 64, 93, 136

Wood, 15

Wrede, Baron Gustaf Woldemar, 138, 193

Wuorimaa, Aarne, 17

Yugoslavia, 70, 159, 161, 184

Zechlin, Erich Wilhelm, 59, 60

Zotov, Ivan S.: presses Finns for reply to Molotov, 73, 74, 110, 111, 116; departs from Helsinki, 112; replaced by Orlov, 162; mentioned, 83, 85, 109